WHEN MEN FELL FROM THE SKY

Between 1940 and 1945, more than 100,000 airmen were shot down over Europe, a few thousand of whom survived and avoided being arrested. *When Men Fell from the Sky* is a comparative history of the treatment of these airmen by civilians in France, Germany, and Britain. By studying the situation on the ground, Claire Andrieu shows how these encounters reshaped societies at a local level. She reveals how the fall of France in 1940 may have concealed an insurrection nipped in the bud, that the "People's War" in Britain was not merely a myth, and that, in Germany, the "racial community of the people" had in fact become a social reality, with Allied airmen increasingly subjected to lynching from 1943 onwards. By considering why the treatment of these airmen contrasted so strongly in these countries, Andrieu sheds new light on how civilians reacted when confronted with the war "at home."

CLAIRE ANDRIEU is Professor Emerita in contemporary history at Sciences Po Paris. Her previous publications include *Resisting Genocide: The Multiple Forms of Rescue* (co-ed. 2011) and *Spoliation et restitution des biens juifs en Europe* (co-ed. 2007). From 2011 to 2018, she was editor-in-chief of *Violence de masse et Résistance / Mass Violence & Resistance.*

Studies in the Social and Cultural History of Modern Warfare

General Editors
Robert Gerwarth, *University College Dublin*
Jay Winter, *Yale University*

Advisory Editors
Heather Jones, *University College London*
Rana Mitter, *University of Oxford*
Michelle Moyd, *Indiana University Bloomington*
Martin Thomas, *University of Exeter*

In recent years the field of modern history has been enriched by the exploration of two parallel histories. These are the social and cultural history of armed conflict, and the impact of military events on social and cultural history.

Studies in the Social and Cultural History of Modern Warfare presents the fruits of this growing area of research, reflecting both the colonization of military history by cultural historians and the reciprocal interest of military historians in social and cultural history, to the benefit of both. The series offers the latest scholarship in European and non-European events from the 1850s to the present day.

A full list of titles in the series can be found at: www.cambridge.org/modernwarfare

WHEN MEN FELL FROM THE SKY

Civilians and Downed Airmen in Second World War Europe

CLAIRE ANDRIEU
Sciences Po, Paris

Translated by

ETHAN RUNDELL

Shaftesbury Road, Cambridge CB2 8EA, United Kingdom

One Liberty Plaza, 20th Floor, New York, NY 10006, USA

477 Williamstown Road, Port Melbourne, VIC 3207, Australia

314–321, 3rd Floor, Plot 3, Splendor Forum, Jasola District Centre, New Delhi – 110025, India

103 Penang Road, #05-06/07, Visioncrest Commercial, Singapore 238467

Cambridge University Press is part of Cambridge University Press & Assessment, a department of the University of Cambridge.

We share the University's mission to contribute to society through the pursuit of education, learning and research at the highest international levels of excellence.

www.cambridge.org
Information on this title: www.cambridge.org/9781009266680

DOI: 10.1017/9781009266659

English translation © Claire Andrieu 2023

This publication is in copyright. Subject to statutory exception and to the provisions of relevant collective licensing agreements, no reproduction of any part may take place without the written permission of Cambridge University Press & Assessment.

First published in English by Cambridge University Press & Assessment 2023

First published in French by Tallandier, Paris, 2021, under the title *Tombés du ciel. Le sort des pilotes abattus en Europe, 1939-1945*.

Printed in the United Kingdom by TJ Books Limited, Padstow Cornwall

A catalogue record for this publication is available from the British Library.

A Cataloging-in-Publication data record for this book is available from the Library of Congress

ISBN 978-1-009-26668-0 Hardback

Cambridge University Press & Assessment has no responsibility for the persistence or accuracy of URLs for external or third-party internet websites referred to in this publication and does not guarantee that any content on such websites is, or will remain, accurate or appropriate.

CONTENTS

List of Illustrations   ix
List of Maps   xi
List of Charts   xii
List of Numerical Tables   xiii
Acknowledgements   xiv

Introduction: The International in the Village   1
The Dupont, Smith and Schmidt War   1
Behavior as a Criterion   3
Piecemeal Academic Knowledge   6
Cult Films and Adventure Stories   12
Debriefings, Depositions and Verified Statements   16
The Book's Arguments   18

PART I   Blitz-Invasion in France, or Resistance Crushed   21

1. ## Finding the Volunteers of the Year 40   23
   Plouguerneau (Finistère), 18 June 1940   23
   In the Midst of the "Débâcle" – War   26
   The Exodus as Referendum on the Invader   29
   Civilians Taken Aback by the Arrival of "Parachutists"   32
   The Last-Minute Creation of the Gardes territoriales   35

2. ## The Repression of the Republic's "Francs-Tireurs"   39
   Arsy (Oise): Between Luftwaffe Ace and Movie Star   39
   "*Schuld Frankreichs*": "France's Guilt"   41
   The Criminalization of "*Freischärlerei*" ("Francs-Tireuring")   44
   Popular Resistance to Invasion   47
   "Without Orders"   51
   Repression Contrary to International Law   56
   Reynaud and Mandel in Exchange for the Territorial Guards   60
   The Defeat Revisited   63

v

CONTENTS

PART II "Imminent Invasion!": A Very Civil War in the United Kingdom 67

3. **Britain into Battle: A People at War** 69
The "People's War," Act I 69
A Situation Worthy of Ancient Myth 71
The Revisions of Later Generations 73
The International Norm of Good Behavior 75
To Arms! An Upsurge of National Resistance 76
Summer 1940 to Spring 1941: The Time of Greatest Tension 81

4. **"British Humor" as an Agent of Civility** 84
Interpreting the Silence of the Sources 84
Reception on the Ground: Comedy Sketches and Genre Scenes 86
Through the Looking Glass of the Press: Some Cases of Brutality 92
The Luftwaffe Ace and the Royal Army Medical Corps Doctor 95
Discussion Forums as a Source of Truth? 98
Smoke without Fire: Bracklesham Bay Beach, East Wittering 99
From Rumor to Fact: Kennington Oval, London 102
Sea Front and Cricket Field: The Refoundation of a Nation 105

PART III The Origins of the Resistance: Hiding Allies in France 109

5. **The Resistance as Mass Local Dynamic** 111
A Journey across France, September to October 1941 112
In the Eyes of MI9, the "Occupied Population" Were Allies 114
The Helpers as Indicative of Mass Resistance 117
The First Stirrings of Resistance on the Ground 120
Assistance as a Form of Emergency Social Service 122
Life in Clandestine Transnational Families 125

6. **The Sequences of Aid: Between Family and Repression** 134
The Three Phases of Evasion Assistance 135
Veules-les-Roses / Rouen-St Aignan – Montpon 137
Plestin-les-Grèves / Bégard – Nantes 140
Les Riceys / Paris – Vierzon / Ste Léocadie – Canet-Plage 142
Back to Phase 1: The Perennial Source of Aid-Based Resistance 144
Women and Children First 146
Repression: Dissuasive or Incentivizing? 149
"People said nothing but horror was written on every face" 154
Civilians at War 158

CONTENTS   vii

7. **A Civil Society against Two States**   162
    Focusing on the Frame of Experience Rather than Motivations   162
    Allied Bombs Cheered from the Balcony, 1940–1942   164
    The Indifferent Reception of Anti-Allied Propaganda   168
    Ineffective Nazi Scenography   171
    A Memory on the Margins   173

    PART IV   **Lynching in Germany, 1943–1945: Defending the Nazi State**   183

8. **The Lynching of Allied Airmen: A Ordinary Practice**   187
    Three Social Patterns: Schleswig-Holstein, 1942–1945   187
    Investigating in Post-Nazi Germany   192
    Petty Local Collective Murders   196
    Lynching, Hallmark of the New Society   199
    A Stage in the Nazi Revolution   202

9. **A Revolutionary Dynamic**   204
    SS-like Civilians   204
    Popular Initiative, Propaganda and the Police Converge   206
    "Deliverance" for the *Volk*: Calls for Murder from Above   212
    Repudiating the Geneva Convention   217

10. **Lynch Mobs: Pre-Constructed Anger and Nazism in Action**   221
    Rüsselsheim, a Model Lynching   222
    Popular Vengeance   227
    Reprisal Violence and Vendetta Violence   230
    Evidence of Residual Civility   233
    Mourning and Ruins: A Political and Cultural Experience   237

11. **Race at Heart**   242
    Race, the Hallmark of Lethal Violence   242
    Blacks as Auxiliaries to the Jews   247
    Airmen Seen as "Jews" and "Negroes"   250
    A Nazified Society   255

    Conclusion: An Archeology of the Moment   257
    British Humor and German Fear of "Francs-Tireurs"   258
    A Franco-Anglo-American Nation   262
    The Making of Civilians   264

viii   CONTENTS

*Appendix: Bombardments and On-the-Ground Responses:
             Maps and Numerical Comparisons   267*
Archival Sources   280
Notes   285
Bibliography   321
Index   342

ILLUSTRATIONS

1.1   18 June 1940. A German crew is captured in the village of Plouguerneau (Finistère). 25

2.1   Mock trial staged by the Luftwaffe in Luchy (Oise), 12 September 1940. 54

3.1   Local Defence Volunteers, 1 July 1940. 79

4.1   "British humor: bomb-proof against wild Nazi raids," *Kent Messenger*, 21 September 1940. 90

4.2   "Is it all right now, Henry?" *Daily Express*, 29 August 1940. 93

4.3   The Battle of Britain: Franz von Werra's Messerschmitt Me. 109 after its forced landing in Marden, Kent, 5 September 1940. 96

4.4   The Heinkel He. 111 of Leutnant Metzger lying on Bracklesham Beach, 26 August 1940, East Wittering, Sussex. 100

4.5   The tail of the Dornier-17 piloted by Robert Zehbe, London, 15 September 1940. 103

5.1a   Telegram from the Royal Air Force to Mrs. Cooke announcing that her son is missing, 8 February 1944. 127

5.1b   Fake identity card issued by the Resistance to Squadron Leader Thomas C.S. Cooke. 128

5.1c   Telegram from the Royal Air Force to Mrs. Cooke announcing that her son arrived at Gibraltar, 30 April 1944. 129

5.2a. & 5.2b   American airmen at home in a family of resisters in Saint-Mandé, Autumn 1943. 130

6.1   Summary execution for harboring Englishmen, October 1940. 139

6.2   On the night of 29 September 1941, the Blenheim made a sea-landing in the bay of St-Michel-en-Grève. 141

6.3   Allied airmen harbored by the Fillerin family, Renty (Pas-de-Calais), September 1942. 145

6.4   Stepped-up repression. German poster, 22 September 1941. 156

6.5   "ZUM TODE," To Death. Poster announcing the execution of two helpers, 14 May 1942. 160

7.1a & 7.1b   Diplomas of helpers issued by the British and the Americans. 176

8.1   Military honors given RAF airmen killed in action, Ütersen, Schleswig-Holstein, 21 April 1942. 188

9.1	An "American air gangster," December 1943. 210
10.1	Rüsselsheim, June 1945: the US Army investigates the lynching. 226
11.1	"Behind the Enemy Powers: The Jew." Nazi propaganda poster displayed in Germany and in the occupied countries, December 1943. 243
11.2	"Forward, Christian soldiers!," *Kladderadatsch*, 18 July 1943. 246

MAPS

2.1   Exodus and incidents between civilians and Luftwaffe airmen (France, May–June 1940).   48

2.2   Areas devastated in 1914–18 and incidents between civilians and Luftwaffe airmen in 1940.   49

6.1   Escapers and evaders in occupied Europe by year, 1940–45.   157

7.1   Helpers of Americans in the Seine département, 1942–44.   179

10.1   The route of lynching: Rüsselsheim-am-Main, 26 August 1944.   225

App.1   Allied bombing in Europe, 1939–45.   270

App.2   Localities crossed by escapers and evaders in Europe, 1940–45.   271

App.3   Allied bombing over Germany, 1939–45.   272

App.4   Lynching of Allied airmen in Germany, 1943–45   273

App.5   Kristallnacht, 9–10 November 1938.   274

App.6   Anti-semitic violence in Weimar Germany.   275

App.7   Allied bombing over France.   277

App.8   Presence of helpers of Americans by commune in France.   278

App.9   Proportion of helpers of Americans in the total population by département.   279

CHARTS

4.1   The capture of an enemy airman: a local event, 1940–45.   87
5.1   Duration of successful escape through France, 1940–45.   126
App.1a Victims of German bombing in the United Kingdom:
        monthly distribution.   269
App.1b Monthly tonnage of bombs dropped by the Allies on France
        and Germany.   269
App.2a Chronology of the lynching of Allied airmen in Germany.   276
App.2b Chronology of the tonnage of bombs dropped on Germany.   276

NUMERICAL TABLES

3.1   Compared civilian and enemy aircrew casualties in the United Kingdom, 1939–45.   82

5.1   Allied military personnel helped in France.   112

5.2   Helpers in France.   118

5.3   Members of the Resistance recognized after the war in France.   119

8.1a   Allied proceedings for war crimes committed against downed airmen on German territory (*Altreich*).   196

8.1b   Cases of airmen lynched on German territory (*Altreich*) investigated by the Deputy Judge Advocate General of the British and American zones.   197

8.2   Socio-professional category of first-tier defendants in the "Flyer trials" conducted by the American Army, 1945–48.   200

10.1   Eleven major lynchings tried by the American Army.   229

App.1   Bombing victims in the United Kingdom, France and Germany, 1940–45.   267

App.2   Tonnage of bombs dropped on the United Kingdom, France and Germany, 1940–45.   268

App.3   Morale on the ground and destruction of cities in Germany.   268

ACKNOWLEDGEMENTS

One does not always appreciate the extent to which an author's work is in fact the product of a collective undertaking mobilizing the assistance and generosity of a large number of institutions and individuals. This book is a case in point. In what concerns institutions, a leading role was played by Sciences Po and its affiliates, the Centre d'histoire and CERI, which provided financial support for my research and granted me a one-semester sabbatical to complete the writing of this book. The original research project that was the inspiration for the present work dates from 2004 but its subsequent progress was greatly assisted by a number of Franco-American academic relationships. Alongside a Fulbright grant, these have included successive invitations from Princeton University's Program in Contemporary European Politics and Institute for International and Regional Studies, Cornell University's Institute for European Programs and New York University's Institute of French Studies. In the United Kingdom, I benefited from invitations to the University of Oxford's OxPo Workshop on European and Global History and the University of Manchester's School of Arts, Languages and Culture. A similar welcome was extended me in Germany and Israel by the Centre Marc Bloch and the Hebrew University of Jerusalem's Institute of History, respectively.

Like all historians, I also owe a great deal to the archivists of the three countries studied here, whether they work in national archives (National Archives and Records Administration, College Park; The National Archives, Kew; the British Newspaper Archive, Colindale, London; the Bundesarchiv-Militärarchiv, Freiburg-im-Breisgau; the Bundesarchiv, Berlin-Lichterfelde; the Politisches Archiv, Auswärtiges Amt, Berlin; the Archives nationales, Pierrefitte-sur-Seine; the Service historique de la Défense, Vincennes; and the Établissement de communication et de production audiovisuelle de la Défense, Ivry), specialized archives (Imperial War Museum, London), départemental and county archives (Oise, Beauvais; and the Center for Kentish Studies, Maidstone) or local archives (Lambeth in London and Greven and Rüsselsheim in Germany). I would particularly like to thank Caroline Piketty and Pascal Raimbault at the Archives nationales, who helped me locate a purge trial that would play a critical role in my argument, and Nicholas Férard of ECPAD, who showed me how to decipher the images of the

ACKNOWLEDGEMENTS

Propaganda Kompanien (PK). Finally, I would like to pay tribute to the professionalism of Gudrun Senska, the archivist of the town of Rüsselsheim, who unfailingly responded to my innumerable questions and helped me bring other sources to light. As my tireless interlocutor, I would also like to thank the Service de cartographie of Sciences Po, which produced and helped conceive the maps in this book in creative dialogue with the author.

It would be impossible to mention all of the colleagues, friends and doctoral students who provided me with advice and constructive criticism in the course of my research. There are so many of them that the list would fill more than a page. But I wish to express my gratitude to those who found the time to reread my writing at various stages, in particular Jean-Marc Dreyfus, Christian Gudehus, Gaël Eismann, Andrew Knapp, Elissa Mailänder, Philip Nord, Nicholas Stargardt and Sidney Tarrow. Among those who directly or indirectly contributed to this book, whether by answering my questions or by way of their thought-provoking reactions, my particular thanks go to Herrick Chapman, Denis Charbit, Sheldon Garon, Dieter Gosewinkel, Harold James, Bruno Leroux, Corinna von List, Deborah Nord, Guillaume Piketty, Antoine Prost, Ezra Suleiman, Klaus-Peter Sick, Susan Tarrow and Dominique Trimbur.

I would also like to recognize my French editor at Éditions Tallandier, Dominique Missika, who welcomed me among her authors with kindness and professionalism. As I was able to work on the English and French versions at the same time, the final manuscript owes much to Michael Watson, executive publisher at Cambridge University Press, as well as to the reviewers of CUP and the team at the Studies in the Social and Cultural History of Modern Warfare series directed by Jay Winter and Robert Gerwarth. The fluidity of the text was also greatly improved by its English-language translator, Ethan Rundell.

I am grateful, finally, to the witnesses of this history. I speak here of Madeline Teremy, posthumous daughter of the pilot Norman Rogers, who was murdered in Rüsselsheim; of Marlies Adams di Fante, who as a little girl was persecuted for her American nationality in the same town; of Maguy de Saint-Laurent (1919–2020), who at the age of twenty-five was orphaned together with her nine younger brothers and sisters following their mother's death in Ravensbrück, to which she had been deported as a helper; of Michèle Agniel, a young helper deported to the same camp when she was eighteen but who returned after the war; of Anise Postel-Vinay (1922–2020), my mother, who was deported to Ravensbrück for acts of resistance but who also returned and whose mother was a helper; and, finally, of a helper, my father André Postel-Vinay (1911–2007), who after his arrest found himself in the same situation as the airmen he had helped, escaped and was taken in hand by his own evasion network.

As can be seen, this book is not the work of a single person. Were it not for the proofreading, support and indulgence of my family, from its youngest member to its oldest, it would surely still be a work in progress.

$\sim$

Introduction
The International in the Village

The aim of this book is to show the extent of civilian involvement in the war. The vantage point I have chosen – a belligerent in the conflict, whether friend or enemy, suddenly arriving among civilians – sheds light on the autonomy of civilians and the ways they took up the fight. In these situations, they appear as direct actors in the war rather than mere subjects of a "Home Front" under strain and beset by mourning, shortages, gender relations and class conflict. This book restores to civilians their concern for a certain common good writ large – that is, for their (imagined) overall community. It seeks to re-politicize war as an interaction between the individual and his or her ideal overarching community, whether national or even international.

The arrival of fallen airmen triggered the emergence of four different social configurations. Each defines a particular type of international relations in which societies act autonomously, with or without support from the state and sometimes even against it. More or less ephemeral micro-international societies in this way emerged, each waging a war specific to them. In a word: French civilians resisted the downed airmen of the invader; the British politely took unlucky Luftwaffe airmen prisoner; the people of occupied France hid the Allies and helped them escape from continental Europe; and, from mid-1943, a good number of German civilians set about lynching airmen.

It is an empirical finding of my research that civilians behaved toward downed airmen in a homogeneous and/or specific manner at the national scale. Each nation at war offered a particular profile. The aim of this book is to deconstruct this homogeneity or specificity so as to better understand the processes at work at the national level. To that end, I have adopted a "constructivist" approach, albeit without bestowing upon this concept the radical meaning it is sometimes given in theoretical debates.

The Dupont, Smith and Schmidt War

It is not to indulge in caricature to ask what factors drove the Duponts, Smiths and Schmidts of the war to adopt behaviors that were so homogeneous and/or specific at the national level yet so variable from one country to the next. An answer may be found in the comparative history of these three countries,

2   INTRODUCTION

conducted at two levels: the local, even microsocial, scale and the national one. By falling or arriving without warning among civilians, the fleeing airman or soldier penetrated deeply into the heart of the societies under consideration. His arrival on the scene was a catalyst for inclinations produced by the political regime, collective memory and cultural tradition. By his appearance, the fugitive acted as a precipitant of national political culture. The actions that followed from this form a typology: resistance to the invader; good-natured reception; the clandestine provision of shelter and assistance in escape; lynching. Does this unequivocal portrait revive national stereotypes? Such is the reproach sometimes leveled at comparative history, which is suspected of reinforcing prejudice. In fact, it is quite the contrary: by identifying the determinants that influenced civilian behavior in wartime, the present study endeavors to deconstruct these oppositions. Three major factors – the nature of the regime, memory and tradition – drove this behavior, with each playing a variable role, differentially entering into sync with or acting as brakes upon one another from one country to the next. Comparison reveals the interaction of these forces.

A comparative history of civilians in wartime, this work also shares some traits with studies of world history. Since the 1980s, the term "world history" has referred to phenomena that are global in scale. In theory, it contrasts with Eurocentric and national history. While the three countries studied here are all located in Europe, they reunite four of the five major situations observed during the Second World War: two sovereign countries, one of which is the aggressor (Germany), the other the aggressed (Great Britain); an invaded and subsequently occupied country (France). Only neutral countries are lacking here. Moreover, American airmen and, in particular, African-American airmen play an essential part in this story. It is thus not particularly Eurocentric. Finally, analogous scenarios are also to be found in Asia, where the Pacific War, or, as the Japanese call it, "Fifteen Years' War" (1931–45), also saw downed airmen. In China and Indochina, some were helped and hidden by civilians. In Japan, others were lynched. As it happens, the most remarkable literary text written on the civilian treatment of a downed airman was the work of a young Japanese writer, the future Nobel Prize winner for literature Kenzaburō Ōe. Published in 1957, *The Catch* is the story of a young boy's adoption of a black American airman who came down nearby.[1] Loved by the children of the village as both pet and fantastic creature, the airman suddenly becomes an enemy when the war reasserts itself in the person of an employee who comes to demand that the prisoner be brought to town for incarceration. The airman retaliates by taking the child hostage and is ultimately killed with an axe. Though rescued, the child remains deeply shocked. Having begun as fable, the story ends in tragedy.

To some extent, the present book swims against the current. The observed situation – the encounter between civilians and isolated combatants – tends to

INTRODUCTION

vitiate both victim-centered approaches and universalist ones that pay little heed to cultural and political contexts. Since the 1980s, an international cultural phenomenon has led to an emphasis on victims at the price of a certain "victimization" (a term that dates from the 2000s) – that is, of a new perspective on social actors now understood as victims. According to some sociologists, a "grand victim narrative" is in the process of replacing the old culture of heroism and the epic story of class struggle.[2] In the discipline of history, the result has been a certain depoliticization of the past as the list of victim categories expands. For the victim is by definition passive. He or she only has feelings and these are those of moral and physical pain. This gives rise to compassion and thus indignation. The focus on the suffering and hardship endured by the victim, however, has tended to efface the idea that the victim can have his or her own political agenda, his or her own choices, that he or she could take pleasure in implementing them and be active and determined. Since the 1990s, moreover, the effects of globalization have contributed to the victim narrative. As considerations of national sovereignty have lost their preeminence, national approaches have lost their legitimacy. This has only further diminished the place of politics and political culture for, in an international conflict, one's involvement on behalf of the nation, one's patriotic engagement, is political in nature. In this respect, our actors – those who received isolated combatants – were politically engaged.

My position is akin to that of the historian Francesca Trivellato. Working on the long-distance trade carried out by two Jewish brothers from Livorno in the early eighteenth century, this author rejects the idea of some economists according to whom such commercial relations, traversing as they did diverse communities (Jewish as well as Catholic and Brahmanical), illustrate the joint efficiency of individualism and the "invisible hand" of the market.[3] Trivellato shows that these highly efficient transnational and intercultural relations coexisted with the persistence of traditional communitarian cultures and prejudices. Our civilian actors of the Second World War were no more fungible from one country to the next and their feelings were only partly universal. Their behavior was governed by their culture and their national traditions as well as, in those countries that retained their sovereignty, the relevant political regime. Trivellato entitled her book *The Familiarity of Strangers*; had I focused on the history of airmen rather than that of host societies, that could just as easily have been the title of this book.

Behavior as a Criterion

Like needles in a haystack – in fact, they often took shelter in these familiar objects – our fugitive airmen and soldiers allow us to put the societies through which they passed to the test. They are like involuntary agents in a "testing" exercise at the scale of the countries they visited. By virtue of their more or less brief but repeated encounters, they offer us systemic experiments allowing us to enter into dialogue with the historiographical theses developed since 1945. This discipline-specific exercise might be of no more than academic interest, however, were it not undergirded by more philosophical, indeed political debates.

The first question concerns the relationship between opinion and action. In this work, the population's stated opinion is only of secondary interest to me. More interesting are their actions, the consequences of which were often grave and irreversible for both the fugitives and those helping them. Spoken words fly away, written words remain but acts are imprinted in the flesh and bind their authors. They reveal a deeper opinion, one that often went without saying because too obvious. In times of peace and freedom, the gap between discourse and action is in general governed by opportunism. Other phenomena emerge when life and liberty are at stake. Many have underscored the prolific anti-Semitic references of French discourse and publications in the 1930s and the "Vichy" years. This vision of the world, in which the "psychology of peoples" plays a role, is even to be found in the writings of some members of the Resistance. If three quarters of the Jews residing in France in 1940 escaped the roundups, however, it is among other things because anti-Semitism and saving lives were not incompatible.[4] Between words and action, the present study will privilege the latter, whether or not it was joined with speech and independently of whether this speech was consistent with the act performed.

Moreover, many social psychology experiments have shown the ease with which any authority can get its subjects to behave in ways contrary to their stated opinions or readily induce them to change opinion. In a now-famous experiment from the 1960s, Stanley Milgram, a professor in the Department of Psychology at Yale University, sought to test "submission to authority" among ordinary citizens. He found that 98 percent of the inhabitants of the United States, then a free and democratic society, agreed to administer strong electrical shocks to a student when ordered to do so by a scientific authority.[5] Milgram's findings have been debated ever since they were first published. It seems that the experimenters exerted more pressure on their subjects than they acknowledged.[6] But less dramatic experiments conducted in France support the same finding. The experiments conducted by Robert-Vincent Joule, a professor of social psychology at the University of Provence, and Jean-Léon Beauvois, a professor of social psychology at the University of Nice, show the ease with which some contexts can provoke subjects to unknowingly change their opinions.[7] It sufficed to exploit the subjects' natural tendency to make their opinions conform with their actions. To do so, they were first induced to freely act in ways that diverged from their opinions. These actions, in turn, changed their authors' conceptions. But the experiments of Charles Kiesler, founder of commitment theory, go farther: they

INTRODUCTION

show that belief can be changed by anticipation, even before the subject has been directly exposed to calls for a "counter-attitudinal" behavior.[8] This aptitude of the mind to anticipate change or interiorize it after the fact broadly captures the instability of opinions and the weakness of their predictive value. Without going so far as to consider individuals as memoryless electrons, these studies are an argument for caution in making deductions from expressed opinion. On the contrary, they insist on the determinant effect of action, the performance of which commits the actor, particularly when such actions are repeated.

The other question at the heart of this book is that of national identity. The comparison of what are in principle similar events in Great Britain, France and Germany leads one to raise the question in terms that do not sit easily with present-day developments in comparative history. The latter is oriented toward "transnational" studies and issues of "cultural transfer." It thus privileges the similarities and circulations between cultures.[9] This new approach is not well suited to the circumstances of war. My tripartite survey of the manner in which downed airmen were greeted upon reaching the ground yields a very uneven picture, full of contrasts, and would seem to legitimate the concept of national political culture. Yet there is a risk of essentializing nations and promoting national stereotypes: that of the English "gentleman," for example, or the Germanic "blond beast" dear to Nietzsche or, in the French case, that of the eternal trouble-maker suffering from a "real predilection for transgressing laws with complete impunity," as a German geography textbook put it in 1923.[10] Yet it must be said that this simple list is predicated on a choice from among the vast repertory of caricatures. Not all of them can be applied to the wartime scenes that concern us. In 1939–45, the situation nevertheless varied greatly from one side of the English Channel and Rhine to the next.

In some ways, the question of national identity has become suspect in Europe. With the unprecedented slaughter of the war, the genocide that accompanied it and the advent of the European construction, "national psychology" – until the 1950s, a discipline in good standing in the university – was gradually discredited. National stereotypes are no longer studied for the realities they might cover but for the uses that are made of them, like a game of funhouse mirrors whose only reality is that of their interaction. As suggested by a book's title, itself drawn from a phrase attributed to Edgar Faure, "*a false idea is a true fact*" – the false idea being the stereotype.[11] Since the 1980s, what's more, the growth of international mobility and the process of globalization that accelerated with the fall of the Berlin Wall tended to relegate the interstate comparisons fashionable in the 1970s–1980s to the warehouse of anachronism. Rather than international relations in the classic sense of the term, historians are now mainly concerned with intersocietal, intercultural and interintellectual relations, particularly in peacetime.

6 INTRODUCTION

My study is thus set in the perhaps outmoded space of nation-states and at the specific point where the unarmed parties of warring nations come into physical contact. My argument is that their affiliation with one of these nations is decisive but that its influence remains to be determined. In choosing a brief and unexpected instant of time during which the individual apparently has a chance of escaping the demands of state and society, one would expect to encounter a great diversity of spontaneous reactions. Yet the opposite is the case. Examining the archives thus requires one to reconsider the question of the formation of national stereotypes.

Comparison will be my control method. In this, I follow Durkheim's dictum that comparison is to the social sciences what experimentation is to the more exact sciences. While the comparative method allows one to better understand the meaning of local phenomena, it also helps identify the cultural filters that color perception and orient action independently of the immediate context. Such is the force of this cultural resonance that it can be argued that the ruins of a bombed building were not perceived in the same way in England, France and Germany. It is for this reason that, in the project he conceived under the Occupation for an apologia for history, Marc Bloch's heartfelt appeal was in vain: "Robespierristes, anti-Robespierristes, we beg for mercy: for goodness sake, just tell us what Robespierre was like."[12] Pro-Ally, pro-Nazi, what were the ruins of the Second World War like? English ruins are not French ruins, which are not German ruins. But his avowed positivism did not prevent Bloch from writing a model article of comparative history in which his professed philosophical realism in no way impeded his critical eye.[13] Yet another example of opinion's dissociation from action.

Piecemeal Academic Knowledge

In this introduction, we shall not review the national bibliographies of the three countries under consideration, as that would require too much space. They will be presented and used in each part dealing with one country or another. Here, I would like to identify the major debates relating to each country and compare the only academic publications that directly address the manner in which fallen airmen and on-the-run soldiers were received by local populations. In doing so, I seek to underscore the main historiographical issues at stake in this research.

In the chronological order of events, the France of May–June 1940 comes first. Its case is doubtless the least well known. No academic work has considered the issue of resistance on the part of civilians and Gardes territoriaux vis-à-vis the invasion. In this area, the lone pioneer consists of an article exploring the local archives of the Manche département.[14] It offers rare access to the subjectivity of French citizens: one there sees the mass levy of citizens against the imminent invasion. This local-level mobilization presaged the

INTRODUCTION

resistance of civilians and Gardes territoriaux against downed enemy airmen. Nipped in the bud by the Blitzkrieg and subsequent repression, however, this resistance has yet to receive a history of its own. French and German archives allow one to uncover its traces. Moreover, some work has already approached the legal and political framework that served as the basis for putting down resistance in May–June 1940. In her book on the German military authorities in France, Gaël Eismann presents the background of German repression.[15] She shows that the restraint supposedly shown by the *Militärbefehlshaber in Frankreich* (MBF) is a myth constructed on the basis of the postwar memoirs of MBF officials. The book does not study the particular case of the repression of civilians who fought the invasion, however. This question is discussed by Barbara Lambauer in her book on Otto Abetz, German ambassador to France during the Occupation.[16] Lambauer's book shows how the ambassador played a decisive role in the bargaining to which each of the parties to Collaboration, French and German, consented and that led a handful of civilians and Gardes territoriaux to be pardoned in exchange for the incarceration of Third Republic ministers Reynaud and Mandel. Yet these books do not give us the view from below, that of these citizens and the actions that they actually carried out. In the debate over the France of 1940, however – generally presented as that of the débâcle, nay of decadence – the determined action of civilians opens a breach in the overall portrait. There is reason to revisit the history of the débâcle.

There has been no academic work on the British case. Yet the manner in which German airmen were received on the ground may stoke the debate that first began in the 1970s regarding whether the People's War was a reality or the stuff of myth. The entire aura surrounding the Battle of Britain, in particular – in which, stoical on the ground and heroic in the air, the British people kept going and ultimately won the day by dint of their endurance and determination – was seriously challenged by social history. It nevertheless turns out that, in the highly civil manner with which they received enemy airmen, the British conformed to the positive image of the People's War. But it is not in academic work that one will find proof of this. Among the large number of books on the "Home Front," in general, and the "Battle of Britain" (10 July–31 October 1940) and "Blitz" (September 1940–May 1941), in particular, the subject is hardly mentioned. Where it is, it occupies no more than a few lines. The least cursory treatment is that given by a professor at the University of South Carolina, Simon Paul MacKenzie, whose study of the Home Guard devotes a very interesting chapter to "the fear of invasion."[17] There, the discussion centers, not on the case of downed German pilots, but on that of an unfortunate twenty-three-year-old RAF pilot, Eric James Brindley Nicolson, who became famous for his bravery and the ordeal he suffered. On 16 August 1940, his squadron attacked a group of Messerschmitts over Southampton. Nicolson's Hurricane caught fire and he was wounded. As he

8   INTRODUCTION

prepared to parachute from his airplane, a Messerschmitt entered his field of view. He resumed his position in the cockpit and fired on the enemy, shooting him down. Seriously burned, Nicolson finally jumped from the airplane ... and was once again wounded, this time by the rifle fire of Home Guard units who had mistaken him for the enemy. Nicolson's story became famous. In November 1940, he received the Victoria Cross for his exploit and in 1942 resumed service in India, where he received the Distinguished Flying Cross. On 2 May 1945, he was killed in a Liberator over the Bay of Bengal. This example, the only one offered by MacKenzie's book, indirectly informs us regarding the treatment of downed pilots once they reached the ground: fewer Royal Air Force pilots jumped from their airplanes than did their Luftwaffe counterparts but the relationship between the number of downed airplanes on each side was less unbalanced than was the case in the skies over France and Germany. During the Battle of Britain, one British airplane was shot down for every two German ones.[18] Among the soldiers on the ground, the possibility that they might accidentally fire on one of their own may in itself have been an argument for restraint.

Another way of testing the British population without wandering from the issue of improvised action is to observe its behavior toward escaped German prisoners of war. Here too, however, the available bibliography is quite sparse. Renate Held's excellent book on German prisoner of war camps in Great Britain does not address the issue of escape.[19] Her bibliography indicates no title referring to the subject. The literature of memoir is no different. Excepting that of Franz von Werra, whose exceptional feat I will discuss later and whose manuscript is for the moment impossible to locate, none of the few dozen German prisoners who escaped seem to have left a written account of their experiences. Their silence raises a question. While it is true that none of these prisoners succeeded in leaving the British Isles or even escaping their guards for more than just a few days, other factors – and particularly cultural ones – may play a role in this domain. For example, the culture of escape may not be equally shared by all nations. And, during the war, it may not have been symmetrically maintained in Britain and Germany. The British created Military Intelligence 9 (MI9), a secret service tasked with helping soldiers and airmen to evade capture, while the Germans established no such service.

As with the examples above, the French case has received little attention from academics. A particular note must be made of two groundbreaking pages written by Jean Quellien for the historic atlas, *La France pendant la Seconde Guerre mondiale*.[20] Quellien shows the extent of assistance supplied fleeing British soldiers and aviators by the French population between 1940 and 1945. After the war, the United Kingdom officially recognized 17,000 "helpers" who had assisted their troops. Laurent Thiéry's book on the repression in Nord-Pas-de-Calais, a zone incorporated into that of the Brussels military command, also contains extensive information on the repression of those secretly

INTRODUCTION

harboring Allies.[21] For the same region, a volume edited by Yves Le Maner contains invaluable information on downed airplanes and crews who were killed, taken prisoner or escaped.[22] One virtue of these works is that they fill a gap in the archives of the Royal Air Force. At the time, the RAF was unable to know precisely where its airplanes came down nor often the precise fate of those who had gone Missing in Action (MIA). Assembled after the fact and with some approximation by the RAF, statistics for killed, captured and "evaders" (soldiers and airmen who escaped arrest) were not correlated with crash or forced landing sites. During the war, the RAF had more urgent matters to attend to. After the war, however, no general survey was taken of the successive totals. It is for this reason that data gathered on the ground is so valuable.

These studies of France are factual in nature. They do not venture into the debate regarding the attitude of the French people, though they indirectly show them to have been overwhelmingly pro-Ally and in favor of resistance. This is the same phenomenon of "mass help" that the historian Roger Absalom studied for Italy. In a pioneering work on the history of helpers, the author reveals the "strange alliance" between Italian peasants and the British soldiers who became fugitives at the time of the Italian armistice in September 1943.[23] Escaping upon the arrival of the Germans, around 50,000 fugitives melted into the landscape of central italy. The author explains this solidarity by reference to a peasant "common sense." Consisting of traditions of survival inherited from centuries of exploitation, this created a sense of fellowship and brotherhood with the fugitives. Moreover, an old millenarianism found satisfaction in the fact of helping the distressed representatives of a rich and powerful country. The inversion of power relations was a sign that the reign of justice was approaching. This social analysis is not applicable to France, where helpers were as active in towns as they were in the countryside and where the condition of the peasantry was not (or was much less) synonymous with social oppression. In France, the "mass help" offered the Allies was based on a revolutionary heritage consisting of ideas of the nation and the right of peoples. Roger Absalom's work nevertheless reveals this characteristic shared by France and Italy: that local help for the Allies was a mass phenomenon.

This understanding calls into question the arguments of specialists of collaboration, who tend to see the population as opportunistic (engaged in a process of "accommodation")[24] and little inclined to resistance, except in a marginal and violent way. In shedding a harsh light on the collaboration between the Vichy government and Nazi authorities, Robert Paxton's *Vichy France*, first published in 1972, contributed to reorienting the historiography of the occupation.[25] Though *Vichy France* concerns state collaboration rather than the Resistance, it was also read as a critique of the place occupied by the Resistance in the history of the Occupation. Published twenty years later,

Philippe Burrin's book, *France under the Germans: Collaboration and Compromise*, contributed to the same historiographical current.[26] In contrast to *Vichy France*, *France under the Germans* does indeed concern the collective behavior of French people under the Occupation but it does not include the activities of those engaged in resistance. Entirely devoted to behaviors of "accommodation," the book paints a portrait in gray and black. These analyses responded to what was at the time a social expectation. The present study seeks to renew the discussion of the place and nature of resistance activities in France and comes to the conclusion that they should be revised upwards.

Since the 2000s, a nascent bibliography has begun to emerge for the German case. A book, an article and three contributions to edited volumes have addressed the lynching of Allied pilots in Germany. They offer general surveys of the institutional mechanisms at work behind local improvisation and seek to give an overview of *Volksjustiz* – the name given "popular justice" by the authorities of the Reich. The clearest contribution to this nascent debate has been that of Klaus-Michael Mallmann, a professor at the University of Stuttgart.[27] This specialist of the genocide of the Jews concludes with the claim that *Lynchjustiz* – a new concept first employed by Wehrmacht staff head-quarters in 1944 – is an indication of the generalization of the war of annihilation launched by Nazi Germany. He adds that this form of "popular justice" involved the population in the same way as its participation in murdering deportees during the "death marches" of 1945. Conversely, Barbara Grimm argues that the authors of these attacks were generally Nazi officials and that popular violence was an exception. This is also the thesis of two recently published (2014 and 2015) and well-documented studies of *Fliegerlynchjustiz* (lynching-justice against airmen) in Austria.[28] Helmut Schnatz's scholarly article, *Lynchmorde an Fliegern*, does not directly take a position, although it is to be found in a volume that puts Nazi and Allied violence on the same level.[29] Finally, an in-depth article by Kevin T. Hall preceding the publication of his Ph.D. ("Terror Flyers," 2021) clearly shows the involvement of civilians in the lynching of airmen and explains it by reference to the anger and desire for vengeance that bombing provoked.[30] This is a point worth discussing: was popular anger a prior fact or rather a political and cultural construction? The fact that such lynching was only committed by German and Austrian nationals helps us to begin to formulate a response. The cases of lynching that took place in occupied countries were perpetrated by Wehrmacht troops rather than the inhabitants of these places. The question of the manner in which Allied airmen were received on the ground in Nazi Germany thus intersects with the debate over German victimization at the hands of Allied strategic bombing.

Alongside this work by historians, there is the particularly useful book by legal scholar Katrin Hassel.[31] She presents the activities of the British military courts that were created in accordance with the 18 June 1945 Royal Warrant to

INTRODUCTION 11

judge war crimes committed in Germany. Hassel thus identifies 92 trials in which 315 defendants were charged with committing war crimes against Allied airmen. This figure is far from representing the total number of Germans charged with this crime since these trials were also administered by other courts, including the French and American military tribunals operating in their respective occupation zones and German tribunals. Hassel's work nevertheless allows us to take partial statistical stock of a subject that has hitherto been an object of ill-founded estimation.

The historiography of bombing also intersects with our subject to the degree that the manner in which airmen were received on the ground may have been influenced by the suffering caused civilians by bombing. In the relevant chapters, we shall see the degree to which the historiography of German bombing of France and Britain is impoverished, in stark contrast to the rich historiography on Allied bombing of Germany and the occupied countries. This imbalance raises questions. It contributes to the historiographical current that tends to present Germany as a victim but is not merely a product of the German historiography of the air war, though the latter has long been culturally imbued with the Nazi past.[32] The historiography originating in former Allied countries is also severely critical of Allied bombing. The wealth of Allied archives, which contrasts with the relative poverty of their German counterparts (partly destroyed during the war), further contributes to this imbalance of information.

By seeking to apply to the French case the issues raised by bombing in Germany, a matter that has been the object of lively discussion since the 2000s, recent research in England has opened another debate. What effect did Allied bombing have on morale and public opinion in French society? First, one must get some idea of the scale of Allied bombing in France: it today seems that it caused as many casualties as German bombing in Great Britain. More than 50,000 French people were killed by Allied bombs, the vast majority of them in the run-up to the D-Day landings of 1944. In 2006, professors Richard Overy, Andrew Knapp and Claudia Baldoli developed a research project to shed light on Allied bombing policies and their material and moral effects. They initially estimated that, "in France and Italy, for example, bombing was carried out against the population by the very forces that promised to liberate them, thereby giving rise to confused and ambivalent responses."[33] The two volumes in which this project resulted drew upon opinion surveys to flesh out this idea.[34] They ultimately concluded that, though it varied according to the intensity of the bombing, French public opinion was less confused than expected and remained solidly pro-Ally. The present study, however, is not based on the evidence of public opinion that we possess for this period of dictatorship. Rather, it seeks to study behavior. Action does not paint the same picture as words. It is unambiguous. The assistance offered to airmen was general.

Cult Films and Adventure Stories

While the local population's reception of airmen on the ground has received little scholarly attention, this moment of the Second World War, repeated thousands of times, inspired and continues to inspire popular culture. It is worth taking a moment to consider this discrepancy.

One reason for it has to do with the attraction exerted by the history of aviation and airmen. Ever since aviation first began, all segments of the public have appreciated the epic story of the air and the legends that have accompanied it. In the United Kingdom, the myth doubtless reached its acme during the Second World War. It is also in that country that the first work of cultural history on the subject was published. Behind the fascination that airmen exerted on the public, *The Flyer: British Culture and the Royal Air Force 1939–1945* reveals the complexity, contradictions and ups and downs of life as a RAF airman.[35] While airmen are not the subject of the present book, the aura that surrounds their activity has given rise to many accounts, novels, comics and films. Starting with the First World War, a transnational popular culture emerged. It plays a role in the present book because, much more so than the work of scholars, these are the vectors that conveyed the memory of the events that concern us.

But this discrepancy is not only a matter of the small number of academic works that have been published as compared with the vast number of stories and films to treat the same subject. The cultural "gap" also has a particular complexion. Works intended for a "general public" do not tell the same story. In what concerns the manner in which civilians received fugitives, they tend either to embellish, idealize or tone down the portrait by passing over or minimizing its tragic or criminal dimension, depending on the place under consideration. These stories and images subsequently set up shop in collective memory and remain there, even when scholarly discourse has subsequently moved on. The result is the coexistence, often within the same citizen, of what may be two contradictory historical analyses, depending on whether what is in question is local or family memory or instead history as it is taught. For example: the polite behavior shown by British civilians sits uncomfortably with the critical approach to the People's War, just as the mass help given the Allies in France does not easily fit into the now dominant historiography of the "Black Years." It is in Germany that this discrepancy has received the most attention, with the book *Opa war kein Nazi: Nationalsozialismus und Holocaust im Familiengedächtnis.*[36] This study, which was conducted in 1985, shows how the past participation of elder family members in the Nazi system has been almost euphemized into oblivion. Yet this has not prevented the teaching of history in Germany from being fully critical of the Nazi regime. Rather, two discourses live side by side – one that defends elder members of the family, holding them up as an example, and another that criticizes the society of that time.

INTRODUCTION 13

If one follows the chronological order of events, the France of May–June 1940 comes first. The local and familial memory of the exodus remains but has resonated little in popular culture. In what concerns civilian resistance to the invaders, no work has attempted to interpret it. Such cinematographic successes as *Jeux interdits* (1952), *Week-end à Zuydcoote* (1964) and *Mais où est donc passée la 7ème Compagnie?* (1973) do not even touch upon the question. Its history remains submerged.

It is perhaps in the United Kingdom, where the arrest of airmen generally remained peaceful, that the discrepancy between local or family memory and school memory is least pronounced. The British configuration is strikingly illustrated by a contemporaneous film. Released in 1942, the American film *Mrs. Miniver* offers an example of a German pilot being received on the ground in England. The film itself was among the war's events.[37] Produced in the United States in 1942 in liaison with the Office of War Information, it was intended to stoke pro-British sentiment in the United States and was a blockbuster in the USA and Great Britain alike. The figure of Mrs. Miniver was already familiar to the English: imagined by the woman of letters Jan Struther, the daily life of this middle-class British woman and architect's wife had been the subject of a column published in the *Times* before the war. In the film, with her husband having left on his boat to assist in the evacuation of Dunkirk alongside some 700 other small craft (27 May–4 June 1940), Mrs. Miniver discovers a wounded German pilot in her yard. Threatening her with his pistol, he demands food and a civilian coat to help him escape. The pilot stirs maternal feelings in Mrs. Miniver, doubtless because her own son is at that very moment fighting in an RAF squadron. Coming to after fainting, the pilot delivers the excited speech of a conqueror: "You'll see, you'll see, we'll bomb, we'll bomb your cities, like Barcelona, Warsaw, Narvik, Rotterdam, we'll destroy them in two hours!" Once again, the pilot faints. Mrs. Miniver calls the police and asks for a doctor. It is interesting to observe how, in 1942, the humane treatment of downed pilots – a depiction not far removed from the reality of the time – was offered as a model to the Anglo-American public.

A similar message is delivered by *The One that Got Away*, an English film released in 1957. It is a documentary-type production regarding Franz von Werra's escape attempts.[38] The film begins on 5 September 1940, when von Werra was forced to land in a field in the village of Marden (Kent) while participating in a bombing mission against the Biggin Hill airfield. With the battle still raging overhead, the Oberleutnant surrenders by handing his pistol to the cook of the anti-aircraft battery who came running in apron and chef's hat to arrest him. The latter is soon joined by the "Ack-Ack boys," armed representatives of the anti-aircraft battery. "It's mine," says the cook, indicating to his comrades that, as the first to reach the scene, the takings were his, as in a treasure hunt. The prisoner is calmly taken back to the battery. This peaceful and picturesque war scene did in fact take place. The question is to

14   INTRODUCTION

determine whether it was always thus and why. One might also mention the celebrated TV series, *Dad's Army*, which depicts the comical adventures and misadventures of a Home Guard platoon in an English village.[39] In a tone of self-mockery, five of its twenty-four episodes recount the painstaking efforts of the platoon to arrest German airmen.[40]

It is in Germany that the gap between history and memory is very likely greatest. For obvious reasons of self-protection, post-Nazi society was silent in regards to the issue of lynching, which was a flagrant violation of international law. Popular culture long excluded the memory of these actions. In the 1980s, however, this began to change, with a few scenes from a hit 1984 television series directly addressing our subject. The series, *Heimat: eine deutsche Chronik*, covers the period between 1919 and 1982. The episode that interests us takes place in 1943 in a town resembling Morbach, the author's native village in the Hunsrück mountains, 50 kilometers from Luxembourg. As indicated by its title and subtitle, the film presents itself as a German account of the German homeland, home and family (connoting a nearly organic conception of home, the term *Heimat* is untranslatable in English). This talented series deliberately sets itself in the context of the German grand narrative, explicitly reacting to another television series, *Holocaust*, which was produced in the United States in 1978. National Socialist crimes are largely absent from *Heimat*. Although the author claimed he chose the title ironically in order to distance himself from the "Heimat" genre that emerged in 1950s Germany and sang the praises of prewar Germany, the portrait he offers of the Nazi years is that of a peaceful village in which the apparent normalcy of everyday life tends to obscure the Nazi dimension of public and private life. It is a vision of German memory that comports poorly with the historiography on Nazism. We shall return to this question of German memory – or, rather, memories – later.

For the moment, it should be noted that *Heimat* is nevertheless original in portraying the murder of an Allied pilot.[41] In 1943, an airplane crashed in the area. Children saw a British pilot enter a forest and led a local SS man, the son of the village mayor, there. Apart from his boots, the SS man was not in uniform. It is thus unknown whether he was on duty or had come in a personal capacity, a distinction that tended to become blurred in Hitler's Germany. The SS man found the seriously wounded pilot on the ground, killed him and returned to the children, telling them he had to shoot the airman because the latter had attempted to flee. Later, the SS man is congratulated by the lieutenant of the local Luftwaffe post. The lieutenant honors him with a coffee and a tirade inspired by Goebbels' speeches on "terrorist pilots" and the "self-defense" measures "the population" had taken against them. Outside, soldiers listening under the window laugh up their sleeves. These scenes thus constitute a rather subtle whole. In addition to showing the population's awareness of the regime's crimes and those who perpetrated

INTRODUCTION 15

them, they suggest that it in some ways stood at one remove from official discourse. This seductive picture does not show close interaction between the population and the elites. The present book, by contrast, shows how, from mid-1943 onwards, social violence and state violence entered into a dynamic of reciprocal emulation.

In France, representations of downed airmen in popular culture significantly depart from the dominant current of historiography. The bibliography on the French case stands apart for its abundance of published first-person accounts. These are primarily accounts written by British or American escapees and published after the war. Nearly three quarters of the few thousand Allied soldiers and airmen who succeeded in reaching London after avoiding capture or escaping from German hands in Northwestern Europe passed through France. Did the accounts of these successful escapes, published after the war, embellish the truth? The portrait they offer of France's people is of a population wholly devoted to the Allied cause despite the threats leveled by the occupiers against those guilty of "helping the enemy." Whether secretly crossing France in 1940 (Jimmy Langley), 1941 (Derrick Nabarro), 1942 (Airey Neave and Lucien Dumais), 1943 (James Hargest) or 1944 (Beirne Lay and Ronald Ivelaw-Chapman), the narrator advanced as if carried on the shoulders of the inhabitants he encountered.[42] Similarly, the many accounts written by members of escape networks give the impression of a France united in its hatred of the occupier and willingness to help the Allies.[43] Even the Anglophobes among them helped young Englishmen return to the fight. Jimmy Langley recounts this exchange with the doctor who tended to wounds Langley had reopened and aggravated so as to circumvent the official repatriation commission headquartered in Marseille. Knowing that the doctor was running a risk by tending to him, he felt obliged to warn him.

> In thanking and offering to pay him, which he refused, I begrudgingly pointed out that he had hurt me.
>
> – I did it on purpose, he replied, I hate the English. You killed my great grandfather at Trafalgar and you stole our colonies.
> – Why then do you take the risk of helping me, I asked in surprise?
> – Only because I hate the Germans more. It's my duty as a Frenchman to help whoever fights them. When you have beaten the Germans, you will be weakened and we will conquer you. Goodbye.[44]

Were the escapees and their helpers mistaken? Did they mistake the part for the whole, attributing what was in fact an unevenly distributed pro-Ally attitude to the entire nation? Or was there some basis to the theme of the nation in resistance?

The cult film, *La Grande Vadrouille*, might for its part also seem to present a storybook image of the French soaked in legend.[45] Dating from 1966, this cult film was still able to achieve record ratings fifty years on when rebroadcast in

16 INTRODUCTION

March 2020 for the first Sunday of the pandemic-induced confinement. The film is set in occupied France. On or around June 1942, three RAF pilots are forced to parachute from their airplane over Paris. One lands in the seal basin of the Vincennes zoo, another on the scaffolding of a house painter and the last atop the Opera. All three successfully make it to the Free Zone with the help of the inhabitants. Thanks to a series of chance encounters, those whom the Allies already called "helpers" assist them in improvising cover stories and thereby escaping the Germans. Though most do not know one another at the outset, they form an escape chain. They are: a Vincennes zookeeper, a house painter (Bourvil), a conductor (Louis de Funès), a young woman puppeteer (Marie Dubois) and her grandfather, who runs the Champs-Elysées puppet theater, Opera stagehands, two postmen, a female hotelkeeper from Meursault (Côte d'Or) and the Mother Superior (Mary Marquet) and nuns of the Beaune hospice. With the exception of the Opera stagehands, who prepare an act of sabotage, and the grandfather, who knows an escape route from the line of demarcation to Meursault, none of these figures has links to the Resistance. But improvisation always leads them in the same direction, that of helping. Together with this series of impromptu actions, the ups and downs of the chase result in what is a deeply improbable (from a sociological point of view) objective social network. For in normal times, it is unlikely that such varied professions would join forces in a single undertaking. This is one of the particularities of this type of Resistance. The fact that it falls outside the scope of any predefined and durable social milieu is a challenge both for the historian and for those who seek to preserve its memory.

The film owes its success to the combined talents of its screenwriter-director (Gérard Oury), his co-writers (his daughter Danièle Thompson and Marcel Jullian), and the famous actors Bourvil and Louis de Funès. At once comedy and action film, it was for thirty years the most widely viewed film in France (17.2 million tickets sold in the year of its release) and was only dethroned by *Titanic* in 1997, *Bienvenue chez les Ch'tis* in 2008 (both of which sold 19 million tickets) and *Intouchables* in 2011, which sold more than 19 million tickets. Part of the success of *La Grande Vadrouille* doubtless also stems from the flattering portrait it offers of the French people of the time. In what regards the specific matter of assistance to the Allies, however, its portrait is not false. From this point of view, the film is in sharp contrast with the "retro fashion" and "cinema of the black years" that would enjoy success following *Le Chagrin et la pitié* (1971), which portrayed the French people as opportunistic and eager to collaborate. This contrast and contradiction are worth exploring.

Debriefings, Depositions and Verified Statements

The sources for this work are of exceptional quality. Often, examinations of wartime societies – of their indifference, mobilization, submission or

INTRODUCTION

resistance – rely on public opinion surveys. For example, historians use "Mass Observation" – the work of a private polling institute created in London in 1937 – and those of the Ministry of Information. For Germany, they turn to the reports of the SD, the Sicherheitsdienst, an SS department that closely monitored German society. For France, the *contrôle postal* (postal censorship commission) and the reports of prefects make it possible to chart the evolution of public opinion. Interpreting these documents is not always a straightforward matter, in part because they depend closely on the service that produced them and in part because their content depends on a collection of opinions.[46]

Central to the sources upon which the present study relies, by contrast, is a set of actions that were carried out and inventoried with the utmost care. The first of these consists of the few cases in which German pilots were roughed up or killed by French people during the invasion in May–June 1940. Its victory freed up the Reich to investigate this handful of cases and carry out reprisals. The many traces left by these investigations are held in the archives of the German Armistice Commission in Wiesbaden, the Wehrmacht's legal department and the German Military Tribunals. For the following period, that of the Occupation properly so called, two serial archival collections offer detailed information on French society. They were assembled during the war (starting in 1940 for Britain and 1942 for the United States). These collections consist of the "debriefings" of soldiers and airmen who escaped from Western Europe – accounts collected by MI9 (British Military Intelligence) and MIS-X (the American Military Intelligence Service). There are more than 4,000 such debriefings of escapees from France.[47] These escape reports are supplemented by a list of the "helpers" whom the escapees encountered. After the war, the two victorious nations carried out a policy of recognizing and compensating those who helped their soldiers. The representatives of these "Awards Bureaus" crisscrossed the formerly occupied countries of Europe to conduct a census of clandestine allies. In London and Washington, hundreds of archival boxes now hold the stories of these "helpers" – the "unknown soldiers," in their way, of the war. In France, they numbered 34,000. Finally, there are also some serial-type sources for Germany: they consist of a systematic and detailed collection concerning the Allied proceedings for war crimes committed against downed airmen. In their respective zones of occupation, British and American military courts conducted a total of 300 trials ("flyer trials") of more than 800 defendants.[48] If one adds the cases of lynching in which the perpetrators could not be identified or located – and thus not tried – cases of lynching increase threefold (to more than 900). On the basis of these selective sources, one can estimate the total number of victims at around 2,500, of whom 950 were killed. Held in the archives of the Judge Advocate General of each country, these dossiers lend themselves to social-statistical treatment. The archives of the trials conducted in the French occupation zone are also available but the inventory does not allow one to identify the trials that

18   INTRODUCTION

concern us among the 15,600 cartons held there.[49] We possess no information concerning trials conducted in the Soviet zone, if there were any, or those of German courts.

The quality of these sources is partly due to their dialectical construction – they are an interaction between two parties, one of whom seeks to verify the other's statements. They are not the analyses of a more or less partial observer but rather documents built from discussion and the tension that sometimes existed between its participants – whether they be representatives of the Wehrmacht and Vichy government, secret service interrogators and escapees, the Awards Bureaus and those requesting recognition after the war or Allied judges and the German attorneys of German civilians. They have been fact-checked, either inside the Allied armies or in literally international manner, and offer a comparative perspective, whether it be that of Germany on France or that of the Allies on France and Germany. In addition to their reliability, these sources have the merit of providing an inventory of verifiable actions free of opinion (unstable) and interpretation (relative).

A gap remains in this summary of essential sources: we possess no comparable corpus for the British side of things. It seems that neither the British nor the Germans took the trouble of noting the conditions in which German pilots were received on British soil. In 1943, the Wehrmacht's department nevertheless established a report on the "British army's war crimes" but Great Britain itself is absent from the theaters of operations reviewed in this document.[50] The archives of the Wilhelmstrasse are also silent on this subject. Whether it be a sign that there were no crimes to report or the reflection of a particular policy, this silence merits further study. We similarly have no information regarding Allied pilots brought down over Germany in 1939–40.

The Book's Arguments

The first part of this book presents the portrait, until now unknown, of local resistance against the Luftwaffe airmen who came down over France in 1940. In so doing, it revisits the image of France's defeat. In place of a moral and military débâcle, we see men fighting to defend their territory (Chapter 1). The exodus of millions of civilians on the roads, which contributed to the defeat, no longer looks like a mass panic but rather like a referendum based on the experience of earlier invasions and occupations. By its brutality, the repression of resistance to the invasion by German military courts shows that, in 1940 no more than in 1914, the German army did not respect the relevant articles of international law (Chapter 2).

The second part immediately follows in chronological order: it concerns the Battle of Britain and the first Blitz. The upwelling of patriotism to which the invasion gave rise, magnified by Churchill's speeches and supported by government measures, calls to mind the mass conscription of patriots during the

INTRODUCTION 19

French Revolution (Chapter 3). This dynamic did not prevent civilians from behaving peacefully toward fallen German airmen. The positive image of the People's War, which has often been challenged since the 1970s, turns out to be well-founded for this aspect of the war. The calm observed by civilians did not come from nowhere. The government played upon the national stereotype of British humor to discipline behaviors (Chapter 4). A cultural fact thus contributed to shaping the behavior of civilians.

The third part of the book shows how, after the defeat, a certain French nation was reconstructed at the local level. The help systematically given at great risk by the population to British soldiers unable to re-embark and downed Allied airmen demands that we revise our image of occupied France (Chapter 5). In contrast with the historiographical current that presents the French as adapting to and even voluntarily collaborating with the occupier, studying the clandestine help given the Allies reveals a resistant France. The brutality of the German reaction did not curb this movement (Chapter 6). Given the violence of the repression brought to bear upon it, "civilian resistance" seems ill-suited as an expression. It was rather a matter of civilians conducting an asymmetric war against an occupation. Their action was all the more remarkable in that it ran directly counter to Vichyite and Nazi propaganda. Strangely, this resistance did not make its way into the national story of the Resistance (Chapter 7). The thesis of "résistancialisme" does not apply here.

The book's fourth and final part raises the question of the Nazification of German society. It shows that the practice of lynching airmen became commonplace among civilians starting in mid-1943 and that this new practice contravening international law was both incited from above and desired from below (Chapters 8 and 9). For townspeople and villagers who participated in these collective actions, lynching represented a moment of free expression. Their outbursts of anger were culturally and politically constructed (Chapter 10). They were a manifestation of Nazism and contained an explicit racist dimension. As surprising as it may seem today, Allied airmen were often perceived as "Jews" and "negroes" (Chapter 11).

In a word, it was a civilian's war, too.

PART I

Blitz-Invasion in France, or Resistance Crushed

Taking place over the course of a few weeks, the crushing defeat of France surprised all protagonists to the conflict. Following immediately upon it, the German attempt to invade the United Kingdom held its actors and observers spellbound in suspense until October. The Battle of Britain, as it once and for all came to be known in 1941, lasted from 10 July 1940 to 31 October of the same year.[1] While it was clear by October that Germany had not succeeded in achieving air supremacy, the threat nevertheless remained. Hitler delayed Operation Sea Lion and the landings associated with it. As the second Blitz (March–May 1941) indicated, this was no more than a delay. Since this fateful summer of 1940, the degree to which the Allies were prepared or unprepared for war has been ceaselessly debated in all areas.

For the civilians of France and Britain alike, invasion or the imminent threat thereof was a common denominator. In one case, a genuine invasion accompanied by a floodtide of refugees several million strong. In the other, the fear of invasion, directly inspired by events in France. Did French, Belgian, Dutch and Luxembourgish civilians give in to panic as is suggested by the many photographs of columns of refugees on the country's roads? Or did they have the time needed to organize themselves to fight the invader, after the fashion of the French francs-tireurs of 1870? And did British civilians, sheltering behind an anti-tank trench more than 25 nautical miles wide, benefit from the lessons of Dunkirk and the collapse of the French Army?

The unpreparedness and improvisations of 1940 seem to dominate the scene. But in truth, when looked at from below and at a very local level, the spontaneity of the French response in all its vagaries showed a potential for resisting the invasion. The announcement of the armistice abruptly nipped this dynamic in the bud. On British territory, which benefited from a few additional weeks to prepare for invasion – an invasion that ultimately never came – this dynamic developed into a national movement to prepare for armed resistance. What would become the legendary story of the Home Guard flourished. The pockets of civilian resistance in France, by contrast, sank into oblivion.

The issues at stake in the Battle of France far exceeded France itself. Imagine, if you will, that the Wehrmacht had slowly advanced across French territory in May–June 1940. The armed mobilization of civilians unearthed in this book thus proceeds apace and gathers steam, these new volunteers of Year II (or, rather, Year XL) efficiently contributing to the defense of the national territory. The press, still free, rediscovers the epic poem of Victor Hugo:[2]

> *O soldiers of year two! O wars! Or epics!*
> *Against the kings together drawing their swords,*
> *Prussians, Austrians,*
> *Against all the Tyres and all the Sodoms*
> *Against the Czar of the north, against this hunter of men*
> *Followed by all his dogs ...*

If France had held out in 1940, how many men, women and children across Europe would have escaped this "hunter of men followed by all his dogs"? The fall of France sounded the victory of Nazism on the continent.

1

Finding the Volunteers of the Year 40

With a few famous exceptions, no history has been written of the fighting soldiers and civilians of May–June 1940. Yet resistance – whether it be the military resistance of Colonel de Gaulle, the resistance of the administration or the resistance to torture with which Jean Moulin opposed the invader – required an infrastructure and the support of troops, civil servants and citizens. The memory of these pockets of resistance has since been engulfed by the fact of defeat, Nazi occupation and the Vichy regime to such an extent that it has seriously skewed the history of the "débâcle," understood as comprising both exodus and defeat. Missing from this portrait is any appreciation of the readiness to fight, whether patriotic or/and republican.

By drawing upon scraps of archive detailing the manner in which civilians resisted the arrival of Luftwaffe airmen on the ground, the two chapters that follow contribute to restoring some balance to this history. The actions some citizens took when confronted with downed Luftwaffe airmen shed light on a French capacity to react that is rarely acknowledged in standard accounts of France's defeat. Given the present state of research in this area, it is still too early to draw any very clear-cut conclusions. This book offers evidence, however, for an emerging thesis that may or may not lead to a larger reassessment of the monochromatic, unquestioned view of the débâcle that has held sway for the past eighty years.

Plouguerneau (Finistère), 18 June 1940

The civilians who apprehended downed German airmen in 1940 did not have the luxury of committing their experience to the page. That would have been risky after the armistice of 22 June. By contrast, one finds accounts by members of the Luftwaffe in the archives of the Wehrmacht's Legal Service. Here is one such example, drawn from a ruling delivered by the military tribunal of the 5th Panzer Division in Brest on 23 June 1940.[1] This ruling sentenced two defendants to death as "francs-tireurs." One of them, a fifty-seven-year-old farmer and father of eight, was executed by firing squad five days later. Jean-Marie Kérandel was doubtless the invasion's first civilian resister to be executed after a ruling by the German Army.

On June 18th, 1940, due to fire on LG1 [Lehrgeschwader 1, a Luftwaffe training squadron] from enemy ships located in the harbor of Brest, the aircraft, which was under the command of Major Cranz, had to carry out an emergency landing around 4km north of Lannilis [in Plouguerneau in fact], near Brest, because the left engine had been shot out by anti-aircraft fire. During the emergency landing in a zone of fields and hedges, the aircraft broke up. The four members of the crew, which also included First Lieutenant Sodermann and corporals Scheidies and Reschke, were wounded to varying degrees. The pilot, First Lieutenant Sodermann, was severely wounded to the head, which was bleeding, Major Cranz had a severely fractured arm, Observer Reschke was wounded to the thigh and knee and Radio Operator Scheidies had a bruised foot.

As the passengers left the airplane and set fire to it, farmers armed with firearms, sharp objects and pitchforks, accompanied by gendarmes, approached the airplane from all sides. They were preceded by women who, according to the witnesses mentioned above, were apparently supposed to prevent a defense [on the part of the airmen]. The peasants opened fire from a distance. In order to defend themselves from the attack, the two lightly wounded corporals fired several pistol shots. The crew, with a dismounted machine gun and their four pistols, headed for cover but were rapidly spotted and surrounded on all sides. As defense appeared hopeless, the crew waved a white handkerchief and loudly shouted in French: "Don't shoot, we're wounded and prisoners!" Despite this call, the peasants once again opened fire. Around 40 to 50 armed peasants and gendarmes threw themselves upon them. Although they must have seen the defenseless state of the crewmen, they tore away their weapons, matériel and uniforms in the most brutal manner. Several peasants and gendarmes pointed their pistols and rifles at the airmen's chests. At the same time, they indiscriminately struck them from all sides with their sticks, pitchforks, sidearms and fists. They also tore off some of the airmen's clothing so that they would be more or less exposed to the blows without clothing.

Presented in the ruling handed down five days after the event in question, this version of the facts raises many questions. The context is not that of a simple training bomber that found itself in distress after falling victim to enemy fire. Starting the previous evening, 17 June, Brest found itself under heavy bombardment on the part of the Luftwaffe. The ships, seeking to embark as many troops and as much materiel as possible, were targeted by German aviation. The population was both witness to and victim of this air warfare. It had also been alerted as to the imminent arrival of Wehrmacht troops. Brest would be taken on the evening of 19 June. Civilians thus found themselves thrust into the middle of a naval, land and air battlefield and their aggressiveness indicates that they felt themselves participants in the war. The behavior of the Luftwaffe crew is not so easily characterized. The tribunal's verdict only shows them on

Figure 1.1 18 June 1940. A German crew is captured in the village of Plouguerneau (Finistère). © Danièle Le Droff.
High school student Georges Le Droff poses on the fuselage of the Luftwaffe plane. The crew was rather roughly arrested by the inhabitants. Following its arrival in Brest the next day, the Wehrmacht arrested some of them. Two men were sentenced to death as "francs-tireurs" and one of them, Jean-Marie Kérandel, was executed on 23 June. Georges Le Droff would for his part become involved in the resistance and helped Allied airmen reach England. He received the title of "helper" after the war.

the defensive. When two airmen fired pistol shots, it was to defend themselves, and when the four men "headed for cover" with their arms and an on-board machine gun, it was not to flee but to prepare their "defense." Yet the possibility of aggressive behavior on their part is not excluded, particularly given that their army would soon be there. The final apprehension of the four airmen by gendarmes and peasants was turbulent: this is one of the only points on which the French and German versions agree, with the arrival on site of a small crowd of hostile inhabitants of both sexes.[2]

On both sides, there were many such undesired encounters. Taken together, the French and British air forces shot down some 850 German airplanes between 10 May and 24 June.[3] Each of these airplanes carried between two and five personnel. In the skies of Europe during the Second World War, however, the mortality rate for airmen whose aircraft was in distress was around 50 percent and this independently of whether they parachuted from their planes, executed a forced landing or were killed in flight.[4] Between 850 and 2,100 members of the Luftwaffe thus reached the ground alive. A portion of them fell behind German lines. At least four hundred of them and perhaps twice that landed their airplanes on or parachuted over territory held by the French.[5] In contrast to army units, they stand apart for having generally been taken prisoner away from the battlefield properly so called. Very often, they encountered civilians before gendarmes or units of the French Army could arrive on the scene.

In portraying the Luftwaffe as innocent victim, the account produced by the 5th Panzer Division tribunal has the merit of raising the question of how French civilians, men and women, behaved when confronted with enemy airmen on the ground. Moreover, by handing down two death sentences even though no airman was killed, the verdict signaled that the right of the civilian population to resist invasion – since 1899 permitted under certain conditions by the first Hague Convention – would not be recognized by the Wehrmacht. The historiography of the exodus and defeat has curiously neglected these two aspects of the story: civilian resistance to the invasion and its brutal repression by the invader without regard for international law. To rediscover these events, one must abandon the vision of the past constructed by most of the work on these subjects published since summer 1940. It is only recently that the understanding of the months of May and June 1940 has been enlarged to encompass other military, social and political realities.

In the Midst of the "Débâcle" – War

Whether it addresses it from a military point of view or a social and political one, recent work on the French defeat of 1940 has contributed nuance to the image of a generalized "débâcle." The military historiography has lately tended to give the French military more credit for its preparedness, deconstruct the "Blitzkrieg legend" and underscore the voluntarism shown by some French Army units. In the social and political domain, recent surveys challenge the idea that French society was "decadent" or in "decline," insisting to the contrary on the very military causes of defeat. Without overturning the dominant historiography of the "débâcle" of 1940, these works attest to the existence of military and civilian resistance along the front of the invasion. The memory of these multiple local undertakings was swept away by later events as well as by the impossibility of recording them at the time. In what concerns the manner in which French civilians received downed Luftwaffe airmen, the present study reveals a dynamic of resisting the invader.

The most incisive work of military history to revisit the image of 1940 is that of the historian Karl-Heinz Frieser. He underscores the fact that Hitler had no Blitzkrieg strategy at the time of the French campaign in 1940.[6] Summarizing his thought, the author offers this striking formula: "The France campaign was a successful but improvised Blitzkrieg, that against the USSR a planned but failed one."[7] Perhaps, as Christian Malis claims, [8] this revision of the received history overstates matters but it has the virtue of unsettling established certainties and reintroducing doubt in regard to what was supposedly an inevitable chain of events. Dennis Showalter and Martin Alexander show that the French Army "had understood modern war" and that its Commanding General, Gamelin, had indeed drawn "the lessons of the Poland campaign."[9] These works do not take up the question of the civilian defense. But they open up a debate that may be useful to us in evaluating civilian preparedness vis-à-vis the aggression of a foreign army.

Whether or not it was planned, the "Blitzkrieg" presented Nazi characteristics. The war "in the West" marked a further stage in the Nazification of the Wehrmacht.[10] The scattered massacres of several hundred – and perhaps even several thousand – Senegalese infantrymen in May and June 1940, the transfer of captured Spanish republican volunteers in the French Army to the Mauthausen concentration camp, and the isolation and mistreatment of Jewish prisoners all reveal the advanced politicization of the Wehrmacht. During the massacres of black soldiers, racist violence was performatively accompanied by specific forms of cruelty.[11] The fact that the German Army should have targeted the enemies of National Socialism – blacks, reds (*Rotspanier*) and Jews – to inflict violations of the law of war upon them indicates collective involvement in racial and political violence. In this connection, one might also mention the massacre of some 200 British prisoners of war (and a few French ones) on 27 and 28 May 1940, or the 600 civilians slaughtered by the Wehrmacht in May–June 1940 in the Nord and Pas-de-Calais départements.[12] It is true that the war in France did not assume the pace of the war in the East, as in Poland where the Wehrmacht practiced a "war of annihilation" (*Vernichtungskrieg*) before openly proclaiming it during the invasion of the USSR, but there was also nothing "normal" or "honorable" about the war in the West.[13] Indeed, can one say this of any war of aggression?

In general, civilians were not spared: 22,000 civilian victims are presently estimated to have been killed in France in 1940, a good portion of them on the roads of the exodus.[14] German bombing is estimated to have resulted in 3,500 victims but it appears that this figure does not include those who died on the roads.[15] The strafing and bombing of refugee columns by Luftwaffe fighter planes and Stuka dive bombers, with their shrill sirens, provoked panic. Finding himself under the bombs of the Luftwaffe, even a hardened veteran of the artillery fire of 1914–18 such as Marc Bloch recognized that "it was only with tremendous effort that I was ever able to keep a similarly even temper."[16] On top of these ordeals came the acts of violence perpetrated by the Wehrmacht, including the massacres mentioned above.

Until the 2000s, the social and political history of the French defeat had not been extensively explored. Published in 1957, Jean Vidalenc's thoroughly researched and little-read book, *L'exode de mai–juin 1940*, long stood alone. Two surveys have recently revisited the subject: Hanna Diamond's 2007 book, *Fleeing Hitler*, and, in 2010, Eric Alary's *L'exode: un drame oublié*.[17] They offer a relatively classic portrait of the exodus as the civilian facet of a generalized collapse. More recently, Nicole Dombrowski Risser's book, *France under Fire*, presented with finesse a social history of families during the exodus and after the armistice. On the other hand, the book does not address the political question: why did people flee from the invader in 1940, while in 1944 they welcomed another with open arms? Other publications, however, have begun to explore new perspectives on the issue. Books by Jean-Louis Crémieux-Brilhac, Julian Jackson and Philip Nord, together with an article by Hanna Diamond, distinguish between various levels of analysis, separating out series of events that are too often compressed into a relentless causal chain. The breach was first opened by Jean-Louis Crémieux-Brilhac, who in 1990 published his monumental study of 1940, which depicts the contradictions of state and population while simultaneously revealing their final engagement in the struggle.[18] Over the course of several publications, Julian Jackson subsequently constructed an innovative analysis that challenged the manner in which the years 1930–44 have often been seen in retrospect.[19] There was nothing necessary about the manner in which five distinct phenomena – the crisis of the Third Republic, the Phony War, the military defeat of May–June 1940, the armistice and the Vichy regime – succeeded one another. Contrary to Marc Bloch, who in *Strange Defeat* acknowledges the military defeat but insists on the social and political weaknesses of French society to explain débâcle and armistice alike, Julian Jackson underscores the multiplicity of factors and their relative independence of one another. This rehabilitation of contingency in what has become an excessively streamlined account – one that partly has its origins in Vichyite propaganda – is an argument for bringing a fresh eye to bear on the few weeks of the French collapse.

Other studies also invite us to revisit our analyses. Philip Nord refutes the interpretation of the defeat as resulting from the "decadence" of French society or the "decline" of France. The defeat was a military event, as the examples of Belgium and the Netherlands show, countries that also fell victim to "Blitzkrieg." In France, it was the enemies of the Republic, well-represented among staff officers, who abandoned it, seizing upon the unhoped-for opportunity to remake France in their image. As the title of the book, *France 1940: Defending the Republic*, underscores, the values of this regime survived beyond its disappearance.[20] A similar argument is made by Hanna Diamond in an article published after her book. Scrutinizing the May–June 1940 exodus of civilians, she sheds light on the determination shown by those fleeing Nazism.[21] By comparing the "official" photographs taken by Army photographers, who tended to assign responsibility for the defeat to civilians, with those taken by Thérèse Bonney, an American special correspondent authorized to travel in combat zones, she offers a version of the exodus that restores their will and autonomy to the refugees. In *Fleeing Hitler*, her judgement is less assured but the very title of the book and that of a brief section, "The Exodus as a First Form of Resistance," had already opened the debate.[22]

Without going so far as to portray refugees as resisters, this new perspective allows one to dismiss any conflation between the "runaways" and the supposed decadence of the Republic. The migration, over the space of a few weeks, of some 8 million people – 1 million Belgians and 7 million Frenchmen[23] – also bespoke a refusal of Nazi and/or German domination and the refusal of forced cohabitation with its troops. The memory of the invasions of 1870 and 1914 and the subsequent occupations remained keen. Following the Allied landing in 1944, by contrast, the population did not vote with its feet in this way, quite the contrary. When several hundred collaborationists made their way to Germany in August 1944, they did not clog the roads. In 1957, the historian Jean Vidalenc, betraying some presentism, even spoke of the exodus of 1940 as "an advance referendum on collaboration."[24]

The Exodus as Referendum on the Invader

The asymmetric encounters between civilians and airmen help us bring a new perspective to bear on the behavior of inhabitants in May–June 1940. Some 8 million civilians fled the German advance. Leaving from Belgium and Luxembourg, this flood of people swept along in its wake a good portion of the inhabitants of northern France, the Paris basin and even south of the Loire all the way to the outskirts of the Jura and the Massif Central. Over the course of two great waves between 10 and 22 May and again between 9 and 22 June, there was no lack of looting, panic and chaos on the roads, the intensity of these phenomena varying from place to place and day to day. This is a phenomenon that must be examined if one is to understand the context in which civilians received downed German airmen.

The image of the débâcle as it is presented in memoirs published during the Occupation or after the Liberation is surprisingly uniform. That the "runaways" and "cowards" should have been described with jubilation by collaborationists like Lucien Rebatet is hardly astonishing: "It was an entire people, frantic and undone, moving house," he wrote, before profusely itemizing the fugitives' woes with sarcastic humor. If one abstracts oneself from the context, there is indeed something comical, a scene worthy of Jacques Tati, about these unlikely processions of ill-assorted vehicles blocked on the road. But it was the Third Republic that Rebatet targeted with this image. Similarly, Alfred Fabre-Luce, a supporter of the Vichy regime, saw this "ghastly exodus" as "the moral foundation of the armistice."[25] This experience of aimlessness and disorder had freed these "runaways," these "millions of uprooted people," from "political ideologies" and converted them to the values of "work" and "soil." They no longer hoped for anything other than "peace" and "order" – Republicans before the exodus, Vichyites after, as it were. But the generalizing moral judgement brought to bear on these events was hardly unique to collaborationists; it enjoyed support across the political spectrum. Marc Bloch himself did not escape this atmosphere of moral order, which he shared with the Vichy government, when in the summer of 1940 he wrote the manuscript of *Strange Defeat*. Though he seeks to qualify his thesis on several occasions, reading his book leaves one with the impression that, foundering in defeat, French society as a whole had failed. There is reason to think that, if the historian had survived, if the Gestapo had not murdered him for acts of resistance in 1944, he would have revised his text before publishing it after the war.

The anti-Nazi writer Léon Werth offers us a day-to-day account of the exodus as he experienced it. Having left Paris on 11 June, Werth found himself stuck for several weeks in the Gâtinais region. His notes make the case for restoring the proper proportions to this experience by taking into consideration the role played by the psychology and sociology of traffic jams in the attitudes of fugitives.[26] Applying a political prism to behaviors largely provoked by these exceptional traffic jams is to indulge in overinterpretation. Yet the nearly unanimous chorus of moral condemnation raises a question. Is this near unanimity anything other than a reaction to the shock of defeat? Does this broad consensus go beyond the search for a scapegoat?

How is one to fit the civilians who armed themselves against the enemy into this portrait of a putative general slackening? We have already seen the position sketched by Jean Vidalenc, according to whom the fugitives of 1940 were proto-resistants after their fashion by virtue of their implicit refusal of coexistence with the Germans. In a study of the Somme in 1940, Philippe Nivet advances another analysis: that there is a distinction to be made between those who remained and those who left.[27] Already bombarded in 1918 and once again under the bombs on 18 and 19 May 1940, the city of Amiens emptied in the space of a few hours. Of the city's 67,000 inhabitants in late 1939, only 5,000 remained in July 1940. The "remainers" (if one is to choose a term to describe them in contrast with those who left) were socially diverse, consisting at once of the poor and isolated – unmarried mothers who depended on charitable institutions, for example – and members of the bourgeoisie, like the company director who chose to stay behind in order to reopen the bakeries. Was the decision to remain political in nature? Did it correspond to a more combative, even proto-resistant population? This is what the account prepared by Jean Moulin, prefect of the Eure-et-Loir département, of the days between 14 and 18 June 1940, in the town of Chartres would seem to suggest. Jean Moulin was himself a good example of this, trying to hold on to the handful of officials specially assigned to him despite the withdrawal order received at dawn on 14 June. Finding himself nearly alone, he surrounded himself with volunteers recruited here and there among the remainers. The bishop and former mayor, among others, placed themselves at his service. In contrast with the civic-minded devotion of these Chartrains who stayed put, the many refugees who had come to the town from elsewhere proved undisciplined and even dishonest.

It is in this extraordinary context that one must consider the behavior of civilians who had to deal with the arrival of a downed airman. Was the airman received in a kindly fashion, a polite one? Or an aggressive and violent one? In the absence of sources, it is not possible to investigate the first of these two scenarios. What information we possess only concerns a proportion of these cases. Fewer than a dozen cases of civilian mistreatment of downed airmen were closely studied by the War Crimes Bureau, an office of the Wehrmacht's legal department.[28] These cases, over the course of which twenty-three German airmen were mistreated, with four of them killed, were tried by the military tribunals of the occupying power. It is for this reason, moreover, that we know about them. In regard to these figures, it is to be noted that between 400 and 700 Luftwaffe air personnel were taken prisoner without the War Crimes Bureau identifying actionable mistreatment. One must thus conclude that, though brutalized by invasion and invader and prey to chaos and the disappearance of structures of authority, the society did not completely lose its bearings.

An incident experienced by Léon Werth gives us an idea of the confusion that could result from unexpectedly encountering the enemy. He experienced this for the first time while stopped in a caravan of cars on a road of Loiret on 14 June. A column of Germans advanced, moving up the line of vehicles.

> The column halts. One of the soldiers stops in front of the car door. His face becomes visible, framed by the window. This private encounter, this proximity was disturbing. And this discomfort goes beyond worry or fear. I have the urge to kill this man or to talk to him about the weather or his health. My wife murmured a few words that I don't recall, to ward off the silence or death. Rather stupidly I tell her: "This man has no desire to kill us." For a few seconds, the three of us form a group at the margins of the war. Perhaps even some fleeting sympathy passed between him and us like a ripple on water. And it seemed to me that the shadow of a smile passed over his tense features.[29]

As an anti-Nazi, Léon Werth was not likely to feel any affinity for the German uniform. His writerly sensibility made him isolate these few seconds during which the story hesitates, where meaning vacillates between an insignificant encounter (a pedestrian bends down to the window) and a deadly confrontation with the Nazi order. Finally, with the help of his wife, he chose to behave innocuously. Perhaps a spark of shared humanity even passed between the two men's eyes. On the French side, the peaceful outcome of this encounter also had to do with the position of weakness in which the couple found themselves as they sat unarmed in their car. It may be imagined, however, that many civilians experienced this same confusion of identity, this same "disturbance," in Léon Werth's words, when suddenly coming upon downed airmen. In nearly all cases in the France of 1940, they overcame this by opting for normal – that is, nonviolent – behavior.

Yet the German military courts identified several cases of violence committed by civilians. Were the French ill-prepared for the events of war?

Civilians Taken Aback by the Arrival of "Parachutists"

In the interwar years, the civilian and military authorities were obviously not unconcerned about conditions behind the lines in wartime. After being mulled over for years, the 11 July 1938 law on the nation's wartime organization contained seven articles relating to "Passive Defense against Air Emergency." It was in this way that the term "passive defense" entered the legislative vocabulary. In 1939, this national organization for protecting people and property against air attack was implemented by four décrets-lois and some fifteen decrees. Of these, the most spectacular measure, alongside the organization of fire and air raid warning systems at the départemental and communal levels, was the distribution of gas masks. In the events that were to follow, oddly enough, the belligerent parties did not resort to chemical warfare, as it had been feared they would; painstakingly manufactured and distributed, the masks went unused.

The 1938 law made it possible to call upon various personnel released from military obligations for the purpose of implementing passive defense measures. Even women could volunteer "as civilians to participate in passive defense" (Article 11). But neither the general texts nor the practical instructional brochures distributed by city halls[30] prepared citizens to apprehend enemy airmen who had parachuted from their airplanes or been forced to land. This terrestrial aspect of aerial warfare was not addressed as falling under the purview of passive defense, a state of affairs that did not change when war was declared in September 1939.

During the Phony War, however, several decisions at the départemental and local levels suggest that the subject was a matter of concern to civilian and military authorities. On 4 September, one day after war was declared, the captain commanding the Fortress of Landrecies (Nord) informed the mayor that "German parachutists might land in the countryside with the mission to destroy telephonic and electrical lines of communication."[31] He asked that the population be alerted and that it join with "the police forces of the Army to track down these parachutists." In December 1939, the chief warrant officer commanding the gendarmerie brigades of Vesoul (Haute-Saône) asked the mayors of the communes for which he had responsibility to post a "Notice to the Population" concerning "the measures to be taken in the event of enemy airplane, aircraft or parachutist landings or any behind-the-lines incursions in the region" so as to "conform to recent instructions."[32] The mayor was to supply him, "as soon as possible, with the list of all able-bodied men from the commune capable of being employed for the creation of a communal search group (this group must include, as far as possible, armed hunters accompanied by dogs)." In conclusion, he underscores the "important mission that may be incumbent upon them [the citizens] in the event of enemy aircraft landings or suspicious movement." Four months later, the prefect of the Manche, the vice-admiral maritime prefect and governor of Cherbourg and the commanding general of the third military region jointly issued a call in the press for a "civil watch":

> All inhabitants of rural villages and more particularly those whose occupations take them outside (rural constables, gamekeepers, farmers) form the civilian watch. Their duty is to report without delay to the mayor of their commune the landings of airplanes in the middle of the countryside, parachutists dropped from airplanes, small suspicious groups and any unknown individual found in the countryside. They must show vigilance at sunrise and dusk. The enemy may be dressed in French or British uniform or civilian clothing. One must not let oneself be fooled by a trick of this kind ... In the present circumstances, all inhabitants must consider themselves as being on permanent alert. By their vigilance, they will effectively aid the military units responsible for defending the territory.[33]

Published in the local press, this text, like other calls to civilian mobilization, allowed a certain confusion to set in regarding "parachutists" and other airmen forced to jump from their planes. Once established, this confusion proved difficult to dispel and contained the seeds of future violations of the Hague Convention of 1907, which prohibits killing or wounding an enemy who has laid down his arms and prescribes that prisoners of war be treated "humanely." The difficulty stemmed from the novelty of airborne assault as a technique of warfare. It was only in 1918 that parachutes first began to be used in a military setting, with Germany leading the way in equipping its pilots with this safety device. Then came the idea of training airborne troops. It would not be until April 1937 that France created its first airborne units in the form of two GIAs (Groupe de l'Infanterie de l'Air), which together comprised 350 parachutists. The Germans and the Soviets had begun training such troops several years earlier and on a larger scale. On 10 May 1940, the Germans carried out the first airborne assault in history, attacking the airfields of The Hague with nearly 3,000 parachutists. The very term "parachutist" thus refers to two, fundamentally different wartime situations. That they were often conflated can be seen in this definition from the 1938 edition of the *Dictionnaire encyclopédique Quillet*: "Anyone who drops from above from an airplane or aircraft by parachute" is a parachutist. In one case, however, an airman, generally unarmed or merely carrying a pistol (if he is the pilot), jumps from his damaged airplane to save his life; in the other, a parachutist in the contemporary sense of the term parachutes to the ground in order to engage in combat.

In the first case, if the enemy airman surrenders, he is taken prisoner. He is protected by the Geneva Convention on the treatment of prisoners of war (1929), which supplements that of The Hague. The Convention was ratified by the United Kingdom in 1931, Germany in 1934 and France in 1935. Article 2 stipulates that:

> Prisoners of war are in the power of the hostile Government, but not of the individuals or formation which captured them.
> They shall at all times be humanely treated and protected, particularly against acts of violence, from insults and from public curiosity.
> Measures of reprisal against them are forbidden.

In the second case, the parachutist attacks and the armed riposte is in conformity with the law of war.

None of the decrees, notices and directives published in France during the Phony War or subsequent invasion referred to the laws and customs of war. By failing to remind its readers of the law of war, the appeal to "armed hunters" opened the way to illegal violence. For those on the ground, more-over, it was difficult to distinguish between "parachutists dropped from air-planes" and disarmed pilots jumping for their lives from their aircraft. It would have been wise to draw the volunteers' attention to this possible confusion. In the heat of action, however, several directives were issued by local military authorities or prefects. On 19 May 1940, an official telegram from the Oise prefecture to the département's 702 mayors thus reminded them that "parachutists in the uniform of the army to which they belong must be treated as soldiers covered by the law of war."[34] In the debate over France's preparedness for war or lack thereof, the paucity of civilian education at the national level tips the scales in favor of a lack of preparation.

This lack of preparation may also account for the tendency among those doing the shooting to confuse German and Allied "parachutists." Not that it was easy to make this distinction from the ground; seen from below, it was hard to distinguish between their characteristic silhouettes. But impetuous fire speaks to a lack of preparation. On 15 May 1940, the fortress of Abbeville (Somme) was thus informed that "soldiers or civilians have recently fired on English and French air personnel as they descended in parachute, thereby causing mortal accidents." The "telephoned message" ordered that, hence-forth, one was "only to fire into the air on groups of at least three parachut-ists." For the number of parachutes in the sky was one way of distinguishing between the isolated descents of distressed airmen and the grouped descents of attack formations. It is nevertheless surprising that the threshold should have

FINDING THE VOLUNTEERS OF THE YEAR 40   35

been defined as "at least three": fighter planes were generally one-seaters but bombers held four or five crew members. Four Allied parachutists could thus appear in the sky at once. . . and thereby expose themselves to the fire of pre-mobilized civilians.

The Last-Minute Creation of the Gardes territoriales

Another sign of this lack of preparation: the belated creation of a "Garde territoriale" (Territorial Guard) responsible for "taking an active role behind the lines in protecting the national territory against the enemy." It was only on 17 May 1940 that a decree was issued creating "military formations of territorial guards."[35] Drawn up at the communal level, these units were collectively placed under the authority of the commandant of gendarmerie of their respective départements. All French men sixteen years old or older who had not already been mobilized or assigned to a Passive Defense formation could volunteer. The Gardes territoriaux were subject to military discipline, wore insignia and were to be "armed with weapons requisitioned from the commercial establishments." They were allowed "to use their personal weapons." The 19 May instructions specified that their weapons could come "from voluntary donations" and they would receive an armband bearing the initials "G.T." and the seal of the gendarmerie brigade.[36] They were authorized to wear their personal helmets and whatever uniform they possessed. These details illustrate the improvisational manner in which these units were created. Of their uniforms, not a single gaiter button had been provided. And, if 17 May seems late, it is not only because France and Germany had been at war since 3 September of the previous year or that German panzers were already in France; though less directly threatened by invasion, on 14 May the United Kingdom moved to create the LDV, or Local Defence Volunteers, the first iteration of the Home Guard. Like the laws preceding 10 May 1940, the decree and directive concerning the gardes territoriaux mentioned neither the Hague Convention (which recognized this type of formation and moreover prohibited killing or wounding an unarmed enemy) nor that of Geneva (which reiterated the principle of humane treatment for prisoners of war).

Considerations of a domestic and international order may also explain this belated decision to create a Garde territoriale. A government may have reason to fear issuing a call to arms after the fashion of the Committee of Public Safety in 1792 or the Provisional Government of the Republic in 1870. Would doing so be to arm the French people or arm the revolution, as was the case with the volunteers of Year II and the francs-tireurs of 1870–71? In 1914, moreover, the German Army had shown that it did not respect international law as it had been established at The Hague in 1907. In defining the "belligerent," however, Articles 1 and 2 had specifically included francs-tireurs under this protected legal category. If they had been respected by the 5th Panzer Division, these articles would have ensured that Jean-Marie Kérandel and his co-defendants were protected:

> Article 1. The laws, rights and duties of war apply not only to armies, but also to militia and volunteer corps fulfilling the following conditions:
>
> 1. To be commanded by a person responsible for his subordinates;
> 2. To have a fixed distinctive emblem recognizable at a distance;
> 3. To carry arms openly; and
> 4. To conduct their operations in accordance with the laws and customs of war.
>
> In countries where militia or volunteer corps constitute the army, or form part of it, they are included under the denomination "army."
>
> Article 2. The inhabitants of a territory which has not been occupied who, on the approach of the enemy, spontaneously take up arms to resist the invading troops without having had time to organize themselves in accordance with Article 1, shall be regarded as belligerents if they carry arms openly and if they respect the laws and customs of war.

Between 1870 and 1945, little changed about the way in which the German Army regarded populations that "spontaneously take up arms to resist the invading troops." The massacres of civilians perpetrated by the Kaiser's armies in Belgium and northern France – a response to (imaginary) attacks on the part of francs-tireurs – were proof that the Convention remained a dead letter. While it is true that it had been included in the 1911 edition of the *Felddienstordnung*, the field reference manual distributed to officers, it appeared only in its annex and its provisions were contradicted by the text of the manual. Two historians who have very closely studied this issue, John Horne and Alan Kramer, have shown that the training they received encouraged German officers to see civilian resistance as illegal and that the memory of the "francs-tireurs war" of 1870 in their eyes justified killing civilians.[37] In the single month of August 1914, some 5,000 civilian inhabitants of Belgium, Luxembourg and France were thus executed.[38] The dispute that these events provoked between Germany and the former Allies carried over into the interwar years. With the Nazi regime contributing its own brand of brutality to a trend in German military culture,[39] Allied governments had no reason to believe in 1939 that the German Army had significantly evolved in this respect. Even though the advances of the Hague Convention had by 1939 been integrated into the Special Criminal Code of War (*KSSVO, Kriegsonderstrafrechtsverordnung*), they were largely nullified by the preceding paragraph, as we shall see below. The crimes committed by the Wehrmacht in Poland, moreover, gave reason to doubt its desire to respect the laws of war, its own included.[40] The legal historian Andreas Toppe has shown that ninety-five Polish "francs-tireurs" or "spies" were sentenced by German military tribunals in 1939; the number of civilians killed without trial by the Wehrmacht in the first two months of the occupation, meanwhile, stands at several tens of thousands.

To organize "militias or volunteer corps" was thus to assume a heavy responsibility. Although true to the letter of the Hague Convention, these units risked being seen by the enemy, not as "belligerents" bearing the rights associated with that status, but rather as irregular units falling outside of the laws and customs of war.

In contrast to the LDV and Home Guard, whose history is well known and has even assumed the proportions of legend thanks to the fact that Britain was not invaded, the short life of the Gardes territoriales has until now been almost completely forgotten, swallowed by the memory of invasion and defeat. Traces of it, however, may be found in local and départemental archives. In some départements, as we have seen, measures that prefigured the creation of the GT had been in place since winter. In the Manche département, a sophisticated alert system, the "civil watch," had already been created in April 1940. But the decree creating the Garde territoriale immediately gave rise to further directives disseminated in the press. In the event of parachutist landings: "Ring the alarm to marshal the gardes territoriaux of the commune and in the same way warn neighboring communes; at the same time, alert the gendarmerie brigade by the quickest possible means (telephone, automobile, motorcycle, bicycle); march on the adversary; seek to capture him and destroy him if he resists." At important crossroads, moreover, the Garde was to erect "barricades with double bends forcing vehicles to stop." "Whomever does not obey the order to stop or who seeks to evade is to be immediately shot."[41]

In the Manche, several thousand men volunteered for the GT. Veterans associations issued the call for mobilization so as to "once again block the way of the Boche" and "drive out the traitors and defeatists." In Cherbourg, the maritime prefect and subprefect invited mayors to arm the gardes as quickly as possible while supplying them with ammunition and the insignia of their post. There was no doubt as to the warlike mood in this département of "débâcle" France. In the fifteen days that preceded the arrival of the Germans on 17 June, the gardes territoriaux carried out their duties. But accidents took place, hardly a surprise given the atmosphere of improvisation and the gardes' lack of training. It was above all the roadblocks that provoked incidents. These could sometimes be amusing, as when the gardes took a few too many drops of calvados after a roadblock had been set up next to a pub, but sometimes they were tragic. Arrested at the wheel of his car, a young man was killed following an altercation with a garde. When Rommel's 7th Panzer Division occupied the Manche on 17 June, the gardes territoriaux did not have time to react. The same day, Maréchal Pétain made it known that he had asked the enemy for an armistice. Some were still thinking about taking action that evening but were persuaded by their elders to abandon these plans. Having closely studied these two weeks of civilian mobilization on behalf of the beleaguered fatherland, Michel Boivin recognizes in them a "spirit of proto-resistance."

While it may not have met with the same enthusiasm, the creation of the Gardes territoriales was accompanied by similar resolve in the Oise département, which, in comparison to the Manche, was located much closer to the front. When instructed by the prefect to create "watch groups" on 12 May, the mayors of the département immediately supported the measure.[42] Where this demand on citizens provoked complaint, it mainly concerned the lack of weapons and ammunition, both of which were urgently requested given the extremely limited range of shotgun fire. Naturally, the creation of the Gardes territoriales was also a source of some tension. At a time of year characterized by particularly intense fieldwork in agricultural zones, farmers were natural watchmen. After one week had passed, however, there were fewer volunteers to keep watch at night. A few citizens refused to sign up. On 30 May, the mayor of Talmontiers, a village of 300 inhabitants, wrote the prefect to report on the refusal of three of his co-citizens: the baker, a rentier and the municipal roadmender. In contrast to this unlikely trio, "factory and farm workers all accepted this duty." This correspondence ends on 6 June, one day after the Germans launched their assault on the Somme.

*

In the English-language historiography, historians who argue for putting France's military defeat into perspective are described as "revisionists."[43] Among other things, they argue that Belgium, the Netherlands and even Great Britain were no better prepared to confront a "Blitzkrieg" than was France and either did not or would not have been able to resist a blitz-invasion of their territory. Surveys by Julian Jackson and Philip Nord may indeed come to be seen as marking a turning point in the historiography. The fierce fighting and high morale of French soldiers on the Somme and Aisne fronts between 5 and 10 June are just one example of what Jean-Louis Crémieux-Brilhac has termed the "upsurge."[44] As for civilians, the pause brought by the armistice did not mean they had abandoned the Republic. This emergent thesis finds support in the manner in which civilians reacted to the arrival of downed enemy pilots in May–June 1940 and the way they helped Allied soldiers and airmen during the Occupation.

2

The Repression of the Republic's "Francs-Tireurs"

Armed citizens attempted to resist the invasion by apprehending downed enemy airmen. Their story, however, is largely unknown and extremely difficult to study. Not only was the phenomenon in question very short-lived but, in cases in which an airman was apprehended in brutal fashion, efforts were immediately made to conceal it for fear of reprisal on the part of the occupying power. The far more traumatic nature of the events that were to follow under the Occupation only further contributed to burying this memory. What we know about the behavior of civilians during these few days or weeks thus for the most part comes to us from the archives of the victorious power, particularly those of its military tribunals. The document that follows, which comes from a French source, is an exception. It offers an alternative, on-the-ground perspective on the sequence of events.

Furthermore, history from below sheds new light on the sesquicentennial debate over 'Francs-tireurs' in France and Belgium. This discussion has lately resurfaced in connection with the wars of 1870 and 1914, particularly as it relates to the book by John Horne and Alan Kramer, *German Atrocities 1914.*[1] Studying the German repression of acts of resistance to the invasion of France in 1940 reopens the question of whether the German Army had at this point effectively integrated the relevant clause of the Geneva Convention.

Arsy (Oise): Between Luftwaffe Ace and Movie Star

The account of gendarme Visse, a member of the Estrées Saint-Denis brigade (Oise département), shows something not found in the German sources: a pilot resisting arrest and the extensive resources that the forces of occupation devoted to finding the civilians who had mistreated him. On 5 June 1940, German flying ace Werner Mölders' airplane was shot down over the Oise département. The report of the gendarmerie recounts the events as follows:

> At 17:15 on 5 June 1940, a German airplane of the Messerschmitt 109 type was shot down by a French fighter plane. It came down near the farm of Villerseau (Canly district). The 29-year-old pilot, Captain Moeller [Mölders], jumped in his parachute and landed in Marival wood in the commune of Grandfresnoy.

He was found by gendarme Visse of the Estrées Saint-Denis brigade with help from Monsieur Pierre Hochedez, from the same village, who spontaneously provided his car for use by this soldier. The airman was arrested near the Arsy [rail] halt after having travelled 3 kilometers and disposed of his parachute and jacket.

Though holding a revolver in his hand, he raised his hands in the air when he saw his pursuers and was then disarmed and brought to the barracks, where he was handed over to military authority (Major Bassous of the 195th RALT, SP 8753) before being taken to BCR 2 in Amiens.

Some inhabitants of the region had already arrived on the scene to arrest the parachutist.

On 16 August, gendarme Visse underwent his first interrogation by a German officer, in the course of which he identified the airman and stated that, together with Monsieur Hochedez, he had protected him against possible blows from the crowd. The officer thanked the gendarme for having supplied the parachutist's identity and protected him. The places where the airplane and pilot came down were identified on site. Monsieur Hochedez was arrested the previous evening and taken to Senlis, where he spent two days.

On 29 September, Visse was interrogated a second time for around two hours in Noailles, where he had been taken. Once again, the investigators thanked him for having protected the airman.

The same investigators simultaneously carried out a series of arrests in the region. The identities of the individuals arrested [eight in all] are given in the attached statement.

Gendarme Visse, having been asked by German authorities on several occasions if he knew the people who had struck the airman, each time answered that he did not.[2]

The fallen airman thus disposed of part of his uniform to avoid being recognized and fled, a revolver in hand. He cleverly tried to get back to his lines by heading for the north, perhaps hoping to jump on a train as it passed the rail halt near which he was finally arrested. According to the testimony of soldiers from the 195th Artillery Regiment, which was stationed nearby, after being spotted, Mölders tried to hide in the wheat, which was already tall at this time of the year.[3] A civilian dealt him a blow, cutting him above the eye. The gendarme and civilian named in the report intervened and were supported by the arrival of soldiers from the RALT.

Held prisoner for several weeks and then freed following the armistice, the ace pilot had thus complained to his superiors of mistreatment at the hands of civilians. Between 28 September and 3 October, eight inhabitants from five neighboring villages were arrested and brought to Gand for trial by a Luftwaffe tribunal. On 7 November, the main defendant, a foreman at the Chevrières beet sugar plant and distillery, was sentenced to twelve years' hard labor. He was energetically defended by his employer, who wrote to Marshal Goering, the air force minister, and then contacted a Luftwaffe officer in Paris to ask that he inform Lieutenant-Colonel Mölders. By chance, the German officer he met in Paris who contacted the flying ace was none other than Arletty's lover, Hans Jürgen Soehring. A veteran, like Mölders, of the Condor Legion, Soehring served as judge at the *Reichskriegsgericht* in Paris from 1941 to 1943.[4] The foreman, who was ultimately released in February 1942, was very lucky.

It was the historian Gaël Eismann who first revealed the operation of German military tribunals in France.[5] Her work builds upon that of Ulrich Herbert, Ahlrich Meyer and Regina Delacor, who challenged "the sanitized image of a 'decent' military occupation in France."[6] Eismann shows that, far from playing a moderating role, German military tribunals from the first months of 1941 exerted a form of "judicial violence" predicated on the policy of the German military administration in France, the Militärbefehlshaber in Frankreich (MBF). Until the 1990s, the collective and scholarly memory of the MBF distinguished its activity from that of the police (*Sipo-SD*, which included the Gestapo), which was solely assigned responsibility for the intensifying violence of the occupying power. The "clean Wehrmacht" (*saubere Wehrmacht*) myth even influenced the history of the occupation of France.[7] This, too, was called into question. For reasons relating to her sources, Eismann was unable to closely study the "legal façade of judicial repression" (the expression is hers) during the first year of the Occupation. The trials of "francs-tireurs" allow one to do so, revealing the immediate violence of legal repression.

"Schuld Frankreichs": "France's Guilt"

Among the 400–700 Luftwaffe aviation personnel taken prisoner by the French in May–June 1940, at least 23 were severely mistreated by civilians upon reaching the ground. Four of them were killed by civilians or with their participation.[8] For several reasons, it is difficult to analyze and interpret these actions. The most obvious of these is their small number, which renders any statistical approach largely random. Another reason has to do with the partisan nature of the investigation, which was solely conducted by the Germans, conquerors of the occupied territory with sovereignty over it. None of the statements gathered by the Wehrmacht among German soldiers and airmen allows one to consider the question of whether their own behavior might have played some role in their misadventures. Instead, they are all presented as innocent victims. The final reason stems from the lack of available data regarding this type of situation in general. Military historical

42 BLITZ-INVASION IN FRANCE

studies have not addressed the subject for any country. This book attempts to do so.

In the summer of 1940, the War Crimes Investigation Office, part of the Wehrmacht Legal Department (Untersuchungsstelle für Verletzungen des Völkerrechts, Wehrmacht Rechtsabteilung), started collecting the testimony of German soldiers who had spent a few weeks as prisoners of war. In November 1940 and then again in April 1941, the Wehrmacht Legal Department gathered together their statements in two successive white books, which were exclusively distributed to general staff, the German Armistice Commission in Wiesbaden, the Occupation authorities in France (Militärbefehlshaber in Frankreich, MBF), and Wilhelmstrasse, headquarters of the Ministry for Foreign Affairs.[9] Over the course of some 700 pages, *France's Conduct of a War Contrary to International Law* (a title that left little doubt as to where responsibility for the war resided) offers an inventory of French violations of the laws and customs of war vis-à-vis German Army personnel during the 1940 campaign. This document took the precedent set by the First World War as its model, repeating the German Ministry of Foreign Affairs' efforts at that time to respond to the inter-Allied campaign to denounce German atrocities. In May 1915, Wilhelmstrasse published a black book entitled *Belgium's Conduct of a War Contrary to International Law*[10] in which it accused the Belgians of having conducted a people's war – a war of "francs-tireurs" – against the German Army. The purpose of the document was to justify the many civilian massacres carried out by the invading army in 1914.

Bearing the heading of general staff headquarters (OKW) and accompanied with the initials of the army's Legal Department (WR), the two volumes of 1940 and 1941 mix investigation, verdict and political interpretation.[11] The tone is set in the introduction, which claims that, in the war of 1939–40, as in that of 1914–18, France's behavior was in total contradiction with the claim that it championed international law. The Prussian Ministry of War had already seen this for itself. This time, however, "the French government, the French Army and the better part of the French people" demonstrated, "in keeping with the history of France itself," "the contradiction between a humanitarian dialectic and humane behavior."[12] The documents brought together in the two volumes, which "overwhelmingly [prove] France's guilt" (*vernichtender für die Schuld Frankreichs*), are presented in the same spirit, with the selected testimony presumed as being at once beyond question and representative of the whole. The transitional paragraphs separating the excerpted depositions repeatedly state that, on the basis of this "evidence," the German government was already convinced that the acts of violence they denounce were not matters of negligence. Rather, these violations of the law of war had been "organized" by the French high command. As these texts show, conspiracy theories and investigations with predetermined outcomes were both characteristic features of the legal and political culture of the Wehrmacht Legal Department.

This anti-French prejudice may be ascribed to a military culture and image of the "hereditary enemy" revived by the third Franco-German war. Yet the National Socialist vision obviously contributed to it. The text is punctuated with Nazi-inspired expressions. On the face of it, these are not omnipresent: mention is not always made of the "race" of those identified as involved in the mistreatment. In general, they are described as "French." Now and then, however, it is specified that they are "French nationals" or "white French people." In some places, there is talk of "Jews" and "Spanish reds" while in others – more frequent – those incriminated are described as "blacks" or "negroes." While the text takes it for granted that humanity is divided between whites, blacks, reds and Jews, it does not further exploit this vein. The question of responsibility focuses on French people in general, in keeping with the instructions of the general staff, who themselves took their cue from Goebbels' portrayal of the situation: "It is the French people in its entirety that is responsible for the policy that has until now been conducted against Germany."[13]

In point of their violence, the argument put forward by Wehrmacht jurists, which among other things reveals a complex relationship vis-à-vis the ideal of "civilization" to which France laid claim, pales in comparison to the instructions given the media by the Reich Minister of Public Enlightenment and Propaganda. Goebbels' instructions, expressed several times a week between May and July 1940, have been preserved.[14] As he stated on several occasions, the goal was "to once and for all eliminate France as a national power of any importance whatsoever" and see to it "that this be the last time in the next three hundred or four hundred years that France is capable of attacking a peace-loving people without justification." France was to be reduced to an "obese Switzerland" and "any attempt at national recovery [would] be nipped in the bud" via a "merciless" and "perpetual" campaign of intellectual terror.[15] The minister was also eager to avoid another Allied campaign against German atrocities of the type that emerged in summer 1914, issuing instructions for "counter-propaganda" to that end.[16]

In addition to serving as documentary "counter-propaganda," the Wehrmacht collections also performed a preventative role. They sought to get out ahead of any effort on the part of the French government to initiate proceedings against the crimes committed by the German Army. According to these confidential volumes, the French were thus guilty of systematically violating the two Geneva Conventions of 1929: that regarding the treatment of prisoners of war and that regarding the amelioration of the condition of the wounded and sick in armies in the field. But as this was not an open investigation and the French party was not invited to testify, it does not allow one to acquire a proper understanding of the facts.

The Criminalization of "*Freischärlerei*" ("Francs-Tireuring")

In spring 1941, the Wehrmacht's Investigative Office collected some 330 depositions. They describe a series of isolated offenses rarely resulting in death. Altogether, the two volumes mention a total of twenty dead from all services, including ten Luftwaffe personnel, their deaths taking place in the sometimes-confused context of battle.[17] The remainder, or more than nine out of every ten cases, concern instances in which prisoners were abused. This covers cases in which pressure was brought to bear on individuals to obtain military intelligence (including a number of brutal interrogation sessions involving threats and blows), instances of prisoners being wounded, conditions of inadequate food or shelter and cases of personal property theft. What may appear a minor offense – verbal abuse – occupies a major place in the depositions, doubtless because Article 2 of the Geneva Convention explicitly stipulates that prisoners shall be protected against insult and public curiosity. Such banal wartime insults as "Hitler's footman," "Hitler's pig," "dirty pig," "murderer," "child killer" and "woman and child killer" (in response to the bombing and machine-gunning of civilians) provoked strong emotions among the jurists who drafted the reports. Their sincere indignation reflects the interiorization of Nazi values. For a German in 1940, being on the receiving end of an insult could be experienced as an attack on the principle of Aryan superiority. The other recurrent grievance concerned the uncleanliness of barracks – not itself a violation of international law. This reproach reflects a culture of cleanliness but may also have a political connotation, as when the prisoners singled out "Spanish reds, Jews and other swarthy bastards" as being responsible for the place's filthiness.

Given the facts, the anger inspired within the Wehrmacht Legal Department by France's "conduct of war contrary to international law" seems disproportionate. Coming from an army with 2 million men in the field in May 1940, a balance sheet of some 300 complaints and 20 or so deaths falls short of establishing that the French Army had violated the laws and customs of war in any "systematic" way (to say nothing of the fact that there had been no massacre of Germans to report). Nor does the number of complaints seem particularly elevated given that the French held nearly 10,000 German prisoners of war at the time of the armistice.[18] One may also expand the discussion to encompass the manner in which each side prosecuted the war. But the asymmetry of information makes this difficult. The victorious country had the resources to investigate the abuses committed by the defeated one at its leisure. The French, by contrast, conducted no investigations into the crimes committed by Germany during the 1940 offensive. The Vichy government was hardly about to investigate the aerial strafing of civilians on the roads (unknown number of deaths), the massacres in the north of British and French prisoners of war (200 dead) and civilians (600 dead) or the killing of black prisoners of war (between 900 and 3,000 victims).[19]

From the point of view of this data, the violence committed by French soldiers and civilians seems minimal. There is one exception: the 20 May massacre perpetrated by French soldiers in Abbeville against twenty-one Belgian prison inmates as they were being transported southwards by the French Security Police. Apart from this case, which does not figure in the German white book as the victims were all Belgian civilians, the offending acts, all one-off affairs, do not correspond to the logic of mass murder. They were directed neither against defenseless civilians nor against the representatives of particular racial or political categories but rather against a uniformed invader. And they were punished by the victorious side.

Prepared in advance, "the edict concerning the introduction of German criminal law and criminal statutes in the occupied territories of France" was postdated 10 May 1940, and disseminated via public bills. While the posted text only informed readers of measures relating to the suppression of freedoms, its title made it known that, henceforth, German law would supersede French law. Anyone attempting to slip away to England, for example, would be immediately sentenced for the crime of high treason and subject to the death penalty. Applied to French people, this measure directly contradicted Article 45 of the Hague Convention, which states that it is "forbidden to compel the inhabitants of occupied territory to swear allegiance to the hostile power." Rulings by the German tribunals in France were not only based on the *Reichsstrafgesetzbuch* – that is, German criminal law. They were also based on the old military criminal code (the *Militärstrafgesetzbuch*, of 1872), an 1899 imperial decree granting greater latitude to commandants, and the *Wartime Criminal Code of Procedure* (*KstVO*) and *Wartime Special Criminal Code* (*KSSVO*), both of which were published on 26 August 1939.[20] In addition to these texts, there were the rulings of the MBF in France and the directives frequently issued by Army High Command in Berlin (OKH) and Wehrmacht High Command (OKW).[21]

In contrast to the German field manual of 1911, the Wartime Special Criminal Code (*KSSVO*) of 1939 appears to incorporate the contributions of the Hague Convention. On the subject of "Freischärlerei" (literally, "franc-tireuring," a noun that does not exist in English), Article 3, paragraph 2 of the Code adopts the language of the regulations appended to the Hague Convention. Under the protected category of "belligerents," these articles – adopted at The Hague and quoted in the preceding chapter – included not just "militias or volunteer corps" equipped with visible insignia, but also the "inhabitants of a non-occupied territory who, on the approach of the enemy, spontaneously take up arms to resist the invading forces, without having had time to form themselves into regular armed units, provided they carry arms openly and respect the laws and customs of war."

The *KSSVO* nevertheless added a threatening paragraph, placing it moreover at the top of the article on "franc-tireurism." Partly contradicting the Convention of 1907, it made it known that, in the absence of visible external signs of membership in a regular armed force, bearing arms and even the mere intention (*Absicht*) of using the arms in one's possession against Germans or their allies was to incur the charge of *Freischärlerei*. The only penalty for this was death.

KSSVO, ORDER RELATING TO THE 26 AUGUST 1939 WARTIME SPECIAL CRIMINAL CODE

Article 3. Francs-tireurs

1. Acts of "francs-tireuring" are to be punished by death in the case of any person who, without being recognizable as belonging to enemy armed forces by the external insignia of membership prescribed by international law,

   > Bears or possesses arms or other means of combat with the intention of using them against Germans or their allied armies or with the intention of killing them, Or otherwise undertakes actions that, according to the customs of war, can only be performed by the units of an armed force in uniform.

   The sentence may moreover include the confiscation of property.

2. Not considered francs-tireurs are:
   1. The members of armed forces in uniform, who are simply under a standard camouflage;
   2. The members of militias and volunteer corps, if they fulfill the following conditions:
      a. They have at their head a person responsible for his subordinates;
      b. They wear distinctive insignia that may be recognized at a distance;
      c. They openly bear arms and
      d. Their operations are in keeping with the laws and customs of war.
   3. The inhabitants of a non-occupied territory who, on the approach of the enemy, spontaneously take up arms to resist the invading forces, without having had time to form themselves into regular armed units in keeping with first article, will be considered belligerents provided they carry arms openly and respect the laws and customs of war.

The beginning of Article 3 of the *KSSVO* thus levels a formidable threat at initiatives taken outside of the regular army, even during the invasion and prior to any armistice. It recognizes neither national sovereignty nor the right to resist invasion. Such legal considerations may appear superfluous given the growing and ultimately overwhelming percentage of extrajudicial arrests in occupied France. Of the 60,400 individuals deported from the Northern and Southern zones as a repressive measure, for example, only 3,400 were sentenced by German military tribunals. These same tribunals categorized 3,180 others as "NN Wehrmacht" (meant to disappear, in keeping with Keitel's decree) in the absence of any sentence.[22] The tribunals of the occupying power thus only examined the case files of 11 percent of all deportees. They were nevertheless active for the duration of the Occupation, prioritizing the repression of communist armed struggle and any actions relating to the non-consent of French people to the Occupation. This seemingly legal system of repression also played a decisive role in the policy for repressing popular resistance to the invasion, mainly carried out between summer 1940 and fall 1941.

Popular Resistance to Invasion

The chronology and geography of civilian use of force or arms against downed Luftwaffe airmen shows that these were indeed acts of resistance to invasion. Nearly all took place in the hours immediately preceding the invading army's arrival.

It is more difficult to form an estimate of their real number. Although the Wehrmacht white book on acts of violence committed by the French Army insists that German airmen were assaulted "countless" times upon reaching the ground, it only presents a dozen such cases.[23] These resulted in thirteen trials.[24] I shall leave aside a case that was purely internal to the army. The twelve others targeted civilians, gardes territoriaux and gendarmes called back into service, sometimes mixed with soldiers in uniform. There are thus twelve trials to be examined, bringing together seventy-eight defendants for twenty-three German victims, four of whom were killed. As regards the trials, it must be recalled that the facts were reread in light of Germano-Nazi law and that, with one exception, I have only been able to consult the verdicts, which very much take the form of briefs for the prosecution. The exact sequence of events is thus unknown.The map of incidents overlaps with the isochronal lines of the German Army's advance. The incidents of 12 and 13 May in the east, near Sedan, took place as Belgian refugees flooded south and German aviation targeted villagers with bombing and strafing. The 18 May lynching in Vimy took place in the midst of the combat zone. The incidents noted in the Oise département on 19 May and 5 June took place in the rear area south of the Somme and Aisne rivers as Guderian's Panzers continued their lightning advance. Amiens suffered its largest bombardment on 18 and 19 May. Similarly, the incidents of Offranville (Seine-Maritime), Plouguerneau (Finistère) and Aumagne (Charente-Maritime) shortly preceded the arrival of enemy troops. Of the twelve cases, two do not so neatly correspond to a state of emergency: while the abuses committed in Curchy (Somme, 10 May) and Anthien (Nièvre, 5 June) did indeed take place during the enemy onslaught, the front lines were still hundreds of kilometers distant.

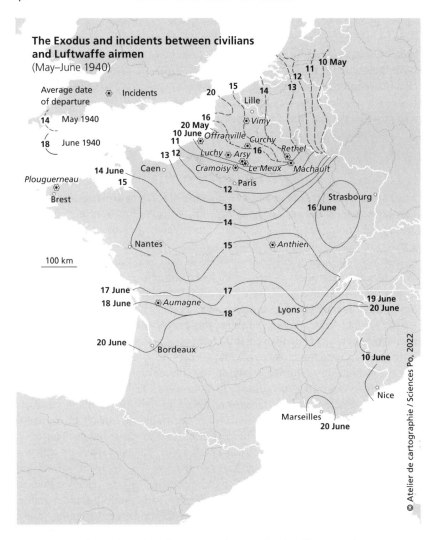

Map 2.1 Exodus and incidents between civilians and Luftwaffe airmen (France, May–June 1940). Average date of departure / May 1940 / June 1940.
Sources: Jean Vidalenc, *L'exode de mai–juin 1940* (Paris: PUF, 1957), 174; and sites of incidents in Oberkommando der Wehrmacht, *Frankreichs völkerrechtswidrige Kriegführung 1939/1940* [*France's Conduct of a War Contrary to International Law, 1939/1940*], November 1940 and April 1941.

These behaviors were influenced, not just by geography, but also by history. The map of incidents is reminiscent of another map, this one from the First World War. Eight of the twelve cases took place on or in the vicinity of the "red zone," that crescent of land that, descending from

REPRESSION OF THE REPUBLIC'S "FRANCS-TIREURS"   49

**Devastated regions in 1914–1918
and incidents between civilians and Luftwaffe airmen in 1940**

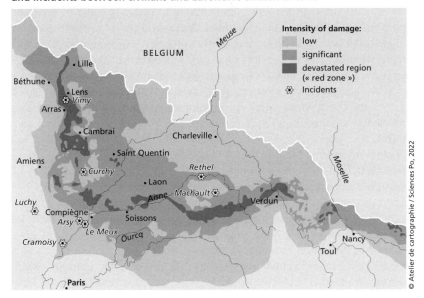

Map 2.2   Areas devastated in 1914–18 and incidents between civilians and Luftwaffe airmen in 1940. Intensity of damage: low / significant / devastated region ("red zone").
Sources: J. Guicherd and C. Maitrot, "Les terres de régions dévastées," *Journal d'agriculture pratique, de jardinage et d'économie domestique*, 34 (1921), 154–56; and sites of incidents in: Oberkommando der Wehrmacht, *Frankreichs völkerrechtswidrige Kriegführung 1939/1940* [*France's Conduct of a War Contrary to International Law, 1939/1940*], November 1940 and April 1941.
Source for base map: Tinodela, Zone_rougeRed_Zone_Map.jpg: Lamiot, CC BY-SA 2.5, via Wikimedia Commons.

the Nord département, crosses the Pas-de-Calais, the Somme and Oise and then turns east towards the Aisne and the Ardennes. For four years between 1914 and 1918, these regions served as a battlefield. They exited the war deeply scarred in both human and material terms and seem to have produced the most intense reactions. We thus have four incidents in the Oise, two in the Ardennes, one in the Somme and one in Pas-de-Calais.

It is perhaps reductive to limit oneself to the geographical area of the invasion properly so called. The experience of invasion can be transmitted via other channels. Combined with radio broadcast news, contact with the evacuees and refugees of the exodus could make for strong impressions. While the peasants and shopkeepers of Finistère who abused airmen at Plouguerneau on 18 June 1940 may thus still not have set eyes on the German Army, which only reached Brest on the 19th, the bombing of that city could be seen and heard from a distance. As it happens, moreover, the plan for evacuating civilian populations in the event of war assigned Finistère and the other Breton départements as the destination for inhabitants of the Nord and Pas-de-Calais. More than 100,000 refugees from various regions thus crowded into the towns and villages of Finistère. With a resident population of some 14,000 inhabitants, the town of Morlaix, 50 kilometers from Plouguerneau, alone provided accommodation for 26,650 of them.[25] Such an unprecedented concentration of population could only leave people shaken. In the northern half of France, moreover, the spectacle of refugee columns tended to extend visions of the battlefield beyond the front properly so called, propagating fear as it did so. With one exception, the assaults took place after the first refugees had passed through.

On the judicial front, as German sovereignty was limited to the occupied zone until November 1942, the geographical distribution of known incidents is confined to this space. But other incidents doubtless took place further south. The lynching of an airman reported by André Gide, for example, which probably took place in what would become the unoccupied zone, did not result in a trial. Meditating on faith after the war, in 1950 Gide drafted an obituary of sorts for the lynched airman:

> In the notebook in which I had once again begun to write, aimlessly, a little like I'm doing here, and that I lost in Rapallo, I recounted the horrid lynching of a very young German parachutist at the start of the war. It took place in a village through which we passed the next day. The indignant peasants had thrashed him, beating him to death with shovels and rakes, but got nothing more out of this fervent young man than a stubborn "Heil Hitler!" These martyrs – authentic for all that – these witnesses to divergent mystiques, are embarrassing indeed. One wonders what other Peter awaits them at the gates of what other paradise?... And what other Pascal will dare write: "I gladly believe those who die for..." etc. (or something of the kind).[26]

The incident was perhaps not as clear-cut and symbolic as the writer would have had it but it does overlap with the other cases in one point: it was the inhabitants of the place who forcibly opposed the intruder. In an effort to determine which populations were more or less inclined to resist, one may here call upon a dichotomy – variously noted by Jean Vidalenc, Philippe Nivet and Hanna Diamond – between fugitives and those who remained in place. It is to be noted that those who would later appear as defendants before German tribunals were all residents of the place. With the possible exception of Luchy,[27] no refugee is to be found among their ranks when they take action. Did the strains of La Marseillaise reverberate in the ears of these new volunteers of Valmy – "Aux armes, citoyens, formez vos bataillons"? Some were later to set out on the roads of the exodus. This was the case of Eugène Andrieux, who left Machault with his family for Sologne, and also of Alfred Mullot, who followed the evacuation of his village a few days later.[28]

During the invasion, civilian combativeness constituted a form of military resistance but cannot be identified with the Resistance properly so called, which played out under the Occupation in the absence of any official support and even contra the authorities. The invasion and Occupation were two, clearly distinct moments of the war. Some actors, however, would provide a link between resistance to invasion and the Resistance. Bernard des Champs de Boishébert, for example, a farmer from the département of Seine-Inférieure who was sentenced to death for having roughed up an airman. Pardoned and ultimately freed in 1943, he became a Resistance fighter. President of the provisional municipal commission of Offranville during the Libération, he carried on in the post of mayor until 1971. More frequently, however, it was the repression of the combativeness of 1940 that inspired resistance in reaction. Between November 1940 and March 1941, ten men were thus arrested in the village of Cramoisy, in the Oise, for having roughed up three airmen on 26 May. Very depressed at finding himself incarcerated without trial, one of them committed suicide in Fresnes in April and was buried in the commune on 1 May. Seven prisoners were freed in September 1941 and the last two sentenced by the Reichskriegsgericht in Paris that October and November. One was condemned to ten years' imprisonment and the other, Henri Heurteur, a father of three children aged nine, seven and one, was sentenced to death. Pardoned by the MBF, he died in the prison of Saarbrücken in August 1943. When this news reached the village in November, a mass was held for him. The morning of the ceremony, these words could be read in capital letters on the wall of the church and the adjacent road:

> WE WILL AVENGE YOU HEURTEUR. THE NATIONAL FRONT MOURNS ITS MARTYRS AND AVENGES THEM. DEATH TO THE BOCHES[29]

"Without Orders"

Having considered the geopolitics of resistance to invasion, we shall now examine four cases that resulted in the death of Luftwaffe airmen in order to shed light on the context. The reproach leveled at civilians by the enemy's tribunals was that they had acted in the absence of superior order and without themselves being soldiers. The tribunals in this way revealed that they were unable to grasp the logic of resistance to invasion. German airmen were killed on 12 May in Machault (Ardennes), 18 May in Vimy (Pas-de-Calais), 20 May in Luchy (Oise) and 20 June in Aumagne (Charente-Maritime). Of these, we shall consider the case of Vimy last, as it stands apart from the others by its resemblance to a collective lynching.

In Machault, the action of Eugène Andrieux, a fifty-year-old family man, farmer and coal and liquor merchant, resulted in the death of an airman. As an adolescent, Eugène had his first experience of German occupation, during which he was subjected to forced labor in the service of the occupying power. May 12, 1940, was Whit Sunday. The flood of refugees from Belgium and Sedan – among them a handful of disheveled soldiers – was already on the march. Others soldiers were on the move in the opposite direction, heading to the front. It was around 2 pm. The sounds of a dogfight could be heard in the skies above. When an airplane came down, landing in a field, the villagers ran towards it. Eugène grabbed his hunting rifle. Having climbed atop a truck, he was the first to arrive on the scene with his friend the cattle merchant. A man in a white flying suit climbed out of the Dornier. Having learned German during the occupation of 1914–18, Eugène called out to him. The man did not reply. Eugène fired: the man collapsed, mortally wounded. The airplane's other survivor was taken into custody by the gendarmes who then arrived and transported him to a military hospital for his wounds. The three airmen who died in flight and the one killed on the ground were buried in the village cemetery. Following the armistice, the Andrieux family returned home. In the meantime, however, the German military authorities had launched an investigation on the basis of the testimony of the wounded survivor. The following spring, on 23 April 1941, Eugène was arrested as he went about his work. Interned in Paris' La Santé prison, he was tried by the German military tribunal on 10 May and sentenced to death. According to the verdict, he "had no orders authorizing him to arrest German soldiers" and he "acknowledged having used his personal weapon against the airman."[30] Transferred to Fresnes, he was executed on 4 June at dawn. Eugène Andrieux would become the first Frenchman executed by the occupant to be buried in what would later be known as the *carré des fusillés*, or "square of those shot," in the cemetery of Ivry on the outskirts of Paris. Unfortunately for both him and the German airman, Eugène was a "good shot" and aimed well, the reflex, perhaps, of a seasoned hunter. It is clear, however, that the weight of history also bore on this improvised deed.

In the case of Elie Pellerin, a farmer from Aumagne (Charente-Maritime), the shadow cast by the war of 1914 would once again play a decisive role. On 5 March 1941, Pellerin was sentenced to death by the German military tribunal headquartered in Matha (Charente-Maritime) "for having opened fire [on 20 June 1940], though not himself a soldier, on a German airman who had parachuted from his burning aircraft."[31] The verdict also ordered that Pellerin's property be confiscated. In keeping with the procedure established following the creation of the MBF (Militärbefehlshaber in Frankreich), the verdict was confirmed on 11 March by Otto von Stülpnagel,

Commander-in-Chief of occupation troops in France. The execution took place the same day. Otto von Stülpnagel, however, had long familiarity with the issue of francs-tireurs, having himself published a book in 1920 entitled *The Truth about German War Crimes.*[32] There, he came to the defense of the Kaiser's army and questioned the reality of the German atrocities committed in Belgium in 1914.

Another Frenchman accused of murdering an airman had more luck. On 20 May in Luchy (Oise), an airman and non-commissioned officer named Wilhelm Ross, born in Duisburg in 1917, was killed by gunfire from a group of refugees marching on the road, among whom were mixed soldiers stationed in the village.[33] In August, the Germans arrested a farmer from the commune, Alfred Mullot. Mullot was taken to Gand to be tried before the Luftwaffe's military tribunal and then brought to Luchy to serve in a German Army propaganda operation. A "Propaganda Kompanie" was summoned to the scene to prepare a report. Mobilized by the army, these professional photographers, who sometimes participated in the fighting, were lavishly financed by the Ministry of Public Enlightenment and Propaganda to film and photograph the front.[34] On 12 September 1940, extras were thus brought to Luchy to play the role of witnesses.[35] So that he be well dressed, his guards returned his suit, cleaned and pressed, to Alfred Mullot.[36] After meeting in a room at the town hall, the "tribunal" headed with the defendant to the scene over a little road through fields where the still-fresh grave of W. Ross was to be found.

The final hearing and sentencing took place outdoors on the public square, which had been abandoned for the occasion by the inhabitants of the place. A table and chairs were set up on the grass of the village square, with the church and monument to the war dead forming the backdrop. In a three-piece suit, his cap in hand, the defendant alternately stood and sat between two helmeted Feldgendarme, their necks draped with chain and chest plate. The proceedings were overseen by a Luftwaffe colonel. Also present was a wounded Luftwaffe corporal – doubtless the source of the testimony upon which the trial was based. This corporal, an observer in the airplane that crashed near Luchy, had been wounded as he parachuted to the ground. Nearly twenty German soldiers were present for duty in this peaceful rural context, which seemed to lend itself to the dispassionate exercise of justice.[37] The defendant was sentenced to death as a "franc-tireur."

One week later, a Luftwaffe airplane dropped copies of a German newspaper recounting the trial and showing the photographs over the city of Beauvais and its surroundings.[38] A few weeks after that, a German in uniform visited the defendant's wife to officially inform her that the sentence had been commuted to five years' hard labor.[39] The supposed "murderer," however, would ultimately be released in November 1941. The fact that the airman had been killed by gunfire – and thus by a weapon of war – while the defendant only had a shotgun perhaps played a role in the sentence's commutation.

Figure 2.1 Mock trial staged by the Luftwaffe in Luchy (Oise), 12 September 1940. © Unknown author/ECPAD/DEFENSE. The forces of occupation wrongly accused a farmer of having killed a German airman after he made a forced landing in the area on 20 May. Sentenced to death, the farmer was imprisoned in Belgium and then freed in November 1941. On 12 September 1940, a Propaganda Kompanie took photos of the trial. These were subsequently distributed as part of a Luftwaffe pamphlet dropped by airplane.

Given the obvious nature of this judicial error, the action undertaken in Luchy by the Luftwaffe seems to have been no more than a propaganda operation intended to intimidate the population. The trial staged by the German Airforce and Dr. Goebbels' reporters was a masquerade.

Whether the deed of civilians or soldiers stationed nearby, the deaths of these three men in Machault, Aumagne and Luchy may be ascribed to ignorance of the laws and customs of war as well as to inexperience. It is not easy to carry out an arrest when the other party is armed. Alongside the constraints of the situation, the lack of civic education and practical training could be fatal in its results, especially when the enemy resisted arrest.

Although the German documents never mention the possibility that Luftwaffe airmen may have behaved aggressively or simply failed to spontaneously surrender, reading between the lines at times allows one to surmise resistance on their part. This is clear in the case mentioned in the last chapter, that of Plouguerneau, near Brest. But it is also clear in the 20 May incident in Luchy. As an official from the prefecture noted:[40]

> A German airplane lands in flames. A group of soldiers stationed at Rouge
> Maison hurry to the airplane at the same time as some gardes civiques,
> among them Mullot (the latter armed with his shotgun).
> The pilot is dead when he reaches the ground. A wounded observer climbs
> out of the aircraft. A third, unwounded one also gets out, threatening and
> holding a revolver. A French soldier fires and kills him.
> Throughout this affair, Mullot was only a witness.

The final case in which an airman was killed – a deadly collective lynching – is
in a category by itself. This lynching took place in Vimy, in the Pas-de-Calais,
on 18 May. In the midst of the combat zone, a Heinkel He 111 bomber carried
out a forced landing in a field near Vimy. Fifteen French soldiers happened to
be there. They fired on the airmen, immediately killing three of them. Some
local inhabitants then arrived on the scene and began to beat the fourth
airman with their fists. Some soldiers shouted: "No prisoners, shoot him!"
A woman who initially opposed the beating began to strike him with a large
door key. A gendarme intervened: "Let him live, I need to interrogate him."
But the blows continued to rain down as the gendarme led the bloodied
prisoner away. A soldier fired a mortal shot at the airman. The four bodies
were buried after having been stripped of their shoes and their pockets
emptied.[41]

Though the mortal shots were fired by soldiers in uniform, in the case of the
fourth airman, civilians were present and participated. And, when repression
came, it was the civilians who would be targeted. Several days after the
incident in Vimy, the German Army occupied the area and arrested eight
inhabitants. They included Franziska Gielnik, wife of Chudalla, Bronislaw
Pchalek and Ernest Virel, all of whom were sentenced to death on 6 June in
Doullens for franc-tireur activity (*Freischärlerei*) in accordance with Article
3 of the *KSSVO*. They were executed on the 29th of the same month. Five
other civilians were transported to Brussels, interned in the St-Gilles prison
and tried on 22 April 1941 – not for "franc-tireur" activity but in virtue of the
VVO, the 5 September 1939 edict "against enemies of the people."[42] Paragraph
4 allowed sentences to be increased due to the state of war, whatever the
charge. Of the five defendants, one was freed but three were sentenced to death
and executed.[43] The fifth, gendarme Georges Bièque, was sentenced to five
years' imprisonment, which he carried out in Germany. Altogether, the occupying power thus executed five men and one woman for lynching one
airman.[44] With thousands of soldiers (particularly Canadians) dying on its
soil, Vimy had become synonymous with the carnage of the First World War.
With the new invasion, a particularly feverish atmosphere thus descended on
the town. The weight of the local past made itself felt and the mining town of
Vimy paid a heavy price: Franziska Chudalla, the daughter and wife of miners
and a mother of three children; Bronislaw Pchalek, a miner, and Ernest Virel, a
former miner and past member of the Communist Party, were executed first.

But the region's geography was also shaped by migration: the fact that two of the first three to be executed happened to be (or have been: the Chudallas obtained French citizenship in 1934) of Polish nationality is no accident. It reveals that, on both sides, there was knowledge or experience of the violence committed in the East.

Repression Contrary to International Law

The fact that the Wehrmacht had not integrated the principles of the Hague Convention as they regarded resistance to invasion is reflected in the manner in which its tribunals dealt with the actions of the Third Republic's gardes territoriaux. Indeed, by spring 1941, the position of German Army jurists had become so radical that they now appeared to be the main proponents of severe repression. In the interests of preserving the policy of Collaboration, by contrast, Wilhelmstrasse and the German military authorities on the ground occasionally sought to rein in the jurists' initiatives. The lopsided discussions that took place between Vichy, Wilhelmstrasse, the Militärbefehlshaber in Frankreich, the German Armistice Commission and the jurists of the Wehrmacht occupy a minor place in the Franco-German history of 1939–45. They nevertheless shed light on the balance of power as it was established by the occupying power at the armistice. Altogether, it appears that seventy-eight civilians and gendarmes recalled to duty were arrested in 1940–41 for having participated in the apprehension of German airmen in May–June 1940. Of these, seventeen were sentenced to death by various German military tribunals. Between June 1940 and June 1941, nine were executed, including eight who had participated or been present when an airman was killed. Eight others who had abused but not killed airmen had their death sentences commuted to years in prison. For five members of this latter group, the commutation of their sentence was determined by a decree signed by Hitler on 27 January 1943. By 1943, the case of the gardes territoriaux had ceased to be an affair of state.

On the balance sheet of German military tribunal repression, nine people were thus executed in reprisal for the deaths of four German airmen. Four of them had already been executed in summer 1940, just a few days after the armistice was signed: a father of eight (responsible for the arrest described at the start of the preceding chapter) was executed in Brest on 28 June, and three of the Vimy assailants (including a woman) were executed in Doullens on 29 June. The remainder were executed in spring 1941: one in La Rochelle, one in Paris and three in Brussels. Of the five sentenced to death in October and November 1941 but subsequently pardoned in January 1943, one – the above-mentioned Bernard des Champs de Boishébert – was freed. A descendant of the lords of Offranville, near Le Havre, he benefited from the intervention of Gabriel Le Roy Ladurie, chairman of the Worms

REPRESSION OF THE REPUBLIC'S "FRANCS-TIREURS" 57

company and brother to the minister of the same name. Those who were not freed were given prison terms greater than or equal to five years, which they were to serve in Germany – an additional punishment. Gendarme Bièque from Vimy, who had tried to protect the airman against assault by civilians and soldiers, thus spent five years of the war imprisoned in Germany. The same was true of a merchant from the village of Leuré-Plouguerneau, in Finistère, whose death sentence was commuted to eight years' hard labor while his co-defendant, mentioned above, was executed on 28 June. Sentenced to death in November 1941, Henri Heurteur, a farmer from the village of Cramoisy in the Oise département, had his punishment commuted to multiple years' imprisonment. After being transferred to Germany, he died in the prison of Saarbrücken in 1943, as we have seen, at the age of thirty-eight.

For some in the Wehrmacht, this repression did not seem sufficient. On several occasions, the German Army sought to increase the repression of acts carried out under the aegis of the Third Republic in arms. The first such attempt, which soon fizzled out, consisted in an effort on the part of the Luftwaffe to implement the principle of the inhabitants' collective responsibility, a method already applied in Poland. In October 1940, Luftwaffe headquarters (Luftwaffenführungsstab) proposed that this measure be applied to the inhabitants of towns in which acts of aggression had been committed against German airmen during the invasion. At the time, for example, 22 men from Le Meux, a 600-person village in the Oise, were arrested and held hostage in retaliation for the mistreatment of four airmen on the territory of the commune on 19 May 1940.[45] But the Army (Oberkommando des Heeres, OKH) and even the Wehrmacht's Legal Department firmly opposed this Luftwaffe proposal.[46] In support of its position, the OKH advanced an argument based on fact, principle and opportunity. The assumption that the entire population had participated in this mistreatment was not "without raising objections" and "considerations relating to the law of nations" ran counter to this measure. Moreover, not only did the time that had passed since the events in question render the proposal inappropriate, but these measures were above all "untenable" (*untragbar*) from the perspective of the future development of political relations with France. The Wehrmacht Legal Department, for its part, underscored that the measure under consideration by Luftwaffe headquarters demanded careful consideration given the efforts being undertaken to reach a political settlement with France (*mit Frankreich politisch zum einem Ausgleich zu kommen*). Furthermore, the measure was contrary to Article 50 of the Hague Convention, which stipulated that collective punishment was not to be inflicted on a population for acts committed by no more than a few of its members. That article read: "No general penalty, pecuniary or otherwise, shall be inflicted upon the population on account of the acts of individuals for which they cannot be regarded as jointly and severally responsible." The head of the Legal Department nevertheless noted that Article 50 applied to the period of occupation, not that of the invasion.

The Luftwaffe's effort to have sentences made more severe and increase the number of defendants was not isolated. In his study of German repression in the Nord and Pas-de-Calais départements, Laurent Thiéry noted the greater severity shown by Luftwaffe tribunals, the Luftwaffengerichte, compared with those of the Army, the Feldkriegsgerichte.[47] More closely associated with the occupation military authorities and thus more concerned with maintaining public order and tranquillity, Army tribunals conducted a somewhat less aggressive policy of repression than those of the Luftwaffe during the first year of occupation. This was the period that Gaël Eismann has described as judicial repression with a legal façade.[48]

Luftwaffe pressure nevertheless led the Wehrmacht general staff (OKW) to consider broadening the indictment to include, not the local population, but rather the mayors and prefects of the Third Republic. These they merged under the general term "administrative authorities" (*Behörde*), reflecting the fact that, since the advent of Nazism, German mayors had effectively been absorbed into the regime. Consulted on the matter of jurisprudential disagreements between the army tribunals and those of the Luftwaffe, in spring 1941 the supreme military tribunal of Berlin, the Reichskriegsgericht (RKG), proposed that the indictment be broadened.[49] Studying four cases in which airmen were subjected to abuse in the Oise, Seine-Inférieure and Nièvre départements, the president of the RKG noted that in May 1940, the prefects of these départements had issued instructions to mayors relating to the formation of Gardes territoriales. In one case – that of Seine-Inférieure – these instructions were first transmitted in November 1939. The supreme judge further singled out a telegram to prefects sent by the Ministry of the Interior on 12 May 1940, and also of course the decree signed by the ministers of National Defense and the Interior on 17 May. His conclusion was simple: it was "unjust" (*unbillig*) to try French people who had borne arms and merely obeyed orders while exonerating those "truly responsible" for these "stupid and blameworthy" measures. He therefore proposed that arrest warrants be issued for the mayors and prefects and that they be charged with inciting "franc-tireur activity" (*Anstiftung zur Freischälerei*). To this course of action, the president only acknowledged two possible objections: it would be "difficult to establish" the "subjective guilt" of the defendant, and the use of Article 3 of the *KSSVO*, which had been conceived to administer nearly immediate, summary and dissuasive justice, might fail to achieve its real aim given the remoteness of the events in question. In conclusion, he noted that all of the Vichy authorities (the Délégation générale pour les Territoires occupés (DGTO), the Délégation française auprès de la Commission allemande d'armistice (DFA) and the secrétaire d'État à la Guerre) had made it known that they did not consider the gardes territoriaux to be francs-tireurs but

REPRESSION OF THE REPUBLIC'S "FRANCS-TIREURS" 59

rather members of a legal organization. As a good jurist, the president of the supreme military tribunal closed by expressing his wish that no political consideration be allowed to restrict the legal action he proposed.

This proposal gives an idea of the referential framework of German juridico-military circles in the Reich's capital in spring 1941. Though inscribed in international law since 1899, an invaded people's right to legitimate defense is not recognized. At the same time, the Nazi belief that Germany was in this war a victim of aggression is treated as an established truth. The defeated party should thus pay for the war it had provoked. All of the conceptual elements of a ruthless "victor's justice" were thus present. This intellectual framework – just one of the ways in which the supreme tribunal was involved in the Nazi totalitarian system[50] – played a central role in efforts to repress civilian resistance to the German offensive.

It is not known whether the Vichy government became aware of this proposal to issue arrest warrants for all mayors and prefects of the communes and départements in question. There is reason to believe that it would have staunchly opposed it if it did. While this chance government had indeed sought to prosecute republican governments in the Riom Trial (February–April 1942), it was not so at war with republican society as to indict mayors and prefects who had served the National Defense at the time of the invasion. At the local level, the many reports by prefects seeking to defend the citizens under their purview are testimony to the incomprehension provoked by repression. In the Oise département, for example, no fewer than forty-one men were arrested for acts of "Freischärlerei," thirty-three of whom were still held prisoner in spring 1941. In April of that year, the eighteen mayors of the canton of Estrées-Saint-Denis petitioned the prefect to secure the liberation of twenty-two citizens from the commune of Meux who been incarcerated for merely having "executed well-known orders that the French Authorities had instructed us to carry out at the time."[51]

The Vichy government, in any case, had no need to make itself heard, as the Reichskriegsgericht's analysis provoked intense opposition from the Militärbefehlshaber in Frankreich (MBF) and the German Armistice Commission. Their vehement response was signed by no less than the head of the MBF himself, Otto von Stülpnagel.[52] Since the French Minister of the Interior and Prime Minister "could not be brought before German courts, French public opinion would see a trial against the administration's subordinate offices as an act of hatred and perhaps even vengeance against a defeated adversary." Taking a resolutely political stand, the general added: "The French government has recently committed itself to a policy of Collaboration (Zusammenarbeit) with Germany. A significant share of the French population is still unfavorable to this policy. Winning over the people will be made more difficult" by embarking on trials of this type. Yet this principled position did not prevent the general from looking favorably upon trying the Republic's ministers nor did it persuade him to accept the idea that those sentenced to death for "franc-tireur activity" should be pardoned. Even as he inveighed against the prospect of generically charging the local authorities of the Third Republic, he thus rejected the pardon of Elie Pellerin in March and that of Eugène Andrieux in May.

The response of General Vogl, who presided over the German Armistice Commission, converged with that of Otto von Stülpnagel. In a more measured tone, he underscored the attenuating circumstances that held for those who had committed abuses (albeit still without questioning whether the behavior of German airmen had played a role in provoking these acts). "The use of parachutist units (*Fallschirmtruppen*)," he wrote,

> is a novelty of this war and doubtless provoked mass hysteria in the population and its leaders, resulting in hasty, entirely ill-suited and illegal (as shown by the information contained in the case file) counter-measures. From this it followed that the rapid advance of German troops and the mass flight of the civilian population towards southern France sparked feelings of panic. There is no doubt that the many legal infractions committed against German parachute troops were the consequence of this hysteria and the prevailing atmosphere of panic.[53]

The general's call for moderation was itself perhaps inspired by his interviews with General Doyen, leader of the French Delegation to the Armistice Commission.[54] Whatever the case, his proposal, converging with that of the MBF, was put into effect: the notion that a number of trials should be reserved for Luftwaffe tribunals as well as the project to indict all mayors and prefects were abandoned.

When the Reichskriegsgericht (RKG) traveled to Paris to hold a session in October–November 1941, it was so as to arbitrate disagreements between army and air force tribunals. Ruthless though they were because based on the Nazi German conception of justice and, in particular, the *KSSVO*, the RKG's rulings nevertheless had some of the trappings of law. The twenty-two inhabitants of Le Meux, for example, were freed for lack of evidence. But in the case of three other trials involving nineteen defendants, five gardes territoriaux who participated in the arrest of German airmen (none of whom were killed) were sentenced to death. These were the inhabitants of the communes of Offranville (Seine-Inférieure), Cramoisy (Oise) and Anthien (Nièvre) who were pardoned by the Führer in January 1943.[55]

Reynaud and Mandel in Exchange for the Territorial Guards

What price was paid for these pardons granted by Hitler? There is no question as to the perseverance with which the French government defended citizens accused of "franc-tireur activity." In doing so, it argued that these were not

REPRESSION OF THE REPUBLIC'S "FRANCS-TIREURS" 61

francs-tireurs but rather Frenchmen obeying legal orders; if some of them lost control of themselves, they could only be tried for this reason and while broadly taking the circumstances into account.[56] On 25 June 1941, Marshal Pétain himself ultimately addressed a letter to "His Excellency Herr Reichskanzler." Appealing to the Führer's "clemency," Pétain asked that in no case should the gardes territoriaux be likened to francs-tireurs. He underscored the putative political interest of this decision "at a time when I am going to great lengths to get the French people to faithfully accept the orders I give it."[57] This request thus evoked the issue of public order and the harmonious pursuit of Collaboration. As the documents of the French Delegation to the Armistice Commission show, however, the French government proved less insistent when it came to defending the German refugees present on its soil (who were to be handed over to the occupation authorities in keeping with Article 19 of the Armistice Convention) or even German personnel in the Légion étrangère. The fact that the population targeted by the charge of *Freischärlerei* overwhelmingly consisted of rural Frenchmen likely made it easier for the Vichy government to take them into account.

But another argument – this one of Nazi and collaborationist inspiration – grafted itself onto the case of the gardes territoriaux. The ambassador to Paris Otto Abetz and his friend, French minister Jacques Benoist-Méchin, doubtless acted in concert. In March 1941, Otto Abetz suggested to his minister, Ribbentrop, that two French ministers responsible for establishing the gardes territoriaux be punished rather than executing "the people who were manipulated by them."[58] He proposed that Paul Reynaud and Georges Mandel – respectively, Prime Minister and Minister of the Interior in May–June 1940 – be extradited. This explains why, in May 1941, the ambassador placed a large question mark next to Otto von Stülpnagel's claim to the effect that the Minister of the Interior and Prime Minister could not be brought before German tribunals. In July, the matter was decided by the German Minister of Foreign Affairs, who ruled out extraditing Reynaud and Mandel, who he described as "the intellectual instigators" (*die intellektuellen Urheber*) of the deeds committed by the gardes territoriaux."[59] He nevertheless asked that, in exchange for pardoning the gardes, Reynaud and Mandel be sentenced to life in prison. The French government should also hand over the archives testifying to these ministers' relations with the United States. In the end, the archives were not handed over. In a speech broadcast by radio on 16 October 1941, however, Marshal Pétain announced that former ministers charged before the Riom Court had been transferred to the Fort of Portalet, in the Pyrenees, together with Reynaud and Mandel, against whom the Court ultimately brought no charges. Though all of these figures had already been imprisoned since early summer 1940, summarily transferring them to a fortress for detention represented a degradation of their condition.

As the chief of state's chargé for Franco-German relations, the writer and Hitler admirer Jacques Benoist-Méchin on several occasions intervened on behalf of the gardes territoriaux with arguments similar to those of Abetz. In October 1941, he hastened to underscore that "M. le Maréchal Pétain ordered, on October 15th, that MM. Mandel and Reynaud be imprisoned in a fortress."[60] The fact that neither of the ministers had been charged by the magistrates responsible for preparing the Riom Trial weakened Benoist-Méchin's position. He did not fail to express his regret to his friend the ambassador: "A verdict should have been delivered in Riom against the ministers responsible for creating the garde territoriale."[61] Following the Allies' November 1942 landing in North Africa and the subsequent invasion of the southern zone, all ministers interned in the fortress were transferred to Germany.

At the same time, from summer 1940 to February 1943, the Wehrmacht Legal Department hoped for a more severe resolution to cases in which German airmen and soldiers were abused. Led by Rudolf Lehmann from 1938 to 1945, the Wehrmacht Legal Department led the fight to have the two volumes of *France's Conduct of War Contrary to International Law* provide the foundation for a policy of repression.[62] The Department first requested that the guilty be tried in Germany, attempting to convince the German Armistice Commission in Wiesbaden of this in August and then again September 1940. The latter, however, objected that the matter was not covered under the text of the armistice and that it would be inopportune to rekindle memories of 1919, when Germany had refused to extradite war criminals identified by France. Rudolf Lehmann thus proposed that the volumes be handed over to the Vichy government so that, under German supervision, French tribunals might try defendants who were not prisoners of war "in such a way that the French admit that they had gravely violated the laws of war."[63] Those who were prisoners of war would in any case be tried by German tribunals. This proposal was rejected by the Minister of Foreign Affairs on political grounds. In May 1941, after the second volume had been printed, the Wehrmacht Rechtsabteilung went back on the offensive but Wilhelmstrasse stood firm: "for the time being," in the ministry's view, it would be inopportune to ask the Vichy government to hold trials in the non-occupied zone. The exchanges continued in this vein without result until February 1943. The generic indictment of the gardes territoriaux thus remained a classified document exclusively available to German military, governmental and legal staff.

The fact of the matter is that, in November 1941 – and thus following the announcement that Reynaud and Mandel had been interned in a fortress – the MBF decided that the fifty or so gardes territoriaux who found themselves in German-run prisons should not be included in the hostage lists.[64] Then, in January 1943 – that is, following the invasion of the southern zone and the

Portalet prisoners' transfer to Germany – Hitler pardoned the five gardes who remained in prison, all of whom had received death sentences. Between 1940 and 1943, in other words, Wilhelmstrasse's policy of *Realpolitik* towards France won out over Luftwaffe efforts and the wishes of jurists in uniform. What were the concerns that drove Auswärtiges Amt policy? The books that have been published on the Nazi-era Foreign Ministry have demonstrated its involvement in the Nazi system and the genocide of Jews.[65] The Foreign Ministry's action was thus driven, not by humanitarian considerations, but rather by a desire to mollify Vichy so as to ensure that government's ongoing cooperation in the policy of collaboration. As the only occupied country to still possess a German ambassador, moreover, France possessed a particular status vis-à-vis Wilhelmstrasse.[66] At least until 1943, Wilhemstrasse thus played an important role in defining Nazi policy towards France, a role that it sought to preserve.

It is also possible that Wehrmacht general staff did not entirely share the punitive desires of the Legal Department and that it, too, had taken political considerations into account. A recent analysis of German general staff writings shows that, as early as 1940, Hitler and the OKW were concerned about General de Gaulle's influence, the creation of the FFL and the expansion of territory under its control.[67] Sparing Vichy such useless provocations as publicly and systematically trying mobilized civilians and French veterans was also a way of ensuring the government's continued compliance. There was no point in fueling the "Gaullist movement."

In the history of the Gardes territoriales' repression, a mistake committed by the German side would give one to smile were it not so revealing of its murderous policy. When the decree concerning the Gardes was drawn up and signed, Georges Mandel was Minister of Colonies, not of the Interior. It was his colleague Henry Roy who co-signed it with Édouard Daladier.[68] Even though Mandel became Minister of the Interior on 18 May, it stands to reason that Henri Roy should also have been incriminated by the occupying power. But Mandel was of Jewish origin. In July 1944, he was finally transferred back to France from the outskirts of the Buchenwald camp where he was interned to be murdered by a member of the French milice. Reynaud only narrowly escaped the same fate.[69]

The Defeat Revisited

By positioning oneself as closely as possible to events and actors, one acquires a more contrasting perspective on the few weeks of the French defeat. By setting the insights collected here alongside other, already published contributions, the outlines of a new portrait of France in May–June 1940 begin to emerge.

Whether it be on the part of the government of the Republic or that of citizens mobilized in the rear, actions intended to resist the invader were not in short supply. Proof of their quiet determination may be found in the 400 or more Luftwaffe airmen apprehended by French civilians and soldiers. These arrests took place in a context of improvisation and were on occasion met by aggression on the part of the airmen. In about a dozen cases, civilians engaged in violence, sometimes with deadly results. These civilians had received no advance preparation for the new techniques of war. Even before 1939, it could have been foreseen that large numbers of enemy airmen would be brought down behind French lines. In the fall of 1939, however, the first efforts to mobilize citizens to meet this challenge were belated and disorganized. When the general mobilization of civilians finally got under way in May 1940, the invasion had already begun and it was too late to educate the hastily recruited gardes territoriaux, teach them how to make an arrest or remind them of the restrictions established by the Hague Convention. Was the government reluctant to mobilize civilians before this point? Did it fear demoralizing the population by suggesting that an invasion was possible? If this was the case, the experience of spring 1940 shows that it underestimated the warlike disposition of French people. This miscalculation might have been corrected had the enemy advance been stopped and the country not been submerged by Blitzkrieg in the space of a few weeks. In the event, the Blitzkrieg nipped in the bud what might have become a franc-tireur resistance similar to that of 1870.

A step-by-step analysis of the manner in which civilians fled south on the country's roads also contributes to dismantling the conflation between fugitives and runaways. On the one hand, this is because a large proportion of the fugitives left their homes after being ordered to do so, sometimes against their will. But it is also because some of them – and not just members of the gardes territoriales – only left after having resisted the enemy. As we saw in the case of Léon Werth, finally, participation in the exodus is not evidence of a predisposition to Collaboration. Whether they left under constraint or of their own free will, the flight of 8 million inhabitants from Belgium and France was above all an immense referendum, a massive example of voting with one's feet vis-à-vis the prospect of German occupation.

At the local level, the ways in which the German Army established itself in France also argue for revisiting the propagandistic depiction of the "korrekt" German soldier familiar from the public notices posted by the occupying power in France and Belgium. The acts of violence perpetrated by the Wehrmacht in 1940 were never accurately catalogued as the events that immediately followed them rendered any such exercise impossible. By the time of the Liberation, they would seem of secondary importance, having in the interim been displaced by the other massacres committed by the occupying power. In terms of the total number of victims, however, it is not clear that the record of the Kaiser's army in 1914 is so different from that of the Wehrmacht in 1940. If one includes the bombing of civilians on the roads, the number of civilian victims was greater in 1940. Moreover, in contravention of the Hague Convention, the immediate introduction to France of Nazified German criminal law retroactively transformed the legal analysis of actions undertaken on that country's territory under the Republic. Starting in summer 1940, a number of citizens who had acted legally in accordance with international and republican norms were thus executed on the basis of Germano-Nazi law.

The historiography of the French defeat would have been different had the outcome not been the 22 June armistice. Had France pursued the war despite this localized defeat, the resistance to invasion put up by soldiers and civilians in May–June 1940 would be better known. For the time being, one can only combine the insights offered by the present study with the perspectives opened up by, for example, the surveys of Julian Jackson and Philip Nord, which reveal moments of intense military resistance as well as the persistence of republican values. One would also need to relieve our image of the exodus of the interpretations that flourished under the Occupation. In place of the a priori image of a "débâcle," one might instead there seek the signs of aggressive and coherent behavior. Altogether, such a research project will above all depend on exhuming remnants and traces at the local level. For the great emergency of May–June 1940 did not lend itself to drafting notes and reports. Once it had passed and the armistice been signed, publicly drawing attention to behaviors associated with resisting the invader would have been dangerous indeed.

PART II

"Imminent Invasion!"

A Very Civil War in the United Kingdom

Seen from below and from the perspective of the civilians under attack, studying the Blitzkrieg in France challenges the traditional portrait of France as a nation in collapse and frantic retreat. To the contrary, it shows the French to have been determined and ready to fight. Examined from the same perspective, the Battle of Britain similarly offers a portrait of a people standing tall to confront invasion. Naturally, the two situations also differ. The French had to repel the enemy on their own territory. Attacked in their homes by the enemy presence, civilians and territorial guards proved themselves responsive and combative. Can this spirit also be applied to the British experience? We shall never know. In part, this is because the German landing never took place. But it is also in part because the British government made good use of the two months separating the German attack (10 May) from the onset of the Battle of Britain (10 July) to mobilize civilians and prepare the country for invasion. Receiving an enemy airman when invasion is no more than a hypothesis, however likely, does not induce the same emotions as receiving him in the context of invasion.

3

Britain into Battle

A People at War

In the way they acted, the British civilians who apprehended downed Luftwaffe pilots generally answered to the characteristics of a "People's War" – that is, a war that was democratic in its recruitment and liberal in its methods. These collective behaviors, which offer a positive image of the morale and political morality of the British people of the time, dovetail with what was until the 1970s the dominant historical analysis. In contrast to French historiography on the France of 1940, which has been almost universally negative from the 1940s to the present, British historiography prior to the 1970s presented a favorable image of wartime English society. Starting in that decade, as we shall see, it became divided over the question of whether the "People's War" was myth or reality.

One can paint a portrait in contrasts of wartime Britain. It offers a good example of a social pattern that was from the outset never free of contradictions. As we shall see, on the particular subject of downed airmen, British behavior was consistent with a certain image of the People's War, conducted from below and in a rather civil manner. This observation contrasts with the limitations and shortcomings of the Home Front as it has been described in the historiography since the 1970s. It adds a colorful touch to the overall picture.

The "People's War," Act I

The expression "the People's War" was itself not much used at the time, even if one comes across it here and there in the press. In the left-wing *Daily Herald* of 6 July 1940, for example, a member of the Local Defence Volunteers created two months earlier put it this way:[1]

> To the L.D.V., anyway, this is a truly people's war bringing back half-forgotten memories of dim stories of other wars, read in history books.
>
> Were there not wars in which horsemen rode through the dawn, knocking on a door, casting a handful of gravel at a sleeping window, carrying the news, "To arms"; wars in which hill-top beacons flared and the villagers filed out silently to their places in the field?

> We have our more prosaic counterparts – a bicycle bell ringing in the front garden just before dawn, a few words to an open window, and then, in ones and twos, men in khaki, carrying their rifles down the lanes, where the cottages slumber, where every footstep crunches loudly on the gravel, and only the distant searchlights reaching to the clouds seem silently awake.

This patriotic meditation, which to the French reader calls to mind, willy-nilly, the volunteers of Year II, the irregulars of 1870 and the Resistance fighters of 1944, was part of a social movement of warlike determination. From the time of the Great Armada to the revolutionary wars and the years of the Napoleonic threat, levying volunteers had been a British tradition. There was thus nothing novel about the notion of a people's war in 1940. As early as October 1939, Churchill, then First Lord of the Admiralty, had suggested that the government form a "Home Guard" of volunteers armed with rifles and supplied with armbands.[2] The idea of a "People's War" had been revived by the Spanish Civil War, with left-wing militants and opponents of the appeasement policy embracing the cause.[3] In June 1940, the left-wing journalist John Langdon-Davies, a former war correspondent during the Spanish Civil War, asked that the "people be armed." The Liberal MP of North Cornwall, Tom Horabin, a notorious opponent of the appeasement policy, also called for "turning the resistance to invasion into a people's war."[4] But the most visible proponent of this cause was Tom Wintringham, a member of the Communist Party of Great Britain until he broke with it in 1938. Formerly commander of the British Battalion of the International Brigades, he supported raising a volunteer army and even created a private training school for its members. It was in this spirit that he published *Army of Freemen* in 1940 and *The People's War* in 1942.

Before seeing how the People's War manifested itself in regards to its enemies on the ground, one must ask whether the Battle of Britain may legitimately be isolated from subsequent events. Whereas the success of the Blitzkrieg marked a fundamental break in French history, the United Kingdom presents a picture of undefeated continuity. It would thus be possible to trace British events across the duration of their democratic framework until 8 May 1945. But the Battle of Britain, affectionately nicknamed the BoB, requires a closer look due to the situation's mythical aspect and the fact that this "battle" played a foundational role in defining the behavior that was to be adopted towards downed pilots. The question of invasion hung over the country like Damocles' sword. Even if invasion fear (or invasion scare) did not subsequently disappear – at least not until the end of the first Blitz in May 1941 – the sixteen weeks of the Battle of Britain were the greatest ordeal. This period presents characteristics analogous to those of the Blitzkrieg in France: a democracy fights for its freedom in constant uncertainty as to the outcome of the fight. This period preceding the stabilization of the front, during which no one knew what would happen the next day, opened up the field of possibilities. In contexts marked by disorderly improvisation, panic, anger, renunciation and stoic determination manifest themselves in unpredictable and sometimes alternating fashion. When social and mental frameworks are subsequently stabilized by victory or defeat, freedom or submission, when actors can once again envision themselves in the duration of a predictable future, their behavior becomes "socialized" in response to the usual parameters – the political system, culture, history – which are now mainly restored. Another period commences. For civilians confronted with the arrival on the ground of a German pilot, the Battle of Britain was thus a moment of individual improvisation within the more general improvisation of the nation's organization. As it happens, however, the collective behaviors adopted at that time served as the mold from which subsequent behaviors arose.

Given that the People's War has been a hotly debated subject in the United Kingdom for the past fifty years, we must begin by identifying the various perspectives on the event in order to understand it in full knowledge of the facts. And there is another reason for this detour through the historiography: the facts that I shall relate here have yet to be studied but are quite present in the memory of British people. Evidence of this can be found in the rather lively discussions of them that take place online. As is widely known, memory and historiography develop in tandem and constant interaction with each other. "Online exchanges" regarding the welcome accorded this or that Luftwaffe pilot in this or that town of the United Kingdom reflect these developments. They are all the more useful for my research given that no archives exist regarding the manner in which downed Germans were received in the British Isles. There is a reason for this absence, as we shall see. But it has the drawback of depriving us of a systemic source that, while just as situated as any other, has the advantage of a certain exhaustivity and proximity to the events. The only serial archives produced at the time are those offered by the contemporaneous press. The handful of archives and eyewitness reports that I have collected allows some things to be verified but most of my information comes from newspapers, which were subject to the censorship and self-censorship of a democracy in wartime. Thus, by focusing more on the reflection of events than on the events themselves, I shall seek to decipher the messages sent by the press in order to reconstruct the likely dimensions of the facts as they took place.

A Situation Worthy of Ancient Myth

It is hardly surprising that the Battle for Britain, or Battle of Britain, should be a matter of continuous debate since the 1970s. The same holds for the Blitz, the systematic bombing of towns – and particularly London – from September 1940 to May 1941, during which the Luftwaffe killed half of its British victims.

It is a story that contains all the elements of ancient myth: the stakes of the battle and the scale at which it was waged were epic, while the besieged island's solitude and the youth and very small number of those upon whom victory depended made it heroic. Seen as such at the time, it offers a bottomless reservoir for impassioned judgement. Today's historiography tends to play down the narrative of the Battle of Britain, presenting it as less than a struggle between David and Goliath.[5] The resources of the British Empire offset the balance of power between the two belligerents. It nevertheless remains the case that Churchill could have ceded to the entreaties of the "appeasers" in summer 1940 and that he did not do so. Following the fall of France, Britain's decision to pursue the war constituted the second turning point of the war in Europe.

The precocious manner in which contemporaries identified and named the war's phases reveals their awareness of the significance of events. The expression "the Battle of Britain" was coined by Churchill in a speech to the House of Commons on 18 June 1940, and immediately taken up by the newspapers. At that moment, the battle properly so called had yet to begin. Starting in 1941, the dates of the Battle of Britain (10 July to 31 October 1940) were set in stone by successive studies conducted by the Air Ministry and Air Marshal Dowding.[6] The Blitz, for its part, began on 7 September with the onset of strategic bombing over England and came to an end on 21 May 1941, when the final preparations for Operation Barbarossa led some of the Luftwaffe's resources to be shifted to the East. In its first days, the Blitz ("lightning" in German) referred to nocturnal bombardment and the beams of light that accompanied it on the ground and in the air. Its meaning was then broadened to encompass the bombing of towns in both day and night. The word first appeared in August and thus once again before the event had begun in earnest.

The two phases of the Battle of Britain partly overlap. The reasons for the shift to the Blitz are worth considering for what they tell us about Nazi policy and, in particular, the future policy of lynching Allied pilots in Germany. In late August 1940, when Hitler diverted the Luftwaffe from its plan of destroying English airfields in order to concentrate on bombing cities, he played into his enemy's hands by relieving the pressure on RAF bases. But what is important for the subsequent history of Allied airmen is that this new strategy corresponded to an aspect of Nazi ideology: reprisal as a mode of government. Opposition deserves annihilation. The concept of regeneration by education or "re-education" was almost wholly absent from this type of totalitarianism. What happened in late August 1940 such that British civilians merited physical destruction? On the night of 23–24 August, German bombers principally targeting oil refineries near London dropped their bombs on residential areas. Churchill decided to retaliate. On the night of 25–26 August 1940, Berlin thus experienced its first bombardment. Nearly one hundred bombers, then at the extreme limit of their range, slightly damaged the city but above all produced a psychological shock. As William L. Shirer, a war correspondent in Berlin, noted in his journal, "The Berliners are stunned."[7] According to a rumor originating in a September 1939 speech delivered by Goering to Ruhr industrialists, Goering had said that "if the Ruhr was bombed, you could call him Meyer," in reference to a folk expression loaded with anti-Semitism. Berliners believed it, or at least the German journalists frequented by Shirer did. At this point, in Summer 1940, Nazi reprisal policy helped save the United Kingdom. Beginning in 1943, however, Nazi vengeance, now increasingly out of reach of British cities, was instead enacted against Allied pilots brought down over Germany.

For a year and particularly during the summer of 1940, it was a situation worthy of ancient myth. Britain stood alone and stood firm. Until Hitler invaded the USSR, the country showed that it "could take it" in total – and this time, involuntary – isolation. The fall of France had left the sky of continental Europe under Nazi control for an indeterminate duration. While the fall of Britain might not have ushered in a thousand-year Nazi reign, the regime would have lasted for decades or longer if Roosevelt had not been re-elected in the fall of 1940. In English-speaking countries, the victory of the Axis has thus become one of the favorite themes of historical fiction. One of the best known of these alternative history novels, *Fatherland* (1992), by the English novelist Robert Harris, takes place in Nazi Germany in 1964. This book belongs to a now long-established literary genre. To some degree, Britain, the new Atlas, had held the free world on its shoulders during the Battle of Britain and even throughout the duration of the first Blitz after 17 September 1940, when Hitler postponed Operation Sea Lion and preparations for landing on the British coast. It was a New Atlas but one that consisted only of a squad of young Hermes, the winged messengers of the British people, who were responsible for keeping watch over the airways and turning back the "bandits," as they described the enemy airplanes in their radio communications. Doubly mythical, this epic and heroic story easily inspires judgements full of emotion.

The Revisions of Later Generations

In Britain, the Ministry of Information poster, "Keep Calm and Carry On," has gone through a series of commercial declensions since the early 2000s. First made available in August 1939, it was ultimately not diffused for fear of needlessly alarming the population. But civilians conformed to its model of their own volition. Their calm laid the groundwork for the victory of fall 1940. A panicked people would have brought the government to the brink of surrender. Hitler moreover patiently awaited "explosions of mass hysteria" ("hysterische Massenerscheinungen") to erupt, and Luftwaffe General Chief of Staff Jeschonek insistently requested authorization to bomb residential areas in order to provoke "mass panic" ("Massenpanik").[8] From this point of view, the Battle of Britain was indeed a "People's War," just as much as the Blitz and the subsequent years of war. Since the 1970s, however, British historians and journalists have called into question the "Blitz spirit," that moment when the British people were said to have been united unto death in the struggle to defend their country and its values.

A generational phenomenon certainly played a role in this change of perspective, very much as the 1970s in France witnessed a historiographical shift towards minimizing the importance of the occupier and the Resistance while maximizing that of collaborators and the Vichy regime. The concomitance of these changes is not without significance. In Great Britain, the initiator of this shift, Angus Calder, was actually the son of a left-wing journalist who during the war became a propagandist and herald of the "Blitz spirit." Published in 1941, Ritchie Calder's *Carry On London* ended with these words:

> London, because it showed so emphatically, by the character and the courage of its people, that a free people cannot be bludgeoned by force and that free men and women can rise to almost any demand made upon them, their spirit, their hearts, and their minds, has become to the world the symbol of a new awakening and a new hope. In peace, as in war, let us say: "CARRY ON, LONDON!"[9]

This emphasis on and display of proud and noble sentiments, which in 1941 had a performative function and served as an incentive, were a generation later seen as salve to the bourgeois conscience, as moralizing cant that would be refuted by a close examination of the facts. With the student revolts of the late sixties, history was revised. The best-known initiator of this shift was thus the son of a former agent with the Political Warfare Executive, one of the inter-ministerial structures responsible for propaganda. In 1969, Angus Calder published his "masterpiece," *The People's War*. Written in lively prose, this work presented the portrait of a people at war but also sometimes frightened and defeatist. Divided by class consciousness and strikes, the people of Calder's book occasionally looted bombed-out neighborhoods, rejected refugees and were little inclined to share their homes with those made homeless by the bombing. With the *Myth of the Blitz*, which he published in 1991, the author once again developed this critical perspective on the unsteady morale and variable morality of the British at war.

Since then, the history of the Battle of Britain and, more generally, the social and political history of the war years in Great Britain have been split between the revisionists and the classics. Some works deliberately invert war propaganda, with titles such as *Their Darkest Hour: The Hidden History of the Home Front, 1939–1945* or, more recently, *Unpatriotic History of the Second World War*.[10] They denounce the "myth" of the People's War, just as in France some denounce the "myth" of the Resistance. For their part, the "classics" pursue their analyses, though doubtless in a somewhat more nuanced fashion than

BRITAIN INTO BATTLE: A PEOPLE AT WAR   75

before.[11] But a third way has now opened with the appearance of a more cultural history that includes gender studies. For the purposes of the present study, the most promising work in this series is that of Sonya Rose, *Which People's War?*, which subtly dissects the mechanisms of national identity and citizenship in Great Britain between 1939 and 1945.[12] Rose's description of Britishness as a complex whole dovetails with my examination of the reception of the enemy on the ground. The "temperate heroes" who were the men of the Home Front and the women restrained by the "contradictory obligations" weighing upon them were precisely the same as those who greeted the fallen enemy with civility.

The International Norm of Good Behavior

What is the result of these debates for our subject? Should the Great Britain that humanely received enemy pilots and cared for the wounded, even during the Battle of Britain and under bombardment, be considered a "myth"? A "moral" people should be able to distinguish between the function – uniform and weaponry – and the individual who operated the machines of death, whether because he had been forced to or of his own consent. Such at least has been the received norm of international law since 1899. As we have seen in connection with the activities of the French Gardes territoriales, prisoners "shall at all times be humanely treated and protected, particularly against acts of violence, from insults and from public curiosity."[13]

In keeping with the Hague Conventions of 1899 and 1907, individuals have a right to respect once removed from battle and delivered unarmed into the hands of the enemy. The 1907 Convention was ratified by thirty-six countries, including the United Kingdom, the United States and France. Germany, Japan and Russia also adhered to it, though they rejected Article 44, which stated that "a belligerent is forbidden to force the inhabitants of territory occupied by it to furnish information about the army of the other belligerent, or about its means of defense."

> **Regulations annexed to the Convention: Article 4 (1907)**
> Prisoners of war are in the power of the hostile Government, but not of the individuals or corps who capture them.
> They must be humanely treated.
> All their personal belongings, except arms, horses and military papers, remain their property.

After the First World War, in 1929, a new Convention regarding the treatment of prisoners of war was drafted in Geneva as a supplement to that of the Hague. Ratified by fifty-three countries, including the United Kingdom, the United States, France and even Germany (but not Russia or Japan), it provided that:

Article 2

Prisoners of war are in the power of the hostile Government but not of the individuals or formation which captured them.

They shall at all times be humanely treated and protected, particularly against acts of violence, from insults and from public curiosity.

Measures of reprisal against them are forbidden.

Article 3

Prisoners of war are entitled to respect for their persons and honor. Women shall be treated with all consideration due to their sex. Prisoners retain their full civil capacity.

Good behavior had thus been clearly and even legally defined before the war. The norms of civilization did not need to be invented. But it was still necessary to want to implement them and have the ability to do so. The mental operation that consists in separating responsibility – the responsibility, that is, of the deadly accoutrements (the uniform, the remains of the airplane) – from the person who wore it and carried these insignia and these weapons – supposes some preliminary reflection or some well-established backstop. It also entails that he who bears the symbols of death not noisily lay claim to the destruction of which he is the immediate author.

To Arms! An Upsurge of National Resistance

The difficulty the host population may have in calmly and peacefully receiving an enemy on the ground also stems from its degree of war mobilization. In these improvised contacts, the civility I will describe below might only be the product of a form of unawareness or indifference to the war. Were civilians at war from the first days of the Battle of Britain or did their mobilization take place later as a result, for example, of the weeks of Blitz over London? On this hypothesis, the People's War was neither beautiful nor ugly during the first phase of summer 1940; it had simply not taken place. Yet this is not very likely after nine months of "Phony War" and following the demonstration of patriotism offered by the voluntary participation of some 700 small private craft and their crews during the evacuation of Dunkirk. The "Dunkirk spirit" and Churchill's 4 June speech transformed a military disaster into a national and moral victory.

It is nevertheless a question that one may pose in reading the press, which offers a very euphemized vision of events. As long as the Blitz had yet to begin, the air war was presented as a match between two teams: the newspapers counted the strikes, as in cricket, with the difference that, here, the strikes were airplanes shot down. The score was sometimes even displayed in the form of a table, as in a sporting event. There was hardly ever any mention of civilian victims. Yet in late August there were already 1,500 of them, including more than 200 for the county of London.[14] But the press did not dramatize things – to the contrary. It developed a new genre, that of the colorful or humorous anecdote intended to defuse tension. Thus, in a school transformed into an emergency shelter for "bombed out" civilians, a doting husband reminds his wife that she had always regretted not attending school longer, telling her, "This is your chance, Ma!"; or the two old women being served a cup of tea, one saying to the other, "Don't you think this is delightful, Martha, we're saving rations!"[15] With the Blitz, the tone became a bit harsher, all the more so as the national press was headquartered in London and the capital was the main target. The 200 dead in August gave way to 5,500 new victims in September and 5,000 in October. More than 1,000 children were killed in two months in the London region. Yet the number of dead and the extent of damage caused by the bombing were rarely specified. This was also a matter of not informing the enemy. The information supplied was allegorical in nature: the ruins of a hospital were supposed to illustrate the enemy's barbarism, full-page photos concentrated on the downing of a German "raider," and the comical predicaments in which those under bombardment found themselves continued to amuse the reader.[16] Clearly, censorship and self-censorship converged to filter information and safeguard the citizens' serenity.

For all that, there is no doubt as to the patriotic mobilization. The rhythm offered by Churchill's speech is one indication of this. Just as he was the precocious author of the expression the "Battle of Britain," and the term "Blitz" also spread in a way that anticipated events, Churchill's speeches to the British in spring and summer 1940 preceded and pre-named the event. They acculturated the citizenry to the war, literally making them into warriors by supplying them with the mental weaponry necessary to identify and combat the enemy.[17] On 13 May, the standing ovation that followed the "I have nothing to offer but blood, toil, tears and sweat" speech in the House of Commons showed that Churchill's rhetoric resonated well beyond his political supporters. The speeches that followed continued to anticipate events by several weeks. They launched the general mobilization of civilians even before the invasion of France, announced the exploits of the RAF before the onset of the aerial battle and insisted on the refusal of any surrender. They occurred at regular intervals: 13 May; 19 May ("This will be the true battle. Faced with the supreme peril ... to call from our people the last ounce and the last inch of effort of which they are capable"); 4 June ("we shall fight on the beaches, we shall fight on the landing grounds, we shall fight in the fields and in the streets, we shall fight in the hills; we shall never surrender"); 18 June ("Let us ... so bear ourselves that, if the British Empire and its Commonwealth last for a thousand years, men will still say, 'This was their finest hour'"); 4 July (Mers-el-Kebir); 14 July ("we will defend every village, every town, every city ... this is a war of the Unknown Warriors"); and 20 August ("Never in the field of human conflict was so much owed by so many to so few," the "few" here referring to the young men of the RAF).

The bellicose message of these interventions has often been underscored, their way of galvanizing enthusiasm for the fight while simultaneously signaling to the enemy that there would be no surrender. But the political message that was repeated nearly every time must also be noted, a message that was sadly absent from war propaganda in France. The fight was clear. It was not merely a matter of defending the institutions and the British way of life; it was also "a war against Nazism,"[18] a fight for the freedom of Europe and the "survival of Christian civilization" (18 June 1940) against "a monstrous tyranny, never surpassed in the dark, lamentable catalogue of human crime" (13 May). It was a matter of rescuing "not only Europe but mankind from the foulest and most soul-destroying tyranny which has ever darkened and stained the pages of history" (19 May) and of not sinking "into the abyss of a new Dark Age made more sinister, and perhaps more protracted, by the lights of perverted science" (18 June) so that "the dark curse of Hitler will be lifted from our age" (14 July). The speeches were short and clear: the enemy was named, the issues of the battle laid out and its means defined.

It was not only the Army, Navy and Royal Air Force that were mobilized; the people were as well. The advent of radio amplified the Prime Minister's direct line to the nation. In his speeches of 1940, Churchill addressed the people, either by preparing them for guerilla warfare, as we have seen, or by inviting them to "show the finest qualities of their race" like the "brave men of Barcelona." "Their finest hour" would indeed include a people's war, after the fashion of the Spanish republicans whom Churchill, though a conservative MP, did not shy away from referencing:

> There remains, of course, the danger of bombing attacks . . . I do not at all underrate the severity of the ordeal which lies before us; but I believe our countrymen will show themselves capable of standing up to it, like the brave men of Barcelona, and will be able to stand up to it, and carry on in spite of it, at least as well as any other people in the world. Much will depend upon this; every man and every woman will have the chance to show the finest qualities of their race, and render the highest service to their cause. For all of us, at this time, whatever our sphere, our station, our occupation or our duties, it will be a help to remember the famous lines: He nothing common did or mean, Upon that memorable scene.[19]

The call to the people transcended national and political divisions, differences of gender, social origin and profession. Men and women would see it through without giving way to panic.

It was in painting this epic portrait of the British people united in a just fight that Churchill most fully gave voice to the "furia Britannica." Speaking of the Home Guard on 14 July, Churchill evoked the prospect of invasion ("should the invader come to Britain, there will be no placid lying down of the people in submission before him, as we have seen, alas, in other countries") and the possibility of a Battle of London, a city that, "fought street by street, could easily devour an entire hostile army." "We would rather see London laid in ruins and ashes," he added, "than that it should be tamely and abjectly enslaved." In accents worthy of La Marseillaise on this 14 July, His Majesty's Prime Minister sung the praises of the democratic conception of the people in arms.

In fact, the Prime Minister's bellicose fervor was buoyed and had even been preceded by an unprecedented patriotic outpouring.[20] In spring 1940, a veritable social movement stirred the British. Announced over the airwaves of the BBC by then Secretary of State for War Anthony Eden on the evening of 14 May, the creation of the Local Defence Volunteers responded to a pressing social demand first voiced in press and Parliament that April. On 10 May, the start of the German offensive sparked a multitude of proposals and letters to the editor and civil and military authorities. Even the respectable *Times* echoed these demands for a call to arms. In some regions of the country, citizens

Figure 3.1 Local Defence Volunteers (LDV) learning rifle drill at Buckhurst Hill, Essex, 1 July 1940. The photograph was taken by Captain Console, a War Office official photographer. It aims to disseminate a peaceful and even smiling image of the general mobilization of civilians. © Imperial War Museum.

began to organize and arm themselves. Whereas the civilian air defense organization, Air Raid Precautions (ARP), had struggled to recruit volunteers ever since it was first created in 1937,[21] the LDV sprang to life in one go. The creation of the LDV on 14 May was a precocious move, even preceding by four days the French decree creating the Gardes territoriales.

The mobilization of the British was linked to the fear of invasion and in particular the fear that airborne parachute troops might land: a fear made all the keener by the fact that, until 4 June, when the last man returned from Dunkirk, a large portion of the army found itself on the other side of the Channel. The fear of parachutists, which was also inspired by events in the Netherlands and Belgium, where the Nazis had conducted airborne operations, became a focal point of demands that the people be armed. Eden's announcement immediately met with enthusiasm from those whom the press for a time called "parashots." By the evening of 15 May – or just twenty-four hours later – some 250,000 men had signed up. By late July, they numbered 1.5 million. Broadcast over the radio, Churchill's 14 July speech, which gave the Home Guard an explicit role in combat, even in the streets of London, was warmly received by public opinion.[22] With this speech, the "LDV" also became known as the "Home Guard," a term Churchill preferred for its symmetry with the "Home Forces" (Army stationed in the United Kingdom) and the fact that it elevated the volunteers from a purely "local" defensive posture to a more properly national one ("home").

The political situation and the people's new self-definition created by the influx of volunteers widely diverged from the Nazis' expectations. On 19 July 1940, in a major speech to the Reichstag celebrating the victory of the "German people," Hitler also addressed a "call to reason" to Churchill. The war would end with the "integral destruction" of England but "naturally, not [of] Mister Churchill for he will certainly find himself in Canada where the fortune and children of the most distinguished war profiteers have already been transported." Together with the "warmongers of Judeo-capitalism covered in blood," Churchill and the British MPs were among those "destroyers of peoples and states" who filled Hitler with "profound disgust." One may to the contrary think that the circumstances of summer 1940 constructed a new British people, that they established a new social and political configuration that, while obviously not eliminating those that had preceded it, was superimposed upon them. The class analysis implicit in the Reichstag speech was further honed in the report submitted by the "England Committee" of the German Ministry of Foreign Affairs in September 1940. The report recommended bombing civilian populations and particularly working-class neighborhoods in order to induce them to rise up against the ruling classes. The Fleet Street district should also be a high-priority target since "without the press, political life in Great Britain will come to an end."[23] These plans attempted to apply to England a method inspired by the myth of the "stab in the back" of 1918. But even the Communist Party of Great Britain (CPGB), which had not been outlawed at the time of the Hitler-Stalin Pact, shied away from calling for a class front. When, on 15 September 1940, the party arranged for the air-raid shelter of London's luxurious Savoy Hotel to be briefly occupied by the residents of a working-class neighborhood, it was merely an expression of social grievances.[24]

It was thus on a population hyper-mobilized in defense of its island and particularly against the arrival of parachutists that the enemy airmen were to fall.

Summer 1940 to Spring 1941: The Time of Greatest Tension

To assess the quality of their reception, one must first understand the context. Alongside the fact of mobilization and the extreme anxiety generated by the fear of invasion, the number of pilots who fell to earth also had an effect, as did their distribution over space and time. The greater the number of downed pilots and the more concentrated the area in which they fell, the greater the probability that there would be a large number of bombing victims and ruins. This very local context might have a decisive influence on the manner in which the airmen were received on the ground.

Is their reception a matter of anecdote, a minor news item or a social fact? Counting the number of Luftwaffe airmen who reached British soil alive during the Battle of Britain is not a straightforward undertaking. Armies in battle are not fond of displaying their losses. When they make statistics public, they generally speak only of losses in matériel and only to contrast them with the correspondingly greater losses of the enemy. After the war, published statistics were provided for large theaters of operation and often organized by calendar year. This public data does not offer detailed information at the local scale.

In April 1941, the Luftwaffe calculated the number of personnel it had lost between 1 August 1940 and 31 March 1941.[25] Among air personnel, it counted 1,741 killed and 2,537 taken prisoner or missing. This total included the Mediterranean Front and, among casualties of the Battle of Britain, naturally also the airmen killed or missing over the Channel or who died upon their return to France (a group not covered by the present study). And yet German pilots dreaded crossing the obstacle of the Channel, particularly on returning from combat when, still shaken from the stress of battle, they brought back planes often damaged and short of fuel. Some were in a traumatized state when they landed, victims of "Channel illness," or "Kanalkrankheit." Among the overall losses, the proportion of 41 percent killed (1,741/4,278) for 59 percent taken prisoner or missing merits attention. If one limits the figures to airplanes brought down in British skies, where dog fights with the Royal Air Force took place, there would be fewer killed but even fewer or none missing.

There, the proportion of losses is around one killed for every one taken prisoner.

Another way to approach the question is by taking into account the number of Luftwaffe airmen graves identified in the United Kingdom. For the years 1939–48, there are 1,926 of them, of which 1,829 date from the period 1939–45. If, as we saw above, one airman was taken prisoner for every one killed, we may thus conclude that roughly 1,800 German airmen were taken prisoner over the course of the war. Thus, 1,800 encounters took place between civilians and enemy airmen – indeed, likely a few more than that since a minority of German families sought to repatriate the bodies of their loved ones after the war. These chance events took place across the country. Even if the bombing mainly affected the southeast, no region of the United Kingdom was spared. The reception of some 1,800 Luftwaffe airmen and the burial of an equal number of them is a social fact indeed.

Moreover, the airmen were brought down in a relatively short period of time. As we see in Table 3.1, 1940 was by far the bloodiest moment, with 40 percent of the war's deaths in this country's skies. And, for that year, the three and a half months of the Battle of Britain (10 July–31 October) represent 80 percent of losses (580 killed). To judge by the chronology of death dates for buried airmen, this number appears plausible as it is roughly equivalent to that for the Royal Air Force. The honor roll of some 3,000 RAF combatants who

Table 3.1 *Compared civilian and enemy aircrew casualties in the United Kingdom, 1939–45*

Year	Civilians killed by German bombing	New German airmen graves
1939	0	14
1940	23,767	725
1941	20,885	462
1942	3,236	182
1943	2,372	199
1944	8,475	199
1945	1,860	48
Total	60,595	1,829

Sources: Statement of Civilian Casualties in the United Kingdom (i.e., Great Britain and Northern Island) Resulting from Enemy Action from the Outbreak of the War to 31st May 1945. TNA, HO 191/11.

New German airmen graves: after the list of the Aircrew Remembrance Society, with the kind authorization of Melvin R. Brownless.

took part in the Battle of Britain includes 544 killed. Summer 1940 was thus characterized by the highest frequency of downed pilots.

This period of maximum frequency of downed enemy airmen also corresponds to the greatest slaughters of civilians killed in bombing. Table 3.1 shows that two thirds of bombing victims died in 1940–41 (43,000 killed out of a total of 61,000 for 1940–45). The heaviest losses took place from September to November 1940 (18,000 dead) and from March to May 1941 (17,000). Over the course of the war, London accounted for half of all victims. In summer–fall 1940, however, 70 percent of all victims were concentrated in this region. Rural zones were bombed less often but the psychological effect could nevertheless be significant there. The County of Kent, for example, between the Channel and London, was directly on the bombers' route. In the daytime, civilians watched the dogfights; at night, they could watch fires burning in London from afar. Within artillery range of the continent, Dover and the coast also sustained shelling. Beginning in August 1940, the county was nicknamed "Hell Fire Corner" and during the Blitz was subsequently rebaptized "Bomb Alley."

But the time of greatest tension extended beyond the Battle of Britain. It included the Blitz, which lasted from September 1940 to May 1941. Starting in fall 1940, the stress of sleepless nights and the emotional pressure afflicting thousands of families in mourning further added to the fear of invasion, even as the latter receded.[26] Yet hundreds of airmen continued to be brought down. With the resumption of the German air offensive in April–May 1941, more than 220 airmen were taken prisoner.

*

"The terrible year" of 1940–41 was perhaps the worst possible moment for an enemy to set foot on British soil. A "People's War" had been launched, driven from above by the passionate eloquence of the Prime Minister and supported from below by a popular outpouring of patriotic sentiment that was still going strong. The anxiety caused by the fear of invasion further increased the tension. Very bloody – the bloodiest of the war in the United Kingdom – and relatively concentrated over the capital, the bombing further shocked by its tactical novelty. In this political, material and human framework, one would expect to see civilians engaging in acts of violence against downed pilots. But this was not the case.

So what considerations of policy and/or political culture account for the success of this subtle balancing act of stop and go, of contained violence and unloosed fury?

4

"British Humor" as an Agent of Civility

Walking a tightrope, the British government exhorted the people to take up arms while simultaneously seeking to prevent the turmoil that might result from this. One risk of this balancing act was to trigger acts of violence against downed airmen contrary to international law. If Britain mistreated its German prisoners, Germany would not fail to take retaliatory measures against the thousands of British prisoners it already held. It was thus necessary to at once encourage and restrain the population, inciting the citizens to a determination that was both resolute and calm. Doing so was all the more important given the fear that a panic similar to that which seized hold of the Belgians and French during the invasion of their territory would once again happen if the Germans crossed the Channel. The exodus of 1940 had contributed to defeat on the continent. Order and calm must thus reign in men's minds at all costs. So how was one to fire and dampen, arouse and soothe, incite and pacify at one and the same time?

Interpreting the Silence of the Sources

The moment has come to more specifically discuss the sources or rather their silence in both the British and German cases. In the case of the Battle of France, we have seen the utility of German sources for studying the manner in which German pilots were received on the ground. Though biased and misleading, they nevertheless had the merit of drawing the attention of – and, above all, provoking a response from – the French, a fact that lends itself to highly interesting comparative study. But it seems that the Wehrmacht's Legal Department made no such attempt to describe the fate of airmen brought down over Britain.[1] The archives of this department, which overflow with information concerning Soviet and Polish atrocities and the mistreatment suffered in France, are silent in regards to the reception of Luftwaffe airmen in Britain.

It can be supposed that, if Britain had been defeated, the Wehrmacht's Rechtsabteilung would have carried out the same type of investigation that it conducted in France, one similarly colored by National Socialist ideology and the refusal to recognize the international conventions of 1899, 1907 and 1929.

In the eyes of the Abwehr (*Amt Ausland / Abwehr*), a spy agency under the direct authority of the OKW, it seemed obvious that the Home Guard was "nothing more than a bunch of francs-tireurs."[2] As we have seen, the same conclusion was reached regarding the French territorial guards. Yet Article 1 of the annex to the Hague Convention of 1907 was clear and the Home Guard, which had had the time to organize itself over the course of May and June, fully satisfied the conditions it stipulated for being considered an army:

> The laws, rights and duties of war apply not only to armies but also to militia and volunteer corps fulfilling the following conditions:
>
> 1. To be commanded by a person responsible for his subordinates;
> 2. To have a fixed distinctive emblem recognizable at a distance;
> 3. To carry arms openly; and
> 4. To conduct their operations in accordance with the laws and customs of war.

Starting in July, Berlin's press accused Britain of conducting, with the Home Guard, "a franc-tireur war against Germany . . . in which men and women will individually threaten the lives of German soldiers via ambushes and the most treacherous means."[3] The myth of Belgian francs-tireurs, which had been used to legitimate the German atrocities of August 1914, was thus intact. Together with the "stab in the back," masked "francs-tireurs" were among the tools of a political rationality that had existed in Germany since the days of Wilhelm II.

It nevertheless seems that the WR (Wehrmacht Rechtsabteilung), the Wehrmacht Legal Department, felt some reluctance in venturing onto this terrain, at least as long as the invasion had yet to take place. Several months later, in March 1941, the Luftwaffe attempted a final all-out assault on Great Britain in order to obtain its surrender before the start of the invasion of the USSR. From March to May 1941, the Blitz killed almost as many civilians as the period between September and November 1940. It was in this context – the renewed possibility of a German occupation of Great Britain – that Reichsführer SS Himmler, the chief of all police services, called upon the Wehrmacht's Legal Department in regard to the Home Guard. The Gestapo doubtless wished to lay the groundwork for subsequent repression. The director of the Wehrmacht Rechtsabteilung, the same man who had allowed the French gardes territoriaux to be tried as francs-tireurs, reacted cautiously. He began by sending the Abwehr a factual description of the Home Guard, asking it whether this portrait was consistent with its own intelligence. His aim, he said, was to lay the groundwork so that the OKW might reach an opinion on the question of whether the Home Guard "was a militia or not."[4] The remainder of the file is missing.

In the same way, no information is to be found in the archives of the "War Crimes Bureau" regarding possible mistreatment incurred by German soldiers on British territory. This "Bureau" had been created in September 1939 as part of the Wehrmacht Legal Department.[5] The archives of the Wilhelmstrasse are also silent regarding the reception of German pilots in Great Britain, whether they be those of Secretary of State von Weizsäcker, the ministry's legal department or the information service, which disseminated the ministry's Nazi propaganda.[6] Unless these files have disappeared in their entirety from both the archives of the Wehrmacht and those of Wilhelmstrasse, it seems likely they never existed. Finally, the sprawling Wehrmacht veterans file (WASt)[7] gives no information on the conditions in which airmen were received on the ground. A good explanation for this would be the absence or rarity of mistreatment, for Germany was well informed regarding the situation in Great Britain. In addition to the work of the Abwehr, it could count on the British press and the BBC as well as reports from its legations in neutral countries and firsthand information sent it by the Japanese embassy in London.

Nor are there more sources regarding the reception of airmen on the ground to be found in the British national archives. A study of the Archives of East Sussex and a visit to the Archives of Kent were equally unfruitful, among other reasons because the day books of police stations were destroyed in 1943 as part of a national recycling program. The absence of sources for Britain is easily understood. In its interrogations and surveillance of POWs, the British Army was interested in the enemy but not in the conditions in which he was intercepted on the ground.[8] Nor were the police and the courts going to gather potential complaints from enemy airmen. The pacifists, for their part, did not establish any system to monitor that the rights of people in this domain were respected. Even "Mass Observation," the association created in 1937 to study the everyday life of ordinary people so as to build an "anthropology of ourselves," as the organization's founders put it, did not conduct any studies of the matter.[9] Yet, with their team of remunerated observers and large number of correspondents distributed across the country (who moreover responded to questionnaires), "MO" was well placed to develop a rather representative picture.

For the moment, the only available continuous source is the press. It is of interest for two reasons. On the one hand, its regular appearance allows one to identify the frequency with which airmen were brought down. On the other, its content, filtered by wartime censorship and self-censorship, informs us as to government policy and also the ideal image the British wished to have of themselves. We shall begin with this agreeable portrait before turning to consider the government's interventions, which will put us on the path of a reality that was at once less uniform and less peaceful.

Reception on the Ground: Comedy Sketches and Genre Scenes

Even in wartime, a democracy's press is a good indicator of the subjects that people are talking about. During the Battle of Britain and until December

The capture of an enemy airman:
a local event (1940–1945)

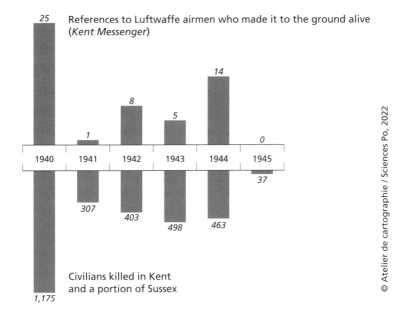

Chart 4.1 The capture of an enemy airman: a local event, 1940–45.
Sources: Kent Messenger, Maidstone; *Statement of civilian casualties in the United Kingdom from 1939 to 1945*, Région 12 (Tunbridge Wells: Kent and a portion of Sussex). TNA, HO / 191 / 11.

1940, the capture of downed enemy airmen was a subject worthy of Fleet Street headlines and sometimes even made the front page. Subsequently, however, the subject almost completely disappeared from the national press, perhaps on account of its repetitive character and because newspapers increasingly devoted their coverage to the war's spread in Europe and beyond. The same did not hold at the local level, where the capture of an airman remained a noteworthy event. The frequency of articles and news items regarding this subject in a Kent newsweekly, the *Kent Messenger*, well reflects the development of the air war if the latter is evaluated by the number of civilian casualties on the ground. Chart 4.1 shows that the curves of fallen airmen and civilian victims of raids are not entirely parallel but also that they are not unrelated to one another. The probability that there were victims and airmen parachuting from their craft is obviously related to the frequency of bombing. But their mention in the press also has to do with other factors, such as the novelty or triviality of the phenomenon and its relative (and rapidly diminishing) place among the war's events. An anomaly in this pattern – the revival of media coverage in 1944 – remains to be explained.

In 1940, all of the popular national and local newspapers seemed of one mind. The encounter with a German pilot is depicted as a comedy sketch or amusing genre scene. Often presented in serial form, the anecdotes remind one of the pages of a book of jokes or amusing stories. Humor is the rule. Although the psychology of peoples – a university discipline until the 1950s – has become politically incorrect, one cannot help but think of the national stereotype of British humor. A brief foray into the catalogues of the British Library (BL) and the Bibliothèque nationale (Bnf) seems to confirm this hypothesis. One finds nearly 200 titles containing the words *Blagues, Histoires drôles* and *Livre d'histoires drôles* at the Bnf. At the BL, by contrast, titles containing the words *Jokes* and *Joke Book* correspond to 2,500 entries, the oldest of which dates from the early eighteenth century. A *history of English Humour* appeared in two volumes in 1878 whereas the history of French humor has yet to be written.[10] But was this really a national practice in the United Kingdom of 1940 or had this stereotype been opportunistically put into the service of political ends? Humor is widely recognized as a distancing technique, a way of defending oneself against a traumatic event. Were newspapers serving as the vehicle for a policy of appeasement, this time targeting the country's interior and intended to keep people calm so as to prevent the "Masspanik" desired by Hitler?

The humor of the situation stemmed from the unexpected character of the situations as well as the collision they brought about between public and private spheres. It was a backdrop that lent itself to humor to the degree that the downed airmen were not aggressive, especially in 1940. The latter willingly surrendered, convinced of Germany's imminent victory, as shown by their interrogations at CSDIC, the Combined Services Detailed Interrogation Centre. The insularity of Great Britain doubtless also discouraged them from trying to escape. Both of these factors were lacking on French territory during the invasion of May–June 1940 and their absence resulted in more aggressive behavior on the part of downed airmen. A brief survey of British newspapers gives an idea of their content:

9/7/40 *Daily Express*	"Woman seizes Nazi airman"
26/7/40 *Daily Herald*	"Miss X gets her German (because she left gas on)"
3/8/40 *Kent Messenger*	"Tractor drowned noise of Nazi plane crash"
14/8/40 *Daily Express*	"Bathroom used as prison to hold German airman"
3/9/40 *Daily Mirror*	"Nazi pilot helps buy a spitfire"
7/9/40 *Kent Messenger*	"Nazi pilot surrenders to Kent man in bathing kit"
21/9/40 *Kent Messenger*	Cup of tea for the Nazi pilot in the presbytery
30/11/40 *Kent Messenger*	"Mind our Messerschmitt, Nellie!" [Legend accompanying a photograph depicting a mule (Nellie) and a horse surrounded by a small crowd of people as they drag an airplane out of a meadow]

The reader is thus offered a series of humorous anecdotes. The image they give of the English is that of a hard-working and restrained people lacking animosity towards the enemy and capable of acting on their own to defend their country without particular supervision. The women are at their stoves or in their dining rooms, the men in the fields. Farmers lend their horses to pull a damaged Messerschmitt out of a field while the station master who arrested the pilot describes him as "quite a pleasant fellow." The person in the bathing suit was sleeping next to his pool after a night on guard and before going back on duty. The style of the tractor story is typical:

> Tractors are noisy things. So noisy indeed that a farmer working alone in a field of South East England did not hear an enemy plane crash in an adjoining field. Imagine his surprise then when two German airmen walked up to him, gave themselves up, and explained what had happened. "Well, you had better come along with me, he said, and have a cup of tea." Off they strolled to the farmhouse where the farmer, after informing a Home Guard of what had occurred, entertained his visitors at the family table. Tea was soon over, a military guard quickly arrived and soon the tractor was working as noisily as ever.[11]

"Business as usual." The war came to the farmer but he was not so at war as to change his behavior. He carried out his British duty just as he worked his field. He was the opposite of a warmonger.

One also sees that women were involved in the country's defense, albeit in their traditional role. Although a Women's Home Defense Corps (WHD) was created on private initiative, women were not authorized to join the armed battalions of the Home Guard.[12] The success that greeted the Home Guard upon its creation (as the LDV in May 1940) was partly due to this instance of gender discrimination. Writing of the ARP (Air Raid Precautions), Lucy Noakes suggests that its difficulty finding recruits stemmed from its mixed character, repellent to masculine pride.[13] Armed and male, by contrast, the Home Guard flattered gender prejudices. Yet, though the war maintained the gender hierarchy, the role played by women in arresting Germans is nevertheless very visible in the press of the time. While women were indeed involved in arresting Germans – where the airmen came down was a matter of chance – their role was doubtless foregrounded as a way of de-dramatizing the air war. If capturing the enemy is women's work, it cannot be frightening. When "Miss X gets her German," she is in the midst of running out of her bomb shelter during an alert to turn off a clothes iron she had forgotten to unplug. She at that point comes nose to nose with a frightened young German, asks him if he is wounded, has him come in and makes him drink a glass of whisky. He thanks her by kissing her hand. The romance was not to be; it is merely suggested. But the irruption of the front line into the humdrum routine of the household's daily life, while it gives the anecdote its flavor, also trivializes the incident. A harmless young woman offers hospitality to a helpless passerby. It was a scene of genre (and gender), not of war.

These good-natured and humorous sketches also send an implicit identitarian message: if humor is, as the saying has it, a British trait, then keeping one's sense of humor is to remain British. By defending one's culture, one defends one's territory. The press sometimes played on this national stereotype to show civilians' capacity for resistance: "British humour: bomb-proof against wild Nazi raids," ran a headline in the *Kent Messenger* after two weeks of Blitz (Figure 4.1).[14] Of course, as long as the invader was not on the scene, the people's ground war constituted a form of remote warfare. Had the troops of

Figure 4.1 "British humor: bomb-proof against wild Nazi raids," *Kent Messenger*, 21 September 1940. © The KM Group. Consisting of euphemism and self-mockery, British humor was part of the inventory of national stereotypes. The British press put this cultural resource to work to discipline and calm the population.

the Wehrmacht made landfall, British behavior and propaganda would most probably have lost their dose of humor.

In the meantime, the image of the enemy that was disseminated was in keeping with the distantiated character of the narrative. Most of the time, the enemy was not "German"; he was a "Nazi." This dominant use of an adjective describing the enemy in terms of his ideology or by the regime that had armed him sharply contrasts with the situation in France, where it was the German who was presented as the enemy. This was a specificity of the British that perhaps reflected the country's history – that is, the fact that the United Kingdom had not experienced three German invasions in the space of a single lifetime and the related fact that the Treaty of Versailles came in for early criticism there. As a "Nazi," the airman was thus the messenger of a condemned ideology, one that he might be persuaded to abandon after a period of re-education in prison camp. But he was not forced to carry the weight of history. Nor was he perceived as the representative of a hateful race or culture. There is no Germanophobia in these newspaper stories. The pacifist newspaper, *Peace News*, itself recognized this in January 1941, noting that "there's little jingoism to be found in the people."[15] It was not a time for chauvinism.

When the press sought to describe the German airmen, it did so along the lines of universal psychology. In August, the *Daily Express* classified the pilots into five categories: the realist who declared on arriving, "English too good"; the philosopher who performed a forced landing with his Messerschmitt in a cabbage field, concluding that "these Spitfires are very good. They were too fast for me. So I'm out of it now"; the financier who parachutes from his Heinkel and exclaims in regards to the plane, "a million marks gone!"; the grouser who bitterly complains, "that's what we get for coming to England"; and the Italian who jumped from a Junker 88 and is saved at sea.[16] Ten days later, the same newspaper distinguished, not five, but six psychological types of Nazi airman: worried, vigilant, happy to be there, combative, melancholic and ever gentleman. Brief legends were accompanied with photos of ordinary faces.

Another mode of categorization may be detected. A class relation often existed between the airman, endowed with an advanced education and social capital, and the average man or woman who came upon him on the ground. This class relation was often suggested when the author of the arrest was an industrial or agricultural worker. The event also stood out for the inversion it produced in the usual social hierarchy. The only case (albeit minor) of ill treatment that I was able to find in the press was clearly a response to class contempt. "The arrogance" of an airman who came down near Newcastle, in northeast England, earned him a punch in the nose from a worker employed nearby. As a fellow worker recounted: "The airman didn't seem in a hurry to put his hands up when challenged and, after looking my mate up and down, passed a remark in German which we regarded as a sneering reference to my mate's working togs."[17] Clearly, even in the mind of a supportive colleague,

92   "IMMINENT INVASION!"

throwing a punch did not go without saying and warranted an explanation. In his mouth, the enemy is "Jerry," a diminutive of "German" – a pejorative expression but less mean-spirited than the French "Boche." "Kraut," an English abbreviation of "Sauerkraut," is the equivalent of "Boche." The press sometimes referred to "Huns," an openly hostile expression so unlikely that it tended to elicit a smile, but "Kraut" is wholly absent.

The model offered by the press is thus that of quiet men and women, peaceful citizens whom the war has surprised as they go about their daily lives but without changing their behavior. The hero of the "People's War" neither flexes his muscles nor thrusts out his jaw; the heroine does not drape herself in the folds of the Union Jack. Both simultaneously refuse chauvinistic posing and fearfully letting themselves go. They keep their cool. Decent people and honest workers, such are the people at war: a portrait that in no way corresponds to representations inspired by the concept of "brutalization."[18] As they are depicted by the press, we find no trace among the British of a type of brutality or "war culture" that might have resulted from the Great War, no disposition to hate nor, among men, to aggressive virility. To the contrary, one observes a general desire to maintain the state of peace around oneself as long as possible and hold the violence of war at arm's length, whether it consist of nervous tension, the shock caused by destruction or hardship and mourning. The heroes are instead anti-heroes – good husbands, good workers, wives and young women at home, attached to their habits and their culture. This portrait nicely corresponds to that offered by Sonya Rose in her book, *Which People's War?*[19] On the basis of the brochures and radio broadcasts of the time, she describes the men of the "People's War" as "temperate heroes," reserved men with little appetite for displays of patriotism and attached to their home and fellow workers. War is a duty. The typical profile drawn from interwar press drawings is that of the "Little Man," the modest fellow in melon hat and folded umbrella, well-meaning and easily disconcerted.[20] The "Little Man" contrasts with the age-old John Bull mobilized by First World War propaganda as well as with that other frequently drawn character of the 1930s, Colonel Blimp, a sort of reactionary "old fogey." War is a duty and nothing more. It was upon this image that the hit TV series of the late 1960s and 1970s, *Dad's Army*, was to draw in making fun of the Home Guard. It brought people's experience into popular culture.

Through the Looking Glass of the Press: Some Cases of Brutality

Although the portrait offered by reading the press on the whole appears accurate, it must be qualified with a certain number of exceptions to the rule if one is not to slide into legend. It is not difficult to cross the looking glass of the press for it supplies the means to do so itself. During the Battle of Britain,

"BRITISH HUMOR" AS AN AGENT OF CIVILITY 93

Figure 4.2 "Is it all right now, Henry?" *Daily Express*, 29 August 1940. © Daily Express.
"Is it all right now, Henry?" inquires the wife from inside the Anderson shelter as fires caused by the bombing rage nearby. "Yes, not even scratched!" responds "The Little Man," who is gazing at a large squash. A devoted husband who loves his garden, this famous figure by artist Sidney Strube is a symbol of the continuity of everyday life. Neither "John Bull" nor "Colonel Blimp," "The Little Man" is just a normal citizen.

several articles reported "mistakes" that led civilians, LDV and Home Guard to inadvertently mistreat RAF airmen. From this, one may easily deduce that Luftwaffe airmen were also subject to hostility upon their arrival. If the press is silent on this point, it is for reasons of security, to protect the British pilots who had recently been brought down over Germany. Retaliatory measures on the part of the Nazis were to be feared.

The examination of these "mistakes" allows one to understand how they took place. In my review of the press, I encountered three cases of mistreatment towards members of the Royal Air Force. Two of these took place in mid-August, the third on 1 September – thus before the Blitz had even begun. The first case presents an RAF airman who came down in a wheat field and was spotted by armed civilians. An older farmer took aim at him while a peasant came up from behind with a two-meter-long iron bar. Though the pilot protested that he belonged to the RAF, the threat was only dispelled after soldiers arrived on the scene. In the press account, the airman described the peasant who approached him from behind as a "yokel" and was himself insulted by the farmer with the gun, who said "I'd like to blow his blue-pencil brain out." Already, the shock of contact between different social worlds stands out. Moreover, two women coming from the farm arrived, one carrying a frying pan and the other a large knife. The fact that this incident was presented by Air Marshal Sir Philip Joubert in a press conference about "British and enemy" airmen who escaped the crash of their planes shows that the subject was a matter of concern for the authorities.[21]

The most memorable incident in this series took place on 16 August, just one day following the press conference. It concerned the same Captain Nicolson we encountered in the Introduction to this book. At the controls of his Hurricane in flames and already severely wounded and burned, the young Captain James Brindley Nicolson raised himself to climb out of the cockpit. Spying a new target, he sat back down to fire a final salvo against a Messerschmitt before leaping from the airplane with his parachute. He succeeded in extracting himself and floated in the sky for nearly twenty minutes. A Home Guard who spotted him coming down took him for a German and wounded him anew with rifle fire. The pilot survived. He would be the first of the "Few" to receive the Victoria Cross.[22] The third misadventure was that of an RAF pilot almost lynched by a crowd that mistook him for a German.[23] Descending in his parachute for more than ten minutes, the airman was spotted by the inhabitants of a neighborhood on the outskirts of London, who were convinced he was German. Reaching the ground in a pub parking lot and threatened by a crowd that included Home Guards, he was saved by the intervention of a bus driver. The police and army subsequently arrived to take him to hospital. The inhabitants "explained that they were enraged by the indiscriminate bombing of non-military targets practised by the Nazi airmen."

As there is no reason to think that only the British were on the receiving end of threats from civilians, one may suppose that some Germans were seriously mistreated. So much is not said but these articles are so many calls for prudence and calm. Indeed, this was perhaps their main purpose. The same may be said for the account of how the anti-aircraft guns of a southeastern town suddenly fell silent in the midst of an air battle in order to allow a parachuting German to make it safely to the ground.[24] On 14 September, a notice was even published that put the matter plainly: "Parachutists Not Always Nazi."[25] The population was called upon to show discernment and only use their weapons if the "parachutist" adopted a threatening attitude or committed hostile acts. They were reminded that Poles, Czechs and Belgians were fighting in the RAF and might very well not speak proper English. "Care and discretion" were required of the "public." Even with invasion imminent, the use of legitimate violence remained reserved to the public authorities.

The Luftwaffe Ace and the Royal Army Medical Corps Doctor

One could take the opposite tack and ask what after all was the real basis for these little stories, all of which end so well or make one smile at the comical aspect of the situations they evoke. For reasons of security – that is, so as not to inform the enemy – the settings of these anecdotes were never precisely specified and their characters were nearly always anonymous. As we have seen, moreover, archival sources for these incidents are almost completely lacking. On the German side, the hope that I would find something in the immense Wehrmacht veterans file (WASt)[26] proved vain. The file supplies standardized information not touching upon the matter at hand. A study conducted among the families of survivors with the help of this service did not yield any usable information. For the period of the Battle of Britain, we possess just a few first-person accounts.

The first of them is that of Franz von Werra, whom we have already encountered in this book. This Luftwaffe ace came down in Kent on 5 September 1940 (Figure 4.3). Immediately taken prisoner, he subsequently tried to escape England on two occasions. Finally transferred to Canada in a prisoner convoy, he succeeded in escaping his guards in January 1941 and took refuge in the United States, at that time a neutral country. Taken in hand by the German intelligence services, he travelled to Latin America, returning to Germany by airplane in April 1941. Von Werra was the only German prisoner of the entire war to pull off the exploit of escaping and returning to his country. He did not survive the war. On 25 October 1941, von Werra disappeared after his airplane suddenly plunged into the North Sea.

Upon his return to Berlin in April 1941, Franz von Werra was called upon by the Air Ministry, led by Goering, its intelligence service and its administration of POW camps for RAF prisoners in Germany. Goebbels and the services of the Ministry of Public Enlightenment and Propaganda also asked him to write an account of his escape. One should thus be able to find the documents he produced.[27] Yet what results from the available second-hand documentation is fairly conclusive.[28] The writings of Franz von Werra differ sharply from the usual accounts that Luftwaffe pilots produced after the war. The latter avoid any allusion to national socialism, like Adolf Galland's *The First and the Last: The German Fighter Force in World War II*, or to the contrary reveal their commitment to the Nazi cause and fidelity to Hitler, as in Hans Ulrich Rudel's *Stuka Pilot*.[29] Writings by the pen of von Werra or published under his name primarily reveal a merry and playful personality who experienced his escapes as a big prank and good joke. Given his complicated youth as the adoptive son of a Bavarian family, these are rather remarkable character traits. Members of the penniless Swiss nobility, his biological parents chose to part with two of their children when the latter were five and two years old.[30] From a political point of view, the remarks uncovered by the

Figure 4.3 The Battle of Britain: Franz von Werra's Messerschmitt Me. 109 after its forced landing in Marden, Kent, 5 September 1940. Aircrew Remembrance Society © 1995–2021 Alexander D. King & David King.
On 5 September 1940, the young Luftwaffe ace Franz von Werra was taken prisoner during the Battle of Britain. He was the only prisoner held by the British to ever succeed in escaping. After several attempts in England, he jumped from a Canadian train transporting him to a prisoner of war camp. Upon his return to Germany, he made himself unpopular by describing his British guards as cordial men with a sense of fair play.

British listening service for German prisoners did not reveal von Werra to have been a fanatic Nazi. Confident in victory and the Führer's capacities and indifferent to the slaughter of French and English civilians under the bombs, this former SA school student nevertheless feared the prolongation of the war and did not go so far as to justify war crimes.[31]

A dose of Anglophobia would come as no surprise given this unexceptional support for National Socialism. Strikingly, however, von Werra consistently presented his jailers and the British police in a favorable light. He was well placed to speak of them. After being arrested following his forced landing in Kent, he was again arrested two times, first after a six-day period on the run in the mountains of the Lake District, and a second time following a trek of several hours that led him all the way to the controls of a Hurricane. Von Werra thus spoke from experience. His enemies had not subjected him to mistreatment or the least strong-arm interrogation. Indeed, on his second arrest, the Superintendent of police comforted him with strong, hot, sweet tea in a pub. "He had never drunk anything better in his life!"[32] When arrested a

"BRITISH HUMOR" AS AN AGENT OF CIVILITY 97

third time, at the Hucknall airfield, von Werra's account of the giant trick he had pulled to reach the plane's cockpit provoked peals of hysterical laughter on all sides:

> [The Adjutant] slapped me madly on the back. All the officers cheered, as though at a football match.
> "Three cheers!" they cried, and "Clever boy!" ... Then everybody started shouting at once : "Don't take it too hard!" "We'll come and see you at the camp!" "You were splendid!" "We'll bring you some whisky, too" ...[33]

Before being confined, the Wing Commander had him served a hearty breakfast.[34] In one of his reports, von Werra is said to have even written that "in general, the treatment of German prisoners by the British is beyond reproach. The few isolated cases of mistreatment that took place were the result of the misconduct of the prisoners in question in the first, decisive moments of captivity."[35]

Though officially commissioned by the German general staff and having received prior authorization from the Reich Chamber for Writers, it comes as no surprise that this light and effectively Anglophilic tale of adventure was never published.[36] Franz von Werra had a ghostwriter, Joachim Bartsch, who at the time worked for Leni Riefenstahl. After the pilot's death, in 1943 Bartsch published an instalment on von Werra for the series of propaganda brochures, "Our Fighter Pilots." But the original Bartsch/Werra text did not make it through the censors of the Ministry of Propaganda. One of Goebbels' deputies, Eugen Hadamovsky, who was the ministry's head of radio, was chosen to supervise the work. He demanded that the book be entirely rewritten. For example, when von Werra was recaptured following his escape to the mountains of the Lake District, Hadamowsky asked that the cup of hot tea given by the Superintendent be replaced by blows administered by "the Jewish police." A year later, the manuscript was resubmitted for authorization but this time it was the general staff of the Luftwaffe that, for reasons of security, refused to allow its publication.[37]

While more nuanced than von Werra's account, the journal kept by a doctor mobilized at the military hospital of Chartham, near Canterbury (Kent), similarly confirms the thesis of British good manners.[38] The son of a Methodist pastor, Kenneth Hulbert was by inclination a pacifist, though he did not refer to himself as such. He received his "first Nazi pilot" on 12 July. The same evening, Hulbert wrote that the latter "was very polite" and "didn't look a bad sort at all." He added: "I wonder if all of them are so bad as they make out. We all seem to be caught up in some infernal maelstrom in which we do things without thinking." On 15 September, the day of "great air battles" (later known as "Battle of Britain Day"), he cared for "four very badly injured Nazi airmen." One died following an operation. Hulbert wrote: "What a futile waste of life this all is!" Between July and October, Hulbert cared for both Luftwaffe and

RAF pilots. Once, on 30 August, he noted the arrival of "several Nazi airmen" who "had been beaten up on landing."

> One had his front teeth knocked out. He had landed in a Kentish hop field full of hop pickers from the East End of London, many of whom had been bombed out of their homes. We saw a photo of him in the paper the next day being taken away in a car by the police with a large woman shaking her fist at him.

These few traces of the past appear consistent with the general portrait one may deduce from the press. There are several darker accounts, however.

Discussion Forums as a Source of Truth?

Since the 1980s, there has been a revival of interest among scholars in the use of rumor. With the publication in 1981 of *The Vanishing Hitchhiker*, the folklorist Jan Harold Brunvand contributed to this revival.[39] He referred to the rumors of his time as "urban legends," thereby indicating that the contemporary period also had its folklore. Since then, specialists have preferred the term "contemporary legends" since rumors spread as much in the countryside as they do in town, as much in the mouths of city dwellers as in those of country people.[40] Since the Internet first arose, a broad public has had access to what until then was spread by word of mouth or occasionally printed in the books of journalists and amateur historians. Today, "netlore" tends to replace folklore. Indirectly contributing to the spread of rumor, "experts" of various types create sites for deconstructing rumor. The news site *About News & Issues*[41] thus includes a section devoted to "Urban Legends," with a column entrusted to "our expert on contemporary legends," a journalist who sees to separating truth from falsehood in more or less extraordinary and alarming "news items."

Since the 2000s, several "discussion forums" have thus indiscriminately published rumors, first-person accounts and discussions regarding the arrival of German pilots on British soil. Examples of these forums include the "Axis History Forum," "LWAG" ("Luftwaffe Archives and Records Reference Group"), the "Luftwaffe and Allied Air Forces Discussion Forum" and "The Battle of Britain Historical Society Discussion Forum." In what concerns the subject at hand, web discussions arise by fits and starts: several dozen posts on the matter were published in 2000, 2004, 2008–09, 2013. The Internet permits anonymity and also allows for all variety of fantasy. Our theme might give rise to macabre and "gory" stories. That has not happened, however, particularly as some of these commentators have written under their real names and are well known for their work as amateur historians. It is easy enough to detect the point of view of the authors of these posts: the moderate and well-balanced ones argue that, "for every action that inspires disgust, there were surely an

"BRITISH HUMOR" AS AN AGENT OF CIVILITY

equal number of gentlemanly, compassionate and human actions on both sides";[42] the crusaders of denunciation, by contrast, single out "the lynching of German pilots by British crowds" and plainly state that cold-blooded murders were committed in Luchy (France, as we have seen), East Wittering and Kennington Oval;[43] the prudent worry about the frequency with which British atrocities are denounced on revisionist sites; and the civic-minded rebel against "revisionist propaganda," "revolting to those who have first-hand information regarding the treatment of American airmen" brought down over Germany.[44]

These exchanges yield no certainty, no more so than does the BBC's otherwise remarkable website, *WW2 People's War*. Between June 2003 and January 2006, the BBC asked the public to send it their memories of the Second World War. The result is a site containing 47,000 first-person accounts. One there finds accounts of the reception of German airmen on the ground but they are of limited reliability. In general, their authors cannot be clearly identified. Moreover, the accounts often come from individuals who were children or adolescents at the time. Inevitably, these first-hand accounts are mingled with images inspired by the accounts of parents and loved ones as well as clichés drawn from the films and books that appeared in the fifty years following the war. In general, no specific date is given for the events under discussion. More often, a place is mentioned. To be used, each story would first have to be passed over with the fine-tooth comb of critical history. It would, in short, be a monumental undertaking but the tone of these accounts is nevertheless worth noting: generally based in fact, they are not without humor and are neither boasting nor self-deprecating. The resulting image of the people at war is the same as that which we have already encountered: a good-natured people that, while sometimes undisciplined, sometimes angry, sometimes valiant and sometimes childish, contain their emotions and urges within certain limits.

Smoke without Fire: Bracklesham Bay Beach, East Wittering

These websites thus do not supply useful material for elucidating the two controversial cases of murderous violence that may have been committed against German airmen during the Battle of Britain. That is two cases involving five real or supposed victims out of some 600 Luftwaffe airmen who reached the ground alive between July and October 1940.

The first case, that of the supposed murder of four Luftwaffe airmen on the beach at East Wittering (Sussex) on 26 August 1940 (Figure 4.4), shows that rumor and its exploitation by the media were not born with the Internet. The facts are as follows. A Heinkel carried out a forced landing on the partly inundated beach. The wounded pilot was extracted from the airplane and the bodies of four other members of the crew were laid on the sand. They were

Figure 4.4 The Heinkel He. 111 of Leutnant Metzger lying on Bracklesham Beach, 26 August 1940, East Wittering, Sussex. Aircrew Remembrance Society © 1995–2021 Alexander D. King & David King.

subsequently buried with military honors in the cemetery of the neighboring town, Chichester. The debate concerns the cause of death of the four airmen.

At the time, with the feverish Battle of Britain in full swing, word spread with the help of the local press that, by chance finding themselves conducting exercises in the vicinity of the beach, soldiers from the Duke of Cornwall's Light Infantry Regiment (DCLI) opened fire on the airplane with machine guns and shot it down, simultaneously killing the crew members. Were the latter killed in flight, as they landed or even a few seconds after having done so? The question is important because it would allow an act of war intended to shoot down an enemy airplane to be distinguished from an act located in an intermediary zone where the legality of the killing could be questioned from the viewpoint of international law. In their chauvinistic-patriotic fervor, the local press ignored these details and praised the victory of Company A of the 2nd Battalion of the DCLI, crediting it without further ado with bringing down the plane and killing the occupants of its cabin.

The event had been forgotten when, in February 1971, a violent storm uncovered the remains of the Heinkel. The story made the *Chichester Observer* and was soon followed up on by a reporter from the *Sunday Times*.[45] In less than a week, the nation's attention was riveted to a scene straight out of a western movie: the "spectacular" crash (there was no crash) of the "Dornier" (it was a Heinkel) before the eyes of a lone corporal who let

"BRITISH HUMOR" AS AN AGENT OF CIVILITY 101

loose on the crew with his machine gun. Very much in the spirit of the times, the newspaper headlined its story "The skeleton in East Wittering's closet." Two years later, the popular tabloid *Tit-Bits* went further: "Was this our secret war crime?"[46] Dating from the nineteenth century, the old technique of the popular press, "Get me a murder a day,"[47] was pressed into the service of an historiographical sea change.

Founded the same year, in 1973 the magazine *After the Battle*, which specialized in the military history of the Second World War, carried out an in-depth investigation. The pilot "Combat Reports" in the archives of the RAF showed that the airplane had been brought down, not by groundfire, but by a series of Spitfire attacks. Yet these documents still left some question as to the cause of death of the four airmen. Sergeant Basil Whall, the last British pilot to have fired on the struggling Heinkel, watched it from a distance, reporting that he saw "the Army take the crew prisoner," which would seem to suggest that the men were still alive at that time.[48] The Air intelligence officer's report included a more precise phrase: "The crew was prevented from setting fire to the airplane."[49] This would seem to indicate that the men had refused to surrender and were killed by the soldiers.

In this instance, the archives were no more reliable than the rumors. Nor were they more worthy of trust than the belated testimony of the commander of Company A of the 2nd DCLI. In 1972, he described how his men, driven by a desire to avenge the dead of Southampton, directed sustained fire at the Heinkel:

> The men went on firing but now at the bomber and officers could not stop them – rapid fire, many weapons, intense noise. The men had seen plenty of women and children killed in Southampton and regarded all German airmen as vile outlaws so they fired rapid until all the Germans had dropped.[50]

In fact, Southampton was first bombed on 11 September. The former commander had doubtless confused it with Portsmouth, which was first hit in July. But that is not the important thing.

Light was finally shed on the matter when the investigators succeeded in finding the pilot who had survived. After being treated in a military hospital, Albert Metzger was subsequently sent to Canada, like many German prisoners in British hands. His testimony is unambiguous. He recalled no longer hearing the onboard machine gun after the first Spitfire attack. Concerned that he was no longer receiving a response from the mechanic and radio operator, he sent the navigator to the rear of the craft to find out what was happening. It was then that a final Spitfire attack (that of Sergeant Whall) raked the fuselage and wounded him in the thigh. The navigator did not return. With the two motors out of service, Albert Metzger initiated an emergency landing. He succeeded in bringing the airplane down smoothly. Upon his arrival, he heard a few gun shots but the not the characteristic sound of automatic weapon fire. Soldiers helped him out of the airplane. As this happened, he glimpsed the immobile corpses in the cabin. As he was receiving first aid on the sand, he saw the inanimate bodies of his crew being carried away.

In this instance, the "crime legend" – a type of widespread rumor that peddles a crime story – is thus unfounded. Other crime legends continue to circulate. It was likewise by locating the pilot that a local historian from Quinton, near Birmingham, in 2002 put an end to what had become a persistent rumor repeated in books concerning the mistreatment of downed airmen[51] Another rumor that continues to be debated concerns the fate of Oberleutnant Robert Zehbe.

From Rumor to Fact: Kennington Oval, London

Robert Zehbe was the pilot of a Dornier-17 that came down over London on 15 September. The facts as we know them are as follows. On that day, the Luftwaffe launched a massive final attack on London with the aim of forcing the British government to sue for peace. The operation was a relative failure and, two days later, Hitler postponed the invasion of England. September 15 would subsequently be chosen by the British to commemorate "Battle of Britain Day." By that date, the city had been subjected to nonstop "Blitz," day and night, for ten days. Nearly 3,000 inhabitants died and roughly 4,500 were seriously wounded. Zehbe's airplane took off from Cormeilles-en-Vexin in the morning. It was part of the first great wave of the attack, which reached London shortly before noon. September 15 was a Sunday, people were out walking, others cleared debris from the ruins. Zehbe's airplane was attacked by several Hurricanes and caught fire, finally coming down over Victoria Station (Figure 4.5). Three men parachuted from the plane. Onlookers saw them fall and some followed them to the ground. Two of the men were taken prisoner and their story has left no particular trace. The pilot, by contrast, remained hanging from the cables of an electric pole in which his parachute had become entangled alongside the famous Kennington Oval cricket field. And this is where the matter becomes more controversial: did the pilot die from the wounds and burns he received in combat or the mistreatment to which he was subjected on the ground? The debate focuses on the few minutes during which the man found himself alone, confronted by a hostile gathering of civilians. What followed is once again certain: an army van came to take him down and conduct him to a nearby military hospital, where he died the following day.

The first author to repeat the rumor according to which Robert Zehbe had been brutalized on the ground was a journalist named Alfred Price. In his 1990 book, *Battle of Britain Day*, Price produced a terrifying and gripping account

Figure 4.5 The tail of the Dornier-17 flown by Robert Zehbe, where it landed on the roof of a building, Vauxhall Bridge Road, 15 September 1940. Aircrew Remembrance Society © 1995–2021 Alexander D. King & David King

inspired by the testimony of a couple who took refuge in a vaulted passage across from the Oval tube station:

> Suddenly, the German airman appeared beside them a few yards away, as if from nowhere. "His parachute was caught over electric power cables and he ended up dangling just above the ground. People came from all directions shouting 'Kill him, kill him!' They pulled him down. They went crazy. Some women arrived carrying knives and pokers and they went straight in and attacked him. In the end, an army truck arrived and the half dozen soldiers had to fight their way through the crowd to get to him. They put him in the back of the truck and drove off."[52]

Other accounts added that, instead of taking the road, which would have been normal, the truck shamelessly drove across the sacrosanct turf of the cricket field. Was this in order to more rapidly reach Vauxhall bridge and the Millbank military hospital or was it to flee the enraged crowd, some wondered? On the website of LWAG, the Luftwaffe Archives and Records Reference Group, a certain Martin Smart vigorously claims that his mother and aunts were at the scene, that they saw the already severely wounded pilot and that he was not attacked, even though the crowd was threatening.[53] Since then, the debate has periodically been revived online, albeit without particularly advancing.

Can one go further? Three contemporaneous documents seem to testify to the start of the lynching. The first is a phrase that occurs in the log book of the Local Emergency Civil Defence Committee. At 6pm on 15 September, the situation report contains the following note: "Enemy parachutist came down among a hostile population in Kennington."[54] The second document is a report by an Air Force intelligence officer written the following day, 16 September, which presents the crash over London of Zehbe's airplane and the airman's arrival on the ground: "The pilot parachuted from his plane and came down in Kennington, where he was violently attacked by the crowd, which tore his parachute and harness to shreds."[55] Two days later, a note in the local newspaper, the *South London Press*, also mentioned mistreatment with this title, "Troops Save Nazi from Angry Women."[56] A witness described the airman pulled to the ground and struck with a coal shovel by a woman crying, "and that's for my son at Dunkirk!" The national newspapers did not take note of the incident.

According to these documents, mistreatment indeed took place. Perhaps due to simple clumsiness in its composition, however, the officer's report nevertheless raises a question. What did the aggression consist of apart from ripping Zehbe's parachute and harness? At this time, the destruction of the parachute could be interpreted – by a man, above all – as a violent gesture or even the symbolic execution of the airman. In fact, cutting up silk parachutes to make underwear or obtain fabric for dresses soon became a widespread practice in the bombed-out country. The downing of airmen was an occasion for running "silk raids" among women, just as downed airplanes set off souvenir hunts among little boys despite the authorities' ban on this type of behavior. In both cases, the participants' haste to be first on the scene created a certain frenzy. In these discussions of whether or not a given incident actually took place, with all their twists and turns, one always observes the same succession of events: a local rumor instantly emerges in which sensationalism and even a taste for gore vies with a heroic-patriotic spirit only further enflamed for entailing no physical risk; intelligence officers, doubtless ill-prepared to investigate the matter, head to the scene; more or less fanciful eyewitness reports surface after the fact. Finally, should there be no "Combat Report" allowing one to piece together the damage suffered by the airplane as it came down and should it be impossible to locate the Heinkel's pilot, as in the first case above, no conclusion can be reached.

It is perhaps no accident that the most animated discussions should concern incidents that took place at the seaside or cricket field. These two symbolic places in the British Isles have the power to mobilize. The cultural mobilization associated with the war and its afterlife in collective memory have obviously drawn upon the repertory of national symbolism.

Sea Front and Cricket Field: The Refoundation of a Nation

If there was a "korrekt" people in 1940, it was indeed the British. These foundational beginnings constituted a norm throughout the duration of the war. British resistance was built around the resistance to invasion. The term is used here without capitalization to preserve its military connotation of response to enemy aggression. This defensive action was not clandestine. It was supported and encouraged by the legal government and was not to know the practices associated with the Gestapo and Wehrmacht. No one can say whether it would have turned into a French-style resistance in the event that the Germans had crossed the Channel. As General Weygand underscored in 1940, it was the United Kingdom's good fortune to find itself ringed by an anti-tank trench *sans pareil*. The people had the time to gather their strength and spirit. But if the people had not supported the principle of defending the territory by massively joining the ranks of the LDV – the Local Defence Volunteers, which Churchill would soon rename the Home Guard – the Prime Minister's position would have been undermined. If, under the bombs, the people had given way to "Masspanik" as Nazi leaders hoped and expected, the party of the "appeasers" would have gained the upper hand over that of war without surrender.

This resolve in the face of adversity is remarkable in two ways. First, it did not erode the respect for good manners that was due the unfortunate enemy who fell upon the islands. Even in the extraordinary framework of a war without surrender and in the context of daily suspense as to the fighting's outcome, ordinary behavior prevailed. This disjunction between mental framework and practice contradicts the usual arguments of social psychology. Some particular factor must thus have impeded the impulses created by this framework from being transmitted and subsequently translated into specific behaviors. The maintenance of democratic norms and the reliance on the British culture of humor helped discipline the population and preserve practices of everyday civility. It is in this respect that the "Blitz spirit," even if it never had the homogeneity and universality suggested by the expression,[57] did indeed exist.

It might be thought that this result is a matter of chronological accident: even though large numbers of airmen fell from the skies of Britain during the first two months of the battle, their bombs made few victims. This situation facilitated the learning of good behavior. All this changed with the Blitz and its tens of thousands of dead. And yet the peaceable behaviors remained. Another factor – one brought out by comparison with the German case – must thus be taken into consideration. Between 1940 and mid-1943, German civilians had three years to practice receiving downed pilots on the ground. With the intensification of bombing, however, their behavior underwent a brutal transformation. In the United Kingdom, continuity. In Germany, rupture. These myriad ephemeral encounters between airmen and civilians reveal distinct political cultures.

It was not that British civilians remained unchanging in their equanimity throughout the entire duration of the war. With the passage of time and the growing number of bombing victims, signs of anger, chauvinism, even blood-thirsty xenophobia, now and then made their appearance in newspapers. Such was the case following the bombing of Coventry in November 1940, which provoked this wild headline in the *Daily Express*: "Coventry cries: Bomb back and bomb hard!"[58] The second intensive phase of the Blitz, which killed 16,000 people between March and May 1941, was also keenly felt. It was at this time that the *Daily Mirror*, a popular left-wing newspaper, published a two-page spread on the "Terror Raid" that took place in the night of 10–11 May. In the black sky, a giant, hideous black gorilla lit by the inferno of the city on fire, is pictured throwing bombs by the fistful.[59] But this type of crude propaganda remained the exception. Until the end and even during the V1 attacks of summer 1944 (the third Blitz), the tone of the press was restrained. Humor, often taking the form of knowing understatement, did not vanish from the pages of newspapers. What's more, though British public opinion found it increasingly easy to accept the practice of area bombing over Germany,[60] this bloody strategy continued to be debated in the media throughout the war's duration. The very fact that there was debate represented a moderating factor in its own right.

Starting in late 1940, anecdotes relating to the on-the-ground reception of downed airmen disappeared from the national press. But they continued to appear in the local press. The *Kent Messenger* continued to report on this news until April 1944. Though humor became featured less prominently in these accounts, the articles retained the same tranquil tone free of animosity towards the enemy. As he waited for the police to arrive, the airman found himself being offered a cigarette or a cup of tea. In April 1944, a physical education teacher gave a pack of cigarettes to a hospitalized German airman in Marlborough (Wiltshire). As he had not followed the administrative formal-ities in this respect, he was brought before the local tribunal. In his defense, he explained that the airman had given four of his cigarettes to the couple who had taken him in at their cottage on the night of the crash. The defendant claimed to have acted from "humanity and Christianity," which he described as "the great things we're fighting for." Deeming that he had "not had bad intentions," the judges ruled that he be acquitted.[61]

Actions reveal more than words and texts. The Battle of Britain provided the mold for British behavior. For the months and years that followed, no evidence may be found in printed sources that civilian behavior changed. The few accounts of Luftwaffe personnel that I have been able to collect corrobor-ate this finding. At worst, a hostile crowd threatened the aviator who had been taken prisoner but he continued to be duly protected by soldiers (Manchester, mid-1941).[62] At best, the civilians stopped by the roadside to pick him up in their car and offered him a comforting cucumber sandwich (near Southampton, May 1941) or women from a village rushed to fetch him a glass of water while a police officer offered him a cup of hot coffee and some cake (Warminster, near Bristol, April 1944).[63] In yet another case, the wounded airman fell into animated conversation with the Home Guard, telling them of his father who had attended hotel management school in London, and later encountering a girl as he was being transferred to London by train who said *Ich liebe dich* ("I love you") to him as a way of telling him how much she hated the war (Harwich-London, January 1944).[64] This portrait converges with that offered by Richard Overy in his masterful study of the air war. Working on public opinion – a subject offering a much richer array of sources – Overy similarly concluded as to the stability of British morale.[65] They could take it.

What is also striking about this British resolve is how, despite many ups and downs, it remained unbroken through war's end in 1945. In retrospect, 1940 witnessed the refoundation of the British nation; it was one of those "finest hours" that breathe life into national cohesion. The "finest hour" of 1940 took on a legendary dimension and is now an object of deconstruction among historians eager to show its limits.[66] But the value of the 1940 refoundation may be appraised by contrasting it with the national destruction entailed by the emergence of a collaborating government in France. There, the break was immediate. It cut the legs out from underneath a national mobilization that was still quite alive and irreversibly split the nation. The first stirrings of resistance, to which the responsiveness of the territorial guards attests, were stopped in their tracks and disrupted. Had the German army advanced less suddenly, the stirrings of resistance that one observes at the local level might perhaps have grown to resistance at the scale of the nation, as had been the case after the francs-tireurs formed in 1870 to support the remains of the regular army. Instead of experiencing Vichy, the French would have had a "finest hour" of their own. The country's occupation, however, radically altered the situation. France's "finest hour" was to take a completely different path.

PART III

The Origins of the Resistance

Hiding Allies in France

Part III of this book seeks to tell the story of civilian assistance to Allied soldiers and airmen in occupied France. Hitherto, the literature has been largely limited to first-person accounts of escapees and the organizers of escape networks together with a few books recounting the history of particular networks. After the war, around thirty specialized escape networks were recorded as having existed – some supported by the British intelligence services (MI6, MI9, SOE), some by those of Free France (BCRA) and some but not all specializing in helping Allied soldiers and airmen.[1] This list does not include networks that were nipped in the bud, as happened to the Oaktree network in 1943. Nor does it cover the help that intelligence and resistance networks sometimes gave those seeking to escape. Above all, it says nothing about the social networks upon which these organizations relied. Upstream of these, very local escape lines, generally following a zigzag path and sometimes doubling back on themselves, took in escaped soldiers and fallen airmen, sheltering them for days, weeks, sometimes months before contact was established with one of the major lines that would take them safe and sound across the Channel or the Pyrenees. It is this on-the-spot population that hastily and haphazardly constructed networks (all without knowing their ultimate destination) that we will consider here. They numbered in the tens of thousands, even more if one includes the families who, by offering the use of their homes, were de facto participants in this clandestine activity.

For two reasons, this aspect of the social history of occupied France is also of interest from an historiographical perspective. It allows one to interrogate the rather well-established current according to which the Resistance was the work of an isolated minority unrepresentative of the larger population. For what we encounter here is a French population that, at its own risk, instantly stood by Allies in distress. Allies remained allies, with ordinary citizens honoring and defending the Republic's alliances. Is this form of mass resistance against the occupier a specifically French phenomenon? In part, yes: it can be seen as a repeated feature of Franco-German wars since 1870. But after the war, the Allies identified about 150,000 helpers across Europe. Civilians helped Allies throughout the German-occupied countries of the continent. In at least three cases – those of Belgium, Italy and France – this help was offered on a massive scale. These countries were also those that suffered the heaviest bombing outside the Reich.

These observations tip the scale in favor of the new historiography of the Occupation. From the 1970s to the late 1990s, mainstream historiography depicted resisters and collaborationists as two active minorities within a passive, wait-and-see population. Since the 2000s, the historiography has shown greater nuance. Academic publications have underscored the fact that the two minorities were not symmetrical, not simply because the ranks of one thinned while those of the other expanded, but also because the population as a whole favored the Resistance. Naturally, this pendulum movement does not invalidate years of research on Collaboration and collaborationism. Rather, it introduces complexity and discontinuities, even hiatuses, into the overall picture.

Yet another notion that has made its way into school textbooks – the concept of "résistancialisme", which would have it that the postwar French significantly embellished and inflated the role played by the Resistance – similarly does not apply here. The assistance provided the Allies does not figure in national memory. While it vividly lives on in local memory, it has not entered the "national grand narrative." Far from being embellished or exaggerated, its existence has not even been acknowledged by the national media.

5

The Resistance as Mass Local Dynamic

A posthumous debate pitted Max Weber against Norbert Elias, two pioneering sociologists born in Wilhelmine Germany. In his book *Economy and Society*, written in the aftermath of the First World War, Max Weber defined "social activity" as a "fundamental concept of sociology." In his view, "if at the beginning of a shower a number of people on the street put up their umbrellas at the same time . . . this would not ordinarily be a case of [social] action, but rather of all reacting in the same way to the like need of protection from the rain."[1] To which Norbert Elias in the 1980s responded that one only has an umbrella if one is located in certain civilizations and that opening an umbrella is thus not socially neutral.[2] This is not the place to consider whether Weber's vision of social activity was really so narrow.[3] But it is clear that opening an umbrella is also not a politically neutral action. For the decision taken in isolation by thousands of individual actors in France to open their umbrellas to protect Allied soldiers and airmen on the run was at the origin of wartime escape networks and thus of one aspect of the Resistance. An isolated action repeated so many times is a social and political action.

The idea underlying Max Weber's reasoning that "social activity" presupposes interaction between individuals or groups is nevertheless essential if one wishes to demonstrate the *national character* of escape activity – that is, not just its geographical extension to all of metropolitan France but also its coordination via interconnected networks. On this condition, the Allies' escape from occupied France assumes the aspect of a national liberation movement. For harboring escapees requires external contacts and even a chain of liaison. First and foremost, this is because their motivating belief – fidelity to the Allied alliance, the moral and political values it entailed and the hope for victory – led those giving shelter to seek out an escape route to England on behalf of the men they were protecting. But it was also in the interest of these hosts – endangered by their activity and afflicted by the difficulties of obtaining supplies in this time of shortage – to seek out additional assistance. At once the symbolic embodiment of a hoped-for liberation and "hot potatoes" in a dangerous game, the airmen were among the catalysts of the national liberation movement that came to be known as the Resistance.

112 THE ORIGINS OF THE RESISTANCE

Table 5.1. *Allied military personnel helped in France*

British and Commonwealth soldiers and airmen who escaped France	⊳1,917
American airmen who escaped France	2,155
Others, recaptured by the Germans	Unknown
Others who remained hidden	Unknown
Total	**⊳4,072**

Sources: British and Commonwealth personnel: "Escape & Evasion Reports," numbers 1 to 3122. TNA, WO 208/ 3297 à 3327.[*]

American personnel: "Escape & Evasion Reports," numbers 1–2953. NARA, RG498, UD 133, UD 134, Boxes 516–73. Available online.[**]

[*] Number of debriefings contained in the series: 2,483 (of 3,122 numbered). The journey of 1,397 evaders (soldiers and airmen together) began in France; others (520) traveled through France by way of other countries; others escaped by way of Sweden, Italy, the USSR or Southeastern Europe or were repatriated via semi-official channels. This yields a minimum of 1,917 British and Commonwealth personnel having escaped from France; 62 percent of those who escaped were airmen. Out of the 2,483 reports consulted, 77 percent of the journeys departed from or passed through France.

[**] 73 percent of those who escaped departed from or passed through France for a total of 2,155 Americans having escaped from France, nearly all of them airmen.

How many of these catalysts of national reconstruction were to be found at the local level? The debriefings conducted in London of successfully evaded soldiers and airmen provide something of a baseline (Table 5.1). Whether these lucky Allied escapees had been brought down over France, found themselves stranded on its territory in 1940 or otherwise travelled through the country, they were no more than a "happy few." There were at least 4,000 of them, divided between "evaders," or those who successfully evaded arrest by the enemy, and "escapers," or those who escaped their prison camp.

A Journey across France, September to October 1941

Upon his return to London in November 1941, the Royal Air Force pilot P.F. Allen described the odyssey that took him across France following a forced landing in Bourgogne. His debriefing reveals the numerous encounters that his escape and that of his crew occasioned between airmen and civilians. From this mass of isolated encounters, there would gradually arise a movement at the scale of the nation.

We had not been hit ourselves, but the condition of our remaining engine made it impossible to continue, and about 0130 hrs on 11 Sep we sent out a signal and immediately afterwards made a forced descent on the top of a small hill near Les Riceys, North-West of Châtillon (Dijon area).

... About 0300 hrs we all set off together on a South-Westerly course. We walked for about three hours and then slept in some bushes till daylight. After walking further we met a peasant girl who told us that 25 Germans were searching for us. She advised us to keep on our course, by which we hoped to reach Dijon. We went on, keeping to the fields. At 1700 hrs we went to a house and asked for water and directions to Dijon. The woman in the house directed us to a farm nearby; there we were given food and at about 2100 hrs we left, accompanied for a short distance by a Frenchman who said he had heard that 500 Germans were to be sent out next day to search for us.

We slept that night in a wood, and went next morning to a farm where we got a meal and from which a young boy on holiday from Paris took us to the village of Channay. We spent one night in a barn and the next three in a wood. The French boy then took Worby and Campbell to Paris in civilian clothes, leaving the rest of us, who were still in uniform, at Channay, where we lived for a fortnight in a barn in the courtyard of a farm.

At the end of that time the French boy returned with two Frenchmen who gave us civilian clothes and took us by train from Nuits St Ravières [Nuits-sous-Ravières] back to Paris. The tickets were bought by the Frenchmen, and there was no inspection of identity papers on the train. We arrived in Paris on 28 Sep.

In Paris, we were split into two parties, and on 3 Oct Sgt. Saxton and I were taken by train to Vierzon. We stayed the afternoon in a small hotel and in the evening were taken in an ambulance to a farm just outside the town. On the instructions of our helpers we posed as Flemings. After spending two or three hours at the farm, we forded the river Cher on foot at a point where the river was about 20 yards wide and knee-deep. We were accompanied by one Frenchman and spent the night in a wood. Next morning (4 Oct) we were taken by car to Charost, and after four days there by car to Chateauroux and then by train, via Lyons, to Marseilles (7 Oct). Five days later we were moved to Perpignan, where we were joined by Sgts. Saxton and Christensen and Pilot Officer Zulikowski, R.A.F. (now at Gibraltar). We remained in Perpignan 14 days and then went by train to Ste Leocadia. Two stations before our destination Saxton and Hickton were questioned by gendarmes and arrested. Christensen, Zulikowski and I picked up a guide at the station at Ste Leocadia and left for Spain on foot about midday on 30 Oct. We crossed the frontier about 2000 hrs and went to a farm where we stayed two nights. The guide was left at the farm, but the farmer conducted us by train to Barcelona, where we reported at the British Consular-General. Two days later we were taken by train to Madrid, and after three weeks in the Embassy were moved to Gibraltar for repatriation.[4]

In the Eyes of MI9, the "Occupied Population" Were Allies

Before plunging into the deepest recesses of what was at the time an invisible aspect of society, a word must be said regarding the exceptional archives that give us access to this part of the past. These archives were produced by the British intelligence services, which first began to contribute to the establishment of escape networks on the continent in 1939. Starting in 1942, the Americans followed their example and began to produce comparably interesting archives. As early as 1939, the general headquarters of the British Expeditionary Force in France requested that an organization be established to facilitate the escape of prisoners of war. It was in this way that, in December 1939, "MI9" (Military Intelligence 9) was established under the aegis of the War Office's Directorate of Military Intelligence (DMI).[5] An interbranch service, MI9 was on several occasions reorganized over the course of the war as its domain of activity grew. In January 1942, a subsection – IS9 (Intelligence School 9) – was created, bringing together the various services actively involved in aiding escape. Intelligence School 9 was itself subdivided into several branches. IS9 (W) interviewed "evaders" (those who had never been made prisoner) and "escapers" (those who had escaped prison camps) upon their arrival in England, verified their accounts and transformed these "debriefings" into reports. The "Escape & Evasion Reports" are now available at the National Archives in Kew. They describe in some detail the path taken by these escapees/evaders between their point of departure and the moment they left France. Contemporaneously drafted, they supply an unusually detailed secret portrait of what was then an invisible society. The "E&E reports" moreover supplied the basis for the escape courses given airmen, naval personnel and infantry. In 1943–44, these "lectures," which were also given by the corresponding American services (MIS-X, Military Intelligence Service X), informed their audiences that between 90 and 99 percent of French people were eager to assist escaping airmen.[6]

Another branch of MI9/IS9, the IS9 (D), also known as P15 or Room 900, recruited and trained the agents who would later be sent into occupied countries to help escapees/evaders get to England. IS9 (D) operated under the aegis of the Secret Intelligence Service (SIS), also known as MI6 ("Military Intelligence 6"). The activities of P15 covered France, Belgium and, to a lesser degree, the Netherlands. While to prepare its activities MI9 had in its early stages interviewed former soldiers who had escaped during the First World War, P15 directly conceived its action by drawing upon the experience of those who had escaped from German-occupied Europe. Its leader, "Jimmy" Langley, had escaped a hospital run by the German Army in Lille, where his arm had been amputated. Escaping on 1 October 1940, he succeeded in reaching Marseille in late November following a journey that took him through Paris, Vierzon, Lyon and Vichy. Interned in Marseille's Fort St-Jean

THE RESISTANCE AS MASS LOCAL DYNAMIC   115

by the Vichy authorities, albeit under a system of day parole, he was repatriated to England after having successfully deceived the Joint Medical Commission responsible for examining candidates for repatriation. After legally departing Marseille in early February, he arrived a month later in Liverpool by way of Spain and Gibraltar.[7] Langley's deputy at MI9 was Airey Neave, who had also succeeded in escaping – in his case, from Colditz in Saxony, a high-security fortress holding prisoners who had already escaped once. After leaving Colditz on 5 January 1942, Neave crossed the snow-covered Swiss border at night four days later. He then illegally entered France, passing through Chambéry, Marseille, Toulouse and finally Perpignan before moving on to Barcelona, Madrid and Gibraltar. He finally made landfall in Scotland on 13 May, four months after escaping Colditz.[8]

An endless series of inter-service battles accompanied the history of MI9, which had to struggle against the demands of various branches of the military, particularly the Air Force Ministry, as well as against the suspicions of the Intelligence Service, which feared that its own work on the continent would be jeopardized by the amateurs of MI9. The IS had already been obliged to reluctantly acknowledge the creation of the Special Operations Executive (SOE) at Churchill's express request. Yet despite the obstacles put in their way by what they saw as a bureaucratic and military mindset, the young escapees of P15 were determined to succeed. Donald Darling oversaw MI9 in Gibraltar. He came from MI6, the Intelligence Service's traditional overseas department, but shared his colleagues' rebellious spirit. Memoirs written by Langley, Neave and Darling bathe in the same British humor, in which understatement is mixed with a form of pragmatism indifferent to formal hierarchies and routines.[9] In pleading their cause vis-à-vis the already existing services, they argued that it was in England's vital interest to recover its lost airmen as quickly as possible, particularly given the cost of their training (estimated at £10,000, or as much as it would have cost to send ten students to Oxford or Cambridge for three years).[10] But it was in unexpected fashion that they stumbled upon their best argument: the spectacular effect on crew morale when missing pilots returned to their bases. Nearly half of all airmen who saw combat, it should be recalled, lost their lives.

In general, MI9 was aware of the crucial role that helpers played in its escape networks. In an appendix to nearly every E&E report, a "list of helpers" recapitulated the assistance that had been provided along the path to freedom. These lists are not complete and suffer from some approximation due to the linguistic obstacles between helpers and their beneficiaries but it was nevertheless on their basis that efforts were made to seek out helpers after the war. MI9 and MI6 were both aware of the severely repressive measures visited upon helpers and wanted their merit to be recognized by the United Kingdom. This impetus in favor of recognition was mixed with other considerations, such as MI6's desire to draw a line under what it saw as an amateurish episode or, for the intelligence services as a whole, the opportunity it represented to create lasting contacts with what might in the future prove trustworthy correspondents on the continent. A number of helpers and intelligence network personnel were thus sought out after the war.

Recalled from Gibraltar after D-Day to take the leadership of P15, in September 1944 Donald Darling was named European mission chief of the Awards Bureau, the office responsible for locating helpers on the continent for purposes of decoration and compensation. Signed in October, the charter of the Decorations Bureaus put them under the joint responsibility of MI6 and MI9.[11] They also cooperated with the Americans and French. Donald Darling was sent to Paris, Airey Neave to Brussels. In his memoirs, a crucial source for our knowledge of the assistance given the Allies, Darling laid out his method. He tells of how he initially had the files of IS9 (D) / P15 merged with those of MI9 before transferring them all to Paris.[12] By way of its field agents, the IS9 (D) / P15 section often possessed more complete information than MI9, which only had access to the debriefings of evaders/escapees that had been conducted in London. The information thus gathered was highly reliable since it had been collected in real time and simultaneously verified as far as possible. On the basis of these archives, the search for helpers thus began in the Paris region. In order to avoid inviting false declarations, it was not publicized. With the re-establishment of road and rail links, starting in January 1945 teams were dispatched to the provinces with lists of helpers gathered before D-Day. These missions included a local escape network leader and were often preceded by a paragraph in the local press announcing their arrival. Their investigations turned up names formerly unknown to IS9. This fine-toothed survey of the territory generally succeeded in excluding potential impostors. The handful of former collaborators who attempted to clear their names in this way – whether or not their claims had a basis in truth – were dismissed, in particular thanks to the assistance given by local prefectures in monitoring local rumors. This Allied purification campaign carried out at the request of the French government (which was also represented on the awards committee) targeted a small percentage of candidates – less than 5 percent.

For all its virtues, however, this investigative procedure also had its drawbacks. The decision to principally rely upon lists of helpers drawn up in advance in London led the investigators to focus on those who had helped the most fortunate escapees, those who had succeeded in reaching England. This approach thus ignored the help given those who had been recaptured or remained trapped in France. It for this reason privileged helpers who had been able to enter into contact with one of the major escape lines, neglecting those who – particularly in the first years – had to proceed by trial and error, often keeping the airmen in their homes for many months. The result was that many known helpers were not recognized as such by the Anglo-American services.

Other candidacies for the title of helper – around 18 percent of the total – were turned down due to the inadequate assistance they had given. To receive this title, it was not enough to have given an airman a sandwich or a civilian outfit or even to have put him up for a single night without being able to give his name. Cases in which more significant assistance was given but the escapee was nevertheless subsequently arrested were also not recognized.

Another limitation of the inquiry stemmed from the fact that the central services of MI9 – first based in London and then at Wilton Park in Buckinghamshire – tended to credit themselves alone for the escape of some 30,000 soldiers and airmen from the continent. This 30,000-strong figure includes all "escapers" and "evaders" who successfully escaped Europe, from Norway to Turkey.[13] Drafted shortly after the war ended, MI9's final report stated without beating around the bush that "90% of 'evaders' [those who escaped the continent without ever being arrested] and 33% of 'escapers' [those who escaped the continent after first being taken prisoner] had been extracted thanks to the organization and activities of MI9."[14] This was to forget the role played by tens of thousands of little people (Pierre Brossolette's famous "soutiers") – the men and women of the occupied countries who contributed to this result while placing themselves and their families in danger. Transferred to Paris in October 1944 as director of the Awards Bureaus for Europe, Donald Darling rebelled against this failure to properly appreciate the role played by members of the Resistance on the ground. This form of service patriotism was also reinforced by social and socio-professional prejudices. As Darling notes in his memoirs: "I felt that MI9 suspected me of inflating the role played by humble people in the escape lines to the detriment of the aristocracy." And later: "I came to believe that the Decorations Committee in London simply did not grasp what the French equivalent of John Smith and his wife had done to help the 'evaders' and that they thought of things in terms of soldiers' wars in which civilians played little part."[15]

The Helpers as Indicative of Mass Resistance

The expression "mass resistance" may seem excessive and awkwardly imbued with a belated "résistancialisme". Thanks to the Allies' work, however, we may now revisit this debate. It is also necessary to agree on terms. Numerically, a mass resistance in an occupied country in times of war bears little comparison to the mass movements of a free country.

Despite these obstacles and limitations, Donald Darling's service identified some 21,000 helpers in France, of whom 17,000 principally assisted British personnel.[16] The Americans, who participated in the search effort as part of the joint French, British and American tripartite committee, identified 17,000 people who had helped USAAF airmen.[17] Given the overlap among helpers

118 THE ORIGINS OF THE RESISTANCE

Table 5.2. *Helpers in France*

Helpers who mainly helped British and Commonwealth personnel	16,929
Helpers of Americans	17,044
Total number of helpers (excluding redundancies)	33,535

Sources: Register of Helpers, IS9, Awards Bureau, Paris, TNA, WO208 5465 to 5474; Jean Quellien, "L'aide aux soldats britanniques," in Leleu et al. (eds.), *La France pendant la Seconde Guerre mondiale*, 184–85; Master List of MIS-X Awards, 1945–48, France, NARA, RG 498, ETO, MIS, 290/55/27/1.

who helped Allies from both armies, the total of identified and verified helpers is 34,000 (or, more precisely, 33,535) for France (Table 5.2). For all of Europe, the Allies identified at least 150,000 helpers. This number is a known minimum value revealing the scale of popular support for the Allies in occupied countries.[18] The 34,000 helpers are important to understanding resistance as a phenomenon in France, not just in qualitative terms but also, as we shall see, in quantitative ones. Since the 1970s, the opening of archives after a delay of thirty years and the rediscovery of the policies conducted by the Vichy government has led the place of the Resistance in the history of occupied France to be called into question. The discovery of the apparently seamless cooperation between "Vichy" and German-occupied France seemed an indication that the French had consented to the new political, economic and social order. Nazism and the "National Revolution," it was claimed, were supported by the people. This thesis reduced the Resistance to a minority of activists who occupied a symmetrical relationship vis-à-vis another minority of collaborationists while the mass of the population was either satisfied with the state of affairs or had at least resigned itself to collaboration. The limited number of Resistance fighters recognized at the Liberation – a figure that can be estimated at more than 325,000 – seemed to confirm this picture (Table 5.3).

These certificates of recognition were parsimoniously distributed. The 20 percent of those whose candidacy for recognition as helpers was rejected are nothing alongside the rate of rejection for CVR (Volunteer Resistance Fighter) cards, which was 46 percent; 325,000 therefore represents a known minimum value for the Resistance. This only covers those who were actively involved in the Resistance and not those who occasionally or belatedly participated in it. Thus, those granted the CVR title had demonstrated that they had regularly taken part in Resistance activities before 6 March 1944 (that is, at least three months before D-Day). At the time, there were 31 million French people over the age of fifteen. This yields a 1 percent rate of involvement in the Resistance or 0.8 percent if one takes the total population of 40 million as one's

THE RESISTANCE AS MASS LOCAL DYNAMIC   119

Table 5.3. *Members of the Resistance recognized after the war in France*[*]

Category	Number
Volunteer Resistance Fighters (CVR)	261,000
Free French Forces	32,000
(coming from metropolitan France before 31 July 1943)	
Non-CVR Helpers	28,000
Righteous	4,000
Total	325,000

[*] These consist of resistance members recognized on the basis of predefined criteria. The Service historique de la Défense holds some 600,000 individual files requesting recognition after the war. Serge Barcellini, "La Résistance française à travers le prisme de la carte CVR," in Douzou et al. (eds.), *La Résistance et les Français*, 151–81. Jean-François Muracciole, "Français libres, définition et décompte" and "Français libres, devenir social des," in François Broche, Georges Caïtucoli and Jean-François Muracciole (eds.), *Dictionnaire de la France libre* (Paris: Robert Laffont, 2010). A survey comparing the helpers of Loiret and the CVR of that département (for which Antoine Prost kindly supplied me the data) shows that only 15 percent of helpers were CVR; 4,000 Justes who assisted Jews under the Occupation were recognized by the state of Israel, a significant undercount that reflects the particularities of the procedure.

denominator. This 1 percent rate may appear low, even laughably so. In fact, it is very high. There are several ways of showing this.

One must first establish a benchmark. What is the average level of resistance to authoritarian or totalitarian regimes? This figure is not known. Since a posteriori definitions of what counts as resistance vary widely, it is difficult to compare levels of resistance from one occupied country to the next. In Czechoslovakia, for example, the combatants who emerged on 8 May 1945 were seen as resistance fighters.[19] We find ourselves confronted with the following question: is the 1 percent who risk their lives, their freedom and that of their families a small percentage or a large one? Sociology has no answer to this question. A few limit cases may nevertheless serve as benchmarks. Stanley Milgram's experiments at Yale in the 1960s showed that only 0.4 percent of subjects – two women, as it happened, which is perhaps not a coincidence – flat out refused to administer electric shocks to an adult considered to be a bad student.[20] A 0.4 percent rate of resistance to authority in a free and democratic country makes a 1 percent rate in a totalitarian/ authoritarian country a remarkable performance. Or take another striking example: that of the Congress of Spanish Deputies on the day its members were taken hostage by Colonel Tejero as part of the 23 February 1981 coup d'état. Only 3 of the 350 deputies, or 0.8 percent, refused to lie down, with one of them going so far as to actively attempt resistance. Another, less convincing example (for neither the life nor the freedom of the legislators was at stake) is supplied by the Grand Casino of Vichy on 10 July 1940. Under pressure from men and events and in a prevailing atmosphere of fear, 12 percent of the deputies and senators present were able to bring themselves to vote no.

Another approach is to examine political engagement. The Resistance was a form of political engagement just as much as (and even more than) membership of a political party in times of peace and freedom. In France, however, a 1, 2 or even 5 percent rate of party membership is commonplace and not taken as evidence of depoliticization or political indifference. The 1930s and 1940s saw a spike in rates of party membership, with the rate of political party membership among the adult population ranging from 5 (1936–39) to 6 percent (1945–46). It subsequently decreased, leveling off at between 1.5 and 2.5 percent between the 1960s and the 1990s. It then dropped once again, reaching roughly 1 percent in 2017. This comparison is too artificial to merit in-depth consideration but it does indicate that the 1 percent of the population who were involved in the Resistance must not be compared to a 100 percent level or even one of 50 or 25 percent. The cost of involvement in the Resistance acted to limit the number of candidates. There is no historical example of the utopia in which 100 percent of the population is engaged in resistance. Talk of mass resistance in this instance merely refers to the fact that more than 90 percent of inhabitants called upon to help an Ally in distress did so on the spot.[21] These repeated and spontaneous actions are surer proof of their attitude than any survey or analysis of the authorized opinion press.

The First Stirrings of Resistance on the Ground

In the academic literature on the history of the internal Resistance, one often finds the same analytical, logical and chronological structure: there first emerges a movement centered on a handful of remarkable figures, which subsequently expands its activity and recruitment and often produces a newspaper for purposes of mobilization. As the Resistance becomes increasingly united, an organizational perspective is adopted and the study concludes with a chapter on the war's final months and the Liberation.[22] These studies have done much to renew the history of the Resistance. In light of the history of resistance as escape assistance, one may nevertheless wonder whether they do not entail a certain bias. This bias stems from the fact, first, that the organizations studied consist of resistance movements rather than intelligence or escape networks. The latter, however, were subject to greater repression, perhaps because the Germans feared them more than they did the movements. Some disappeared or ceased all activity. In *Comment meurt un réseau*, Rémy recounts the disappearance in November 1943 of his own network, la Confrérie Notre-Dame (CND), which was the main intelligence network

THE RESISTANCE AS MASS LOCAL DYNAMIC

working on behalf of the London-based BCRA.[23] The story of the Resistance would doubtless be different if one only studied short-lived organizations. Julien Blanc has examined an example of this, that of the Musée de l'Homme network, whose leading members were arrested by the Germans in early 1941, with some executed the following year.[24]

The best contemporary work involuntarily relies upon a success story, that of groups created in 1940 or 1941 that continued to grow throughout the Occupation. The trajectory of these edifying stories, which were not without their setbacks and tragedies, is only further enhanced by the fact that they seem to organically grow from their initial nuclei. This growth process took place by way of horizontal enlargement and the absorption of small organizations willing to join what from 1943 onwards would become a sort of oligopoly of resistance. At the same time, the organizational chart became hierarchical and the founders and pioneers who were there from the beginning found themselves at the summit of a federative structure. The story of these "leaders," many of whom were drawn from the Parisian elite, is all the better known because they wrote their memoirs. The fact that so many histories favor an "organo-centric" approach presenting the Resistance from above reflects their reliance on these memoirs as well as the archives produced by organizations that survived the conflict.[25]

Stories of escape, by contrast, present a multitude of starting points, with decentralized segments intersecting in haphazard fashion depending on the location of downed airplanes and the path taken by wandering soldiers. They took place throughout the country and did not particularly involve its elites. The growth of these escape networks was often interrupted by repression, sometimes even before the network had a chance to perceive itself as such. In the best cases, there was a gradual specialization of tasks and hierarchization of roles but the leaders' names are not remembered by posterity. Only one of them wrote his memoirs: Georges Broussine of the Bourgogne network.[26] Furthermore, neither escape nor intelligence networks participated in the process whereby the Resistance was unified. The founders of the National Resistance Council (the initiatives for which came from both London and the French interior) deliberately left them out on the grounds that they were excessively dependent on the military authorities – a surprising consideration given the humble origins of the helpers. In any case, it is thus entirely likely that, treated as a history of organizations, the history of escape networks would yield a picture different from that of the history of resistance movements.[27]

Three surveys have recently been published on the Resistance. Though significantly differing from one another in point of sensitivity and approach, they all ignore or nearly ignore resistance as evasion assistance to Allies.[28] It is doubtless no accident that the only book to briefly mention it is the work of a British historian.[29] Moreover, since the history of the Resistance ultimately ended on a positive note with the Liberation of France and the establishment of a government drawn from its ranks, these books rightly privilege the stages by which the movement developed. Encompassing the entire history of the Resistance, they necessarily adopt a flattening perspective, reducing its various peaks and valleys to the same level. Robert Gildea's book and the volume by Sébastien Albertelli, Julien Blanc and Laurent Douzou nevertheless compensate for this leveling of lived experience by reconstructing the trajectories of particular individuals. The perspective I adopt here is not simply that of grassroots actors, seen from below. It is also spatial (the terrain of their activity) and temporal (that of the emergence of their activity). This approach casts the Resistance in a new light.

Working on the debriefings of escaped airmen and the recognition files of individual helpers independently of their membership of a recognized group allows the history of the Resistance to be doubly decompartmentalized. First, this method allows one to transcend what is a necessary but not sufficient history of organizations. By questioning some 2,000 escape network agents after the war, the French intelligence service, the Direction Générale des Études et des Recherches (DGER), left out ... 94 percent of the helpers.[30] The archives produced by the Allies at the time of or immediately after the event allow one, not just to get a better grasp of the nature of the helper population as a whole, but also to revisit the origins of the Resistance. They reveal that ever-repeated first moment, a time and place when there was no question of organization, when all that mattered was to take immediate action despite danger. By shedding light on the role that territorialized endogenous development played in the growth of the Resistance, they underscore the decisive importance of local dynamics.

Assistance as a Form of Emergency Social Service

The scale of citizen assistance to Allies in distress can be measured in various ways. As their presence increased, so too did the demands it placed on helpers in terms of individualized social service. We will later consider the political significance of the constantly repeated acts they performed and the human costs of repression. In what follows below, however, I would like to examine the Resistance as a practice on the ground, together with its social and economic consequences for the local population.

As we have seen, there were thousands of Allied soldiers and airmen hidden in France during the war and perhaps more. Alongside the 4,000 British, Commonwealth and American personnel who succeeded in escaping France or passed through it while escaping from elsewhere must be added those who were recaptured before crossing the Pyrenees as well as those who, unable or unwilling to try their luck, remained hidden. If one takes as an indicator the number of British military personnel who escaped from Northwest Europe

THE RESISTANCE AS MASS LOCAL DYNAMIC   123

and reached London before May 1945, 60 percent departed from France. Either their airplanes had been shot down over France (for the airmen) or they had avoided capture or escaped from camps in 1940 (for the soldiers). If one adds to this those who departed from Belgium, the Netherlands, Luxembourg or Switzerland, 77 percent of those escaping Northwestern Europe traveled through France. One must also add those – a small but exceptional group – who set out from camps in Germany, Poland and Austria. It is likely that 80 percent of Allied fugitives from Northwestern Europe thus passed through France. The reason for this is geographical in nature: the least difficult escape route passed through the Pyrenees and Spain. The Mediterranean and the English Channel were particularly complex and dangerous options and the North Sea no option at all.

The 4,000 or so British (or Commonwealth) and American men who succeeded in leaving the continent were clearly the chosen few of the fugitive population. But to what degree? How many men did the helpers take on? To answer this, one must know, not only the number of those who remained in hiding with their helpers, but also the number of evaders and escapers who were recaptured after having received assistance for some longer or shorter period of time. Some of these itineraries – those involving assisted freedom in France followed by internment in German prison camps – are recounted in the "Interrogation" and "Liberation" reports that the Allies had POWs fill out following their liberation.[31] Among British ex-POWs, one finds some 1,400 cases of this type gathered together in accordance with an unknown criterion in four archival cartons at Kew. Of these, several hundred passed through France. But this collection does not appear to be exhaustive. Their initial plan notwithstanding, the Allies were unable to interrogate all POWs liberated from Germany. It would have been necessary to interrogate more than 250,000 people, without counting those who had individually joined up with Allied troops once the latter reached the locality where they were hidden.

Many cases thus escape the statistics of the "Escape & Evasion Reports" that supply my principal source. In August 1941, the airplane flown by Wing Commander and ace pilot Douglas Bader was shot down over northern France. In parachuting, he lost one of the two artificial legs that had supported him since undergoing a double amputation as a result of a prewar airplane accident. Shortly thereafter, friends from the Royal Air Force parachuted in a spare pair. From the Saint-Omer hospital where he was an inmate, two nurses, a young man and a retired couple helped him escape on 19 August. He was recaptured and four helpers were arrested and sentenced to death by a German military court in Brussels for "assisting the enemy" (the helpers were recognized as such after the war). Their sentence was commuted to hard labor. They spent the remainder of the war in German prisons under terrible conditions. Another well-known example is that of Air Commodore

124 THE ORIGINS OF THE RESISTANCE

Ivelaw-Chapman, whose airplane was shot down over the département of the Sarthe on 7 May 1944. Significantly, he had been informed of D-Day preparations. Upon learning the news of Ivelaw-Chapman's downing, Churchill is said to have given the order to "exfiltrate or eliminate him." With the assistance of local helpers, including a series of families, Ivelaw-Chapman successfully evaded capture for a month. Picked up by Annie Rospabé (the future Annie Guéhenno), an envoy from General De Gaulle's Delegation in France who worked for the Bureau of Air Operations, he was finally arrested with her on 8 June. The D-Day landing had taken place in the meantime. Ivelaw-Chapman is also absent from the "debriefings" of airmen who succeeded in escaping Europe.

The last relatively famous example – and also the most tragic – is that of the 168 airmen and their helpers who were found out, many having been given away by a professional traitor, Jacques Desoubrie. After having infiltrated the escape lines running north and west of Paris as well as in Eure-et-Loir, this double agent gradually betrayed hundreds of helpers and airmen to the Germans. In summer 1944, 168 of the young men he had betrayed, all of whose airplanes had come down between May and August, were sent, not to a prisoner of war camp, but to the Buchenwald concentration camp – a punitive measure in violation of the laws of war. Arriving by convoy on 15 August, they were removed from the camp in October, two of them having died in the meantime, and sent to Stalag Luft III in Sagan. The arrested helpers were deported to concentration camps without trial. Several hundred citizens had thus mobilized themselves to protect the Wing Commander, the Air Commodore and the 168 pilots. Until now, however, history has above all remembered the most prominent heroes of this adventure.[32] Occupied with repetitive, material tasks, the run-of-the-mill helper had few great deeds to boast of.

One may form an idea of the labor that this involved by considering the example of the UK and Commonwealth citizens who succeeded in making it to London. First, in point of its duration: on average, 198 days – or between six and seven months – passed between the initial escape (some were recaptured and had to escape again) and arrival in England. The average period spent in hiding in Northwestern Europe was shorter: 116 days. This is due to failed escape attempts followed by arrest as well as frequent arrests in Spain, which were followed by periods of internment in the Miranda-de-Ebro camp in the province of Burgos. In France, escapees spent an average of 87 days in hiding. Over the duration of the war, it thus took three months to get a British airman out of France. In the case of Germany, a country from which few succeeded in escaping, it took six days. There, successful escape depended on extreme speed and the absence of any contact with the population. The contrast is all the more striking with the average duration in hiding for prison camp escapees on

THE RESISTANCE AS MASS LOCAL DYNAMIC   125

what had formerly been Polish territory: 134 days. This lengthy duration, perhaps the greatest in Europe, reflects the alignment of the Polish people in the war.

Helpers sheltered those being pursued. A minimum of 4,000 men spent an average of 87 days in the country "in freedom." They thus received a minimum of 348,000 days and nights of assistance from helpers. Perhaps a little less since American airplanes only started to be shot down over France in 1942 but doubtless also a little more since this 4,000-person minimum does not include those who did not succeed in escaping the continent.

Chart 5.1 shows how the escapee population was distributed over time between two groups. On the one hand, there are the British and Commonwealth soldiers who found themselves trapped in France in 1940 but who succeeded in evading capture by the Germans, gradually making their way to England. The corresponding clusters of dots observe a straight line that regularly rises as time passes before their ultimate escape. On the other hand, there is a cluster of increasingly dense dots oscillating around the 200-day mark while slowly diminishing. This corresponds to the helpers' activity, which intensified as the number of arrivals on the ground increased. The establishment of networks made itself felt starting in summer 1943, slowly reducing the time required to escape.

The fate of Squadron leader Thomas C.S. Cooke and his crew illustrates the joint performance of airmen trained for special operations and local people and resisters on the ground. On the night of 7–8 February 1944, on their way to the dropping zone in the south of France, this SOE crew and the SOE secret agent they were transporting had to bale out because of an engine failure. All eight men, parachuting blind, arrived alive on the ground and none was taken prisoner. By the evening of 8 February, four of the crew had already been picked up by maquisards of the Drôme département, and the other three by the 12th. Consequently, their debriefings stop on these dates, with the conventional phrase: "The rest of our journey was arranged for us."[33] The first group crossed the Pyrenees on 30 March and landed at Lyneham (Wiltshire) on 12 April. The other three, including Thomas C.S. Cooke, arrived a month later, on 5 May, at Whitchuch (Shropshire). The following three documents (Figures 5.1a–5.1c) summarize their odyssey. . . and provide a glimpse into the range of family wartime emotions.

Life in Clandestine Transnational Families

What does it mean to house, feed, clothe, supply false papers to and transport several thousand young men for weeks or months as they cross several borders, those of the incorporated zone (*zone rattachée*), the forbidden zone (*zone interdite*), the line of demarcation and the Swiss or Spanish border? At

Duration of successful escape through France (1940–1945)

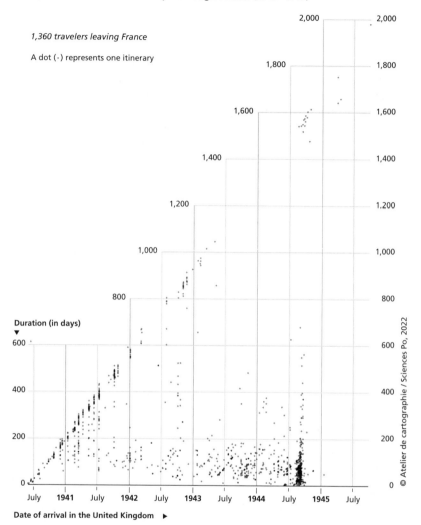

Chart 5.1 Duration of successful escape through France, 1940–45 (1,360 travelers leaving France).

This diagram depicts the escape history of two groups of Allied servicemen. The soldiers who remained stuck in France after Dunkirk form a straight line starting in 1940 and continuing to summer 1944. Some thus remained in hiding for four years. Airmen represent the bulk of the cluster that grows denser in 1943–44 while oscillating and slowly diminishing. They in this way reflect the accelerated returns made possible by the growing organization of assistance. The rising column of summer 1944 reflects the speed of the Allied advance as it recovered the airmen. Over the duration of the war, 75 percent of all successful escapes were performed by airmen.
Source: TNA, WO208, 3297–3327.

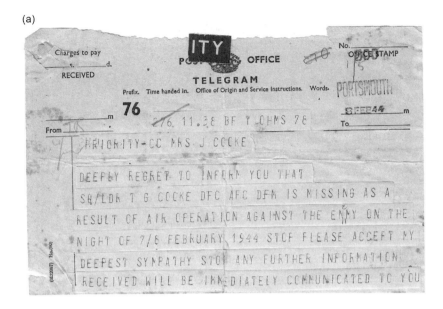

Figure 5.1a Telegram from the Royal Air Force to Mrs. Cooke announcing that her son is missing, 8 February 1944. © Collection Maurice Bleicher.

the same time, the families of France hid or assisted some 100,000 people in avoiding hard labor in Germany (from 1943) and an unknown number of Jewish families, parents and children. Assisting the Allies was thus not the only form of unanticipated social work that the inhabitants had to shoulder on their own in this period. Each group had its specificities. Assisting the Allies resembled assistance for grown children. It entailed a series of heavy and repetitive tasks, such as locating suitable civilian clothing and shoes – the Americans' great height and large feet drove their helpers to despair (see Figure 5.2a) – and long hours queuing for a greatly increased quantity of food (a costly and dangerous task as it required the use of false ration tickets and could provoke the unwelcome curiosity of shopkeepers). There was also the additional housekeeping, cleaning and general upkeep, of course, which extended women's workdays, to say nothing of the household congestion caused by additional residents. On top of that, specific tasks were necessary, including finding a doctor who would agree to care for the wounded, finding a way to manufacture false papers and locating French people capable of speaking English, something much less commonplace than today. In Italy, which had historically been a country of emigration, it was easier to find village residents who had spent a few years working in the United States or the United Kingdom. The tension associated with having young men in the home

(b)

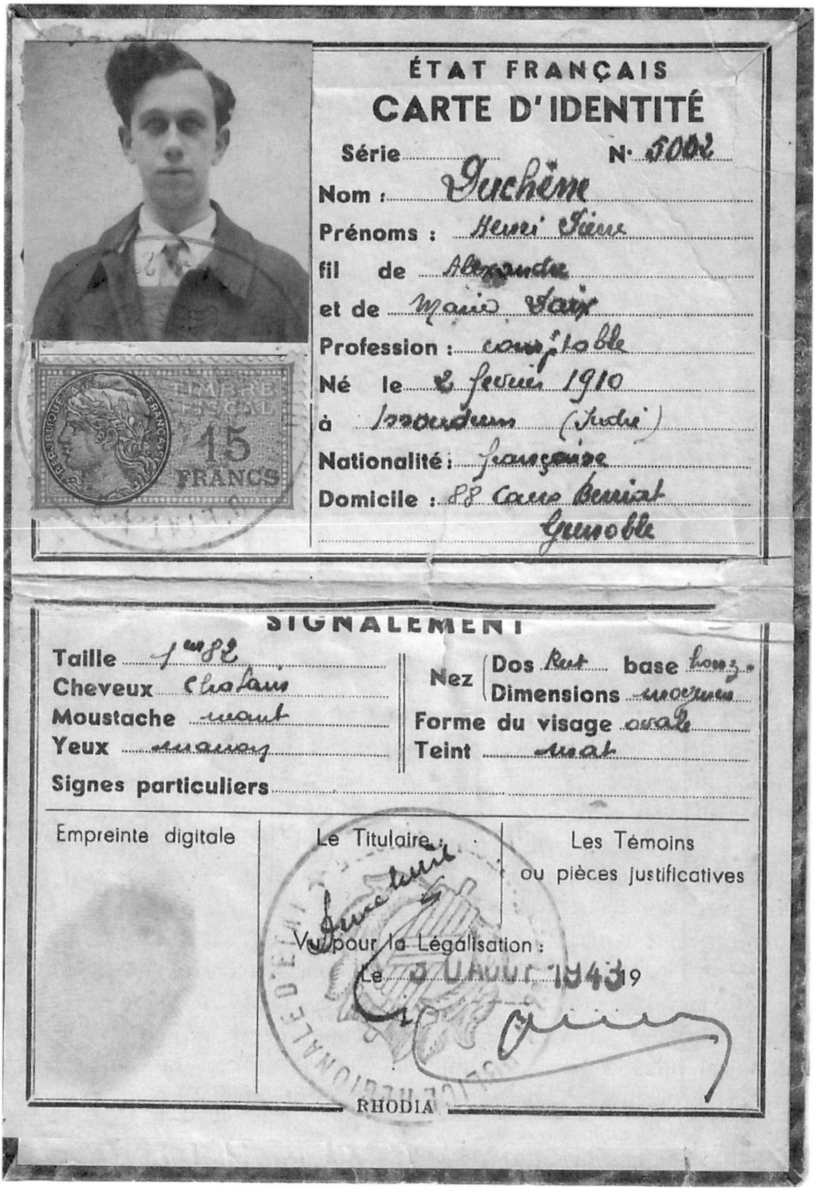
ÉTAT FRANÇAIS

CARTE D'IDENTITÉ

Série .... N· 5002

Nom : Duchêne

Prénoms : Henri Pierre

fil de Alexandre

et de

Profession : comptable

Né le 2 février 1910

à Issoudun (Indre)

Nationalité : française

Domicile : 88 cours Berriat Grenoble

TIMBRE FISCAL 15 FRANCS

RÉPUBLIQUE FRANÇAISE

SIGNALEMENT

Taille 1m82

Cheveux châtains

Moustache

Yeux marron

Nez Dos base

Dimensions moyennes

Forme du visage ovale

Teint mat

Signes particuliers

Empreinte digitale

Le Titulaire :

Les Témoins ou pièces justificatives

Vu pour la Légalisation :

Le 1943 19

RHODIA

Figure 5.1b Fake identity card issued by the Resistance to Squadron Leader Thomas C.S.Cooke. © Collection Maurice Bleicher.

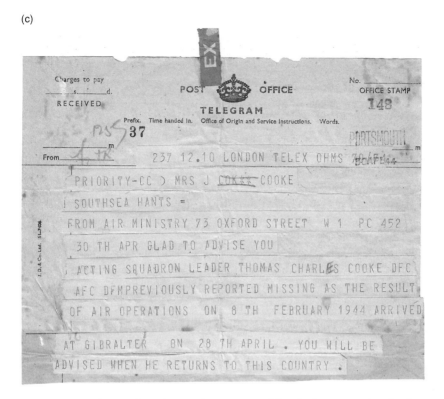

Figure 5.1c Telegram from the Royal Air Force to Mrs. Cooke announcing that her son arrived at Gibraltar, 30 April 1944. © Collection Maurice Bleicher.

could increase when, as was frequently the case, they failed to observe security precautions. For fugitives and helpers alike, silence, the need to stay clear of the windows and to hide at the least unusual noise were additional burdens of everyday life. In order to help these young men pass the time, their hosts sometimes accompanied them on dangerous outings (Figure 5.2b). They did not go unremarked by the French. Their particular way of walking – what the young Michèle Moët, a seventeen-year-old escort for the Bourgogne network, called the Americans' "gait" – easily betrayed them, as did their facial features and the redness of their hair in some cases, to say nothing of their speech should a few words escape them.[34] A "thank you" or a "sorry!" could be enough to lead to the arrest of Ally and helper alike.

In a country where economic exploitation by the occupying power had rapidly reduced agricultural production – by 1944, it had reached 60 percent of its prewar level – supplying food to the men they sheltered was a heavy burden on family life. Upon arriving in France, the agents of the Awards

(a)

(b)

Figures 5.2a and 5.2b American airmen at home in a family of resisters, in Saint-Mandé, Autumn 1943. © Michèle Agniel.
(5.2a) Autumn/winter 1943. The American airman Burkowsky poses near the radio where he listened to the BBC at the Moëts' home in Saint-Mandé, Seine département. One notes the

Bureaus were struck by their interlocutors' poverty. Three years later, the poverty in which a portion of the helpers lived, often aggravated by the death or illness of one or several of their loved ones as a result of repression, could still be read in the moving thanks addressed to the American Army for its packets of provisions and textiles. These packages were delivered by the CARE organization.[35] Founded in the United States at war's end and bringing together twenty-two civic, religious, cooperative and labor union humanitarian organizations, CARE (Cooperative for American Remittances to Europe) saw to the distribution across Europe of 2.8 million US Army surplus packages. The helpers received some of these in January 1948. Even at this distance from the Liberation, their emotion on discovering chocolate, sugar, white flour, powdered milk, canned meat or perhaps wool and needles for knitting or pieces of fabric for sewing well captures the conditions of poverty in which they lived. In often awkward writing characterized by shaky spelling and punctuation, these letters reveal the extreme poverty in which these former members of the Resistance lived.[36] Their misfortune was material, of course, but also moral, a result of the mourning that repression left in its wake.

These thank you letters are a type of family correspondence. They contain almost every detail of family life: births, deaths or illnesses, the holy communion of children and family photos. Their authors also ask for news of those they had protected or request that their interlocutor (whom they generally did not know) also send them photographs of their own families. Here is the letter of a helper, a female farmer from the Ardennes village of Stonne. Her husband also received the title of helper. On pages of a school notebook, she wrote her "Dear Benefactor," sending him a photograph of her family. Posing in the mud in front of the home she temporarily occupied as the family waited for their farm to be rebuilt, she seems to have gathered together all of her wealth: her five children, her husband and the old horse.

Figures 5.2a and 5.2b (*cont.*) too-short sleeves of his suit. The Americans' average height, which was greater than that of the French, complicated the search for civilian clothing. After having been accommodated in France for over three months, in early 1944 the airman was arrested in transit to the Pyrenees as he descended from a train at the Toulouse station.

(5.2b) Autumn 1943. Vetter, an American airman who had piloted an airplane shot down over Beauvais on 15 September 1943, and was harbored at the Moët home in Saint-Mandé, is here photographed standing behind two German soldiers as he is accompanied on a walk to the Vincennes zoo. The photographer Jean Carbonnet and the guide Michèle Agniel (born Moët) clearly savored the humor of the situation. For the young airmen, their reclusive life was a source of much frustration. The hosts sometimes took the risk to organize an accompanied walk for them. Arthur M. Vetter made it to Spain on 18 November and to Gibraltar on 11 December. Both members of the Bourgogne escape line, Michèle Agniel and Jean Carbonnet were arrested in early 1944 and deported to concentration camps.

132   THE ORIGINS OF THE RESISTANCE

St., Les Cendrières, le 24-2-1948

Dear Benefactor,

I hasten to thank you for your packet. Everything was in perfect order and delighted the entire family.

It is good of you to think of us and you could not have found a family in greater need.

I am a mother of five children

16-year-old Françoise

12-year-old Louis

10-year-old Emile (both take 1st communion in July 1948)

5-year-old Julien

2-year-old Eveline

My oldest daughter fell seriously ill in August 1947. She suffered a great deal. On December 1st of last year, I had her operated on and she suffered greatly but she is getting better now. I sent her to stay with her aunt, she'll fully recover there. We haven't been able to find anything else and live in wooden huts. It's cold in the winter and you suffocate in summer. Though we work all of the time, we hardly eat. 200 grams of bread per day and per person, children up to age 4 get 100 grams and 300 grams of fat per month. 1 kg of sugar per month for the children and 500 gr for the adults.

Everything is in short supply here in France: you can't find affordable clothing or shoes and always with rationing coupons, older and younger children are often blue with cold and nearly always barefoot. I think that where you live children fortunately don't suffer from this poverty. That's what makes so many young people sick. And yet my children are strong. I'm enclosing a photo that was taken in April last year. It's the whole family with my husband and his horses, my oldest daughter whom I almost lost holding her little dog, our two big boys who are going to take their 1st communion in July 1948, Julien standing near them and me holding my youngest, who is now two years old.

I hope this letter finds you and yours in good health. In closing, I send you our kind regards.

Please accept our warm thanks, dear Benefactor.

V.M.L.

(Les Cendrières) St. par R. Ardennes France

P.S. Would it be possible to have news of an airman who parachuted to the ground in Raucourt on 25-2-1944 whom we took in for a few days. We haven't had any news since. His name is John Jerome Bajenscki No. 96, his airplane came down in flames.

Thank you for your kindness and be well.

V.M.L.

In his debriefing, written up in London in June 1944, the Radioman taken in by this helper, Jerome Bajenski, described the primal scene of assistance to the Allies:

As soon as day had come, I knocked on the door of an occupied house. The woman who opened the door drew me inside as soon as I told her

THE RESISTANCE AS MASS LOCAL DYNAMIC

133

who I was. She and her husband were very poor but they straightaway made a fire, gave me the little bit of food they had and put me to bed. That day, the woman made alterations to some civilian clothes for me and gave me a pair of wooden-soled shoes.[37]

A scene worthy of a children's tale, where the brave orphan finds a caring family and home. This traditional picture at once reflects the emotional shock felt by the fallen airman, the emotion of isolated peasants as they take in an American fallen from the sky and also the political engagement that their actions entailed at a time when efforts to locate the airman were in full swing.

In the letters written by helpers after the war, it was women more than men who expressed familial and maternal feelings towards the airmen they had sheltered and whose news they requested. Indeed, most of the letters came from women, either because expressing thanks tended to feature more prominently in feminine culture or because they believed that the content of the packets concerned them in their role as homemaker. But men also sent photos, mentioned their children and invited their correspondents to visit them. Thus this dialogue between children recounted by a father and Resistance member from the commune of Lepuix-Gy in the Territory of Belfort:

Lepuix-Gy, 1 March 1948

As my little children feverishly spread over the table the magnificent gifts pulled from the supply parcel you sent us, the youngest of them enthusiastically cried: "I want to write and thank Father Christmas of America." And his older brother replied: "You don't know how to write that in American."

"Yes, I do," he responded in triumph, "You write it 'Eisenhover'!"

. . .

Constant B.

From the local to everyday life and everyday life to family ties, this data on assistance to Allies in distress reveals a dynamic of grassroots resistance and is confirmation of its popular nature. For the paths taken by downed airplanes and fugitives on the run were alike matters of chance, introducing Allied personnel to all variety of social environments. It also shows that the Resistance pushed its roots deep within families – for these defenseless young men were adopted as sons. Extended families were in this way created at the local level, multinational families built from one day to the next under circumstances of urgency and risk. A transnational society *avant la lettre* thus emerged. It would not be soon forgotten.

But it was not enough to house, care for, clothe and feed the young men. Aid was not, or not only, humanitarian. It was also tantamount to taking the Allies' side in the war, of helping those whom the helpers protected escape so that they might once again take up arms against the enemy. In this sense, aid was at once a reflection of political engagement and an act of war.

6

The Sequences of Aid

Between Family and Repression

The local nature of much Resistance activity helped sustain it. From its emergence to its regeneration following destruction by the occupier, aid-based resistance resembled a perpetual motion machine. Others have already recounted the escape network experience. In addition to the handful of memoirs written by their participants, a large number of accounts by former fugitives have been published in Great Britain and the United States – so many true stories of adventure and occasionally love unfurling across the length and breadth of France. In this chapter, however, I shall seek to shed light on the first two phases of aid supplied on the ground. These consist of the first moments following the downing of an Allied aircraft or the escape of an Allied serviceman and the weeks that immediately followed, during which efforts were made to locate go-betweens who might escort fugitives to Spain and, from there, Gibraltar and England. Located upstream of escape networks and fully dependent on the willingness of local people who enjoyed no other source of support, these two phases of assistance ensured that pro-Allied energy was a renewable resource. The third phase of aid – which was also the most difficult to attain for those concerned – consisted in the establishment of organized networks requiring money, permanent agents and relay points to the border. This is why, though the Allies recognized 34,000 helpers, only 2,000 escape network agents were interviewed after the war by the French secret service.

But the various temporalities of aid do not suffice to define it. It was also characterized by two constants: the role of the family and the prospect of repression. More so than in other resistance activities, the family played a decisive role. The crime scene – that is, the place where Allied airmen were harbored – was the family home and the authors of the crime included and sometimes mainly consisted of women and children. A supposedly peaceful and non-belligerent population thus found itself at the heart of combat. For given the ubiquity of repression, it was indeed combat, even if the activities in question were peaceful in nature. German posters, newspapers, the arrest and deportation of men and women and the information filtering out of prisons regarding the occupier's interrogation methods all contributed to the menacing environment in which the helpers carried out their activities. An

134

awareness of risk and the very real prospect of repression were part and parcel of the resistance experience.

The Three Phases of Evasion Assistance

In the first moments, assistance was offered blindly, without any other thought than helping a person in distress who was also under imminent threat of capture by the enemy. The debriefings conducted in London contain fleeting traces of this assistance. Two of the three phases of evasion are clearly in evidence in the debriefing of Arthur Vetter, whose photograph taken in hiding is reproduced in this book: after being rescued on the ground, he was taken in hand by a network (the Bourgogne network). On 15 September 1943, Vetter was flying a bomber on mission over Boulogne-Billancourt. Returning, the airplane was hit by anti-aircraft fire and came down outside Beauvais.

> I jumped at 3000 feet and opened my chute immediately. I saw no chutes on my way down, but it was getting pretty dark. As I landed, I saw my plane crash and burn. I landed without any difficulties in a back yard. A crowd of Frenchmen were waiting. One took my chute and my Mae West and ran off with it. I asked where I should go and was told to head for a nearby wood. One of the crowd spoke a little English and this helped to take matters clear. I ran a half mile to the woods and sat down. When it got really dark, three men came for me. I was taken to a kitchen where I was joined by Sgt Wagner (E&E #254) and another member of my crew. Sgt Wagner had broken his ankle while parachuting. We were fed and given civilian clothes. We spent the night in a hay loft.
> The next morning, we were hidden in a nearby thicket. This was done because the Germans had started to search for us that morning by going into the barns in the vicinity. The news travelled to our helpers and we were moved. A light German plane flew very low over the area. It was also searching for us. We had taken bread and wine with us when we went to the thicket and that was all we had to eat all day, as the French were afraid of betraying our location by bringing us food. Somehow we were not hungry anyway.
> That night the French returned after dark. We walked across the fields until we came to a deserted farmhouse. From here on, our journey was arranged.[1]

These first, high-risk twenty-four hours were decisive. Without them, the network, located further downstream, would not have had a "package" to pick up. If the entire local population had not supported the effort, the airmen would have been unable to evade capture. In the present instance, this involved a small crowd, including a man who immediately set off to hide the incriminating evidence, three other men, an indeterminate number of people in the kitchen, including the women who prepared the meal for the three survivors, and then more guides to lead them to the abandoned farm.

136   THE ORIGINS OF THE RESISTANCE

Finally, there was an inhabitant who knew how to go about contacting a network. The entire village, in a word, knew what was happening and kept quiet.

And the crew of this bomber was lucky that their airplane came down in 1943, a time when organized networks existed. Three months later, on 11 December 1943, Vetter once again laid foot on English soil. The networks did their best to cover the zones where airplanes most often came down – that is, directly underneath the principal bombing routes over Brittany, Normandy, the Paris basin and the Nord. Air fleets en route to Germany also passed over the latter two areas and, to a lesser extent, northern Italy. For during the first years – 1940–41 and even 1942 – networks were few and far between. Sentences of the type, "From here on, our journey was arranged," appeared in only 35 percent of the debriefings of British servicemen who reached England from France (Chart 6.1). Often established on the initiative or with the support of MI9, the networks were thus clearly not the sole force driving assistance – far from it. These proportions are not to be taken literally, however. Given the compartmentalization of information, they are perhaps

**Proportion of evasion journey overseen
by an organization** (1940–1945)

in whole or in part, from:

Belgium

54 %

129 out of 240 journeys

Netherlands

40 %

56 out of 141 journeys

France

35 %

475 out of 1,360 journeys

Distribution by year (number of journeys organized)

	1940	1941	1942	1943	1944	1945	40–45
Belgium	0	0	60	47	22	0	**129**
Netherlands	0	0	5	20	30	1	**56**
France	1	11	90	189	184	0	**475**

Distribution by year (as a % of total number of journeys that year)

	1940	1941	1942	1943	1944	1945	40–45
Belgium	0	0	81	94	28	0	**54 %**
Netherlands	0	0	83	91	38	3	**40 %**
France	1	4	61	90	30	0	**35 %**

© Atelier de cartographie / Sciences Po, 2022

Chart 6.1   Proportion of evasion journeys overseen by an organization, 1940–45
Source: TNA, WO208, 3297–327.

underestimates. For obvious reasons of security, the helpers were at certain moments not aware of the framework in which they sometimes found themselves operating. The rate of successful evasions overseen by an organization proved higher for Belgium and the Netherlands, perhaps due to the difficulties that had to be overcome in crossing additional borders.

The first, most dangerous instants and the moment when the evader was taken in hand by a network were thus separated by a variable span of time during which individual actions gradually laid the foundations for the future network (provided it was not repressed before regular contacts could be established). This second phase of evasion, during which a chain of contacts was haphazardly assembled without external help, also participated in the same bottom-up process that spawned the Resistance as a national liberation movement. Phase 3 – that of the fully developed network – above all obtained for 1943 and 1944. On some occasions (the case of Arthur M. Vetter, for instance), the network operated with such efficiency that phase 2 could be skipped altogether. In all cases, however, phase 1, the primeval scene of evasion, remained. It was this phase that, like a self-starting perpetual motion machine, tirelessly drove the creation of new networks.

We shall examine three cases that illustrate the process by which aid-based Resistance developed. The first began on the Norman coast in June 1940, the second in Brittany in September 1941. These cases of aid-based Resistance covered phases 1 and 2 before being brutally put down. The third case also began in September 1941, this time in Bourgogne. It covered phases 1, 2 and 3. Illustrating the first stirrings of resistance as a type of action, these cases demonstrate with particular clarity the bottom-up genesis of a movement that was national in scale. They took place, moreover, in the first fifteen months of the Occupation, a time when the expansion of the Third Reich was in full stride and only the United Kingdom stood in its way. At this time, engaging in resistance was not a matter of flocking to the winning side. Rather, the people in question rushed to rescue those who had been struck down and thereby see to it that they might fight another day. Theirs was a rearguard action in the European war.

Veules-les-Roses / Rouen-St Aignan – Montpon

Located at the foot of a chalk cliff in the Pays de Caux, the village of Veules-les-Roses was home to some 600 inhabitants before the war. Veules was also a vacation spot, its streets thronged with tourists in season. It was from there that, until 12 June 1940, British and French soldiers attempted to reach the ships that had come to pick them up. A minority of them succeeded but most were captured, with an unknown number escaping the Germans. Once it had settled in, the occupying army transformed the landscape, razing seaside villas, transforming the beach into a field of metal stakes and barbed wire, constructing three blockhouses and placing several anti-aircraft batteries on the level ground.[2]

138   THE ORIGINS OF THE RESISTANCE

In late June, six British soldiers looking for a way to cross the Channel arrived in Veules and hid in an uninhabited villa. Dirty and famished, they could see in the distance below them the garden of "La Pomponnette," a boarding house run by Marcelle Bochet. The boarding house had been partly destroyed by German fire on 11 June but several rooms remained habitable. The soldier with the best command of French – later described as a "witness" in the ruling of the German military tribunal of Greater Paris – went down to ask for food. The hotelkeeper, an unmarried thirty-six-year-old woman, immediately agreed and showed the fugitives a little house located behind her garden. Every day, she brought food and drink there. In October, she moved them to her home, supplying them with shelter and meals and even arranging for a barber to visit to see to their hair until they departed for what was known as the Free Zone on 28 February 1941. After having drawn from her savings and sold her stock of wine to provide for them, the hotelkeeper appealed to the solidarity of local people. On several occasions, the hairstylist and barber gave money; the woman farmer at the end of the street donated money and provisions; a Parisian woman who had grown up in the village, a hardware store owner by trade, gave nearly 6,000 francs in all and her daughter brought clothing, English-language books and a radio post; a school principal from Fécamp supplied clothing and provisions. And nearly all of them spent New Year's Eve in the refugees' company.[3]

In the meantime, the German military high command in October began posting notices informing the public that harboring enemy soldiers was punishable by death (Figure 6.1). This notice did not frighten the helpers of Veules for it was at this very moment that the hotelkeeper of La Pomponnette decided to move the soldiers she was protecting into her home and local solidarity was expressed via gifts of provisions, civilian clothing and money. No, it was the cost of their presence that motivated the search for a way to evacuate the young men. That, at least, is what these resisting civilians told the occupying forces after their arrest. It would have been unwise to acknowledge their political motivation: to help liberate France by ensuring that the Allied soldiers could rejoin their army.

The second phase of assistance thus began after Christmas, when the hardware store owner and his daughter sought a way to obtain material aid from the Allies and/or escort the soldiers to the southern zone. After various attempts, they made contact with what the tribunal's ruling referred to as an "organization." This network was nameless. Centered around the well-connected owner of an industrial clothing cleaning factory in Rouen-St Aignan, it did not operate in a systematic and regular fashion but rather depended on several short chains of acquaintance. Nor was it specialized, with its members also sometimes carrying out acts of espionage (most importantly, drawing up blueprints of the neighboring airfield of Triqueville). This second group in our explanatory schema had more members, at least if one is to judge by the number of individuals who were later arrested in connection with it.

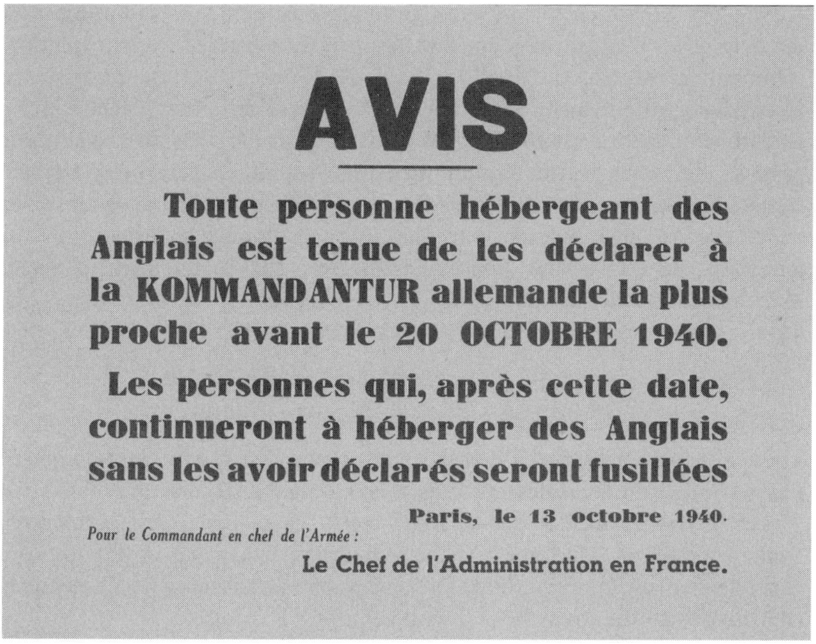

THE SEQUENCES OF AID

AVIS

Toute personne hébergeant des Anglais est tenue de les déclarer à la KOMMANDANTUR allemande la plus proche avant le 20 OCTOBRE 1940.

Les personnes qui, après cette date, continueront à héberger des Anglais sans les avoir déclarés seront fusillées

Pour le Commandant en chef de l'Armée :

Paris, le 13 octobre 1940.

Le Chef de l'Administration en France.

Figure 6.1 Summary execution for harboring Englishmen, October 1940 © Archives nationales (France). Public notice posted in the départements of the occupied zone in October 1940 following the German order of 10 October 1940, relating to defense against acts of sabotage (Verordnung über die Anmeldung englischer Staatsangehöriger vom 10. Oktober 1940, *VOBIF*, S. 109).

Working with the factory owner were a doctor, one of the factory's directors, an engineer, his wife, an accountant, a pharmacist, a tailor, two shopkeepers, a precision mechanic, a secretary, a stenographer, a clerical worker, a shop assistant, a police secretary who helped produce counterfeit papers, a textile worker and a domestic servant. It was a cross-section of society at the intersection of several social milieus and included both workers and employers. Resistance decompartmentalized society, increasing the number of unlikely encounters.[4] The type of social transgression involved in this activity contributed to the stimulating sense that the entire nation was behind the Resistance. In the postwar years, by contrast, the return to ordinary sociological frontiers acted as an impediment to efforts to establish associations rooted in this shared memory.

Between November 1940 and February 1941, this "organization" (as the German military tribunal referred to it) succeeded in evacuating some twenty British soldiers over the course of five or six voyages. Three of the group's young women – a secretary, a stenographer and a clerical worker – alternately accompanied the men to Marseille, crossing over the demarcation line with the help of a smuggler. In Marseille, the men were handed over to what the tribunal referred to as an "English office." On 1 March 1941, the escorts were arrested with the men in their charge – the six soldiers from Veules and a seventh who had been harbored in Pont-St-Pierre (Eure) – as they sought safe passage, the smuggler for whom they were waiting having been arrested earlier. The story of the Veules-les-Roses and Rouen-St Aignan groups ends there, even though assistance to the Allies continued to expand in the following years. Over the duration of the war, the département of Seine-Maritime counted an unusually high number of helpers; only the départements of the Paris region, Nord and Pas-de-Calais had more.

Plestin-les-Grèvres / Bégard – Nantes

Though it took place nearly a year later and at a distance of 500 kilometers, this second example of nascent resistance strongly resembles the first. Their points of resemblance underscore the constants of their genesis. In both, women were a driving force and their children participated. And both were characterized by improvisation and a lack of specialization – all elements contributing to the strength (and weakness) of this dynamic.

Around one in the morning on 29 September 1941, a bomber returning from a mission to Saint-Nazaire was hit by anti-aircraft fire over Brest. It carried out an emergency sea landing in the bay of St Michel-en-Grève on the territory of Plestin-les-Grèves in the Côtes-du-Nord département (Figure 6.2). Luckily, its crew was uninjured on impact with the water. Discovering to their relief that the aircraft was not floating but instead resting on its nose on the seabed, the three men destroyed the cockpit and walked to a bathing cabin, where they tried to sleep. In the morning, a little crowd rushed to the beach to admire the Blenheim. A young woman saw the three men and indicated by gesture that they should hide in the cabin's ceiling, accessible via trapdoor. The Germans began their search. In the afternoon, her mother, Anne Leduc, a housewife and mother of three children, accompanied by her sister and another couple, brought the airmen hot tea and food and then left. Shortly thereafter, soldiers – "Huns," as the pilot would later write – inspected the cabin's straw but did not notice the trapdoor. The airmen remained there for two days. On Wednesday, the same women took them to an old abandoned mill, where they stayed two more days. The two sisters brought them provisions. On Friday evening, a mother of ten, Marie de Saint-Laurent, came for them with one of her sons, taking them through the woods to her château and giving them civilian clothing. On account of the searches being carried out in the sector by the Germans, the following Monday she hid them in a cellar in the forest. After two more days had passed, a woman with a car and an *Ausweis* permitting her to travel as a physiotherapist (yet another mother,

Figure 6.2   On the night of 29 September 1941, the Blenheim made a sea-landing in the bay of St-Michel-en-Grève. © With the courtesy of ABSA 39–45.

Alexandrine Tilly) came for them to put them up with peasant families in Bégard (two children) and Langoat (four children), 40 kilometers away. Seen from the perspective of the airmen, this simplified account does not reveal the difficulties that had to be overcome in arranging for such movements in such a context. The first phase thus lasted eight days.

The second phase of the evasion began in Bégard, where the pilot had been put up. The farmer and his family had already put up two British soldiers (and perhaps also a third), who were successfully evacuated to the Free Zone by way of Nantes.[5] The same woman driver, who, as a bonesetter-physiotherapist, possessed an *Ausweis*, took the fugitives to Guingamp, the neighboring town, to take the train for Nantes. This was on 14 October, eight days after they had been placed in Bégard and Langoat. In the meantime, they had been supplied with counterfeit papers and a photographer from Paimpol had come to take their photos. A large meeting took place on Sunday at the Le Gacs' home, where a photo was also taken. The pilot spoke of a constant stream of visiting neighbors – "perhaps one hundred people." The same guide who had earlier escorted other evaders accompanied the three of them to Nantes, a one-day trip in trains filled with German soldiers. They were put up with a housewife who was already giving shelter to three escaped Poles. Six days later, on

142   THE ORIGINS OF THE RESISTANCE

20 October, the city's commandant was assassinated by a member of the special organization of the Communist Party. The state of siege tightened around the fugitives. On 10 November they were arrested, as were all of the helpers between Nantes and Plestin-les-Grèves in the days and months that followed.[6]

Les Riceys / Paris – Vierzon / Ste Léocadie – Canet-Plage

This third case initially seems happier than the preceding ones. Though it was contemporaneous with that of Plestin-les-Grèves, since the airplane in question carried out a forced landing on 11 September 1941, it presents a higher degree of organization, reaching level three, that of the organized network. We have already encountered its pilot, P.F. Allen, at the beginning of the preceding chapter.[7] Yet another indication of the performance of helpers may be found in the fact that the Wellington's six-man crew were led all the way to freedom. Ten weeks after arriving on the ground, four members of the crew were already safe and sound in Britain or Spain. Two were missing, having been arrested in the little train that conducted the six from Perpignan to Ste-Léocadie, from which they were to cross the Pyrenees on foot. One year later, the same network once again took them in hand, arranged for their escape and included them in a collective evacuation leaving from Canet-Plage on a trawler chartered by MI9.[8]

Phase 1 of assistance once again featured women. With one of their two motors out of service, the crew successfully landed the airplane around one in the morning near the village of Les Riceys, in the Aube. After having walked for part of the night, in the small hours they crossed paths with a peasant girl who warned them that twenty-five Germans were looking for them. She advised them to carry on in the same direction (towards Dijon). Around 5pm, the group stopped at a house to ask for water and provisions. A woman led them towards a neighboring house, where they were fed. After their meal, a man accompanied them for some way and warned them that 500 Germans were going to resume the search the next day. They slept in the woods and the next morning were received at a farm, where they were served a meal. There, they met a young boy on vacation from Paris, doubtless called by the farmers, who took them to the village of Channay, in Côte d'Or. They spent three more nights in the woods, a mere 15 kilometers from the place where their airplane had come down. Once these three days had come to an end, some farmers from Channay put them up in a barn in the farm's courtyard. Adding up the number of people who helped during this six-day phase of maximum alert yields two lone women and three couples, together with their children. Years later, rear machine gunner Pat Hickton recalled the solidarity of local inhabitants who, questioned by uniformed Germans and threatened with being shot, claimed they had seen nothing.[9] It was perhaps

THE SEQUENCES OF AID 143

with some exaggeration that Hickton added, "even the three or four-year-old kids looked them in the eye and said 'non'."

Phase 2 began when the young vacationer took two of the airmen, now outfitted with civilian clothing, to Paris. The "young boy" sought a contact. Fourteen days later, two men supplied with civilian clothing came to get the four remaining airmen. The crew was taken in hand by Parisian helpers, who supplied them with false papers, train and car transportation and had them cross the demarcation line in two separate groups at Vierzon and La Haye (Indre-et-Loire). In Vierzon, they crossed the Cher on foot. Still accompanied by escorts, the fugitives carried on until they reached Spain. The only snag in the voyage: Saxton, the airplane's navigator, who as a civilian had been a beer advertiser at Burton-on-Trent in Staffordshire, and Hickton, a railroad fireman from Manawatu, New Zealand, were arrested by two gendarmes before reaching Ste-Léocadie, at the foot of the Pyrenees. They were interned in the Free Zone but not given over to the occupiers. The Vichy government had not declared war on Britain and the Free Zone remained a "nonbelligerent" area until it was invaded in November 1942. But since Article 13 of the Hague Convention gave neutral powers the right to intern escaped prisoners of war present on their territory, starting in July 1940 the Vichy government opted for a policy of internment.[10]

This journey across France underscores the risk of simplification inherent to any effort of historical analysis, which necessarily carves up reality into convenient slices. Phase 2 may be defined as a form of assistance implemented by an as yet unnamed embryonic organization also engaged in gathering military intelligence and distributing leaflets produced elsewhere. At this stage, the group operated by seizing upon the various opportunities that presented themselves to harm the occupier. It had not specialized in evasion and was financed via its members' personal assets. But the case of the evasion assistance given the Wellington crew that came down in Les Riceys blurs the boundaries. In order to cross the occupied zone and the demarcation line, the group did indeed participate in phase 2. This was the case of the two men who came for the airmen in Les Riceys, André and Jacques Postel-Vinay. André also actively participated in S.R. Guerre's parallel intelligence network, an army intelligence service based in Vichy that supplied information to the British Intelligence Service. In the Free Zone, however, these helpers delivered the evaders over to an already established and structured network that extended as far as the départements of the Nord and Pas-de-Calais. This thus qualifies as level 3 evasion assistance. The group still possessed no name but was led by Ian Garrow, a Scottish officer who had himself evaded. Segments of variable maturity thus came together. The network branched out at the national scale.

The nascent organization based in Paris had thus already linked up in September 1941 with its better-established counterpart in Marseille. It was

Pierre d'Harcourt, a student at the École libre des sciences politiques, who first put the two in touch with one another. At the beginning of the 1940 academic year, d'Harcourt recruited his professor, André Postel-Vinay, to the Resistance. In January 1941, d'Harcourt had been called upon to help evacuate eight Seaforth Highlanders who found themselves stuck in Honfleur. Postel-Vinay helped him hide them in Paris. When he later drove them to Marseille, d'Harcourt became aware of Ian Garrow's efforts to set up an evasion network for British troops. In his memoirs, d'Harcourt estimates that he crossed the line or arranged for others to do so roughly forty times before his arrest in July 1941.[11] Postel-Vinay then succeeded him at the head of this as yet nameless network that would soon be integrated into that of Marseille. The transition from level 2 to level 3 of assistance activity thus took place in a gradual way, with the group's willing absorption into the older and more developed network. Garrow's group, for its part, reached level 3 as soon as it linked up with the northern départements in May 1941.[12] It was still on a precarious footing at this point, depending for its funding on local business figures, the Intelligence Service and Varian Fry. This initial group was at the origin of the "Pat O'Leary" network, one of France's largest evasion networks. Following Ian Garrow's arrest in October 1941, Albert Guérisse assumed leadership of the network. A Belgian military doctor, Guérisse went by the name Pat O'Leary and had previously worked for the SOE.

Back to Phase 1: The Perennial Source of Aid-Based Resistance

Lavishly funded by MI9, the "Pat Line" was typical of the established evasion networks, those I refer to as level 3. Cutting clear across France from Belgium to Spain, the network operated from 1941 to March 1943, when it was dismantled by the Gestapo. It was based on a territorial network of local volunteers, an inexhaustible source of energy. Though the network was ultimately brought down, with some of its members tortured and sent to concentration camps, its activities did not cease. In the southwestern region, the proprietor of a fashion boutique, Marie-Louise Dissard, took over the network's Toulouse-Pyrenees-Spain leg, with other networks seeing to the "packages" elsewhere.

The enduring sources of rescue activity are illustrated by a family from the Pas-de-Calais, the Fillerins. Hailing from the village of Renty, 20 kilometers from Toucquet, their case also is also worth considering as it demonstrates the limits of the history of organizations.[13] The Fillerins first worked for Ian Garrow and then his successor, Pat O'Leary. Following the latter's arrest in March 1943, they became involved in the Bordeaux-Loupiac organization, the OCM and others still. Fundamentally, the assistance they provided was "unaffiliated." It did not depend on a job offer from above or elsewhere but

Figure 6.3 Allied airmen harbored by the Fillerin family, Renty, Pas-de-Calais, September 1942. © Centre de ressources de La Coupole, Helfaut (Pas-de-Calais).
The Fillerin family harbored Forster, Barnard and Glensor, whose airplane came down on 16 September. The airmen are flanked by the mother and her two daughters. The German French-language poster specifies the punishments for this action: the death penalty or hard labor. The family's father, Norbert Fillerin, was arrested and deported in March 1943. The mother was arrested in January 1944 and imprisoned in Germany. Both survived. The three men made it back to London with the help of the Pat O'Leary network in early 1943. CNRD brochure. Supplementary online dossier.

rather on local solidarity with and a desire to provide immediate assistance to downed Allies as well as available opportunities for evacuating "packages."

The case of the Fillerin family was also typical in the prominent role that women played in it, as illustrated by the photo reproduced in this book (Figure 6.3), which features the Fillerin daughters, Geneviève and Monique, and their mother, Marguerite (at right). Dating from September 1942, the snapshot shows three airmen whose aircraft had come down a few days earlier. Taken in hand by the Pat O'Leary network, they reached London in January and April 1943. The smiling faces of the women helpers as they stood alongside their charges contrast with the text of the German poster ("Seeking British Airmen"), which lays out the repressive measures to be taken against those found to have harbored Allies. Clearly, the threat of repression

146   THE ORIGINS OF THE RESISTANCE

failed to dissuade this hearty family of helpers, who took pleasure in thumbing their nose at the occupier by posing next to the poster with the "objects of the crime." After their father was arrested in March 1943 and their mother in January 1944, the sisters and their little brother Gabriel remained active until the Liberation. Just after the war, the parents and their three children each received the title of helper. Without this abundance of local initiative, even such a professionalized and efficient network as "Pat" would have been almost completely ineffective.

The severity of the repression brought to bear on assistance to the Allies in the Incorporated Zone (Nord and Pas-de-Calais incorporated into Belgium with an eye to their future annexation) was based both on the German military code and the orders of General Niehoff, commander of the Lille Oberkommandantur. Rigorously applied by Luftwaffe tribunals, the penal code prescribed the death penalty. But the Wehrmacht's military tribunals preferred to apply the General's orders, which stipulated that assisting the British was "punishable by death *or* forced labor." As Laurent Thiéry notes in his book, the repression may have been less brutal in this case.[14] Nevertheless, the relative severity shown by military tribunals must be judged with an eye to the notion of "forced labor" as it was practiced in the Reich. It is generally agreed that the rate of return for prisoners sent to German prisons and concentration camps was around 60 percent. It is fortunate that both Fillerin parents survived their deportation. Ultimately, repression in the incorporated départements was arguably no less brutal than in Occupied France.

Women and Children First

The example of the Fillerin family and, in general, those drawn from phases 1 and 2 of evasion assistance shed light on several recurring traits. The first of these is the crucial role played by women. Without them, the first phase of assistance would not have taken place on such a scale. Their unfamiliarity with the terrain and ignorance of the country's language as well as their hunger and fatigue would have quickly got the better of the fugitives' willpower. In both Plestin-les-Grèves and Veules-les-Roses, men are nearly absent from this initial phase of assistance. In Les Riceys, women played a frontline role and, in Renty, a dominant one. This is no accident. The women were there in their traditional role as nurses and mothers. Though their action was politically meaningful, it was in this respect an extension of their gender role.

In 1940–41, the flow of evaded soldiers meant that the assistance of Channel coast women was particularly solicited. The case I mentioned above of the eight Seaforth Highlanders escorted by Pierre d'Harcourt offers yet another illustration of this. In their remarkable escape, Lieutenant Richard Broad and his seven Seaforth Highlanders – nicknamed by one of the helpers "Snow

THE SEQUENCES OF AID 147

White and the seven dwarves" –made it to Honfleur in July after escaping Saint-Valéry-en-Caux on 12 June. It was not until the following January that they gave up hope of crossing the Channel. For six months, the crew was given shelter by two women, a housewife from the Parisian bourgeoisie and a single woman who lived with twelve large sheepdogs, the two women having distributed the crew across their large homes. In January 1941, the crew members were handed over to escorts for the trip to Spain. Contact was made in characteristic fashion. Two factors triggered the decision to seek an external liaison: the realization that it would be impossible to cross the Channel by boat and a growing awareness of the high cost of caring for the eight men. The helper Nicole Bouchet de Fareins thus delivered a letter from the lieutenant seeking financial assistance to an acquaintance of Broad, a British banker in Paris. The banker saw no way to contribute but called upon a client, the young Prince André Poniatowski, who himself contacted Pierre d'Harcourt. The action of Joshua Campbell, director of the Paris office of Guaranty Trust, sheds light on one aspect of the French Resistance. The incremental assistance he supplied – that of contacting someone who might know someone who could fulfill the request – illustrates both how resistance was embedded in society and the manner in which it expanded by way of networks of acquaintance. Located at one extreme of a chain of relations (Broad – Bouchet de Fareins – Campbell – Poniatowski – d'Harcourt), Pierre d'Harcourt devised a way to escort the eight men to Paris and Marseille.[15] On 15 May 1941, they landed in Liverpool.

Among these Channel coast women must also be included the founder of "Sidonie's group," which joined the Georges France network in late 1940. Residing on the Island of Bréhat, Suzanne Wilborts succeeded in persuading France libre and the British Intelligence Service to take an interest in her project.[16] Created for the purpose of gathering intelligence, the group also helped evacuate Allied soldiers and airmen in 1940–42. It was members of this group who escorted the three airmen who came down in Plestin-les-Grèves to Nantes. Phase 2 was thus implemented here via the participation of a group resembling that of Rouen-St Aignan (both groups carried out espionage operations and helped Allied fugitives). But it was less ad hoc than its counterpart to the degree that it already had a name – the Sidonie/Georges France network – and was in direct contact with London. The destruction of Sidonie's group began with the repression of its Nantes and Côtes-du-Nord branch of helpers in November 1941.

After the war, little effort was made to acknowledge women's participation in the Resistance. In her book, *Le genre de la Résistance*, Catherine Lacour-Astol studied the origins of this negative discrimination.[17] Given the actual scale of resistance activity and the fact that, with the exception of maquis, the only available premises were private homes, it is hardly credible that only

12 percent of the Resistance's 260,000 volunteer combatants (CVR) were women. Female self-censorship, increasingly narrow criteria focused on military-type action and exclusively male award boards all contributed to this misunderstanding of the Resistance. In contrast with this massive under-representation, the 30 percent rate of women helpers present in Allied files seems more realistic, though it is still likely an underestimation. The fact of the matter is that all selection procedures tend to narrow the filter in keeping with a group dynamic that depends on the jury's preconceptions.

Resistance activities naturally permeated the life of the household, all generations included. Even when parents were able to conceal the presence of those they were harboring within the house, the resistance spirit of the household contributed to the political socialization of the children who lived there. Where airmen were concerned, the prestige of aeronautics – an as yet new and marvelous technology – only contributed to making an impression on the children, especially (but not only) little boys.[18] This fact held for all countries and expanded in the interwar years, as recently illustrated by Miyazaki's film, *Le vent se lève* (2013). A number of children's games were inspired by the air war. The following example is particularly revealing in this regard: even as Jean (nine years old) and Étienne (seven years old) were filling in the pages of their "crew book," their mother was hiding or had just hidden three airmen who had come down on the beach of St-Efflam in the Plestin-les-Grèves commune. Hostility towards the occupier was quietly expressed by use of the term "boche," made commonplace by the First World War. The German military post was called the "boche post" and pleasure in mocking the conqueror may be read in the exclamation, "how it makes us laugh when we think that it [the airplane] came down right under the boche's nose." The familiar expression, "under the nose of," regularly recurred during the Occupation. It did not necessarily indicate a spirit of resistance but rather the pleasure of playing what was a relatively harmless trick in ridiculing or even mocking the forces of occupation. This rebellious spirit could lead to incivility (severely punished by the occupier) or indeed resistance.

This familial dimension is one of the factors that differentiates the Resistance from other modes of political engagement. A sociology of the Resistance that privileges official surveys (lacking children and heavily biased in favor of men) would not be meaningless but would overlook almost half the story. Its share of women and children structured the Resistance into clusters of families. At this level, the collective responsibility of involvement weighed heavily when repression struck. The lives of those who remained – the children whose parents were shot or deported, as was the case of the mother of these children, who was arrested in April 1942 and never returned from Ravensbrück – were not simply permeated by the Resistance. For them, the Resistance represented an existential caesura.

Repression: Dissuasive or Incentivizing?

The history of efforts to put down the Resistance is at once well known and unfamiliar. We know, for example, the overall number of those deported as a result of repression: around 90,000 men and women. But we do not precisely know how many of them were arrested for acts of resistance. They represented between 50 and 75 percent of the total. Around 40 percent of them never returned. We moreover know how many were shot as hostages or sentenced to death: around 4,000. But we do not know how many people were imprisoned by the Germans or the Vichy government on political grounds, the number of those tortured or even the number of civilians killed on French territory by these two authorities.[19] Moreover, the history of the repression has developed independently of the history of the Resistance. Efforts to chart the course taken by members of a resistance group or organization as they passed through the labyrinth of the Reich's courts, prisons and camps exist only in outline or in the form of overall figures. It is true that the Germans and, in particular, the Gestapo destroyed their archives en masse in 1944–45 but there are many traces and victim accounts allowing for research in this area.

While the history of repression falls outside the scope of the present study, the fate of the three groups examined in this chapter is of interest from several points of view. On the one hand, it allows us to take stock of the severity with which repressive measures were applied starting with the first months of the Occupation. On the other, it offers us an opportunity to assess the dissuasive effect of arrests on evasion assistance activities. The tragedies resulting from this repression are profoundly etched in the memory of the Resistance and to this day influence our understanding of it. Though distorting, moreover, German sources constitute a revealing mirror of resistance involvement.

The repression we shall study in this chapter is limited to its initial wave: that overseen by the Wehrmacht before the SS was given de facto supreme responsibility in the area with the arrival of Carl Oberg in Paris. The latter took up residence in the capital in May 1942 with the title "Higher SS and Police Leader" (*HSSPf, Höhere SS- und Polizeiführer*) for France. But as Gaël Eismann has shown, the first phase of repression was no less brutal for coming first and was inspired by Germano-Nazi principles foreign to the liberal rule of law.[20] As we saw in the first part of this book in connection with the repression of the resistance to invasion offered by the gardes territoriaux, the German military tribunals applied what may be described as Germano-Nazi law. It was Germanic law in the sense that the German Army had not integrated the clauses of the Hague conventions (1907) into its orders. Ratified in Geneva in 1929, the Convention in some cases authorized the population of a non-occupied territory to put up armed resistance against an invader. And it was Nazi law due to its indifference to the law of occupied peoples. Beginning in summer 1940, young men who attempted to cross the Channel by boat in

150 THE ORIGINS OF THE RESISTANCE

order to reach England were thus sentenced to death and executed for "high treason." It was also Nazi law to the degree that it possessed only fictitious value – when the "ruling" was not itself merely a masquerade meant for propaganda, that is. The Party and the SS were at pains to eliminate their enemies on their own terms and this whether they had been given a sentence or not. In his book, *The Dual State*, which was published in the summer of 1941 after he had taken refuge in the United States, the jurist Ernst Fraenkel showed the inner workings of this mechanism.[21] In the occupied Europe of the time, however, the dualism examined by the jurist had largely been eclipsed by the monopoly of arbitrary Nazi rule. Over the course of the Occupation, military tribunals were directly responsible for only 11 percent of all deportations and this despite the fact that they were applying thoroughly Nazified law.[22] The rest were decided without a ruling.

On the basis of the two examples of Veules-les-Roses and Plestin-les-Grèves, the human death toll of repression proved very heavy.[23] Among the fifty-four people arrested, fifteen were killed, including one by firing squad, four by beheading and ten from exhaustion in prison or KL, including six women.[24] Most of these legally sanctioned murders only came to light following Germany's capitulation. If one wishes to measure the intimidatory effect of this repression, one must discover what information was available to families under the Occupation. It was already sufficiently upsetting. Of fifty-four defendants, eighteen were sentenced to death – one of them was immediately shot at Mont-Valérien, and thirty-seven (among whom the seventeen others condemned to death) deported to Germany. In 1941–42, French people were still largely unfamiliar with survival conditions in German prisons (often industrial labor camps) and concentration camps. For family morale, however, "deportation," though yet to be referred to as such, represented an additional blow. A portion of these deportees – seventeen in all – were classified "NN," or "Nacht und Nebel," a status that prohibited families from being supplied with any information so as to inspire a kind of terror by disappearance. NN were to disappear "without a trace." To various degrees, some sixty families thus found themselves plunged into the suffering of absence and material difficulty after one of their own had been arrested. About 200 people found themselves the collateral victims of repression. Was this enough to intimidate the population and stifle their good will or did the indignation it provoked, to the contrary, stoke resistance?

What exactly was the case? One finds signs of these moments of hesitation that followed the direct experience of repression. In the report she prepared after the war, Geneviève Fillerin cites two moments of interruption or slackening in the family's assistance activity. The first was between 1941 and "early 1942" and was due to the first wave of arrests that took place in early December in Lille, St-Omer and Paris as a consequence of agent "Paul's" betrayals. The second followed the arrest of her mother in January 1944, at which time Geneviève and her sister found it difficult to resume their assistance activity: "It was all rather difficult because, seeing what had happened, the friends who had helped before Mother's arrest no longer wanted to do anything."[25] The young woman did not indicate any difficulty following the arrest of her father but perhaps this is because her mother was in charge.

But among those imprisoned one also finds signs of redoubled commitment in response to adversity. For some of them, the reduction to impotence at the hands of the enemy inspired them to retaliate in remarkable and quite literally extraordinary ways, acts that were at once celebrated far beyond the walls of the prison and contributed to the aura of the Resistance. Without wishing to do so, the example offered by these victims and, at times, martyrs of repression was itself a form of propaganda and testament of faith in the Resistance.

Traces of this may be found in the text of the sentences handed down in the case of the women of Veules-les-Roses. Very gendered and stamped with hostility, this document nevertheless gives one a glimpse of the defendants' resolution vis-à-vis their judges. As it notes in regards to one defendant:

> She is an attractive person, a pleasant woman, cunning, determined, educated, a self-confident and fanatical Frenchwoman who conceals nothing of her hatred for all that is German and her love for England. We thus find the following sentence in one of the letters she sent (Volume II, Annex III): "The French should not dream of killing the women and children of the Germans and Italians." In a letter intercepted in prison (Protocol Annex), she writes: "Supposing that we should be executed, I wonder if our example would really have a point, if an ever-growing number of new people find a way to follow our path. For my part, I think that I've done my duty as a soldier ..."[26]

Notwithstanding the remarks of this uniformed Wehrmacht jurist, the writings of the defendant do not seem stamped with hate-filled Germanophobia but rather inspired by feelings that are entirely human and even tinged with doubt. To see hatred and fanaticism in them requires one to have been blinded by a Germano-Nazi reading imbued with the superiority of the Aryan man in colonized territory. Two other women in this trial were also described as "fanatics" and one was even said to be "hysterical." In keeping with the canons of misogynist analysis, no male defendant was subjected to the same description. Yet it seems that this depreciation of feminine involvement was not a matter of unanimous agreement within the court. In an intercepted correspondence, the defendant Renée Guitton described the counsel for the prosecution as a "wonderful man." She describes him as saying that the battle would not have been won as rapidly in June 1940 if the Wehrmacht had had to fight "such brave, faithful and selfless" women as these.[27] Several defendants thus laid claim to their patriotic faith before a tribunal that could sentence them to death for doing so. A more commonplace attitude would have been – and often was – to hide behind what one hoped (wrongly) to be attenuating circumstances, such as the humane sentiments provoked by Allied soldiers in distress. Of the twelve death sentences that resulted from this trial, five were handed to women, including the three so-called fanatics above.

As soon as it was transmitted by the word of mouth of civil society, news of the defiant conduct of some defendants and the severity of the sentences imposed upon them added to the remarkable aura surrounding the Resistance. Upon returning home, the four detainees (men and women alike) who had been set free out of twenty-eight arrested wasted no time in speaking of their experience. Not surprisingly, the Wehrmacht was eager to put an end to the unwanted publicity this offered resistance activity. Adopted in December 1941, Marshal Keitel's decree creating the status of *Nacht und Nebel* (NN) was partly a response to the threat of proselytism that the trials presented. Particularly targeting assistance to members of the enemy armed forces, Keitel's decree and accompanying letter stipulated that the only dissuasive measure consists in the death penalty, rapidly executed, or disappearance without a trace by means of secret deportation to Germany.

The assistance given refugees in Les Riceys offers an example of a type of repression that caused resistance activity to leave the rails of ordinary engagement. It was not levels 1 and 2 of assistance that were concerned here but level 3, that of the Parisian branch of an established network. The repression originated, not in the arrest of fugitives and their helpers, but rather in a deliberate act of paid betrayal. The emergence of this phenomenon in Lille and Paris starting in December 1941 points to the advent of a market of helpers for sale and thereby reveals the extent of aid in these regions. The betrayal in question was the work of Harold Cole, an English agent of the network who went by the nickname "Paul." Following the arrest of its previous leader, the network had adopted the name Pat O'Leary in October 1941. As we saw above, the segment of the network established in Paris by Pierre d'Harcourt and André Postel-Vinay had merged with the older and better-financed (thanks in particular to MI9) Marseille network.

The story of Harold Cole has all the makings of fiction. A word must be said about his trajectory even though little is known about it as he died before his trial could begin, having been killed in a clash with French police as they attempted to arrest him in January 1946.[28] Born in London's East End, his main concern seems to have been to secure a life of comfort for himself on the basis of women and money. After several stints in prison for fraud, in 1939 he was drafted into the British Expeditionary Corps. He deserted at the time of Dunkirk and took up residence in the home of a woman whose husband had been taken prisoner. Called upon to help hide the British soldiers wandering the region, he presented himself as having been sent by the Intelligence Service. Having become a regular helper, he helped escort evaders between Lille and the Ian Garrow group in Marseille and expanded his contacts in Paris. But this helper was also a crook who put the funds entrusted him by the

THE SEQUENCES OF AID 153

network to personal use. In October 1941, he was unmasked and threatened by Pat O'Leary in Marseille. Cole fled to Lille, where he resumed his activities. On 6 December he was arrested in the company of his landlady by the Geheime Feldpolizei (GFP), the police force of the Abwehr, or German counter-espionage. Between 7 and 14 December, there followed a series of arrests in Lille and Paris, some of them in his presence. It seems that turning him was the work of just a few hours for the GFP, who offered him a new source of income and protection against other members of the Resistance. Fully versed in the workings of the network, "Paul" chose the objects of his commerce. In Lille, between eleven and thirty-five men and women were handed over; in Paris, there were between three and seven of them.[29] That was just the beginning but what followed falls outside of the present discussion.

In Paris, "Paul" included two choice bits in his first delivery: Fernand Holweck, a director of research at the CNRS and research physicist at the Curie laboratory, and André Postel-Vinay, a high-ranking civil servant and auditor at the Treasury. They were respectively arrested on 11 and 14 December and taken to the German headquarters at La Santé.[30] Holweck was almost immediately tortured. On 17 December, he was found hanging in his cell but was resuscitated. He died on 21 December after a second suicide attempt. On the same 17 December, Postel-Vinay also attempted to kill himself, throwing himself from a third-floor balustrade. Wrongly fearing he had left a coded address book at home, he did not want to run the risk of talking under torture. Despite broken bones, he survived.

In his Note, the German captain responsible for this part of the prison reported to his superior to explain why two prisoners meant to be placed on a convoy for the Lille Geheime Feldpolizei could not be transported. This text, which in its sobriety attempts to cast the occupier in a "decent" (korrekt) light, is all the more valuable for what it does not say. The German doctor who was "immediately called" left Postel-Vinay without care and handcuffed on a board for three days. Suffering at once from the effects of torture and strangulation, Holweck doubtless shared the same fate. On 20 December, the two men were taken half-conscious to the German wing of La Pitié hospital. Following a second suicide attempt, Holweck died on the 21st. Nine months later and still walking with difficulty, Postel-Vinay succeeded in escaping. Taken in hand by his own network, he was evacuated from Canet-Plage on 21 September 1942, as part of one of the network's four maritime exfiltration operations. That night, as he crouched in the dunes waiting for the clandestine embarkation that was to transport around thirty men to freedom, Postel-Vinay was surprised to come across Hickton and Saxton, the airmen he had gone to fetch in Les Riceys a year earlier.

As with the nearly sacrificial patriotism shown by the women of the Veules-les-Roses trial, hand-to-mouth reports of Holweck's martyrdom and the heroism of the two prisoners of La Santé immediately contributed to the

154   THE ORIGINS OF THE RESISTANCE

Resistance's image as a cause transcending ordinary commitment. These acts of extreme resistance immediately resonated. According to the historian Michel Pinault, Holweck's death marked a turning point in the life of the Parisian university.[31] As Fernand Holweck's body had been returned to his family, his funeral ceremony in the church of Montrouge was well-attended, with several bouquets of tricolor flowers laid in homage. The underground newspaper of the Front national universitaire, *L'Université libre*, published an article on Holweck and other tributes were paid him over the course of 1942.

"People said nothing but horror was written on every face"

Did these extraordinary acts help broaden resistance? In any case, they contributed to the unpopularity of the occupier. Repression may frighten people but it can also stimulate their commitment by provoking indignation. The occupier was himself aware of this. Two good examples of this phenomenon may be found in the measures taken to crack down on assistance to the enemy.

In the Nord and Pas-de-Calais, the extreme severity shown by Luftwaffe tribunals against the helpers ultimately became a source of concern for the German military command of Belgium and the Incorporated Zone (Nord and Pas-de-Calais). The latter administration and, with it, the German military tribunals of the same jurisdiction, which also answered to the German Army, criticized the Luftwaffe judges for ignoring the requirements of the policy of Collaboration.[32] In July 1942, the open conflict between the Army and the Luftwaffe made its way all the way to Berlin. Territorial officials feared that the cycle of provocation and repression would spread. Their fears for what this might mean for the maintenance of order were sharpened by the fact that the incorporation of these départements into Belgium was in principle a step towards their annexation by the Reich.

The other example of a conflict of interpretation over the effects of repression comes from the Occupied Zone. There, German military tribunals did not feel the same hesitation as in the Incorporated Zone and freely dispensed the death penalty, as we saw in the Veules-les-Roses and "thirty Bretons" trials. Signed by the German military commander in France, von Stülpnagel, in September 1941, the decision made public through posters announced an intensification of repression: summary execution for men, deportation to concentration camps for women and bounties for those who denounced them. In the eyes of the SS, however, these measures were insufficiently severe. It was in this way that the Militärbefehlshaber (MBF) came into conflict with a decision taken by the recently created SS authority in France. For the MBF, the creation of this competing authority represented a *capitis deminutio* but it was also worried about the boomerang effect that be might be produced by these ferocious new SS measures. Curiously, the conflict between the general

THE SEQUENCES OF AID 155

from Lille and the Luftwaffe under his jurisdiction was exactly contemporaneous with the conflict between the general from Paris and the SS of the Occupied Zone. The month of July 1942 represented a new stage in the history of the repression.

Though it ultimately played a role in their application, the MBF was displeased when new methods for repressing sabotage were publicized in the corridors of the Paris metro and the newspapers of the Occupied Zone in July 1942 (Figure 6.4).[33] These new measures included executing all close male relatives of the guilty party, sentencing their close female relatives to forced labor and interning their children in reform schools. These measures of summer 1942 principally targeted those who carried out attacks but also covered "acts of sabotage." As the 10 October 1940 German decree regarding "protection against acts of sabotage" stipulated, assistance to Allied soldiers and airmen figured among these acts.

This notice, which earned Oberg the nickname "the butcher of Paris," did not go unremarked. As Jean Guéhenno noted in his journal for 10 July:

> For some time now, our guests have been committing their crimes in silence. They have been executing people every day in the prisons but no notice was published. Just today they were tempted by publicity once again, as if not having the glory of all their crimes was finally beginning to weigh on them. At five o'clock in the corridors of the République metro station, I saw a crowd gathering around an already-ripped yellow poster. People said nothing but horror was written on every face. It was so badly torn it was hard to read. But fifty yards away, another gathering. And this time the poster was intact. It's an announcement by the head of SS in France, who, moreover, does not give his name. He first addresses his revolting compliments to the great mass of the population for its discipline at work and good conduct but, he explains, the sabotage committed by a few obliges him to take new measures; since the saboteurs run away and hide, he has therefore decided: [there follows a summary of the measures to be taken][34]

Whatever the effect of repression on the decision to engage in resistance, the number of helpers continuously grew between 1940 and 1944. Of course, the number of downed airmen also grew. One must calculate the month-to-month relationship between the number of airmen assisted and the number of those taken prisoner over the course of the Occupation. This work has been done for the Nord-Pas-de-Calais. The curves show that, despite the intensification of bombing, the proportion of RAF airmen who evaded relative to those taken prisoner constantly increased over the course of the Occupation.[35] From summer 1943 to summer 1944, the number of evaders sometimes even exceeded that of those taken prisoner. The curve for USAAF airmen exhibits the same progression, albeit somewhat less sharply. In a general way, the scenario below, presented in Map 6.1, nicely captures the growth of the assisting population as the number of Allied personnel in flight increased.

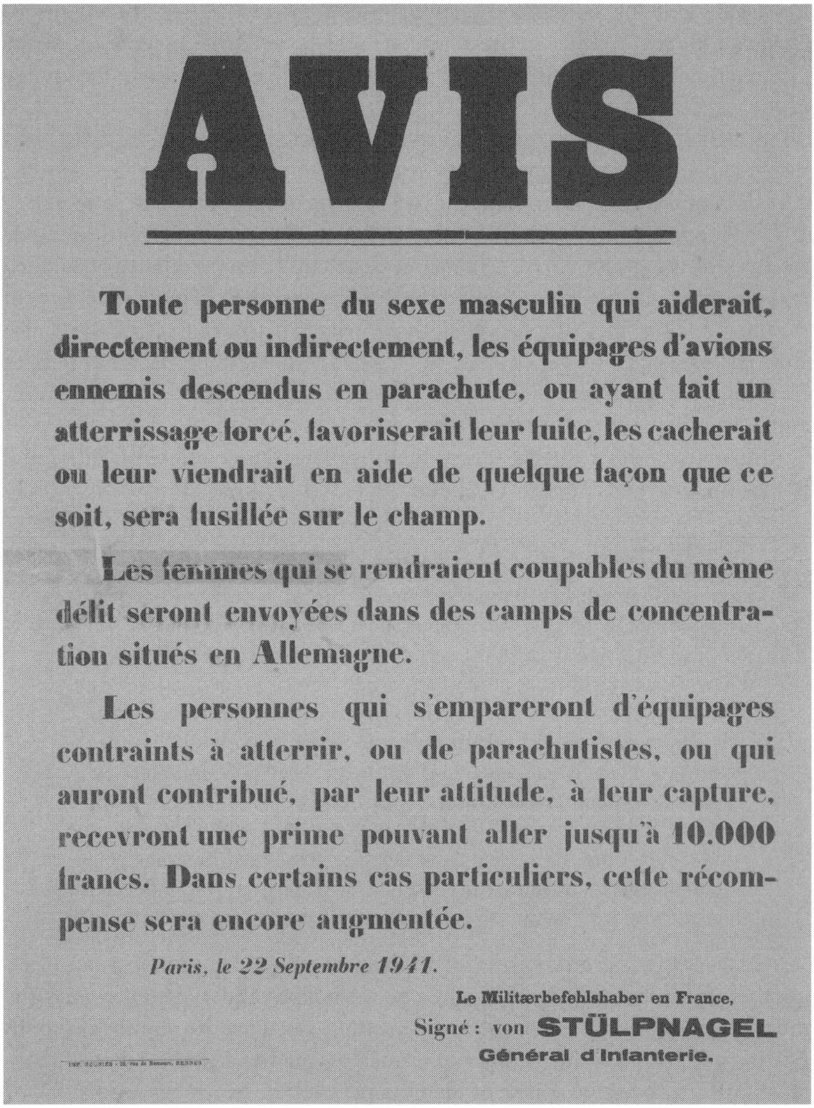

AVIS

Toute personne du sexe masculin qui aiderait, directement ou indirectement, les équipages d'avions ennemis descendus en parachute, ou ayant fait un atterrissage forcé, favoriserait leur fuite, les cacherait ou leur viendrait en aide de quelque façon que ce soit, sera fusillée sur le champ.

Les femmes qui se rendraient coupables du même délit seront envoyées dans des camps de concentration situés en Allemagne.

Les personnes qui s'empareront d'équipages contraints à atterrir, ou de parachutistes, ou qui auront contribué, par leur attitude, à leur capture, recevront une prime pouvant aller jusqu'à **10.000** francs. Dans certains cas particuliers, cette récompense sera encore augmentée.

Paris, le 22 Septembre 1941.

Le Militærbefehlshaber en France,

Signé : von **STÜLPNAGEL**

Général d Infanterie.

Figure 6.4 Stepped-up repression. German poster, 22 September 1941. © Archives nationales (France). Repression for harboring Allied airmen intensifies. Provision had been made for the death penalty since 1940 (decree of 24 August in the North and Pas-de-Calais "rattachés" and 10 and 14 October in occupied France). The poster specified the form this would take: summary execution for men, deportation to concentration camps for women. In addition, those who denounced them were to receive a bounty of 10,000 francs.

THE SEQUENCES OF AID 157

Escapers & evaders in occupied Europe by year
(1940–1945)

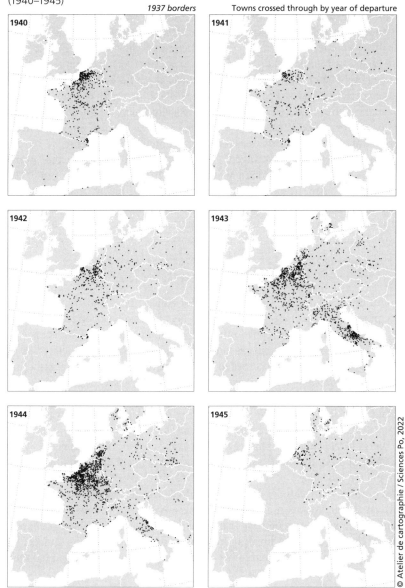

Map 6.1 Escapers and evaders in occupied Europe by year, 1940–45.
Source: TNA, WO 208, 3297–3307.

Arranged by year of departure, these six maps show the places in Western Europe through which "escapers" and "evaders" passed before successfully reaching England. The map shows how the number of such places – and thus the number of helpers – clearly increased between 1940 and 1943. The fact that there were fewer for 1944 is due to the gradual liberation of France.

1940 was a foundational year. The map for that year reveals a series of clusters: in the northwestern quarter of France, along the demarcation line, the Rhone corridor, the coast as far as Perpignan and in the Pyrenees. One may also make out the Toulouse route. Paradoxically, there would be even more dots on the maps for 1942–44 if the escape networks had not grown. In these years, escape route accounts were often interrupted with this sentence: "From here on, my journey was arranged." The effect is to supply no further information as to the towns through which the airman passed. Futhermore, the paths taken by American airmen are not represented on the map, nor those taken by hidden Allies who did not succeed in escaping from France. If all places of shelter were represented, the magnitude of the clandestine migration of thousands of young men across Europe would be even more visible.

Civilians at War

To sum up, phase 1 of evasion assistance for Allied troops and crews gave rise to a practice of resistance and phase 2 geographically extended it. These nascent acts of resistance contributed to the emergence of the Resistance as a national movement. There is reason to believe that the same principles led to the creation of organizations devoted to other activities (intelligence-gathering and propaganda, for example, or sabotage) and they also depended on the initiative of volunteers. Yet the case of sabotage – the most dangerous and brutally repressed activity, to which the occupier responded with a policy of hostage-taking – is perhaps more complex. There was no clear link between the very local, "elusive sabotage" that was carried out throughout the Occupation and the little sabotage groups that were first established by national organizations in 1941–42.[36] It was the "Green Plan," launched in collaboration with London on D-Day, that consummated the encounter between the grassroots movement and these top-down actions. The mythic image of the volunteers of Year II is nevertheless not out of place in characterizing the subterranean uprising in all its varied manifestations. Indeed, by drawing upon the revolutionary image of Valmy, Resistance propaganda often capitalized on the precedent of 1792.

As a form of resistance, Allied evasion assistance also has the merit of revealing the flimsiness of categories constructed a posteriori. Though it represented a useful advance in the historiography when first introduced, the notion of "civilian resistance" here reveals its limits. Since the 1990s, the historiography of the Resistance has expanded its purview to cover acts that, though opposed to the occupier, did not for all that involve direct assaults upon him. These include such actions as listening to the BBC, deliberate negligence at work, public incivility and demonstrations – all severely repressed activities. To this must be added the help given Jewish children and adults, a form of resistance that had formerly been pigeonholed as "humanitarian" and neglected as such.[37] It is now fully part of the academic history of the Resistance. As this assistance to the persecuted was not systematically repressed, in contrast to that given the Allies, the concept of "civilian resistance" is more pertinent here.[38] As soon as they were identified, however, the evasion assistance networks that endeavored to exfiltrate Jewish children and adults to Switzerland or Spain were vigorously repressed. Indeed, such was the violence of this repression that the notion of "civilian" resistance still appears inadequate.

Jacques Semelin's 1989 book, *Unarmed against Hitler*, played an important role in promoting the concept of civilian resistance.[39] At the time of its publication, the book helped underscore the phenomenon of unarmed resistance and thereby counterbalance a representation of the Resistance that was excessively centered on its military aspect. As part of the same revival of interest in society as a whole, François Marcot distinguished the Resistance as a movement from the Resistance as an organization.[40] More recently, Jacques Semelin has argued for separating "social reactivity" from "organized action."[41] One advantage of approaching the Resistance from the perspective of collective behavior is that it offers a counterweight to the organizational and institutional history of the Resistance. The organizational point of view is of course not without interest. But by adopting it in too exclusive a fashion, one risks neglecting the particular context in which this story took place, a context that made organizations particularly dependent on society at large. The study of resistance movements can sometimes even verge on caricature, coming to resemble the history of political parties in times of peace and freedom. By contrast, adopting a bottom-up approach that focuses on the process of engagement encourages one to more closely attend to the particular context and the everyday experience with which it was associated.

But the evasion assistance supplied the Allies blurs the lines. Was this a species of civilian resistance because unarmed and fundamentally implemented by civil society? Or was it a form of military resistance to the degree that its beneficiaries were military personnel and it was repressed by the Germans as an act of war? "Aiding the enemy" and "harboring members of an enemy army" were often punished by the death penalty (see Figure 6.5) or – what was very often the same thing – hard labor in Nazi camps and prisons. It is unknown how many were imprisoned for "aiding the enemy" but we do know that nearly 15 percent of helpers, or roughly 4,600 men and women, were deported.[42] Fewer than two thirds returned. Due to the central role played by the household in this type of resistance (a role reflected in the

Figure 6.5   "ZUM TODE": To death. © Centre de ressources de La Coupole, Helfaut, Pas-de-Calais. With these posted notices, the occupying forces informed the population of its repressive measures. After having come down over the territory of Beussent (Pas-de-Calais) on 16 August 1941, Polish RAF pilot Alexandre Franczak was hidden for two months by the village mayor Irénée Chevalier, its parish priest Georges Haudiquet, and a woman from the neighboring village. Discovered in January, the two men were sentenced to death and executed in the moat of the fortress of Arras on 14 May 1942.

Nazi practice of collective responsibility), roughly a quarter of those deported shared their fate with a spouse or adult child.[43] Several adolescent minors were also deported. Such was the case of Michèle Agniel, who worked as an escort for the Bourgogne network and had yet to turn eighteen at the time of her arrest in April 1944. She was deported at the same time as her mother and father, who had also helped put up Allied airmen in Saint-Mandé. After being roughed up by the Milice, her little brother, just twelve years old, was handed over to a distant relative. Their father never returned.

But if the expression "civilian resistance" falls short due to the radical asymmetry of the conflict, much the same might be said of all resistance activities, with the exception of armed struggle. How can one describe as "civilian" a nonviolent action that is nevertheless repressed with the brutality of an army in the midst of battle? In response to the May–June 1941 miners' strike in the Nord and Pas-de-Calais, the occupier carried out a number of executions, including the decapitation of a woman, and deported nearly

300 miners. Clearly, civilian resistance could require that one's moral commitment be as strong as steel and that one accept combat. The asymmetry between the bare-fisted resistance of citizens and the armed repression of the occupier is simply too great to allow one to readily apply the adjective "civilian." Or, if one does use it, it should be placed in inverted commas to indicate that, in this context, civilian action was tantamount to entering unarmed into an armed struggle. As one of the Veules-les-Roses defendants wrote from her cell, "I believe I've done my duty as a soldier." In the Resistance, experienced as a federation of citizen-soldiers, the divide between civilian and military life was not so clear-cut. As an historian named Marc Bloch wrote in the summer of 1940, "I hope, in any case, we still have blood to spill."[44] Until then, Bloch had never stood out for his militancy; for his "civil" resistance, he was to die under a hail of German bullets. One might speak of "civic" or "citizen" resistance in the sense that the *res publica* in which those who were involved in resistance were able to recognize one another was not that of occupied France or even Vichy. But then that is the general definition of resistance engagement. To call it "civic resistance" would be redundant. Resistance, armed or not, and civilian warfare are synonymous.

7

A Civil Society against Two States

Drawing upon a field analysis – that of the concrete spatial framework in which evasion-assistance actions arose – we have seen how, despite many setbacks, a collective local dynamic rapidly expanded, gradually giving rise to a national-level resistance network. The study of the repression has shed light on the warlike and thus political dimension of these actions of inter-Allied clandestine solidarity. Another way to bring out the political commitment underlying these apparently humanitarian acts is to change scale and take into account the moral, material and national context that accompanied these collective behaviors and that on the face of it should have hampered their development. Evasion assistance did not develop in a peaceful and neutral universe but rather against a backdrop of destruction and mourning caused by Allied bombings and in opposition to a media sphere fully committed to the anti-Allied cause. A paradoxical situation, in short, one that reveals the helpers' social autonomy vis-à-vis the French and German authorities.

Until now, we have focused on the society of helpers and their supportive social environment. A more complete picture should include the burial of fallen airmen and the flowering of their graves which were the occasion of thousands of popular, not always silent, demonstrations. Moreover, a picture of French society as a whole should include the professional and occasional informers, paid or not by the Abwehr or the SD, who denounced the helpers. This is where we lack information. French double agents, *V-Männer* or *W-Personen*, infiltrated the networks and caused most of the arrests. Carelessness and bad luck did the rest. Unfortunately, neither the tributes to the airmen killed in action nor denunciations and treasons have been studied yet on a national scale.

Focusing on the Frame of Experience Rather than Motivations

The Resistance may be seen as at once product and cause of civil society – that is, a society relatively independent of the two states that governed its living space. By its action, the Resistance indicated that a minority of citizens, perhaps even a majority, were restive under the new order that had been imposed upon them by Nazi Germany and the Vichy government. The

A CIVIL SOCIETY AGAINST TWO STATES 163

question has often been raised of why some resisted – that is, actively rebelled – while others did not, as has the question of why some did so very early on and others very late. This is the question of motive.

Psychologists have spent much of the past two centuries trying to answer the question of motive. Dozens of theories have been developed to account for the concept of motive, none of them of much value for the purposes of the present discussion. Either the debate intersects with the philosophical issue of free will and determinism, its arguments supported by what are, from an historian's point of view, disconcertingly simple examples, or motive is dissected into the various phases that characterize an action, its definition appearing relatively tautological.[1]

In studying the Resistance, it is useful to take a political sociological approach, particularly as it has been elaborated in social movement research. In what concerns the issue of motivation, however, such analyses are based on an a posteriori classification that does not address the question of "why some and not the others." One separates the demand for protest from its supply and distinguishes between three types of motive: an instrumental motive, or participation in the aim of influencing the social and political environment; identification with the other participants and organizers; and expressiveness, or participation as a way of expressing one's opinions and feelings.[2] The analysis thus focuses on a moment subsequent to the initial engagement – that is, a time when the choice has already been made. Moreover, while it neatly applies to the democracies that supply the terrain for these studies, it has greater difficulty accounting for dictatorial systems in which the cost and conditions of engagement are very different.

How is one to identify the principle of resistance? For a time, historians debated the motives of those involved in resistance. Were they patriots or anti-fascists? The *Dictionnaire historique de la Résistance* adopted and examined these terms, adding a category for resisto-Vichyists.[3] Each of its contributions reveals the limits of these categories. Patriotism was invoked as often in Vichy as it was in London. Anti-fascism had been in crisis since Munich, with former anti-fascists involved in Collaboration and even figuring among the collaborationists, to say nothing of the effects of the Hitler-Stalin Pact on the communists. Early in the Occupation, even such well-known members of the Resistance as Henri Frenay (Combat) and Jacques Ripoche (CDLL) advanced partly Vichyist arguments in their underground papers. The distinctions in question are nevertheless useful for deconstructing the phenomenon as a whole. To these must be added a category for anti-Nazism. Curiously, this word is absent from French dictionaries such as *Le Petit Robert* and the *Trésor de la langue française*. In contrast to anti-fascism, which arose within an organized political milieu, that of the 1930s left, French anti-Nazism had no developed social existence before 1940. Though it was expressed by such thinkers as Robert d'Harcourt, father to the same Pierre d'Harcourt we

164   THE ORIGINS OF THE RESISTANCE

encountered in the previous chapter, anti-Nazism had no organized social base. Under the Occupation, its best representative was doubtless the clandestine publication, *Cahiers du Témoignage chrétien*. Whatever the case and useful though they may be, these labels – patriotism, anti-fascism and anti-Nazism – do not account for the transition to action.

Instead of surveying opinions, a less ambitious but more reliable way of proceeding would be to consider the experiential framework of those who assisted the Allies. This framework reveals what they were opposing and thus illustrates both the direction and the intensity of their involvement. In the case of evasion assistance, it would moreover be very difficult to assign labels to those who engaged in this type of resistance since no underground publications were associated with it. This is perhaps significant in its own right. The fact of exclusively engaging in action suggests that the need for action was perceived as urgent; from this perspective, the idea of using pamphlets to "influence the social and political environment," as it is termed in sociology, may appear of secondary importance and even derisory. The itinerary of the philosopher Jean Cavaillès sheds light on the fact that, even within the Resistance itself, there was a growing awareness that the enemy needed to be dealt a crushing blow: after helping write the newspaper *Libération* in the Occupied Zone, Cavaillès headed an intelligence-gathering network and ultimately took direct action, carrying out a sabotage mission.[4] He was subsequently arrested, tortured and ultimately executed in April 1944.

This sense of urgency is one of the distinctive traits of the helper's experience of resistance. Otherwise, the helpers shared with all other inhabitants the everyday experience of living under a double dictatorship. But certain aspects of this context especially concerned them, in particular the expansion of Allied bombing and anti-Allied propaganda.

Allied Bombs Cheered from the Balcony, 1940–1942

In her book on official propaganda in France from 1940 to 1944, Dominique Rossignol showed the preponderant place occupied by the anti-Anglo-Saxon theme – well ahead of anti-Bolshevik propaganda, which occupied half as much space, or the third most prominent theme, that of the "fatherland."[5] This assessment is based on an examination of the iconographic stock produced by the German and Vichy authorities, including images, pamphlets, posters, caricatures and posted bills. The same proportion presumably held for books, brochures, newspaper articles and the news reels shown in cinemas. To the degree that it took place in complete opposition to this framework, the helpers' action attests to the existence of an invisible and autonomous society standing apart from the official society of authorized media.

The continuity and expansion of the assistance supplied the Allies over the duration of the Occupation has been established. Yet this continuity covers

A CIVIL SOCIETY AGAINST TWO STATES 165

two successive political contexts. Paradoxically, it was perhaps easier to help fugitives in 1940–41, when it seemed mad to hope, than in 1943–44, when the likelihood of Allied victory was becoming apparent. With the rapid expansion of Allied bombing starting in 1943, the scale of destruction and human loss presented a challenge for those engaged in resistance. The British historians Samuel Kitson and Andrew Knapp have already remarked upon the protests they addressed to the Allies but I would like to revisit the question more specifically as it concerns the helpers.[6]

Until 1942, British bombing was above all concentrated on ports and other military objectives. The deaths caused by the RAF between September 1940 and late 1942 would ultimately represent less than 10 percent of civilian bombing victims in France over the duration of the war.[7] In this period, the bloodiest episodes of bombing took place in Boulogne-Billancourt (3 March 1942: 400 dead) and Saint-Nazaire (9 November 1942: 200 dead). The enthusiasm with which French people greeted the arrival of RAF airplanes, their transports of joy, were so broadly shared that they were expressed without fear. Civilian losses were even slightly increased by passersby who remained in the street to wave handkerchiefs or applaud their hoped-for liberators from balconies.[8] To the collaborators' surprise, the loss and destruction caused by the RAF even reinforced pro-English sentiment among the population. This is noted in contemporaneous reports by prefects and the writings of the time, whether private diaries or accounts published by witnesses who made their way to London or the United States. Two politically moderate British observers who lived in France from 1939 to 1942 thus unequivocally claimed that, even when families were directly affected, these tragedies in no way affected their "feelings of friendship and admiration for England."[9]

After taking refuge in the United States in 1943, an American helper from Paris, Etta Shiber, described Parisians' attitude towards the bombing. Her account is striking in several respects. A housewife and the widow of an American posted to Paris, Shiber lived with another single woman without occupation, an Englishwoman by birth named Kate Bonnefous who was separated from her husband. In 1940, Etta was 62 years old and Kate 54. Starting in June 1940, these two women set about helping British soldiers on the run. Etta was first imprisoned in November 1940. Following her release, she was rearrested alongside Kate in December. In March 1941, the two women, the abbot who helped them and two other helpers were tried for "assisting the enemy." Sentenced to death and later classified NN, Kate spent time in several of the Reich's prisons. An externally organized escape allowed the abbot to avoid being executed. The fate of the two other defendants, respectively sentenced to four and five years of hard labor, is unknown. As an American and thus the national of a neutral state, Etta was for her part "only" sentenced to three years' hard labor. In May 1942, she was freed/expelled to the United States. No sooner had she been released than she set

166   THE ORIGINS OF THE RESISTANCE

about writing her account, a fact that lends it greater authenticity. Here is what she had to say about the first RAF raid against Paris, in October 1940, which she witnessed from her apartment near the Place de l'Étoile.

> The very first night I remained alone, the air-raid sirens sounded. I was undecided what to do, whether to stay in the apartment or seek shelter, when the concierge arrived to tell me that a very comfortable shelter had been fixed up in the cellar of the house next door and to suggest that I go there with her. I accepted – and that gave me an opportunity to see the very remarkable reaction of the French people to an air raid by the British.
>
> They came hurrying out of their apartments to the shelters, not in fear but with exaltation. Some of them were singing for joy, others embraced, with tears streaming down their cheeks. One man shouted up at the sky: "Come on! Drop your bombs! We don't care! We're on your side!" and someone else, up the street, called through the darkness: "Vive les Anglais!"
>
> It was only a few days before that that hated traitor, Marcel Déat, had written in *L'Oeuvre* that people were "naïve" who listened to "false rumors" about the ability of British flyers to appear over France. "Don't allow yourself to be misled," he wrote, "by this collective hallucination which seems to delude hundreds of Parisians into believing that they have seen English airplanes over the city every day. The German anti-aircraft is strong enough to see to it that not one British plane will ever cross the Channel. Those who say the contrary are liars."
>
> ... For two hours, we stayed in the cellar, while outside we could hear the roar of the plane motors, the staccato barking of the machine guns, and the distant explosions of bombs. Every time we heard the dull crushing explosion of a bomb, the people in the cellar seemed to take on new life and gaiety. They didn't seem to realize that they may be killed or wounded themselves. They were too happy about this attack against the common enemy!
>
> Someone in the shelter struck up God Save the King and followed with Tipperary. Everyone else joined in. A few knew the English words. The rest followed the tune wordlessly.
>
> In the darkness of the cellar, where identification was difficult and all felt free to talk, tongues were loosened and pro-British and anti-German stories were told.[10]

Still vibrating with the collective emotion of the neighborhood, this is not an isolated account. It shows how unpopular the collaborationists were as soon as they appeared. Described by this helper as a "hated traitor," Marcel Déat was indeed the inventor of what he took to be the flattering label of "collaborationist." The word, which he first set down in the columns of *L'Oeuvre* for 4 November 1940, referred to those of the collaborators of Paris, who by 1941 had fully thrown their support behind Nazism. While her use of the expression "hated traitor" to describe events taking place in October 1940 was perhaps informed by her knowledge that Déat would fully embrace the cause of National Socialist Germany in 1941, one may think that this helper had correctly identified the French Nazi camp as early as fall 1940. Not only did its propaganda not reach her; it may even have reinforced her pro-British convictions.

An additional first-person account may be found in the journal kept by a woman of the same age under the Occupation. In 1940, Berthe Auroy, sixty years old and unmarried, was a retired schoolteacher living in Paris' eighteenth arrondissement. Although she remained faithful to the values of the Republic, Berthe was not a regular participant in resistance action. On several occasions, however, she took risks to help Jews of her acquaintance escape capture. She was representative of a latent resistance that manifested itself in occasional gestures of solidarity. Berthe recorded her observations in her notebook. From Montmartre, where she watched the bombing of the Renault factories in March 1942; from Vinerville (Eure-et-Loir), where she admired "the perfect formation of squadrons, like groups of migratory birds" in the sky during the summer of 1943; from Paris, where she watched the 24 August 1943 bombing of the Villacoublay aviation facilities from afar. On each of these occasions, she noted the festive atmosphere in the streets, the passersby who refused to take shelter, those who applauded at their windows or climbed the steps to Sacré-Cœur the better to see the fireworks. Of the media spokesmen of enemy propaganda, she ironically wrote:

> September 1943
> Enemy propaganda profits from all our misfortunes. These killings of women and children, these destructions of homes serve their cause. Radio-Paris gives horrible details in a maudlin and indignant tone. And the newspapers publish horror photos. The collaborators rub their hands. The more things get smashed to a pulp, the greater their hope of drawing French people into the party of collaboration. The truth is that, despite it all, almost all of us remain faithful to the Allies. "That's war!" sigh the people.

It was only when her neighborhood was directly struck in the bombing of the La Chapelle station in April 1944 that fear took hold and the inhabitants, including herself, began to seek shelter when the sirens sounded at night. The 20 April bombing killed 600 people in the neighborhoods of Montmartre and La Chapelle. A touch of anger rose in this staunchly pro-Allied woman.

> [April 1944]
> Who would have thought that Montmartre would be struck by bombing? Everyone said: "Our neighborhood will escape it. No factories. No military objectives." Surely, no one had thought of La Chapelle station and, had one thought of it, it would have been reasonable to think that the hill [Montmartre] would not be hit.[11]

The Indifferent Reception of Anti-Allied Propaganda

It was this marked change of mood in spring 1944 that worried the Allies and members of the resistance. Over the course of the war, Allied bombing is known to have caused around 60,000 civilian deaths in France. This figure is close to that for England but its distribution is nearly inverted. Two-thirds of British victims were killed between summer 1940 and spring 1941. In France, by contrast, more than two-thirds of all victims were killed in 1944. Starting in 1943, the French National Committee in London and then the French Committee of National Liberation in Algiers sought to alert the Allies to the political risks entailed by the bombing in France.[12] Their requests that they be allowed to participate in Allied strategic decisions went unheard. In 1943, the warning signs from Occupied France above all came from members of the Resistance who found themselves placed in a difficult position after the intelligence they had passed on regarding German positions and the industrial installations working on their behalf led to bloody and ineffective bombing raids. Following a significant increase in bombing in 1944, criticism on the ground became more widespread and pointed. In a word, the Allies should not be allowed to flatten the French like an enemy people. Delayed-action bombs (or those that were taken as such after exploding in the course of rescue efforts) should be forbidden. The Americans, who were responsible for most daytime flights, dropped their bombs from such high altitudes that accurate aim was impossible. Members of the Resistance, for their part, argued that it was better to rely on sabotage and thus parachute in weapons. Though they were taken into account and discussed by the Allies at the highest level, these recommendations went nowhere.

Public opinion reports must be approached with caution, particularly in what concerns societies living under dictatorships. Did the empirical criticism of bombing as it was seen from the ground diminish French people's support for the Allies? The answer depends not just on the sources that have been used but also on the motives of the report's author. A striking example of this comes from spring 1944, when two offices in the same Algiers-based CFLN Secret Service Directorate (DGSS) produced divergent reports within three weeks of one another.[13] This divergence reflects the political duality of the DGSS, at the time split between its Giraudist heritage and the contribution of Gaullists from London. The first report is uncritically based on partly questionable sources, including the messages intercepted by Vichy's telephone, telegraph and postal censorship bureau, whose authors obviously only allow themselves to say what they believe can be said without putting themselves at risk. This same report, which hardly distances itself from Vichy propaganda themes, concluded that French people would hold a much more severe opinion of the Allies were it not for the fact that official propaganda showed "a total lack of psychology." "Were it not for this unexpected impediment, reactions would be much

A CIVIL SOCIETY AGAINST TWO STATES

169

harsher," it notes. Three weeks later, the same DGSS, though this time at the level of the General Direction and on paper bearing the heading of the CFLN presidency, entirely revisited the question. . . and inverted the answer. Precise, sober and methodical, the report was more dispassionate. According to this report, the danger resided as much in "enemy propaganda" as in poorly conducted bombing. The bombardments that provoked local anger were those that were both ineffective and bloody as well as those in which "delayed-action bombs" pointlessly took lives. With the help of press clippings and radio listening transcriptions from Occupied France, the report shows the orchestrated power of "Germano-Vichyist propaganda." It worried as to its effects and held that it "is not unconnected to the type of disaffection vis-à-vis the Anglo-Saxon allies that has increasingly taken hold of the hearts and minds of French people over the past few months."

Once the collaborationist orator Philippe Henriot was appointed the Vichy government's Secretary of State for Information and Propaganda in January 1944, anti-Allied propaganda radicalized and intensified. In April, wrote the second report's author, media outlets "sought to surpass one another in terrifying and pitiful portraits." In contrast to the British policy of calling for calm during the Battle of Britain and the Blitz, "Germano-Vichyist" policy did its best to "inundate France with a wave of fear and enervating pity." It also cast suspicion on the intentions of the Allies, suggesting that they were perhaps seeking to destroy French industry for the purposes of subsequent economic domination or in order to provoke social discord, "to combine civil war with the war of invasion." Behind this policy, wrote the collaborationist newspaper *La France socialiste*, "looms the Soviets, their demands and their ever-greater control over the Committee of Algiers."[14] The Anglo-Americans and the communists were the primary targets of collaborationist eloquence, with the CFLN occupying a secondary place.

But two items were missing from the picture painted by the Secret Services of Algiers: the Jews and Marshal Pétain. In pro-Nazi anti-Allied propaganda, the Jews were linked with those whom, in the aftermath of the bombing of Juvisy (18 April 1944), Philippe Henriot called the "assassins," "terrorist aviators" and "liberator-killers" [*libérateurs*]. The reports of the DGSS make no mention of this latter theme of Parisian collaborationism, according to which the Jews were the instigators of Allied bombing. Is this an indication that this fantasy of Nazi propaganda was without effect on the population? Possibly so. For the reports also ignore the speeches of the head of state, which were similarly without practical effect. Though few of the Marshal's speeches touch upon this theme, they clearly denounced "the criminal aggression" of the British after the Renault factories were bombed in March 1942. Their tone, however, is above all one of sorrow and shared mourning. They are not calls to action but rather for meditation and do not participate in the sensationalist and at times voyeuristic rhetoric of official media. In these speeches, Pétain only once gives voice to anger, referring to the "terror" provoked by "bombardments of unprecedented cruelty and violence" the day after the deadly bombing of Rouen and Paris. But this short speech ends with a call to "believe in providence and hope for the future."[15] There was doubtless no reason to fear the impact of these sorrowful condolences.

By contrast, the encouragement of anti-Allied hatred, omnipresent in the official media, was not far from incitement to murder. This is what worried Allied observers and members of the Resistance. Expressing himself twice daily on the radio, the sensationalist lyricism of Philippe Henriot played on the nerves and might trigger acts of violence against fallen pilots if they came to be seen as the advance guard of "horror merchants":

> Ah, my French compatriots from the Parisian banlieue, my compatriots from Rouen and its surroundings, watch from afar, your fists clenched and tears of rage and distress filling your eyes, as your cities burn like volcanoes. Listen as the delayed-action bombs explode. Think of the loved ones whose corpses you will perhaps never find. And honestly say where the horror merchants are. (National radio broadcast, 19 April 1944, 12:30pm)

The two Algiers reports also diverged in what concerned the issue of assistance to downed Allied airmen. Not surprisingly, the first singles out the case of the inhabitants evacuated from a building in St Cloud who were said to have made violent remarks one day in September 1943. The author adds: "We have heard it said that, had American parachutists come down alive that day, the crowd would certainly have beaten them up."[16] By contrast, the other report quotes three specific, dated cases (February and March 1944) of evasion assistance given by helpers at great risk to themselves and the flowers widely laid at the tombs for killed airmen.[17]

By the spring of 1944, the official press had long since taken sides. It is not an exaggeration to describe it as a French-language German press. According to the newspapers, however, on 31 May or 1 June 1944, an unsigned communiqué written, without further precision, by "the competent authorities" reiterated "what must be the population's attitude towards downed Anglo-American airmen in France."[18] The vocabulary it employed ("airmen," for example, rather than "terrorists," "air pirates" or "murderers") as well as its content are surprising in this pro-Nazi environment. The communiqué reiterated that, "by the right of peoples" and international law as it had been defined under the Hague Convention and that of Geneva, airmen were to be protected and under no circumstances mistreated. The text claimed that several airmen had been mistreated and in a "few specific cases" lynched. This communiqué represents an example of gray propaganda. Under the cover of an apparently neutral source, it seems to condemn violence even as it suggests it. In his notebooks, the journalist and Resistance member Pierre

A CIVIL SOCIETY AGAINST TWO STATES 171

Limagne commented on the communiqué, the object of mandatory publication order no. 1552, as follows:

> A stupid paper transmitted by the OFI [Office français d'information] but doubtless of German origin – its publication obligatory and without any indication of its origin (or signature, – it was called in), that is, like the occupier's dreadful "notices" – which tells the French: "You do not have the right to lynch English or American airmen who come down in France." It seems that that has happened. However, while we have often noted a certain irritation among our compatriots towards the clumsy Allied aviators, we have never noticed a stronger feeling, except perhaps among a few madmen from the Milice. If the Wehrmacht fires on the Allied airmen forced to come down in parachutes, it is because they well know that, if alive, they would actually have every chance of being hidden by the French.[19]

That day or the next – on purpose? – the same newspapers published a communiqué from Berlin that appeared to vindicate the journalist, stating that "Germany will not leave the crimes of Anglo-American airmen unpunished."[20] At the same time in Germany, a threshold had been crossed in the Nazi policy of encouraging lynching. Joseph Goebbels, Minister of Public Enlightenment and Propaganda, published an article in the *Völkischer Beobachter* inciting violence against the "terrorist pilots" and the instructions that had been issued to this effect to the police since summer 1943 were transmitted within the Nazi Party and thereby reinforced.[21]

The difference between Nazi propaganda properly so called and the propaganda of French Nazis was not ideological in nature but rather a matter of circumstantial positioning and resources. For example, the collaborationists could display the number of dead and macabre images in the newspapers as so many indictments against the Allies. The German media, by contrast, was restrained and sometimes held to secrecy by Goebbels' services. The Nazis feared that shedding light on the people's suffering and the Luftwaffe's inadequacy would provoke popular discontent. This concern did not exist in France, though the official press did occasionally wonder over the Luftwaffe's failure to react to "Anglo-American terrorist raids."[22] But the forces of occupation also possessed specific resources relating to audiovisual propaganda.

Ineffective Nazi Scenography

Drawing upon the "occupation costs" paid Germany by France, the occupier extensively subsidized the press and radio as well as French-language cinema. Shown on screens in March 1944, the short cartoon *Nimbus libéré* (sometimes referred to as "Mickey bombs France") was produced by a French team and paid for by a pro-Nazi French agency, the Comité d'études antibolchéviques.

172   THE ORIGINS OF THE RESISTANCE

Headquartered at 21 rue La Boétie in the apartment of the despoiled Jewish gallery owner Paul Rosenberg, this Committee received funding from both the German authorities and the Vichy government.[23] Although anti-Gaullist, anti-English, anti-American and anti-Semitic, this cartoon must have been more successful in bringing a smile to the faces of Walt Disney fans than it was in drawing its viewers into the Nazi camp. The seductive power exerted by the images of American culture certainly got the upper hand over the (grotesque) content of the film's message.

But the Nazis also had their own resources. The Propaganda Kompanien thus produced a pseudo newsreel in which, with the help of a clever production, extras brought to Paris' Gare du Nord booed captured American airmen as they were being prepared for transfer to Germany.[24] In the first week of August 1944, the viewers of cinema newsreels in Germany and also doubtless France thus saw Parisians mistreating Allies. The extras, consisting of both men and women, were sentenced after the war: they had come there at the request of the Majestic. For the occasion, the German military authorities in France (MBF) had appealed to Paris' small collaborationist milieu. On the morning of 29 June, the henchmen of Bony and Lafont, the leaders of the "French Gestapo," joined the male and female personnel of the Légion des Volontaires Français contre le Bolchevisme (LVF) and the Parti Populaire Français (PPF) in booing and jostling the "Anglo-American" prisoners as they were escorted from the Gare du Nord to the Gare de l'Est.[25]

The next day, the collaborationist newspaper *La France socialiste*, copying Nazi texts, noted that, "someone having found an untimely word of commiseration [for the prisoners], there was a short scuffle, a brief exchange of fists." The "untimely word of commiseration" here is a near literal transcription of the terms employed by chief of the RSHA Kaltenbrunner's circular, which in April announced sanctions against Germans who exhibit "wrongly understood commiseration" towards downed airmen ("falsch verstandenes Mitleid").[26] In mid-July, before the Parisian "fake news" film was produced, images were published in the *Völkischer Beobachter* with the ironic title, "The Parisian population welcomes its liberators."[27]

While it could produce results in Germany, pro-lynching propaganda never produced its intended effect in France. To my knowledge, the only indications of such behavior are to be found in two news items that appeared in official newspapers.[28] The first, which curiously appeared in Saigon's *Echo annamite: organe des intérêts franco-annamites* in 1941, improbably mentions an "indignant crowd" ready to lynch a RAF pilot after he fell into German hands at an unspecified location on the Channel coast.[29] The other news item – less simple and perhaps pure fabrication – appeared in *Le Petit Parisien* in July 1944, that is, at the very moment the Propaganda Kompanien was producing its fictitious lynching mentioned above.[30] According to the article, the "sympathy" initially shown by the population of Laon towards a German pilot who had been saved

A CIVIL SOCIETY AGAINST TWO STATES   173

by a Wehrmacht motorcyclist gave way to "violent invective" when the population realized he was in fact an Allied airman. Some such incident may have taken place – who knows? – but the event in question may well have taken the opposite form, as had already occurred in northern France in 1943, where the population had on several occasions taken the side of Allied airmen as they were arrested.[31] In the case of this incident in the Aisne département in 1944, one should thus perhaps read the notice backwards: the population had believed that an Allied pilot had been arrested and rushed to the scene to defend him. Discovering that he was in fact a Luftwaffe pilot, they booed.

If one takes the activity of the helpers as reference point, the extent to which the authorized media was a closed world, disassociated from the population, becomes clear. Paper "hardly fit for wrapping eggs," as one helper put it. The Allies themselves were surprised by the warmth with which they were greeted despite the destruction caused by bombing. Unexpected testimony to this effect is supplied by no less than Arthur Harris, the head of Bomber Command from 1942 to 1945, who in September 1944 publicly underscored "the warm reception apparently reserved for everyone wearing the blue uniform of the RAF" in France. "Even in places where the destruction has been more significant, the men and women under my Command have been received with open arms and gratitude on the part of the people of France."[32] Gratitude towards the liberators was nevertheless sometimes mixed with bitterness. The inhabitants of Caen had no trouble appreciating the strategic value of their town in June 1944; those of Le Havre, by contrast, found it difficult to understand why their town should have been destroyed by bombs between 5 and 11 September, or more than fifteen days after the liberation of Paris.[33] "We joyfully awaited you, we greeted you in mourning" ran the headline in the first newspaper published in Le Havre following its liberation.[34] Joy and mourning combined.

A Memory on the Margins

It is perhaps due to the complexity of the situation created by friendly bombing that it has not been given a place in the national historical narrative. Yet one may wonder why the memory of Allied evasion assistance also remains excluded from the nation's grand narrative. By "grand narrative," I mean an account of the past that has won the assent of the majority and been given a place in school textbooks. Such narratives are not necessarily rose-tinted. Indeed, in what concerns the period of the Occupation, the national narrative has since the 1970s been rather bleak. The history and memory of Collaboration occupy a dominant place in high school textbooks. In the small place still accorded the history of the Resistance, institutional (the unification of the Resistance), political (parties and movements) and military history (the maquis) figure most prominently. The textbooks of the years 2011–16 do not mention evasion assistance activities,[35] with one exception: a single textbook provides a map of Second World War memorial sites that includes the monument to the Evaders and Smugglers of Donon Pass in the Vosges mountains. And even this solitary reference disappeared in subsequent editions. Since the 2000s, however, a particular type of assistance activity has made it into textbooks: the assistance given Jewish children and adults. This reflects the new centrality of the Shoah to the history of the Occupation.

Academic literature offers another indicator of the absence of Allied aid from the national narrative. Three recently published surveys of the Resistance (2013, 2015 and 2019) have little or nothing to say about aid to the Allies.[36] It is perhaps no coincidence that the only book to bring it up is by an English academic, Robert Gildea, who devotes five pages to the subject.[37] Serge Barcellini and Annette Wieviorka's book, which inventories Second World War memorial sites in France, provides another indicator of the absence of Allied assistance in the nation's grand narrative.[38] Their chapter on the Resistance includes the places where movements held their meetings, the demonstrations of 11 November, radio liaisons, parachute drops, places of asylum, resisting towns and villages, the maquis, the martyrs of the Resistance, foreigners and heroes and major national figures. But there is no mention of the assistance given fugitive Allies or even of the activity of assistance in general. The subject is at most broached by one example, that of the specialized hospital of Saint-Alban (Lozère), which sheltered refugees of various origins.

At the local and départemental scale, however, the memory of the assistance given Allied soldiers and airmen is alive and well. It is driven by two considerations: first, to satisfy the popular interest in aviation and the material culture with which it is associated, an interest stoked by the many thousands of crashes that took place in France during the war; second, to maintain the direct or inherited memory of assistance itself and thereby rekindle the ties of friendship that were established between airmen and inhabitants during the war. These two objectives most often merge in a single association. Today (the 2020s), it comes as no surprise that the most active aerial memorial associations – that is, the départemental associations created by the rescuers of Allied airmen – are spread between the Nord-Pas-de-Calais and Brittany, départements that each received, in the form of crashes or forced landings, hundreds of Allied airplanes between 1940 and 1944.[39] Other private initiatives further contribute to keeping the memory of assistance alive. The creation of online sites, often the work of the sons or friends of those who received or gave assistance, perpetuate the helpers' memory. These databases are sometimes truly encyclopedic in scope, identifying and locating crews and helpers, supplying interactive monographs on evasion networks and reproducing serial archival collections.[40] Anyone who has traveled around these départements or in the country's mountainous border regions – above all, the Pyrénées, Jura and Vosges – has come across the plaques and steles recalling the sojourn or risky passage of thousands of men led by escorts and smugglers, male and female alike.

This raises the question of why the memory of a type of resistance action that took place across the entire expanse of France has not been fully acknowledged at the national level. For one thing, no centralized organization was created for helper groups after the war. In contrast to the United States and the United Kingdom, where national-scale associations were established by those who had received assistance (in 1964 and 1945, respectively), no federation was created to represent helpers of all networks. The Royal Air Forces Escaping Society, or RAFES, not only contributed to the memory of helpers but operated as a charity, raising funds to come to the aid of impoverished helpers and those suffering from health problems as a result of their incarceration. With support from the RAF, RAFES carried out its activities until its dissolution in 1995, at which time it was succeeded by an entirely private charity, the ELMS, or Escape Lines Memorial Society. In the United States, the AFEES, Air Forces Escape and Evasion Society, was created in 1964 on the initiative of an evacuee from Shelburn. The ELMS and AFEES are still active in 2022.

The type of society to which the phenomenon of assistance gave rise might help explain the marginal position that the helpers have occupied in the nation's memory. In ascending order, the role played among the helpers by women, the social heterogeneity of helpers as a group and the multinational nature of the undertaking and its actors all ran counter to securing national recognition.

As we have seen, 30 percent of recognized helpers were women. This rate is high when you consider that women accounted for only 12 percent of those issued a volunteer resistance combatant card and between only 10 and 24 percent of those recognized as members of certain movements and networks.[41] The two helpers' diplomas reproduced in Figure 7 show that the Allies did not hesitate, when necessary, to recognize the actions of the wife independently of those of the husband. In the case of the De Esturos, the Awards Bureau judged that Louise and Théo had assisted the British together but that Louise alone had helped the Americans. Among the roughly thirty recognized evasion networks, four were led by women. Apart from the Comète network, these networks were known by female Christian names: Françoise, Marie-Claire and Marie-Odile. This is at once a small proportion (4 out of 36, or 11 percent) and much higher than what one observes for resistance movements (multi-activity organizations centered around newspapers, 0 percent). It is also higher than the rate found among intelligence networks (7 percent, or five out of seventy networks: Alliance, Gloria-SMH, Hi-Hi, Prosper, Robin). At a time when only half of all women held a job, with factory workers and clerks overrepresented

(a)

This certificate is awarded to

Monsieur et Madame Théo de Esturo

as a token of gratitude for and appreciation of the help given to the Sailors, Soldiers and Airmen of the British Commonwealth of Nations, which enabled them to escape from, or evade capture by the enemy.

1939-1945

Air Chief Marshal,
Deputy Supreme Commander,
Allied Expeditionary Force

Figures 7.1a and 7.1b Diplomas of helpers issued to "Monsieur et Madame Théo de Esturo" by the British and to "Louise de Esturo" by the Americans. Living in Conflans-Ste-Honorine (Oise), this couple hosted several Allied airmen. © Collection Maurice Bleicher.

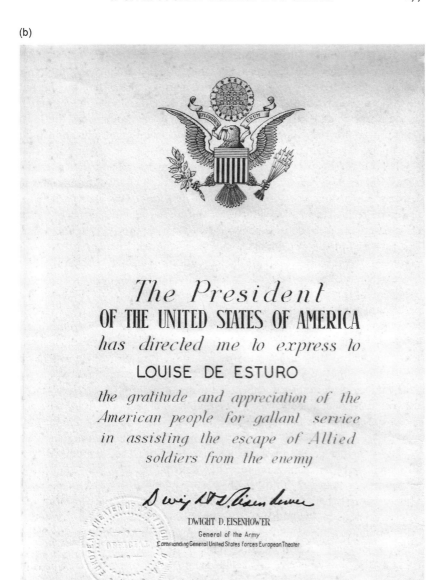

Figures 7.1a and 7.1b (*cont.*)

among these active women, it would not be surprising should the relatively high percentage of women involved in evasion activities have impeded national recognition of their action.

The socio-professional composition of the world of assistance was also more broadly distributed across social categories than was the case of intelligence networks and movements, where recruitment was heavily weighted in favor of the urban middle classes. The assistance networks drew from the most isolated parts of the countryside, called upon urban communication hubs and finally recruited in the hills and mountains of the country's border regions. Taken together, these populations formed a particularly heterogeneous whole, even when compared to the average population engaged in resistance, which also transcended social divisions. The map of helpers' places of residence in Paris illustrates the unprecedented social bridge it created between rural départements and the smartest precincts of the capital. For, in terms of the evasion assistance given the Allies, western Paris was indeed overrepresented. Perhaps the fact that more people spoke English in these neighborhoods, where apartments also tended to be larger, favored involvement in assistance activity. Nor can one exclude the possibility that a political factor – to wit, solidarity with western democracies – played a role in the decision to give aid (indeed, there seem to have been few communists among the helpers). Once freedom was restored, the paths of these helpers, now returned to their usual activities, no longer crossed. There was never much chance that they would come to constitute a pressure group.

The minor place accorded helpers in the national narrative also stems from the fact that their activity was, by definition, multinational. It is generally acknowledged that it took some time for the nation to recognize the role played by foreigners in the Resistance, a process that first began in the 1980s. Taking as his gauge the method by which the title "Died for France" was attributed, Serge Barcellini has shown how difficult the 1945 edict made it for foreigners to obtain it. [42] While the helpers were indeed French citizens, their activity was oriented towards foreigners. The fact that the Service historique de la Défense is, as of 2020, unable to locate archives specifically relating to the recognition of helpers would seem to confirm this hypothesis. Even though an officer from the Direction Générale des Études et de la Recherche (DGER) going by the nom de guerre of Captain Lefort took part in the procedure for awarding titles, it seems that the Service did not conserve the corresponding archives. To this day, the white papers that would have defined the French government's policy towards helpers have yet to be found. The silence of the archives seems to suggest that what was a multinational and even transnational resistance was a source of some embarrassment at the national level. In the 1970s, the term "transnational" was employed as a synonym for "multinational." It was above all applied to the world of large corporations. In the human sciences, it gradually became accepted as a way to describe

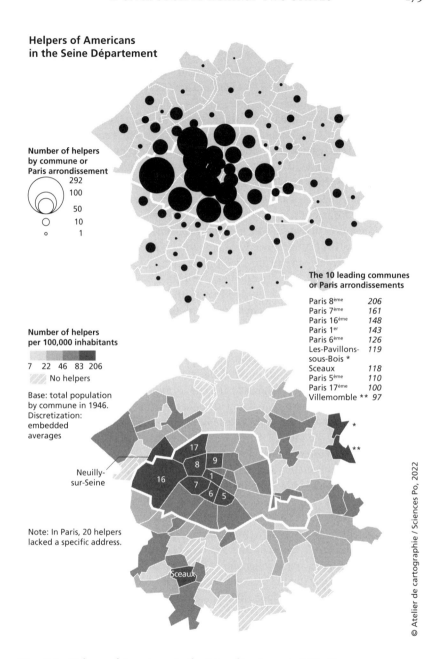

Map 7.1 Helpers of Americans in the Seine département, 1942–44.
Source: NARA, Master List of MIS-X Awards, France, 1945–1948. Helpers' place of residence in 1945–1946. Only recognized helpers.

180   THE ORIGINS OF THE RESISTANCE

international relations that exceeded the framework of states. In reality, the evasion networks for Allied soldiers and airmen were a mixture of international and transnational elements. A recent book has underscored the transnational nature of the Resistance in Europe by showing the role that foreign combatants played in it.[43] Allied evasion assistance also deserves to be described as transnational resistance. In this instance, however, the resisters were local inhabitants who on the whole lacked foreign ties.

This aid was not only intended for non-nationals; it was also partly financed and co-organized from abroad (the British and, to a lesser extent, the Belgians and Dutch).[44] The involvement of the British state is evident at several levels. In terms of financing, the Pat O'Leary network was ultimately supported by MI9, an agency that itself struggled to obtain funds and recognition within the War Office administration. Another, particularly successful creation of MI9 was the Shelburn network, which sprouted from the ruins of the Oaktree network, also a British initiative. Between January and August 1944, Shelburn pulled off the exploit of returning nearly 150 men to England over the course of nine Channel crossings. Its operating principle was as follows: the Royal Navy lent a Motor Gun Boat (MGB) that, with its lights extinguished, would enter the Bay of St Brieuc under cover of darkness, drop off funds and weapons and take on English and American airmen for the return trip, as well as a few Frenchmen seeking to join up with France libre. On dry land, this network employed several hundred people, from the rural helpers of Nord-Pas-de-Calais and the Oise to those of Paris and its western banlieue and the helpers of Côtes du Nord, who escorted the airmen and provided them with shelter before their departure. Passing across a minefield and along a steep cliff at nighttime, the "packages" were taken all the way to Bonaparte beach. A dory then took them to the MGB. Often, its navigator was David Birkin, who would later become the father of Jane Birkin.

The Dutch and Belgian governments in exile also helped finance the escape lines. On the initiative of a Dutchman living in France named Jean Weidner, the Dutch state in exile in London also played a crucial role in financing the Dutch-Paris network.[45] This textile merchant succeeded in leading some 800 (mostly Dutch) Jews to freedom in Switzerland and Spain as well as 120 Allied airmen. He was arrested four times: on one occasion, he was beaten by the gendarmes of Savoie; on another, he was tortured by the Gestapo of Lyon; once, he was picked up in a street roundup in Nancy as part of Aktion Meerschaum (Operation Meerschaum), an effort to supply manpower for the German concentration camp system; another time, he was arrested and tortured by the Toulouse Milice. Each time, he escaped his abusers. It was a rare performance in the domain of evasion. In Belgium, the population was heavily involved in helping Allied soldiers and airmen. Created by a young woman and her father, Andrée and Frédéric de Jonghe, the Comète network crossed France to move men from Belgium to Spain in the sector of the

A CIVIL SOCIETY AGAINST TWO STATES 181

Bidassoa River. Together with Pat O'Leary, Comète was the largest Allied evasion assistance network of the war. It was financed by the British and the Belgian government in exile and, like other networks, it drew from local pools of helpers.[46]

We shall not examine the manner in which the thirty-six commonly identified evasion networks were financed as that would take us far afield from the subject at hand.[47] Moreover, some networks did not particularly rely upon the Allies for funding. One such was the Bourgogne network – the source of the photograph of a clandestine "package" presented in this book – which relied on funding from France Libre's Action and Intelligence Office (BCRA).[48] Active between March 1943 and June 1944, "Bourgogne" succeeded in helping some 300 Allied airmen escape.[49] It was in the nature of things, however, that the sole Allied state in Europe still prosecuting the war should have contributed to the clandestine assistance given to exfiltrating its soldiers and airmen.

Given the involvement of the British, Belgian and Dutch states, evasion assistance was an international undertaking. Its reliance on the spontaneous assistance of helpers in the places where Allied airplanes came down and over the full length of their journeys also meant that it was transnational in scope. Once the nation-state had been restored following the Liberation, however, this assistance received little attention. For the most part, its contribution to the memory of the Resistance has remained a local matter. The "résistancialisme" thesis does not apply to it. Carried out in conditions of urgency and producing an immediate effect in the war, moreover, this action did not require any thought be given the postwar world. There was no time for that, in any case. This is also one reason why evasion and intelligence networks were not invited to the table by the National Council of the Resistance. They remained – the evasion networks, in particular – largely absent from the nation's grand narrative.

PART IV

Lynching in Germany, 1943–1945

Defending the Nazi State

In this fourth part, I shall examine the manner in which German civilians behaved towards downed Allied airmen on the soil of the *Altreich*, or "Old Reich," the pre-1938 territory of Germany. The academic bibliography on this subject is still in its early phases. As we saw at the outset of the present work, the relevant publications are all quite recent. In 2014 and 2015, two monographs were published concerning Austrian territory.[1] These copiously documented books present the Nazi leaders as the main agents of lynching. In the 2000s, three contributions to edited volumes were also published addressing Germany properly so called.[2] Of these, two take a clear stand. Klaus-Michael Mallmann presents the violence committed against downed airmen as indicative of the generalization of the war of extermination and a sign of civilians' willing involvement in this process. Drawing upon a Master's thesis on this subject, by contrast, Barbara Grimm casts blame for this violence on Nazi leaders. Kevin T. Hall's article is also worth noting. Underscoring the important role played by civilians in attacks against airmen, Hall explains this violence by reference to the anger provoked by their experience of large-scale bombing.[3] The book that followed this article takes up the thesis and enriches it.

The present discussion in large measure accords with that of Klaus-Michael Mallmann. The problem is how to go about evaluating the involvement of German society in the severe abuse directed at downed Allied airmen. This is not simply a matter of determining who killed or assaulted them but also of assessing why they did so: was it merely a mechanical reaction to the destruction and loss of life caused by bombing or did it instead reflect their adherence to prevailing Nazism? As it happens, these questions nicely dovetail with the contemporary historiography on Nazi Germany. In his 2013 survey, *Nazism as Fascism*, Geoff Eley shows how the 1980s represented a watershed moment in the historiography.[4] His chapter on "The Return of Ideology," in particular, underscores the manner in which the history of everyday life and efforts to take into consideration the central role occupied by the Nazi concept of *Volksgemeinschaft* contributed to this process. Historians continue to debate whether this "community of the people-race (*Volk*)" can be considered the organizing principle of Nazi society. Was *Volksgemeinschaft* merely a theme of

183

184   LYNCHING IN GERMANY: DEFENDING THE NAZI STATE

propaganda, an at once egalitarian and identitarian ideal reserved for "Aryans," or did it become a social reality, fueling a dynamic of active participation in the regime? By virtue of its frequency and geographical extent, civilian violence against Allied airmen tips the scales in favor of the *Volksgemeinschaft* as social reality. The popular dynamic of racial exclusion was extended to other populations, like that of downed airmen, and gave the *Volk* an opportunity to reaffirm its power in the Nazi political community. What Michael Wildt observed for anti-Jewish violence in the Germany of 1933–39 also holds for anti-Allied violence.[5]

Increasingly, present-day historiography describes the Nazi empire as a "racial state," in keeping with Michael Burleigh and Wolfgang Wippermann's book of the same name.[6] As an aberrant manifestation of the nation-state, the expression "race-state" would perhaps be more appropriate. Over the past thirty years, the social history of Nazi Germany has been transformed by studies of the everyday life of "ordinary" Germans and the question of "Nazi appeal." As this has happened, considerations of class have increasingly taken a back seat in discussions of social structure, with social actors no longer understood as the socio-professional groups that benefited from (the aristocracy, industrial bourgeoisie and lower middle classes) or lost out under (workers) Nazism. *Kulturgeschichte* now enjoys the same prestige as *Sozialgeschichte*. Indeed, the "social revolution" heralded by the rise of Nazism, brilliantly expounded by Ralf Dahrendorf[7] and David Schoenbaum[8] in the 1960s, now finds itself inverted: since the 2000s, it is often seen as a cultural revolution in which social, religious and regional identities became distinctions of little importance vis-à-vis the racial utopia.

Indeed, such has been the success of the expression "racial state" that it has sometimes become a screening concept. The central place occupied by race in the Nazi state notwithstanding, other imperatives – in particular, economic and military ones – did not disappear, nor was the racial system itself always coherent.[9] These flaws and contradictions prevented the racial state from achieving "best of all possible worlds" perfection. Nevertheless, the choice of race as founding principle of the new Germany gradually eroded inherited hierarchies and undid traditional beliefs. Even by 1945, it had yet to reveal its full potential in all of its immense, subversive power. World war and genocide were merely the preliminary result. To the degree that Nazism's reliance on race from the outset fostered an exacerbated national consciousness throughout society, it can be argued that its vision of the world contained the seeds of war. What is clear, in any case, is that, by establishing biological selection as its supreme principle, the biological death of the nonconforming was written into its DNA. The advent and powerful appeal of the race-state altered Germans' relationship to killing. Beginning in 1933, forced amputation and murder became routine aspects of the everyday life of doctors and nurses (between 1934 and 1936, 160,000 patients were forcibly sterilized, resulting in 400 deaths) as well as of members of the SA and Nazi Party.[10]

In 2016, the historian Johann Chapoutot applied the expression "cultural revolution" to the creation of Nazi ideology.[11] For what Germans experienced and followed was indeed a cultural revolution, one that had this in common with events in the People's Republic of China: that the Nazis eagerly sought and received the population's active participation. As the historian of Nazism Michael Wildt underscores in *Die Ambivalenz des Volkes* [*The People's Ambivalence*],[12] the idea of the people is ambiguous, its value varying according to how it is defined.

It would be easy to make the Germans of 1933–45 shoulder responsibility for a cycle of brutality that began in the aftermath of the revolution of 1848–49 (strikingly manifested in the rise of Bismarck as Prussian minister in 1862) and came to an end in 1945. Direct responsibility for two genocides (of the Hereros and Namas, on the one hand, and of the Jews, on the other) and responsibility for the onset of two world wars – shared responsibility in the case of the first, full responsibility in that of the second – confers a particular place upon Germany in the concert of nations of that time. From a French point of view, one might add the three successive invasions of its territory in 1870, 1914 and 1940 as well as (in a way that is significant for the present study) Germany's failure to respect international law as it regarded civilians in the context of invasion. The historians of the 1960s and 1970s often described the singular trajectory of Germany as a *Sonderweg*, or special path. At the same time that Walt Whitman Rostow pondered *The Stages of Economic Growth* – the title of a 1960 book he published in the United States – historians examined the stages of "political development," taking note of Germany's "political lag." Having never experienced a liberal or democratic revolution of the British, American or French type, Germany remained "illiberal" (Dahrendorf). It had "skipped a step" and never caught up with the group of Western powers. This linear vision of history, according to which peoples follow a predetermined path towards Progress, has today lost much of its credibility. Pushed too far, this type of explanation takes a deterministic culturalist turn. The answer would seem to be contained in the question itself; research on the Nazification of German society would thus lose its object.

Studying German civilian behavior towards downed airmen therefore requires, not simply that one establish the context, but also that one break actions down into their constituent parts. Doing so is a twofold process. On the one hand, one must break them down in descending order, following the chain by which orders were transmitted from the apex of the state all the way down to grassroots institutional actors. At the same time, these actions must be reassembled in ascending order – that is, from the point of view of ordinary Germans on the ground as they were confronted with the sudden emergence of the event. And one must continue to entertain the hypothesis that, as the title of a pacifist and republican newspaper banned in 1933 had it, an "other Germany" existed – an *Andere Deutschland*[13] – and this despite any doubts that might arise via comparison with British behavior at the same time. Even when crushed under the extreme phase of the 1860–1945 cycle, an "other" Germany may have struggled to hold on.

8

The Lynching of Allied Airmen
An Ordinary Practice

Studying the lynching of Allied airmen in Germany raises questions of fact and interpretation alike. For, in attempting to establish the facts, one must rely on an indirect source: the war crimes trials brought by the Allies after the war. When conducted by an occupying power, such a posteriori investigations necessarily meet with more or less obvious resistance on the part of the newly occupied perpetrators. Interpreting these events, moreover, is made more difficult by the chronological conjunction of two main factors: from below, a violent popular reaction to the intensification of bombing and, from above, a policy of inciting murder against downed airmen. It is thus necessary to separate spontaneous anger from voluntary compliance with Nazi incitement and reveal their respective contributions to inducing men and women to take action. Provided that it was not the interaction of these two factors that provoked aggression.

Three Social Patterns: Schleswig-Holstein, 1942–1945

The three examples that follow do not offer a representative portrait of all behavior. In their diversity and geographical proximity, however, these scenes from a society at war allow one to define the range of questions to be resolved.

21 April and 11 August 1942, Ütersen, Schleswig-Holstein: military honors

On 18 April 1942, two British airplanes crashed shortly before 4am on the territory of the towns of Hasloh and Glasshütte, located north of Hamburg near the airport of Ütersen (Holstein). The six-man crew of the Wellington all died in the crash. Five men parachuted from the other airplane and were taken prisoner by the *Flak* (anti-aircraft personnel). They were sent to the transit camp for captured airmen in Oberursel, near Frankfurt am Main. A sixth member of this crew was killed in the crash. On 21 April, the Kommandantur (*Fliegerhorstkommandantur*) of the Ütersen air base arranged for the seven Royal Air Force airmen to be buried with military honors (Figure 8.1). There was music, floral wreaths from the Wehrmacht and Luftwaffe and a speech by the pastor recalling that these men had "fallen for their fatherland."

188   LYNCHING IN GERMANY: DEFENDING THE NAZI STATE

Figure 8.1   Military honors given RAF airmen killed in action, Ütersen, Schleswig-Holstein, 21 April 1942. © Bundesarchiv-Militärarchiv, Freiburg-im-Brisgau.

The twenty soldiers present for the occasion fired three salvos of blanks and wooden crosses were erected over each grave. The following 11 August, this ceremony was once again performed for two other RAF personnel shot down on 30 July. Apart from the pastor's Nazi salute as the coffins were lowered into the ground, all rites were observed, one might even say with zeal.[1]

Until early 1943, Allied airmen who came down in Germany were treated according to the laws of war. Sometimes, they were even buried with military honors as was the case here, in Ütersen, Schleswig-Holstein, on 21 April 1942. The ceremony only stood out for the Nazi salute given by the pastor.

18 June 1944, Elmshorn, town adjoining Ütersen: non-deadly lynching opposed by one of those present

The report comes from the local police (*Schutzpolizei*).[2] In the course of an 18 June air raid – or "terrorist attack" (*Terrorangriffe*), as they were now known – a bomber crashed on the territory of Elmshorn. Parachuting from the airplane, an airman landed in a nearby meadow. Farmers ran to the scene, apprehended the airman and gave him a "concrete expression of their legitimate anger, particularly as the property of one of them had been damaged in the terrorist attack" of 3 August 1943, one year earlier. On that day, the village of

LYNCHING OF ALLIED AIRMEN 189

Elmshorn had been a collateral victim of the bombing of Hamburg, 35 kilometers to the south; 62 inhabitants had been killed in Elmshorn. Taking place between 25 July and 3 August 1943, the bombing of Hamburg, during which some 40,000 inhabitants lost their lives, was the deadliest suffered by Germany during the war.

On this 18 June 1944, a sixty-seven-year-old landowner and nurseryman by trade from Elmshorn attempted to interpose himself between the farmers and the airman. He described the blows directed at the prisoner as scandalous (*Gemeinheit*) and recalled that he had seen no such behavior during the last war (that of 1914). In his subsequent report, the chief of police found that Rudolf Frahm had thereby "insulted" his comrades of the *Volk* community (the *Volksgenossen*) and that he should consider himself lucky to have escaped without a beating in his turn. The "Schupo" thus transmitted this information to the local branch of the Gestapo in Itzehoe, a few kilometers away, asking that the latter take all necessary measures.

Some of what followed is known to us from the response that came from the district office of the Nazi Party (Kreisleitung), located in Pinneberg, 20 kilometers south of Elmshorn. It was thus the Party that transmitted Herr Landrat's opinion (the head of the cantonal administration) to the mayor of Elmshorn. The police investigation showed that Rudolf Frahm, unlike another nurseryman of the same name from that village, was a member neither of the Party nor of the National Socialist People's Welfare Association (NSV). He was "only" a member of the sole peasant corporation created in 1933 (*Reichsnährstand*). The senior-ranking member (*Oberabschnittsleiter*) of the NSDAP in Pinneberg thus demanded that Frahm be discharged from his duties as president of the Elmshorn water and soil association. Did other sanctions follow? The question is worth asking given the virulence with which the local party leader presented the facts:

> In the course of the 18 June 1944 terrorist attack [*Terrorangriff*] against Hamburg and its surroundings, an air gangster [*Luftgangster*] parachuted to the ground in Elmshorn. The population was very agitated, all the more so given that he was a Swedish emigrant. In their anger, a few comrades from the Volk [*Volksgenossen*] physically assaulted the murderous gangster [*Mordgangster*]. A German man [*Deutscher*] at this time intervened to protest the fact that an unarmed soldier was being struck. The population [*Bevölkerung*] rightfully objected against this intervention. This strange *Volksgenosse* nearly received a thrashing from the population himself.

One here sees how, even at the local level, the facts of the air war were now being redescribed in the language of the Third Reich. *Terrorangriff*, *Luftgangster* and *Mordgangster* had replaced the bombing raids, enemy army members (*feindlicher Wehrmachtsangehöriger*) and crew members (*Mann der Besatzung*) featured in the reports of 1942. At the very foundations of society,

190   LYNCHING IN GERMANY: DEFENDING THE NAZI STATE

the manner in which the war was perceived had thus changed. It had become a war of aggression conducted by murderers as well as an ethnic war in which the origins of the combatants taken prisoner were a decisive factor. The process of Nazification does not seem to have been entirely complete, however, since the troublemaker was not excluded from the *Volksgemeinschaft*. He was merely described as a "strange" member of the *Volk* – or so one must conclude on the basis of these documents. The very attitude of the old nurseryman, born and raised in the Wilhelmine era, is another indication of the society's incomplete Nazification. In the case of this veteran of the war of 1914, the "brutalization" of social behavior often imputed to the First World War had not taken place. He was doubtless a survivor of "the other Germany."

The same day (18 June 1944), Appen-Etz, another municipality adjoining Ütersen: deadly lynching in the presence of a small crowd

Around 11 in the morning that same day, 18 June 1944, an American pilot parachuted on to the territory of this village.[3] He was immediately arrested and handed over to the local police. Around noon, the latter received a telephone call from the district authorities (the Pinneberg Kreisleitung) asking that the airman be surrendered to the custody of Party member Wilhelm Langeloh, who would be arriving in a few minutes. Pinneberg is only 3 or 4 kilometers from Appen-Etz. This, it was claimed, was on order from the Landrat (administrative authorities). Wearing his uniform as a First Lieutenant in the SA, Langeloh arrived by motorcycle at Appen-Etz and led the POW on foot towards the airport of Ütersen, 2 kilometers away. A local police officer named Runge followed. A few hundred meters from the village, Langeloh fired a nearly pointblank pistol shot into the airman's neck as he walked ahead of him. With a kick of the boot, he rolled the body into a ditch. Langeloh headed back to the village to get his motorcycle so as to subsequently inform the airport's military authorities of this death. He thus once again passed the scene of the murder on motorcycle. Testifying before the tribunal in April 1947, Runge had this to say:

> Langeloh arrived and asked me: "What's he doing?" and I said, "The airman is still alive." I said: "But why torture him this way?" He answered: "He should die in this ditch" [In his written deposition, Runge reported this as "Let him croak in this ditch!"]. He wanted to personally go to the airport to make the report ... then Langeloh returned from Ütersen on his motorcycle and stopped again. I told him that the airman was still alive, that he had spoken in bad German, calling "Father! Mother!" and asking me to "Finish me off!" Then I told Langeloh that he had probably shot too low. It was a throat shot. He then told me: "This isn't the first. This isn't a matter of a single human life." He fired several shots in the air with his pistol. There were many people around at this time. Then Langeloh said he had a lot to do. He said "Heil Hitler" and moved off.

On the same day and at a distance of just a few kilometers, we have an opponent of abuse faithful to the law of nations and a voluntary murderer who looks upon the suffering he has inflicted with scorn and boasts of having killed before. With the reception of enemy airmen on the ground, he was able to launch a career as serial killer. As an added benefit, this social role offered him an opportunity to display heightened masculinity by playing upon the attributes of power, firing in the air while mounted on his motorcycle like a comic strip cowboy.

But the murderer was not alone. It is here that the legal archives of a state observing the rule of law only offer a partial idea of direct responsibility. Obliged to define individual guilt, liberal democratic legal systems struggle to come to terms with group phenomena and responsibilities. The postwar trials of concentration camp officers and guards well demonstrate the near total incapacity of liberal legal systems when it comes to grasping systemic individual responsibility in cases where victims can neither specifically name their abusers nor give exact dates for repeated acts of violence. As noted by the ethnologist Germaine Tillion, a former Ravensbrück deportee present for the trial of that camp's leadership in Hamburg in 1947: "We are alive, too bad for us."[4] To glean information regarding the sequence and site of violence, one must look to the archives. In Appen-Etz, Langeloh was alone in having fired the fatal pistol shot but police officer Runge testified that, as he left the village, he heard cries of "Beat him to death!" These cries came from ten or twenty passersby on their way to or from Appen. One inhabitant who joined the trio on the road had earlier cried from his window, "Beat him to death!" Soldiers from the base of Ütersen saw the airman in the ditch as they passed by. They indicated their surprise but neither they nor any civilian on the road objected or, more than that, took the "serial killer" to task. There was perhaps a single act consistent with the principle of humanely treating prisoners of war, that of a soldier who, it seems, went to warn the police sergeant in Appen so that he might bring a cart to transport the wounded airman. The latter died in a Hamburg hospital the next day.

These three scenes of war, drawn from a single region (*Gau*) and from a group of adjoining villages, illustrate the terms of the debate. In 1942, the army seemed to enjoy mastery on the ground and behaved in keeping with the laws and customs of war. Civilians were absent from the picture. In June 1944, the army had receded to the background. When it intervened, it was only in secondary fashion, hospitalizing an airman as he died from a "civilian" gunshot wound. The initiative was now in the hands of civilians and their aggressive gatherings. Just a few kilometers away, one nevertheless observes a statistically aberrant case: at his own risk, a civilian objected to the mistreatment inflicted on another airman. We thus have two hate-filled crowds, a killer and a lone man who attempted to oppose what was happening. Does this portrait describe German society as a whole? Did these pastoral scenes – more

192   LYNCHING IN GERMANY: DEFENDING THE NAZI STATE

likely to take place, one would think, in bombed-out cities – occur in the same way in urban areas? And what happened between 1942 and 1944 to produce such radical changes in civilian/military relations and behavior? The intensification of bombing obviously played a role but how so, by way of what processes?

And what is one to conclude regarding Nazi mobilization of the people from the killing of a former anti-Nazi which took place in Meldorf after the cessation of hostilities? The Nazi mayor of this town, located approximately 80 kilometers north of Elmshorn, remained in power. On 11 May 1945, when an old prewar social democratic activist, a peaceful wine merchant, came to ask him to resign, the mayor answered with two lethal gunshots and these words: "Traitor! Bastard!"[5] Would the campaign to purge Germans have successfully eliminated the last non-Nazis if the Allies had allowed it to happen? An upside-down purge, as it were, carried out by the defeated? This counterfactual look at a possible way out of the war in Germany is not as far-fetched as it may seem.

Investigating in Post-Nazi Germany

It is necessary to precisely define the type of event I am referring to as "lynching," a term that first appeared in Nazi documents in May 1944 but had already been practiced on the ground for a little under a year. As we have already seen for events in the French and British contexts, since 1899 prisoners of war had been protected by international conventions. Germany, the United States, France and Great Britain had all ratified the Hague (1899 and 1907) and Geneva (1929) conventions, which provided that prisoners of war were to be "humanely treated." The version adopted in 1929 had reinforced the definition of the humane treatment due to prisoners:

> **Article 2**
> Prisoners of war are in the power of the hostile Government, but not of the individuals or formation which captured them.
> They shall at all times be humanely treated and protected, particularly against acts of violence, from insults and from public curiosity.
> Measures of reprisal against them are forbidden.[6]

It is the irony of history that it was Nazi Germany itself – and not the Weimar Republic – that ratified the Geneva Convention in 1934. Be that as it may, Article 2 specifically describes the opposite of what happened to thousands of Allied airmen in Germany. They found themselves in the power of individuals who treated them without humanity and encouraged or committed acts of violence against them, hurled insults and displayed them to public curiosity. Arriving in Germany, the Allies thus faced no legal difficulties in preparing trials on this theme. The law had been clearly established before the war and ratified by all the relevant powers.

The archives of the "War Crimes Trials" in the British and American occupation zones are today held in London[7] and Washington, DC.[8] Those of the French occupation zone are in Paris.[9] Those for the Soviet zone remain to be located. Some number of trials were moreover conducted by German tribunals.[10] In the war crimes trials, one must single out the Flyer Trials, or those that specifically concerned downed airmen. And, among these trials, the present study must single out those that solely concern the territory of the *Altreich*, or Germany before 1938. Downed airmen in Austria do not fall under this domain and nor do those who came down over occupied territory and were assaulted by the forces of occupation (rather than the inhabitants, as is sometimes claimed). Moreover, the present study concerns the civilian population (*zivile Bevölkerung*). Violations of the laws and customs of war committed by guards in such places of incarceration as prisons, POW camps and concentration camps do not concern us, even if they resulted in hundreds of victims. To cite just a few of the better-known cases of this type, one may mention the fifty airmen of the "Great Escape" who escaped Stalag Luft III on the night of 24–25 March 1944, and were subsequently executed by the Gestapo or the 168 airmen who came down over France and were dispatched to Buchenwald concentration camp.[11] The latter remained there from 20 August to 19 October 1944, a two-month period during which two of them died. The survivors were transferred to a prison camp. And then there were the forty-seven airmen shot dead in the Mauthausen quarry on 6 and 7 September 1944, two days after their arrival, and the many other airmen brought there to be killed.[12] These various restrictions on the purview of this study are intended to focus our discussion on the German civilian population acting in an open framework free of military-type discipline, their actions taking place outdoors, in public and of their own volition.

The archives that best lend themselves to our subject are those of the American Office of the Judge Advocate General (T-JAG), the branch of the US military concerned with matters of justice. Each ruling for a war crime was verified, or "reviewed," by military judges, either in the jurisdiction of the relevant territory or, starting in October 1946, by the Deputy Judge Advocate General (DJAG), headquartered in Dachau. These Reviews and Recommendations have been gathered together in the American archives. They provide summaries of the offending acts, a list of defendants and the resultant ruling. They have also been sorted by trial type. We thus have at our disposal the series of Reviews and Recommendations for some 200 Flyer Trials conducted by the American Army in Germany. While they give an overview, one must open the case files of the trials themselves to properly get a sense of civilian involvement.

For many reasons, precise information is not to be had regarding the total number of assaults and murders committed by the population against downed airmen in Germany. At most, one may hazard a low estimate. In war, some portion of an army's losses are reported as "missing." Even today, in 2019, the Allies are far from having found the remains of all downed pilots, whatever the cause of their deaths. Some 800 US Air Force personnel who came down over Germany are still listed as Missing in Action.[13] But if it is impossible to exhaustively account for them, this is also due to the attitude of the newly "occupied" population. Even Allied teams simply tasked with the job of recuperating their side's war dead came up against the hostility of those who had only the day before formed the *Volksgemeinschaft*.[14] It was not unusual for them to be on the receiving end of cries of *Terrorfliegern* (terrorist pilots), a sign of continuity with the language and practices of the Third Reich. Sometimes, the teams had to employ threats to convince mayors to tell them where the bodies of downed airmen were to be found. One team led by an RAF lieutenant thus used its amphibious tank to frighten a mayor from the North Frisian Islands, in Schleswig-Holstein. Finding himself in water up to his belt, the mayor yielded, supplying the information they were seeking. It was not just the population that practiced a kind of "omertà" by holding its tongue; defendants also denied their responsibility, pleading not guilty in nearly all cases.[15] A member of the British Missing Research and Enquiry Service summarized the situation in these terms:

> Whatever the witnesses' social level, job or education, three common factors emerged. Sooner or later in the course of the interrogation, they continuously repeated in their statements that: 1. They had never belonged to the Nazi Party; 2. They had never voted for Hitler; 3. They had never known or heard anything about the concentration camps.[16]

This stereotyped argument is worth pausing over for two reasons. For the observation made by this British air force lieutenant was very widespread. It overlaps with the analyses of war reporters like Martha Gellhorn. Writing from the Rhineland in April 1945, Gellhorn reported frequently hearing remarks to the effect that:

> "No one is a Nazi. No one ever was. There may have been some Nazis in the next village and as a matter of fact that town about twenty kilometers away was a veritable hotbed of Nazidom." There follows an involuntary confession of support for Nazism by way of the self-portrait presented to the occupier: "To tell you the truth, confidentially there were a lot of Communists here. We were always known as very Red. Oh, the Jews? Well, there weren't really many Jews in this neighborhood. Two maybe, maybe six. They were taken away. I hid a Jew for six weeks. I hid a Jew for eight weeks. (I hid a Jew, he hid a Jew, all God's chillun hid Jews.)"[17]

Jews and allies of the Bolsheviks: such was the image presented of Americans by Nazi propaganda from 1942 onwards. These selected scraps of discourse from the mouths of the defeated concur with the remarks of the Mitscherlichs, a married couple of German psychoanalysts. In their book, *The Inability to*

Mourn, they apply the concept of derealization to the negation of the Nazi past observable in 1960s Germany.[18] This psychological process transforms the external world into an unreal space that arouses no emotion.

In its exchanges with the forces of occupation, the occupied population's arguments also demonstrate the limits of opinion surveys in a context of defeat and following twelve years of racist and totalitarian dictatorship. Statistically speaking, the first of these ("never belonged to the Party") is not implausible since Nazi Party membership only stood at around 8.5 million people in 1945, or roughly 20 percent of the adult population. Yet the second argument ("never voted for Hitler") is less credible to the degree that the Party received 43 percent of all votes in the Nazi general elections of 1933 (March and November) and then between 92 and 99 percent of all votes in those of 1936 and 1938, respectively. It is nevertheless true that, under the Weimar Republic, the Nazi Party never received more than 38 percent of the vote. The third argument – that one did not know of the existence of camps – is not plausible. It is now commonly acknowledged that the German population was aware of the genocide and concentration camp system. One of the best confirmations of this is to be found in Nicholas Stargardt's book, *The German War*, which is based on the lived experience of ordinary Germans.[19] But it is the first two arguments that are of interest to us here. Support for the Nazi conception of the world did not require that one formally be a member of the Party or any of its various satellite organizations, nor even that one vote for it. This support developed as if naturally thanks to the attraction exerted by the Nazi *Weltanschauung* (worldview). The image of a German world superior to all others in point of its power and race was flattering to one and all. The creation of the *Volksgemeinschaft* represented a tremendous springboard for the population that suddenly found itself promoted to the status of "Aryan." It was an unprecedented framework for social, national and international self-promotion.

There are also more trivial reasons for why there is no complete inventory of the severe abuse to which airmen were subjected – the staff shortages about which the British complained when comparing themselves to the Americans, for example.[20] In January 1946, the Office of the Deputy Judge Advocate General for the British zone only had three investigative teams; its American counterpart had nineteen. But the limited time set aside for research also played a role, with the BAOR (British Army of the Rhine) and US teams withdrawing following the creation of the Federal Republic in 1949. Due to the political and material difficulties of the investigation, their work went unfinished. This is particularly apparent when consulting the American archives, which contain a voluminous series of "Cases not tried."

These untried cases are of great interest to the historian. There are various reasons that these assaults did not go to trial: the abuse was not considered sufficiently severe or there was a lack of evidence or the defendant had fled. At

196 LYNCHING IN GERMANY: DEFENDING THE NAZI STATE

times, the reason the case was abandoned is not specified. It might simply have been for lack of time on the part of the services of the DJAG. Some case files are nevertheless very specific. In sorting through them, it gradually becomes clear how lynching is to be defined: it consisted of murder or severe abuse taking place in public and/or outdoors and in the more or less immediate presence of a crowd of civilians. When ending in killing, I shall refer to these cases as petty local collective murders.

Petty Local Collective Murders

How many downed airmen were lynched in this way on German soil? Tables 8.1a and 8.1b offer some idea. Nearly 300 cases were tried. To judge by the American archives, however, three times as many cases went untried. Moreover, the disproportionate number of cases examined by the American

Table 8.1a. *Allied trials for war crimes committed against downed airmen on German territory* (Altreich)

Trials for war crimes against airmen (*Flyer Trials*)	Trials	Defendants	Victims	
			Killed	Abused but not killed
British zone	92	315	Unknown	Unknown
American zone	193	520	237	84
French zone	Unknown	Unknown	Unknown	Unknown
Soviet zone	Unknown	Unknown	Unknown	Unknown
Total	285 + n	835 + n		

Sources: Hassel, *Kriegsverbrechen vor Gericht*. TNA, WO 235 and 309.

NARA, micr M-1217, *Reviews of US Army, War Crimes Trials in Europe*, 1945–48, Roll 1, 2 and 3, *Reviews and Recommendations of Cases. Deputy Judge Advocate's Office.*[*]

French occupation zones in Germany and Austria: Affaires judiciaires. Direction générale de la Justice, 1945–55, subseries FRMAE 1 AJ. 15,625 files.[**]

* These *Reviews* may also be found on two websites: ICWC, International Research and Documentation Center for War Crime, University of Marburg, Dachau trials, https://www.uni-marburg.de/icwc/forschung/2weltkrieg/usadachau and *Jewish Virtual Library*, https://www.jewishvirtuallibrary.org/nazi-war-crimes-trials

** These boxes may contain very few trials of lynching since, as early as 1946, a French court judged that French tribunals could not judge events that had neither taken place on French territory nor involved French citizens. See further Hugo Grüner case, Chapter 11.

Table 8.1b. *Cases of airmen lynched on German territory investigated by the Deputy Judge Advocate General of the British and American zones*

Lynching cases examined by Allied military tribunals	Total number of cases examined (tried and not-tried)	Victims		
		Killed	Abused not killed	Total abused and/ or killed
British	122	164	61	225
American (estimate)	783	851	1,386	2,237
Estimated total	905	1,015	1,447	2,462

Sources: British investigations: *Index Cards of Place Names for War Crimes*, WO 353/20–21. This file is perhaps incomplete.

American investigations: *Cases Not Tried*, RG 549, Entry A1–2239, Box 84 to 255. Survey of 7 boxes distributed across the entire subseries: 85, 122, 150, 175, 200, 227, 254.[*]

[*] In these boxes, which contain 94 cases of possible war crimes spread out over the period 1943–45, I identified 24 cases involving the lynching of airmen, corresponding to 25 killed and 53 abused but not killed. Cross-multiplying for 172 boxes yields an estimate of 590 cases, in which 614 victims were killed and 1,302 abused.

services relative to their British counterparts – roughly, six to one – raises questions. For the British zone included northwestern Germany, a region subjected to particularly heavy bombardment. Finally, the results of French and Soviet investigations are absent from these tables. There is thus reason to believe that the 285 Allied trials for lynching of airmen on German soil do not accurately reflect events on the ground. Rather, this figure corresponds to a very minimal estimate. A more likely minimum is that several thousand such incidents took place, corresponding to two or three thousand victims.

Are one or two thousand cases of lynching over the span of two years few or many? This was a unique event in Western Europe, something that distinguished Nazi Germany from the war's other belligerents. While Luftwaffe airmen may have been subjected to abuse on a handful of occasions in Britain and France, as we have seen, nothing even remotely resembles in quantitative or qualitative terms the lynching phenomenon in Germany. One exception to this rule should be noted, however: the aforementioned lynching of a German airman on 18 May 1940, at Vimy, France. Furthermore, the few members of the British Army who committed abuses

198   LYNCHING IN GERMANY: DEFENDING THE NAZI STATE

were court-martialed.[21] Starting in April 1944, by contrast, Germans who opposed lynching risked being sent to prison or concentration camps.[22] The lynching that took place in Germany was thus an entirely different phenomenon. Over the course of this two-year period (June 1943–May 1945), however, around 18,000 American airmen came down over Germany and were taken prisoner as well as 7,000 RAF airmen.[23] If one adopts the low estimate of 2,500 lynched airmen, 1,500 of whom subsequently became prisoners, the rate of lynching would thus stand at 10 percent.

For several reasons, this 10 percent rate is an underestimate. Compared to the number of trials conducted by the Americans, the small number of trials conducted by the British in what was nevertheless a very heavily bombed zone speaks to their paltry resources and failure to carry through their work to completion. Nor were the cases of lynching tried in the French and Soviet zones taken into account in reaching this estimate. Finally, the Liberation Reports distributed to some former Allied POWs did not raise the issue of possible abuse at the hands of civilians. It was thus only after they had been repatriated that Eugene Brown and William Adams, the survivors of the Rüsselsheim lynching (Hesse), learned from a summer 1945 story in an American newspaper that the event had been the object of a trial in Germany. In July 1945, the American judges were still unaware that there had been two survivors.

It is significant that the minimum rate is 10 percent. For a point of comparison, one might refer to the rate at which African Americans were lynched in the United States. The comparison is not incongruous, as we shall see below in studying the racial dimension of lynching. With around 500 cases of deadly lynching per year, Nazi Germany surpassed the scale of American lynching at its worst, in the 1890s. For a population comparable to that of Germany in the 1930s (63 million in the USA in 1890; 60 million in Germany in 1935), the average annual number of deadly lynchings in the United States stood at around 155 over this period.[24] If one restricts the area of lynching to the fourteen states of the American South, the region where that practice was most widespread, there were an average of 140 lynchings for 20 million inhabitants, or 420 theoretical cases for 60 million inhabitants. This is still fewer than the minimal estimate for Nazi cases.

Just as in the American South, the population was more involved in this practice than may first appear since the number of participants involved in a given incident could range from ten to several hundred inhabitants. As can be seen in Map 4 in the Appendix to this book, moreover, the geographical extent of the phenomenon, which was general in scope and not restricted to bombed areas (lynching also took place in the Hessian countryside, Lower Saxony and elsewhere), shows how widespread this practice was across the population. It was indeed a social fact. In the space of a few months, lynching became as ordinary a practice in Germany as it had been in the post-Reconstruction South.

Lynching, Hallmark of the New Society

Just as in the United States, those who did the lynching were inhabitants of the place, not specialized teams that traveled around Germany after the fashion of the *Einsatzgruppen* in Poland and Russia. These were indeed ordinary Germans, carrying out the trades that one finds in small towns and villages. If police officers constitute the most frequently encountered professional category among them, this is due to our sources. Legal investigations naturally privilege cases of murder and those directly responsible for them. As the only people to legally possess firearms, police officers necessarily occupied an outsized place. The legal filter therefore tends to minimize cases of lynching that did not result in the victim's death as well as the role played by anonymous members of the crowd who actively participated but did not directly kill their victims. But even with this double filter, police officers only represent a quarter of those found to have been primarily guilty of murder. As the cases in Schleswig-Holstein examined above suggest, moreover, the army is largely absent from these cases. By not protecting prisoners under its escort, the army nevertheless played a decisive role. Yet since it was not soldiers who generally fired the fatal shots, they did not occupy a prominent place among the defendants.

Apart from the police, self-employed rural tradesmen and their workers were the most heavily represented milieu among the lynchers. More than 40 percent of the total consists of farmers, bakers, butchers, rope makers, innkeepers, shopkeepers, locksmiths, carpenters, painters and mechanics – age-old trades exuding self-respect and stability. The list contains few factory workers but more of them were to be found among second-tier defendants (those who struck but did not kill). No marginalized people (the homeless, unemployed, criminals and so on) are to be found among the defendants of either group. But then Nazi Germany had of course already labeled them "asocials" and set about eliminating them.

There were also few women among the accused, although they were present in the lynch mobs, small or large. The role played by women in the onset of collective violence is a general phenomenon reflecting their socially and physically dominated position. To signal their engagement, they usually shout and hurl challenges at the men, a phenomenon that the historian Edith Raim has also observed for the mobs of Kristallnacht.[25] Of the 520 defendants of the American Flyer Trials, only 9 were women, or 2 percent. This is fewer than in the British Army's trials, where women constituted 10 percent of all defendants.[26] The women accused by the US Army did not merely cry and shout for murder like many other women; they also took a role in beating the airmen. The women who used shoes, sticks and boards to beat the airmen or threw bricks and stones were housewives. On 26 and 29 August 1944, a district of Hesse witnessed a cluster of lynchings. The headquarters of Opel, now converted to an arms factory, was located there. Its bombing resulted in destruction of property and civilian deaths in the vicinity. Of the nine women defendants, five of them participated in lynching in Rüsselheim (six killed airmen, two wounded), Gross Gerau (two killed) and Trebur (several cases of abuse). These women were not members of the Nazi Party (which had few women members in any case) nor of other Nazi organizations.

In contrast to these ordinary women, the case of Therese Gebhardt, local leader of the *NS-Frauenschaft*, the Nazi women's league, stands apart from the rest for her higher degree of commitment to Nazism. Gebhardt was a forty-five-year-old married woman who lived in an apartment in the Bavarian village of Attenkirchen, one floor above the local police post. On 13 June 1944, two airmen parachuted onto village land. The same day, Gebhardt invited the NSDAP Kreisleiter and five or six other members of the Party to her home; some of them had just killed a downed airman. A second airman had been brought to the police and put in the cell downstairs from her

Table 8.2. *Socio-professional category of first-tier defendants* in the "Flyer trials" conducted by the American Army, 1945–48*

Soc.-prof. category	Number	NSDAP	Non-NSDAP	Unknown membership
Farmers	17	10	2	5
Agricultural workers	1			1
Artisans & small shopkeepers	17	8	2	7
Senior management and liberal professions	12	9	3	0
Midlevel management	11	7		4
Employees	6	4		2
Workers	24	12	4	8
Domestics	3	3		0
Police	34	16	3	15
Army	6	2	1	3
Clergy	1	0	1	0
Artists	1	1	0	0
Students	1	0	1	0
TOTAL	134	72	17	45

Source: US Army, JAG, Reviews and Recommendations, for German territory, M-1217.

* First-tier defendant: one who played a major role in the lynching, either by killing or by initiating the murderous lynching.

apartment. Serving food, beer and coffee to all present (as well as cognac to the Kreisleiter), this militant insisted that the second airman be killed. She went downstairs with the group to watch as he was beaten with a hammer before being finished off. A whiff of orgy hangs over this scene, with the pleasures of food, drink and murder inextricably linked in Nazi morality.[27]

In the sociology of lynchers, no single characteristic thus stands out. The factors that brought this population together are to be sought elsewhere. The proportion of first-tier defendants who were also Party members is indeed considerably higher than among the population at large: over 50 percent as compared to a national average of 20 percent. This is partly an effect of our sources. Allied criminal courts had declared the NSDAP a criminal organization. In the context of the occupying forces' investigations, this increased the visibility – and thus vulnerability – of party members. Moreover, were one to consider all 520 defendants rather than just those in the first tier, the rate of party membership would be lower. But the disparity is nevertheless significant. It is an indication that lynching was at least partly a Nazi phenomenon, one that transcended social strata while reorganizing them into a new socio-political elite. As indicated in the table above, Party membership was also distributed across all socio-professional categories. Only senior managers and members of the liberal professions were perhaps more Nazi than the others. As members of the NSDAP, a portion of the lynchers thus belonged to the avant-garde of the Nazi revolution. They were the elite of this new society and among them were to be found a few members of the elite of the elite, individuals drawn from the upper reaches of the Nazi hierarchy. Jürgen Stroop, for example, who, as HSSPf ("Höhere SS-und Polizeiführer"), was chief of all police and SS for Gau Rhein-Westmark. Stroop was accused of having ordered the deaths of nine airmen and was, among other murderous deeds, also responsible for putting down the Warsaw ghetto uprising and deporting some 50,000 Jews. There was also Friedrich Hildebrandt, Gauleiter and Reichsstatthalter of Gau Mecklenburg, who was tried for murdering more than eleven airmen. And Kurt Gross, an Austrian jurist who alternated between fighting with the Waffen-SS and overseeing ideological instruction at the SS school for non-commissioned officers in Radolfzell, on Lake Constance. Gross was tried for the murder of two airmen.

Apart from these three high-ranking members of the new society's elite, it was thus average Germans, smallholders and good workers, who made up the lynch mobs of whatever size. Although they often testified in their depositions as to the state of excitement ("Erregungszustand") the action had provoked, they were not excitable young people. With a mean age of forty-five, the age of defendants was regularly distributed between twenty-three and sixty-six.[28] Though many were present when the action took place, children and adolescents only rarely found themselves under investigation after the war. Taken together and in terms of their distribution by age, sex and profession, the lynch mobs resembled those of Kristallnacht, which were just as representative of local populations.[29] They were nothing if not a cross-section of German society.

A Stage in the Nazi Revolution

The profound changes brought about in German society by the Nazis' rise to power were nothing short of revolutionary. These transformations were not limited to the social and political order. By redefining the people as a race and condemning the outsiders and deviants of this definition to exclusion and death, they affected the moral order as well. Initiated in 1933, this revolution was still underway in 1945. In the final weeks of the war, Goebbels was still talking about "radicalizing our entire propaganda and information policy."[30] He railed against those "whose thinking is 'revolutionary' but [who] do not act accordingly" and congratulated himself on the "revolutionary spirit" of the militia then in training ("Werwolf").[31] Until the very end, the Nazi rhetoric of "burned bridges"[32] and the "destruction of inhibiting bridges"[33] continued to emphasize the radical break with civilization. The policy and practice of lynching airmen marked a new stage in this revolution – yet one more bridge had been burned.

According to statistics for the trials conducted by the British and American occupation authorities, the practice of deadly and non-deadly lynching took root in mid-1943 and carried on until the German capitulation two years later. This period was a time of ever more intense Allied bombing over Germany. But no mathematical or at any rate causal relationship can be established between bombing and lynching. In the first eight months of 1944, for example, the tonnage dropped on France was twice as great as that for Germany and yet no lynching took place in France on the part of its inhabitants. While there were a few cases of lynching in eastern France, they were the work of Wehrmacht personnel. From the point of view of German civilian involvement in Nazi violence, 1943 thus marked a new stage in the downward spiral of Nazi revolution. It was a new stage but not the ultimate one. Other thresholds would be crossed in 1944 and 1945 before this revolutionary process was brought to an end. And, when it was, it was due to the intervention of outside forces – the Allied armies. The Nazi revolution had yet to reveal its full potential.

Other historians have already taken note of the intensifying radicalization of the regime that began in 1943. The defeat of Stalingrad played a major role in this effort to regain control of the domestic situation by intensifying propaganda. Its immediate expression was Goebbels' 18 February 1943 speech summoning the German people, the *Volk*, to "total war." But the institutional repercussions were above all felt later, in the summer of 1943. Nicholas Stargardt has convincingly shown how relations between Nazi centers of power – and, in particular, between Goebbels and Himmler – were thrown into "crisis" in spring and summer 1943.[34] Dietrich Orlow coined the expression "partification" to describe the Nazi Party's growing hold over state, army and society.[35] While the process of politicization had been underway since 1933, it accelerated in 1943. Hans Mommsen and Doris Bergen debated this in 2000.[36] Taking a top-down approach, Mommsen's article was entitled "The Dissolution of the Third Reich: Crisis Management and Collapse, 1943–1945." In order to preempt the much-feared dissociation of society and regime, propaganda and ideology further strengthened their grip over the state administration and military strategy in this period. But is it appropriate to speak of the "dissolution" and "collapse" of the Third Reich? Adopting a bottom-up approach, Doris Bergen would appear to doubt it. Popular involvement in the Nazis' fight ensured the regime's solidity: "We need to ask what made people not only tolerate it but fight and kill for it until the bitter end." In this debate, Doris Bergen above all traded on her knowledge of the *Volksdeutsche* and, in particular, the German "stock" people living in Poland whom the Nazis wanted to reintegrate into the *Volksgemeinschaft*, the community of the German people-race. By concentrating on the Germans of Germany, the chapter that follows shows how the "Aryans" of that country – or at least a significant portion of them – until the bitter end consented to propaganda and as a consequence freely acted, often in deadly fashion. It also shows that the years 1943–45 were not a homogeneous whole. From above and below alike, society was tirelessly transformed by this dynamic of radicalization.

9

A Revolutionary Dynamic

DO NOT SURRENDER TO CIVILIANS, CIVILIAN POLICE, GESTAPO, HITLERJUGEND OR SCHUTZSTAFFEL.
THE SUGGESTION TO SURRENDER IS PERMISSIVE BUT NOT DIRECTIVE.

For the attention of Escape & Evasion Officers for dissemination to aircrews, 14 March 1945.[1]

SS-like Civilians

However belated, this warning directed at American aircrews by their evasion officers is revealing. Enemy civilians had become the greatest danger facing downed airmen, more so even than the Gestapo and SS. They also outdid the Hitler Youth, who were nevertheless heavily involved in hunting down fugitives. The fact that civilians should be the ranking champions of violence against downed airmen took Allied intelligence services by surprise. It took them nearly two years, from 1943 to 1945, to recognize that the usual hierarchy of wartime violence had in this way been inverted.

It was not until February 1945 that the Allies first clearly perceived the danger that German civilians posed for airmen. The February 1944 evasion handbook produced by MIS-X (US Military-Intelligence Service-X) seems unaware of the acts of violence committed on the ground.[2] That had changed by November, as indicated by an MIS-X report released the same month.[3] It asked that crews "revise their ideas on evasion and escape" in enemy territory and insisted that they regard the population in Germany, Austria and Hungary as "unfriendly." Their instructions remained the same, however, albeit now stated in more pressing fashion. It was only in late February 1945 that the American Strategic Air Force's intelligence service became alarmed:

> The situation is definitely becoming increasingly alarming and serious in regard to flying personnel – particularly to fighter pilots. The greatest danger seems to be to personnel bailing out in target areas, or in areas

which have been subjected to severe bombings in the past. There is ample evidence of physical violence, and in some cases of lynchings. The Hitler Youth, Gestapo and SS personnel seem to be mainly responsible for the more violent incidents. Depending to some extent upon the geographical area, civilians can also be placed in the category of being especially dangerous to American airmen. Men have been spat at and threatened with violence by civilians when travelling in various parts of Germany.[4]

Three weeks later, in the warning quoted as an epigraph to this chapter and written in capital letters, the same services ranked German civilians among the most dangerous threats. Until April, however, they still believed that the Wehrmacht and Luftwaffe were respecting international law and protecting the prisoners who had fallen from the sky. It was only on 26 April 1945 that MIS-X learned, through the chance discovery of a file left at a German air base, that the Luftwaffe had been instructed to no longer protect downed airmen from the "people's anger" (*Volkswut*).[5] Here as elsewhere, American soldiers were far from imagining the extent or nature of the violence that had been deployed on the home turf of National Socialism. They had failed to recognize the specificity of the regime.

In what respect does lynching violence express a revolutionary dynamic? This chapter seeks to demonstrate the dynamic nature of the relationship between state and society, the constant dialogue established between the people-race (*Volk*) and its leaders. Their positive interaction resulted in a permanent radicalization of the system. Since the 2000s, the very rich historiography on Nazism has moved away from the more or less functionalist arguments of the past. Without returning to a reductive form of intentionalism, it now insists on Nazi Germany's regnant social consensus and the population's voluntary participation in the regime's objectives.[6] This does not mean bracketing the terror wielded by the regime against its own "Aryan" people; rather, it is a question of shedding light on the spaces of freedom and material opportunities that the regime made available to the *Volk*. The streets, fields and woods where lynching took place were among these spaces of free expression, places where the participants gathered of their own free will. Nazi terror was not such that it could have forced the population to take part in these acts of collective violence.

Numerous and approved from above, these local undertakings were revolutionary in nature at several levels. First, they defined a new kind of democracy, one in which the people immediately rendered justice on their own and in which the separation of powers between the police and the legal system on the one hand, and the executive power and the law on the other, had been abolished. From the point of view of the centuries-old evolution of the rule of law, these events also represented a setback for the progress made since the seventeenth century in what concerned the protection of prisoners of war. After three centuries during which the "uses and customs of war" had become increasingly moderate, this evolution would have been brought to a definitive end in February 1945 had Germany acted on plans to repudiate the Geneva Convention. It would have been a counter-revolution had these events not so clearly entailed the people's will. In the mind of its supporters, this was indeed a new democracy, one that rivaled the other models, whether Western or Soviet. It was a democracy based on the fusion of race-masses and their Leader. In May 1945, it had still not reached its final form.

Popular Initiative, Propaganda and the Police Converge

At first glance, examining the Nazification of German society from the perspective of its reactions towards downed airmen has something of the chicken and egg story to it. The three parameters at work here went into action simultaneously: the intensification of bombing, the establishment of a policy of lynching and popular initiative responded to one another in immediate and synchronous fashion. To demonstrate this, one must revisit the chronology of 1943–45, where three phases, corresponding to the growing involvement of the population, may be distinguished. As shown on the charts that may be found in the Appendix, the new practice first took hold between summer 1943 and spring 1944. For the country's Promethean rulers, however, the most thrilling period was certainly that which began in May 1944. At that time, a sharp and (as the following months would bear out) sustained rise in lynching coincided with a set of discursive and policy innovations. The month of January 1945 was an exception, the combined result of the German offensive in the Ardennes and bad weather, which had the effect of reducing the number of sorties and thus the number of downed airmen. As we shall see below, incitement to lynching almost entered a new, more intense phase in February. But even in the absence of this stimulus, lynching reached an unparalleled height in March. The reduction in April reflects the rapid contraction of the *Altreich*'s territory. By late April, the Allies were on the Elbe and the Red Army had encircled Berlin.

To prop up the morale of bombing victims and the population in general, Nazi rulers initially took measures similar to those taken by other countries at war, implementing a social policy consisting of indemnification, housing, furniture and clothing distribution, anti-aircraft shelter provision and more or less forced evacuation.[7] These measures were immediately stamped with the National Socialist seal: bombed-out Jews had no right to compensation; redistributed apartments had often belonged to them prior to their expulsion and resettlement in camps or "Jew Houses" while they awaited deportation; the furniture, clothing and consumer goods had been plundered from

A REVOLUTIONARY DYNAMIC

occupied countries and the property of deported Jews throughout Europe. Independent minds were the object of rampant repression, moreover. In Britain, pacifists, most conscientious objectors and critics of strategic bombing were allowed to freely circulate and express themselves. In Germany, by contrast, the nonconforming soon lost their freedom and even their lives. Such was the case of the pastor of the Lutheran church of Lübeck, who was arrested and guillotined for having delivered what was considered a reprehensible sermon on 29 March 1942, the day after the town had been bombed.[8] His observation – that, "in the woes of our native city, we hear the voice of God" – was taken as an act of treason.

Another way of watching over the morale of the nation was to offer it reprisals. The theme made its first appearance in the press in 1942, following the bombing of Lübeck and Rostock. When it came, the riposte – *Vergeltung für Lübeck und Rostock* ("Reprisals for Lübeck and Rostock") – would take the form of the so-called "Baedeker" raids, after the name of the German tour guides, against the historic cities of England. But the weapon of reprisal, or *Vergeltungswaffe*, was not ready. It would only become available in 1944: the first V1 flying bombs and V2 rockets exploded in England in June and September 1944, respectively. Together with the atomic bomb, on which work was still underway, the Nazi regime counted on these new weapons to resume the strategic bombing abandoned in 1941. It had not created a bomber fleet comparable in size to that of the Allies nor established air defenses capable of seriously hampering the Allied fleets. These crucial shortcomings deserve a study in their own right. While specialists of the air war have concentrated on the Allied offensives and the German air defense, the German strategic and tactical bombing policies implemented in East and West between 1939 and 1941 have received little attention. With *The Bombing War*, Richard Overy is among the pioneers in this area. As the historian Bastiaan Robert von Benda-Beckmann has shown, the lopsided nature of research in this domain is not without political significance.[9]

In spring 1943, Joseph Goebbels, the Reichsminister of Public Enlightenment and Propaganda, was worried. In one of his daily meetings with fifty media and army propaganda service officials, Goebbels described himself as "seriously concerned about the air war." The minutes of the meeting put it as follows:

> The question of the air war is a serious worry at the moment. The minister is afraid that the German people might fall into a certain mood of resignation. Such resignation is very easily possible since no one knows when this unnerving air war will end. We must make an all-out effort to eliminate this danger and plan all our measures with this in mind. He does not wish the word "mood" to be used in future since one cannot

208 LYNCHING IN GERMANY: DEFENDING THE NAZI STATE

speak about mood when people's homes have been burnt down and cities devastated.

In future he wants mention to be made only of a high morale ... The minister believes that the air war can be eliminated only when a counter-attack is made on British on a major scale. Our defensive measures are not able to deter the British from further attacks ... The minister therefore requests that caution should be practiced in the propaganda treatment of this subject. It would be totally wrong for our propaganda today to make great promises of retaliation. The only reply that can be given is a counter-attack. The sole task of propaganda therefore is to stiffen the spirit of resistance – but here, too it must on no account cause annoyance among the public.[10]

These considerations are crucial to understanding the hiatus of summer 1943. In March, the minister groped for an answer. His instructions were purely negative: do not make big promises of reprisals, do not run the risk of irritating the *Volk*.

It was Himmler, Reichsführer SS and chief of police of the Reich, who found a positive solution the following August: to allow the people to lynch pilots, somewhat after the fashion of the Roman *circenses*. More so than the brutal measures of repression visited upon a few authors of nonconforming deeds, it was this practice of suggesting violence that constituted the originality of Nazi policy. The police were secretly ordered to abstain from intervening "in altercations between *Volk* comrades (*Volksgenossen*) and British and American terror pilots (*Terrorfliegern*)."[11] As a description, *Terrorfliegern* was not restrictive; it targeted all British and American airmen. The decree consisted of one sentence:

Reichsführer-SS   Headquarters, 10 August 1943

RF/Bn

48/16/43g   **Secret**
   It is not the duty of the police to intervene in conflicts between the Volk
   comrades and English or American terror airmen who have parachuted to
   the ground.

                                                      H. Himmler

The accompanying letter asked that the supreme leaders of the SS transmit the order to civilian and security police commanders (Befehlshaber der Ordnungspolizei und Sicherheitspolizei). The order was only to be transmitted orally to lower-level personnel to help ensure that this violation of the Geneva Convention would be kept secret.

In keeping with the technique of discursively cloaking reality so as to provoke a specific behavior, a new vocabulary took hold in the aftermath of the bombing of Lübeck and Rostock. What Victor Klemperer called the "language of the Third Reich" also applied to the air war. As early as 1940, General Jodl, General Chief of Staff of the Wehrmacht, had remarked on the need for "terror attacks" (*Terrorangriff*) against English population centers.[12] Though it had disappeared by 1943, the verb "to Coventrize" (*coventrieren*) was also in use in the language of the Reich following the November 1940 bombing of Coventry. In 1943, as Victor Klemperer notes, it would have been dangerous to remind Germans of their responsibility for ushering in the practice of indiscriminate bombing.[13] The inhabitants of Coventry, for their part, held that their town had been "Guernicaed," or destroyed after the fashion of Guernica.[14] Starting in 1942, the events of the air war were thus no longer treated in the classic propaganda terms that had been in use since the First World War.[15] What had formerly been described as an air attack now became a *Terrorangriff*, a raid became a *Terrorüberfall*, the air war a *Terrorkrieg* and a bomber a *Terrorbomber*. Airmen, for their part, had become *Terrorfliegern*, air gangsters (*Luftgangster*) and murder-bandits (*Mordbanditen*). New terms were constantly introduced along these lines.

When they asked the police to allow the "*Volk* comrades" (*Volksgenossen*) to give free rein to their anger in August 1943, the Nazi authorities were going along with popular violence more than provoking it. The lynching curve presented in the Appendix does not supply a detailed picture of events but only indicates a trend. It nevertheless demonstrates that the August 1943 order was not followed by an increased incidence of lynching; on the whole, the number of lynchings remained stable between June 1943 and April 1944. Yet, while the impetus from above did not affect the tendency, it may have ensured its stability. The authorities certainly cannot be faulted for not having tried hard enough to further redirect popular dissatisfaction against downed airmen. The bombing of Hamburg, which resulted in the death of some 40,000 people, came as a shock. Although the press offered no information apart from its usual talk of air pirates driven by a desire to exterminate (*Vernichtungswillen*) alongside stereotypical praise for the courage and solidarity of the *Volksgenossen*, concrete news spread by word of mouth, notably by way of the victims of bombing, some of whom were evacuated as far away as Bavaria. In his journal, Goebbels spoke of the "tragedy" and "catastrophe" of Hamburg. The rulers passed through a crisis of relative unpopularity.[16] Local party dignitaries and officials were taken to task by enraged civilians. After the defeat of Stalingrad in February, the loss of Tunisia in May and the arrest of Mussolini on 25 July, the Führer's inability to protect the Reich from air attack fueled worry and dissatisfaction. It was in this context that Himmler, Reichsführer SS and chief of police, signed the order to allow "altercations" between *Volksgenossen* and

Figure 9.1 "An American air gangster," December 1943. © 2021 Österreichische Nationalbibliothek. Photograph published on the front page of the *Völkischer Beobachter* on 20 December 1943 (Berlin edition), 22 December (Munich edition) and 23 December (Vienna edition, reproduced above). Kenneth D. Williams was shot down over Bremen on 26 November 1943.

Terrorfliegern to take their course. In doing so, he was offering a distraction to popular anger. On 24 August, Himmler was promoted to Minister of the Interior by Hitler.

The lynchings continued at a constant rate through April 1944. When propaganda seized upon an anecdote to ratchet up the anger, it had no noticeable effect. On 20 December 1943, the *Völkischer Beobachter* ran the headline "An American Air Gangster Calls Himself a Member of 'Murder Inc'." The subtitle read as follows: "Photographic Evidence of Gangster Involvement in Air Terror."[17] The article was immediately picked up in the regional press.[18] It was accompanied by a photograph taken from behind of prisoner of war Kenneth D. Williams, on whose jacket appear the words "Murder Inc." "Murder Incorporated" was an organization of killers working for the New York Mafia that had been dismantled in 1940. Bomber crews often baptized their aircraft with fanciful and provocative names. While we do not know whether the article's readers took it seriously, it ended on a threatening note: "They have sown death and will harvest a burning and undying hatred. With each new victim of their cowardly and treacherous terror, this hatred continues to grow until the time comes for righteous punishment." This was followed by the final sentence of the article, intended to provoke cold rage in the population: "But beyond punishment, there will remain burning contempt for a rabble that, employing the mafioso methods of New York and Chicago, its spiritual origin, rages against the German civilian population."

In April 1944, the authorities sought to give new impetus to popular violence. In our very incomplete survey, we see that fifty airmen had already been severely abused since early 1943, with half of them dying from their wounds. Since early 1944, Ernst Kaltenbrunner ran the RSHA, the Reichssicherheitshauptamt, with authority over all police forces as well as the SS intelligence service (SD) and the Abwehr. Kaltenbrunner issued a second secret order relating to the "treatment of enemy pilots who have parachuted to the ground." The order reiterates the terms of Himmler's decree and adds new measures intended to crack down on the population's behavior in cases in which it does not observe "the necessary distance vis-à-vis the pilots" it arrests. With this ambiguous expression, the order makes reference to non-aggressive behavior, not to be confused, it specifies, with the "crime of assisting escaped pilots."

Chief of Security Police and SD   Berlin, 5 April 1944
                                                  Secret Business of the Reich!

. . .

-VI-

In recent months, individual cases have shown that the German population is indeed capturing enemy airmen but that, while waiting to hand
them over to the police or army, it subsequently does not keep the
appropriate distance. Excessively severe measures on the part of the state
police against Volk comrades (Volksgenossen) would dissuade them from
readily capturing enemy airmen because *these cases must not be confused
with the criminal act of assisting escaped enemy airmen* [underlined
in text].

The SS Reichsführer has ordered the following measures be taken against
Volk comrades [*Volksgenossen*] who maliciously or from misplaced pity
[*aus böser Absicht oder falsch verstandenem Mitleid*] behave in a disgraceful manner towards captured enemy pilots:

1. In particularly severe cases, internment in a concentration camp with
   announcement in the region's newspapers;
2. In less severe cases, protective detention [*Schutzhaft*] by the competent
   state police for no fewer than 14 days. To be employed clearing rubble
   in bombed areas.[19]

212   LYNCHING IN GERMANY: DEFENDING THE NAZI STATE

This text is revealing. It shows how the legislative, judicial and executive powers were conflated in the Nazi state. It also shows how, in a state in which fanaticism was regarded as a positive value, the people were never sufficiently mobilized. Examining the use of the word "fanatical" in the Nazi-era German press, Victor Klemperer described the conceptual revolution by which evil became good and the abdication of reason was transformed into a fundamental virtue.[20] Several cases of normal behavior towards airmen on the ground sufficed to trigger sweeping police measures. Kaltenbrunner's order must not be read from the perspective that we have inherited from the Enlightenment. It is not a negative indicator of popular reluctance but rather the hallmark of a totalitarian state whose horizon of expectation is the people's generalized involvement in the political struggle, however bloody it may be.

In April 1944, the addition of a repressive measure alongside the incentivizing measure of August 1943 had no immediate effect. Between June 1943 and April 1944, the population's involvement in lynching seems to have been relatively constant. The impetus from above in August and December 1943 and then again in early April 1944 did not noticeably affect the curve, although it may have contributed to maintaining it. Indeed, it seems that lynching evolved somewhat autonomously. Taken together, these serial actions constituted a social movement, one that, though encouraged by the police, propaganda and repression, was nevertheless autonomous.

The initial measures taken by the police in August 1943 and April 1944, however, were not made public; the orders given were strictly internal. In May 1944 began the next stage of this policy to support the nation's morale, and this time it took place in full view of the public. It sheds a clearer light on the specifically Nazi character of this mobilization.

"Deliverance" for the *Volk*: Calls for Murder from Above

This incitement to murder was publicized in an article from the Minister of Public Enlightenment and Propaganda. Appearing in the Party newspaper, the *Völkischer Beobachter*, in the last days of May, Goebbels' article, "A Word on the Enemy Air Terror," pounded away at the image of the "defenseless women and children," the "old people, women and children as well as churches, ancient cultural monuments and densely populated residential neighborhoods" upon which the "Anglo-American terrorist airmen" have visited their destruction. But "in these questions," the minister added, "the thinking of our *Volk* is much more radical than that of its government." It was as if the government had to bend to the will of the *Volk* against its better judgement:

A REVOLUTIONARY DYNAMIC 213

No one will be surprised that the population concerned, which is known throughout the world for its full understanding of all types of conventional warfare, has become enraged by these cynical crimes. Guns alone can ensure the security of these downed enemy pilots, who would otherwise be killed by the sorely tested population. Who is right? The murderers who after their cowardly crimes expect humane treatment from their victims or the victims who wish to defend themselves in keeping with the principle, "an eye for an eye, a tooth for a tooth"? The answer is not difficult. In all cases, it would be too much to ask that we use German soldiers to protect child killers from parents who, seized by fury and rage after having lost their dearest treasures because of the enemy's brutal cynicism, take steps to defend themselves. If the English and the Americans want, as they themselves say, to treat us as a tribe of inconvenient natives, it's up to us to know what to do. The German people is known throughout the world for giving to war what war demands. But enough is enough. And here, the limits of what is tolerable are behind us.[21]

Beginning in the seventeenth century, Western countries slowly evolved towards a codified protection of prisoners of war. The Reich minister's suggestion that the population be allowed to re-establish "eye for an eye" justice was thus revolutionary in nature. It amounted to publicly repudiating a long civilizational process. By suggesting that civilians carry out reprisals explicitly prohibited by the Hague and Geneva Conventions, moreover, the minister legitimated in the full view of everyone the path opened one year earlier to private justice. The people's justice or *Volksjustiz* had the force of law.[22] As was usually the case, the article was immediately reprinted in almost identical form by regional newspapers.[23]

This was an exhilarating moment for the Reichsminister of Public Enlightenment and Propaganda. In June 1944, he felt himself to be in symbiosis with the people. Published in the *Völkischer Beobachter* on 26 May (Berlin edition), his "Lynch-style" article on the air war had an "extremely strong impact." "The German people saw it as a deliverance. Given how the air war had developed, one otherwise had a feeling of total impotence."[24] One week later, he again wrote in his journal:

From the letters I've had, I conclude that my article on the "lynching" of pilots was wonderfully received. In the conduct of this war, upon which our fate depends, the German people no longer want to hear talk of the spirit of chivalry or humanity. Rarely has one of my articles had as much impact as this one. In short, the people demand that we conduct a more confident and total war.[25]

The public reception of the article, at least as the minister presents it, reinforced his analysis. As he wrote the same day, "our people," "when they are properly led, never disappoint." Goebbels' journal is not to be taken literally, of course. Any product of a rationality based on a genocidal imaginary is a dubious source. Some facts nevertheless suggest he had reason to be satisfied: for example, the manner in which a Kriegsmarine captain on the island of Borkum reacted to the article. Though he was not even a member of the NSDAP, this captain interpreted the newspaper article as an immediately applicable "decree" and set about orchestrating the lynching of seven airmen by a mob. The article was followed by several others and the minister gave a number of speeches along the same lines. As Goebbels told the ecstatic crowd that on 4 June had assembled at Nuremberg's Adolf Hitler Square for the "district Nazi Party festival" (*Kreistag*):

> Eight days ago, I addressed the public to point out that the German police and German Wehrmacht are obviously not there to hold back the German public when it acts aggressively against such murderers [who strafe villages and streets]; that's not their duty! (rounds of bravos and enthusiastic cries, applause, a chorus of young women chanting "Murderers! Murderers!").[26]

The fact that the Kriegsmarine captain cited above could in August 1944 consider a speech or newspaper article as tantamount to an order is illustration of how the rulers' cult of personality had replaced any notion of legislative procedure, legality and even military regulation. Such behavior was not isolated, however. The incidence of lynching sharply increased in May–June 1944 and then once again in July of the same year, reaching an elevated level that would persist until the capitulation. The appeals to the public from above were heard below. And the route from one to the other was extremely short, indeed nearly instantaneous: half of all lynchings in May took place within forty-eight hours following the publication of Goebbels' article in the *Völkischer Beobachter*.[27]

The direct involvement of the Nazi Party only further contributed to merging the people with its leaders. A 30 May 1944 order from Martin Bormann, chancellor of the NSDAP, was distributed to all levels of the Party.[28] In what regarded the "People's Justice (*Volksjustiz*) against the Anglo-American murderers," the order claimed that several defenseless civilians – and "women and children, in particular" – had been killed by aerial machine-gun fire in the preceding weeks. The text continued: on several occasions, airmen who had carried out forced landings or parachuted to the ground "were lynched on the spot immediately after their arrest by the utterly enraged population." In closing, the order pointed out that no charges had been brought against the "Volksgenossen" (*Volk* comrades) by the police or courts.

A REVOLUTIONARY DYNAMIC

German National Socialist Workers Party
Party Chancellery

Chief of the Party Chancellery   Headquarters of the Führer,
                                                             30 May 1944
                                                             Secret

Circular 125/44 g.
(Not to be made public)

Purpose: People's Justice against the Anglo-American murderers

On several occasions in recent weeks, English and North American airmen have fired while flying at low altitude on children's playgrounds, women and children working in the fields, peasants at work, carts on the country roads, trains and so on and have in this way murdered defenseless civilians, in particular women and children.

It has happened several times that crews that parachuted to the ground or were forced to land have been immediately lynched on the spot by the extremely indignant population. These *Volk* comrades (*Volkgenossen*) have not been charged by the police or been the object of criminal proceedings.

Signed M. Bormann

Distribution: Reichsleiter,
                    Gauleiter,
                    Verbänderführer
                    Kreisleiter
F.d.R.:   Unterschrift

----

                                                             30 May 1944

To all Gauleiter and Kreisleiter!

Purpose: Circular 125/44 g

The Chief of the Party Chancellery asks that the Kreisleiter only orally inform the Ortsgruppenleiter (district-level leaders) of the contents of this circular.

Signed Friedrichs

F.d.R.: Harms

This joint intervention on the part of the Ministry of Propaganda and Nazi Party also shows the growing power wielded by politicians over the military – a contrast that must not be overstated, to be sure, as the officers in question were also convinced Nazis. Faced with such objective realities as the activity of armed enemies or shortages of fuel and heavy weaponry, however, soldiers were in no position to give such free rein to their imagination. Politicians looked upon these external constraints from a greater remove. But why did the minister and Party embark on this offensive? At some point around 19 May, or eight days before the publication of Goebbels' article, Hitler complained that German civilians had been attacked by low-flying Allied airplanes.

216   LYNCHING IN GERMANY: DEFENDING THE NAZI STATE

He demanded that the pilots of these aircraft be immediately executed should they come down. Although the leaders surrounding Hitler possessed no verified information to substantiate the crime with which the airmen had been charged, they immediately set to work. This time, it was not just the Police and Propaganda services that rallied in support of lynching but also the Nazi Party, Wehrmacht and Luftwaffe.

On 21 May, a day or two after Hitler expressed his murderous designs, a round of meetings and exchanges got underway. These brought together Reischsmarshall Keitel, head of Wehrmacht Oberkommando, Wehrmacht General Chief of Staff Jodl and his adjutant, General Warlimont, Colonel von Brauchitsch, representing the Luftwaffe Oberkommando, and SS Lieutenant General Kaltenbrunner, representing the SS and police. From 6 June, it was understood that "lynching justice" (*Lynchjustiz*) was the order of the day and that the SS Intelligence Service (SD) would also be called upon. Since nearly 200,000 Germans were already being held as Allied prisoners, any too open break with the Geneva Convention was to be avoided. As it did not appear to implicate the state, lynching by the civilian population was thus welcomed. But the population was in no position to identify pilots who had specifically attacked civilians at low altitude. The idea was thus for the Luftwaffe to sort through the airmen in its custody and investigate those "suspected" of having fired at low altitude. If their guilt was confirmed, the pilots would be handed over to the intelligence service (SD) for "special treatment" (summary execution after torture). The Ministry of Foreign Affairs "essentially agree[d] with this solution, despite obvious objections based on international law and foreign policy." The decision was thus taken and, on 9 July, the OKW instructed Wehrmacht personnel to refrain from interfering in "altercations" between the population and airmen. The Luftwaffe was less sure. It was only on 2 October that the OKW was informed that Goering agreed to this policy and only on condition that the order not to interfere be transmitted from the OKW rather than the Oberkommando der Luftwaffe (OKL).[29]

One point of military history remains to be elucidated. What is the true reason for this headlong plunge into lawlessness? Did low-altitude attacks on civilians become more common in May 1944 or was this merely a pretext seized upon to take measures meant to bolster the nation's morale? On 30 and 31 May and 1 June, newspapers featured reports on localized attacks on passersby, tourists and peasants. As always with the Nazi press, there is no way of knowing whether this was information or disinformation. A cruise ship transiting between Cologne and Düsseldorf was also said to have come under fire. Six passengers were killed, it was claimed, including three women and two children.[30] It is possible that, recalling Stuka attacks on civilians in Poland, Belgium and France, some pilots wanted to give German civilians a taste of their own medicine. In the case of the American Air Force, however, the first systematic attacks targeting transportation on German soil, including railroads and canals, would not take place until October 1944.[31] As Goebbels noted in his journal that November: "We have inflated the extent of low-altitude air attacks and this has increased anxiety in the population, who fear a worsening of the situation."[32] It does indeed seem that, in spring 1944, such attacks were merely a false pretext for emphasizing the policy of lynching.

Repudiating the Geneva Convention

Yet the situation in the skies changed in late February 1945. On 22 February, the US Air Force launched Operation Clarion, its "General Plan for a maximum effort attack against transportation objectives."[33] As a matter of necessity and even of pilot choice, this policy was to directly impact civilians. The resulting low-altitude strafing of civilians had many witnesses. I shall limit myself to the accounts supplied by two victims of persecution. The first is Victor Klemperer, a Jewish survivor who was at the time wandering southwestern Germany with his Aryan wife. In February 1945, the bombing of Dresden and ensuing chaos provided him with a last-chance opportunity to save himself from being deported the following day, as scheduled. Klemperer offers several examples of deadly fighter attacks, sometimes along railways but also in the countryside and in the absence of any obvious military objective.[34] As he notes on 21 April: "And the country roads are treeless and dusty and threatened by low-flying aircraft." To the northwest, a ten-year-old girl and her brother, persecuted for their American nationality in the town of Rüsselsheim (Hesse), had to leave the place in 1944 after their home was rendered uninhabitable by bombing. They took refuge with their mother in Heimersheim (Rhineland-Palatinate), not far from the Remagen bridge. In this little town, Marlies witnessed two cases of deliberate strafing, one targeting a passerby in the street, the other directed at herself and her brother as they gathered apples in an orchard.[35]

In March 1945, the number of lynchings increased sharply. Was this precipitous rise a civilian response to Operation Clarion, a reflection of surging nationalism as German territory came under invasion, or the outcome of a popular dynamic that first got underway in 1943? It seems safe to say that this showing was the result of the conjunction of all three factors. There is no doubt, by contrast, as to the desire of the country's leaders to push the "revolution" ever further. This was particularly the case with Goebbels. This was already in evidence in 1944, when he spoke with the Ministry of the Interior's Wilhelm Stuckart on the need to declare the "most radical revolutionary war" in the event that German territory was invaded.[36] The same may be said of the pains he took to develop the propaganda of the "revolutionary spirit" of the *Werwolf*, a volunteer militia recruited among the SS and Hitlerjugend and tasked with carrying out guerilla warfare against the invader,[37] and his repeated evocations of the "good old days of our struggle," the "heroic era" of the revolutionary conquest of power. All point to growing radicalization.[38] In the final months of the war, the minister vociferated against the newspapers, which he saw as guilty of defeatism. Thus *Das Reich*, the official Nazi Party weekly,[39] where Goebbels himself wrote the editorial, had allowed one or two insufficiently "revolutionary" articles to appear following the bombing of Dresden. Similarly with *Das Schwarze Korps*, a mouthpiece for the SS, which had entertained the prospect of defeat in battle while still affirming the survival of the National Socialist idea.[40] In response to these writings, the minister announced an "energetic" reaction, up to and including "the most brutal methods." More radical than the most extreme radicals, Goebbels was at this moment the living embodiment of the Nazi dynamic.

It would be a mistake to think that the minister reserved this revolutionary fervor and the various excited declarations that accompanied it for his dictated journal. For this journal contains traces of an attempt to repudiate the Geneva Convention, an attempt that really took place. Starting in late March 1945, Goebbels complained that he had not been heeded when he had requested, in February of that year, that Hitler do precisely that:

> I am very pleased that the Führer should stress that I was the only one to be right over the question of withdrawal from the Geneva Convention. All the others opposed it, he says. But they are after all only bourgeois people gone to seed; they have no conception of revolutionary conduct of war and so could not be expected to support it. It is really tragic to see the Führer, who is a revolutionary of the highest order, surrounded by such mediocre people.[41]

In February 1945, Goebbels thus reacted to the bombing of Dresden with a revolutionary proposal. The bombing had caused the death of 25,000 people and led to the city of art's destruction, including the burning of the Frauenkirche, a jewel of Baroque art. The announcement of this news had even shocked the Allies. On Goebbels' suggestion, Hitler wanted to repudiate the Geneva Convention.[42] Exiting this framework – the result of several centuries' work to regulate the violence of war – would supposedly have had two advantages: it would gratify a population tormented by "terror bombing" by allowing them to "personally deal with enemy pilots."[43] And, by holding out the prospect that they might find themselves on the receiving end of the same abuse meted out by the Allies, this time, by way of reprisal, it would serve to frighten Wehrmacht soldiers who might otherwise be tempted to surrender. Both the Wehrmacht and the Kriegsmarine had doubts regarding this project. An initial draft response dated 20 February 1945 began by asserting, as if it were a matter of established fact, that "the daily terrorist air attacks against the German civilian population exceed in scale all of the atrocities of history." Since the population was "already settling its scores" with the terrorist airmen, however, it was "not necessary to abandon international agreements for that."

Moreover, while the Germans held 230,000 Anglo-American prisoners, the Anglo-American forces now held 441,000 German ones. There was a risk that withdrawing from the Geneva Convention would be disadvantageous for the Germans. Nor would "the problem of our deserters ... be eliminated by abusing prisoners" in Germany for the Anglo-American enemy would certainly continue to attract deserters with false promises of good treatment.[44] General Jodl's conclusion offers a sort of anthology of Nazi reasoning: "In this case also, it seems that the best method, already tested many times over, is to fight terror with counter-terror and not follow the path of law and the violation of law, which is generally the least favorable to us"[45] (an allusion to the fallout from the violation of Belgium's neutrality in 1914). When all was said and done, the idea of withdrawing from the Convention was abandoned, severely vexing the Minister of Propaganda. The intensification of lynching activity in the course of March proved the soldiers right: it was not necessary to officially repudiate international law. The *Volk* had already decided the matter.

* * *

The manner in which civilians treated Allied airmen on the ground in the Germany of 1943–45 is only one small chapter in the history of German society of that time. This vantage point nevertheless sheds light on the close interaction between the population and its rulers. Just as the *Volk* seemed to act autonomously in 1943 even as it was encouraged by the authorities, it responded as if with enthusiasm to the incentives of propaganda in the summer of 1944. This momentum proved lasting and even became more vigorous in March 1945. Here as elsewhere, the National Socialist regime was based on a revolutionary dynamic. In abandoning a development that was centuries in the making and thus civilizational in nature, the practice of lynching reflected a process of decivilization. It is striking to note that, in his masterpiece, *The Civilizing Process*, the sociologist Norbert Elias did not see or did not want to include in his discussion the countervailing process that was very rapidly unfolding before his eyes in 1930s Germany even as he wrote.[46] After the war, he returned to the subject in the context of the Eichmann trial in 1961–62.[47] As a sociologist, he explained German "national hubris" and the Germans' unbroken support for the Nazi regime by reference to the long-term process of state formation, arguing that an exalted and idealized image of Germany had provided the foundations for a consensual process of decivilization.[48]

The intensification of bombing is often presented as a factor contributing to German disaffection with the regime. Drawing upon reports from the SD – the SS intelligence service of the RSHA, or Reichssicherheitshauptamt, which had authority over all branches of the police – the historian Gerald Kirwin showed how pessimism and defeatism gradually made inroads from summer 1943.[49]

220 LYNCHING IN GERMANY: DEFENDING THE NAZI STATE

On the basis of these same police reports, Ian Kershaw has also underscored the proliferating signs that the Reich was "disintegrating" in its final year, with German morale collapsing as the desire for peace grew both on the home front and within the ranks.[50] Yet did these expressions of demoralization – as alarming for the regime's policemen as they were for the dignitaries of the single party – reflect an abandonment of the mental universe of National Socialism? Not really. Rather, it seems, given the constant and even increasing rate of lynching, that they remained circumstantial. The weariness caused by bombing and growing hopes for peace did not signify a rejection of National Socialist thought.

The involvement of the *Volk* in lynching shows the population in a new light: that of combatants in their own right. Without going so far as to supply a counter-narrative, it brings perspective to bear upon the narrative of Germany as victim. As we know, the memory of bombing has served as a vector for German self-victimization and made it easier to turn the tables on the Allies in regards to accusations of crimes against humanity. The historian Dietmar Süss has shown how the memory of bombing in Germany is a cyclical affair.[51] The success of popular historian Jörg Friedrich's *The Fire: The Bombing of Germany, 1940–1945*, first published in German in 2002, represents one of its key moments. In that book, there is no indication of popular involvement in the Nazi struggle. The inhabitants are presented as nothing more than the victims of appalling destruction. Only two paragraphs mention the practice of lynching, as it if were an insignificant footnote.[52] To the contrary, it seems to me that a more faithful portrait should reintroduce the fighting spirit of the *Volk*, its commitment to Nazi values and methods. For, however tragic it may be, lived experience is tinged with social and political subjectivity.

10

Lynch Mobs
Pre-Constructed Anger and Nazism in Action

The time has come to address the political dimension of lynch mobs. Were the mobs that attacked defenseless prisoners expressing legitimate (*berechtigte Empörung*) or extreme (*äusserste empörte*) indignation, as was claimed in the administrative documents that encouraged or approvingly took note of the assaults? Were they driven by anger (*Wut*), fury (*Zorn*), rage (*rasende Wut*) or even hate and fury (*in seinem Hass und in seinem Zorn*), as Goebbels, Minister of Public Enlightenment and Propaganda, maintained?[1] One must not neglect the scale of destruction visited upon Germany. Over the duration of the war, Germany lost six times as many inhabitants as Britain or France, with a population between 1.5 and 2 times as large.[2] Once a certain threshold was crossed, a social mathematics proportionally linking the number of deaths under the bombs to a degree of violence may have been set in motion. But this mechanism demands closer study. Until now, there has been no effort to scrutinize the shift from anger to violence against the subaltern agents of destruction. The handful of books and articles that consider the fate of airmen in Germany and Austria present this link as obvious. It is here, however, that any discussion must begin.

A second issue concerns civilian adherence to the values conveyed in top-down calls for violence. Until now, these encouragements have been presented in stand-alone fashion and without any effort to identify the paths by which they were internalized by those below. Yet these paths inform us as to support for the National Socialist regime. In a general way, history books often neglect to consider civilian participation in Nazi violence, among other reasons because contemporaneous archives have little or nothing to tell us about their contribution. At the time, the active participation of a part of the population in mistreating airmen, forced laborers and deportees during the death marches left no trace. As this violence was considered legitimate and desirable, the authorities felt no need to monitor (or keep a record of) it. The same is true for the other part of the population, that which did not participate in the lynchings. Whether or not it signified a refusal to join in, its passivity left no trace. Did this silent majority approve of the violence on the country's streets and roads? We have thus far assumed that the quantitative and geographical data presented in Chapter 8 are an indication of public acceptance. But what about

222   LYNCHING IN GERMANY: DEFENDING THE NAZI STATE

potential German helpers? Was the German population heterogeneous, like the Hungarian one in which helpers and lynchers co-existed?

During the first semester of 1945, some 10,000 foreign workers and 250,000 deportees died on German territory.[3] During this time, bombing claimed some 95,000 German lives.[4] How many of these 260,000 forced and concentration camp laborers succumbed to exposure, the blows of civilians or their refusal to give them so much as an apple or glass of water during the death marches? Robert Gellately and Ulrich Herbert have examined the fate of forced laborers and/or slaves but the role played by German civilians in this overall picture has yet to be fully elucidated.[5] The same holds for Daniel Blatman's otherwise very thorough book on the death marches.[6] For a good view of civilians in action, one must have sources. The historian Sven Keller, a specialist on the years 1944–45 in Germany, was one of the first to use serial sources to examine the question of the relationship between society and Nazi violence.[7] To do so, he relied on the postwar trials conducted by tribunals, not just in West Germany, but also in the East, where some of the crimes committed against foreign workers and the deportees of the death marches were tried. He devotes a few pages to the subject in his book, *Volksgemeinschaft am Ende: Gesellschaft und Gewalt, 1944/1945* (*The End of the Volksgemeinschaft: Society and Violence, 1944–45*). They represent a first step. For Austria, the historian Eleonore Lappin has also used the postwar trials to study the fate of Hungarian Jews in the death marches of spring 1945.[8] And, once again for the Austrian case, the historians Gerwin Strobl and Georg Hoffmann have, as we have seen, drawn upon the same sources to shed light on the lynching of Allied airmen.[9]

The trials conducted by the Allies after the war, particularly those relating to lynching, partially open a window on the question of civilian behavior but the rules of liberal judicial inquiry did not allow them to directly attack the question. The trials subsequently conducted in the Federal Republic of Germany encountered the same liberal constraints. It is up to the historian to reconstruct the theater of operations, as it were, in which the action took place as well as the role played by each of the various actors. A twofold question cuts across this effort to shed light on the matter: what is the meaning of the civilian violence that may be observed on the ground and that one encounters in neither France nor the United Kingdom? And what local-level considerations were behind this deadly dynamic, which was only brought to an end by the arrival of the Allies?

Rüsselsheim, a Model Lynching

On 24 August 1944, the crew of an American bomber returning from a mission over Hanover were forced to parachute from their airplane, their B-24 having been seriously damaged by Flak anti-aircraft fire. The airmen landed on the territory of the municipality of Greven, a small town in North Rhine-Westphalia, 20 kilometers north of Münster. Upon reaching the ground, two of the crew members were humanely picked up by farmers. A third, Eugene Brown, was immediately subjected to abuse by a small mob in the fields. Upon arriving in Greven, he was manhandled and insulted by a row of hate-filled inhabitants. One by one, the nine men were led to city hall. Inside, the rank-and-file airmen were beaten bloody by civilians. William Adams was then brutally interrogated by the uniformed man who seemed to be in charge of the operation. He came away from this with his face covered in blood. Two members of the crew were "accused" of being Jews: Sergeant Adams and Navigator Tufenkjian. Faced with their denials, those holding the prisoners forced the nine airmen to drop their pants and underwear to examine them. They were finally transferred to the local air base, where the Luftwaffe treated them decently. Sergeant Brininstool, who had been wounded by Flak fire, received cursory first aid and was dispatched to the military hospital in Münster. The next day, 25 August, the eight remaining prisoners of war were sent by train towards the Luftwaffe transit and interrogation center in Oberursel, near Frankfurt. From there, they were to head to a prisoner of war camp.[10]

But on the night of 25–26 August, the RAF bombed Opel factory head-quarters in Rüsselsheim, a small town 30 kilometers from Frankfurt with an at once industrial and rural economy. Its factories produced the Junkers-88, the famous frontline fighter bomber, for the Luftwaffe. The vast area occupied by the firm ran along the railway all the way to the center of town. The night bombardment of 25–26 August cut the railroad leading to it. Escorted by two Luftwaffe guards, the eight Americans thus arrived on foot in Rüsselsheim on the morning of the 26th. There, the soldiers of the escort hoped to find an in-service train. The atmosphere was tense in this little town of 16,000 inhabitants. After a sleepless night, the inhabitants were outside, clearing debris and discussing the night's events. It was the tenth time the town had been bombed since the start of the war (the first, in 1940, was the result of an error on the part of the Luftwaffe) and the third such bombing in five weeks. The deadliest attack took place on 20 July 1944, when 65 of the town's inhabitants were killed alongside 92 other Germans, for a total of 157 dead. On 26 August, the town lost 20 inhabitants (for a total of 21 Germans, including a resident of a neighboring village) and recorded the death of 177 forced laborers and POWs, whose barracks adjoined the factory. A few isolated bombs continued to fall that December. Over the duration of the war, fully 45 percent of the town's buildings were damaged or destroyed by bombing.[11]

Entering the town one after the other as they took turns supporting Dumont, whose ankle had been injured in landing, the airmen marched down

224 LYNCHING IN GERMANY: DEFENDING THE NAZI STATE

Mainzer Strasse, which runs parallel to the Main River, flowing east to west. To their left, they may not have noticed the synagogue that had been vandalized by inhabitants on Kristallnacht. It had not been completely destroyed because "Aryan" tenants lived above it. Since that 9 November 1938 night, the building had been converted into a residence and purchased by a local architect. Some 200 meters further on, the escorted prisoners reached the marketplace, cluttered with the debris of buildings. The evangelical church was still standing but the square was covered with girders, pieces of brick and tiles. As they gathered around the airmen, the hostility of the inhabitants was palpable.[12] To reach the station, the little convoy could not directly turn right onto Marktstrasse as it had not been cleared. The men thus continued heading east down Frankfurterstrasse, which remained passable. Increasingly pressed on all sides by the little crowd, they passed by the police station. To their left, just behind a row of houses, was the town's old Jewish quarter. The "Jew House," or "Judenhaus," in which the last Jews had been gathered before their deportation in 1942 was merely a stone's throw away on Schäfergasse.[13] At the end of this little street – in front of number 10 Frankfurterstrasse or a few meters further on – some women cried out, "Beat them to death!," "Kill these dogs!," "They're the ones who destroyed our homes!," "They're the terrorist flyers!" These calls to murder were leveled by two sisters, wives and mothers both, who owned a little tobacco shop at 10 Frankfurterstrasse. They literally created the event. As she shouted, Käthe Reinhardt – at thirty-eight, the youngest of the two – threw a brick at the head of an airman. There was blood. She followed up with punches. Her fifty-year-old sister, Magarete Witzler, followed suit.

The lynching thus began on Frankfurterstrasse and continued along Taunusstrasse and Grabenstrasse in the direction of the train station (see Map 10.1 and Figure 10.1). Josef Hartgen, a foreman at Opel and the local NSDAP head of propaganda, arrived on the scene and fired a shot in the air, adding to the uproar. He asked the Luftwaffe guards to leave town by the Frankfurt road. The guards refused, however, as they still hoped to find a train. The lynching then unfolded without hindrance over a trajectory of some 800 meters. The guards let it happen. A policeman who was present let it happen. A retired local schoolteacher, Christoph Keil, asked these representatives of the army and police to intervene but in vain. Surrounded by a shouting mob that hurled stones and bricks at them while striking them with shovels and the shafts of farm tools, it took the airmen three quarters of an hour or more to cover this distance.[14] Confronted with cries of "Jew! Jew!" ("Jude! Jude!"), William Adams once again tried to convince the mob that he was not Jewish.[15] As someone of Pennsylvania Dutch origin, he spoke a little German. This was not the case of Haigus Tufenkjian, who did not understand. Halfway up the Taunusstrasse, a

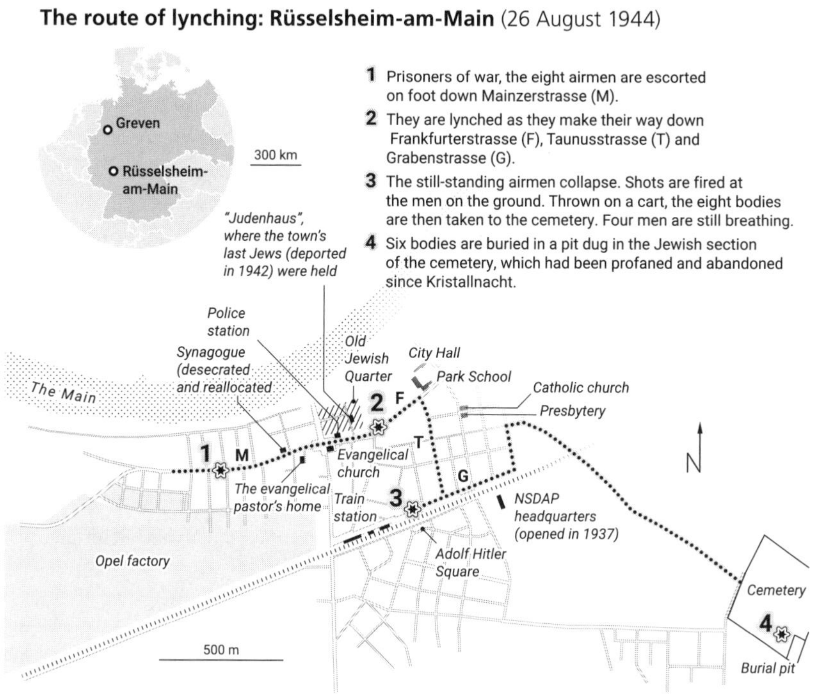

PRE-CONSTRUCTED ANGER AND NAZISM IN ACTION

The route of lynching: Rüsselsheim-am-Main (26 August 1944)

1 Prisoners of war, the eight airmen are escorted on foot down Mainzerstrasse (M).

2 They are lynched as they make their way down Frankfurterstrasse (F), Taunusstrasse (T) and Grabenstrasse (G).

3 The still-standing airmen collapse. Shots are fired at the men on the ground. Thrown on a cart, the eight bodies are then taken to the cemetery. Four men are still breathing.

4 Six bodies are buried in a pit dug in the Jewish section of the cemetery, which had been profaned and abandoned since Kristallnacht.

Map 10.1 The route of lynching: Rüsselsheim-am-Main, 26 August 1944.

Map Source: Strassen-Plan, Gemeinde Rüsselsheim, 1931, Municipal archives.

Map creator: Atelier de cartographie, Sciences Po, 2022

bloodied airman with a piece of tile protruding from his skull dropped to a sitting position. He was finished off with kicks to the throat and chin by a sixty-seven-year-old farmer.

The mob grew in size, perhaps finally reaching 200 people. It grew gradually at first and then grew again when two groups of workers and railway men, rendered idle by the bombing, arrived from the train station and the southern district to take part in the event. One by one, the still-standing airmen collapsed. As Eugene Brown would put it in his testimony: "I fell shortly afterward and played possum. They must have thought I was dead because I was covered in blood due to the blows I had received on the head."[16] A forty-seven-year-old blacksmith-farrier knocked several airmen to the ground with

Figure 10.1 Rüsselsheim, June 1945: the US Army investigates the lynching. © US signal Corps, NARA. Investigators examine the wall along which the airmen tried to protect themselves during the lynching. On the right, a soldier climbs the pile of bricks that allowed three residents from another neighborhood (on the right in the photo) to strike over the wall.

his hammer. Some of the participants threatened Christoph Keil: "Get out of here or you're next," a railway man shouted at him.[17] After having heavily beaten them and encouraged the mob to do the same, the local propaganda chief emptied the magazine of his pistol into the heads of four fallen airmen. The mob dispersed. Several participants returned home. Along the way, they expressed their satisfaction to passersby. A farmer-innkeeper complained of pain in his hands from having struck the airmen so many times with his stick.[18]

Later that morning, a group of eight- to twelve-year-old children, some of them wearing the uniform of the Hitlerjugend, loaded the airmen's bodies onto a cart. They were led by a participant in the lynching, a man in SA uniform and carpenter by trade. Children had also actively participated in the lynching.[19] They now merrily pushed the cart to the cemetery.[20] As they reached its central square, an air raid siren sounded, scattering the group. In the cart, at least four men were still alive. The SA man climbed onto the vehicle and once again began to beat them, after which only two airmen remained conscious, Eugene Brown and William Adams. Taking advantage of the air raid siren, they slipped into the adjoining chapel and from there escaped into the countryside. They would be recaptured several days later and sent to a prisoner of war camp. At the Rüsselsheim cemetery, Hartgen, the factory foreman and head of local propaganda returned in the afternoon and once again shot the airmen. None of them survived this final gesture. Russian prisoners were requisitioned to dig a grave. The place chosen for it was located in the former Jewish section of the cemetery, which had been profaned and disused since Kristallnacht.[21] The six bodies were thrown directly on the ground. The pilot Norman J. Rogers Jr., copilot John R. Sekul, navigator Haigus Tufenkjian, radio operator Thomas D. Williams Jr., ventral machine gunner William A. Dumont and left-side machine gunner Elmore L. Austin all lost their lives.

In the meantime, at around 11:30 in the morning – roughly when the boys were loading the bodies into the cart – eight other airmen were brought by firetruck to the police station. They had just been arrested south of the town. A hostile little crowd gathered around the truck, stirred up by an SA man who sought to force the airmen to climb down. Happening to find himself there for an inspection, the fire chief of Mainz then ordered the firetruck driver to take the airmen to Mainz. A second lynching was thus narrowly avoided.[22]

What happened in Rüsselsheim on 26 August 1944 in two respects represents a model lynching. In point of its scale, the size of the crowd involved and the number of airmen who were mortally lynched, it precisely corresponded to the practice that the country's elites wished to see generalized. But it is also a model in the heuristic sense of the term. The duration of the event and the large number of participants make it a tremendously rich object of study, as does our extensive documentary record of the lynching, thanks in part to the unexpected survival of two of its victims.

Popular Vengeance

Starting in 1943, Nazi directives and propaganda emphasized popular anger. They presented it as a primordial fact that had spontaneously appeared in the civilian population (*zivile Bevölkerung*) independently of the will of the rulers of the Reich. This was the case of the first directive, signed by Himmler, SS chief of all police, in August 1943. The secret order given the Police to not "interfere in altercations between *Volk* comrades and English and American terror pilots"[23] gave the impression that these "altercations" were already widespread. Similarly, when Goebbels resumed the policy of lynching in May 1944, this time in full view of the public, he gave the impression that he was merely bowing to the will of the *Volk*: "In these matters," wrote the Minister of Propaganda, "our *Volk* thinks much more radically than does our government."[24] Two days later, the circular regarding *Volksjustiz* towards downed airmen, which appeared under the signature of Martin Bormann, head of the Party chancellery, also pointed out that the "intensely outraged" population had already "lynched" (*gelyncht*) airmen on the ground.[25]

How is one to assess the validity of the diagnosis advanced by the chief of police, minister and Party chief? As we saw in the last chapter, a dynamic interaction took hold at the national level between bottom-up initiatives and top-down encouragement. What was the case at the local level? What proportion of the population was so convinced of the legitimacy of murder or even that they were duty-bound to kill Allied airmen such that they were willing to take action? Something of an answer may be had by studying the postwar trials conducted by the American Army. In half of them, an aggressive "mob" of smaller or larger size was reported to have surrounded the victims or been present at the scene.[26] This represents a minimum estimate for, when one looks more closely at certain trials, one discovers bystanders who actively contributed by way of their cries or whose mere presence spurred on first-time or practiced killers to take action. The deadly lynching at Appen-Etz mentioned in the last chapter is one such case. This overall proportion may be confirmed by examining major cases of lynching (Table 10.1), defined as those that brought together a large crowd (as many as 300 people) or produced a significant number of victims (five or more).

It is to be noted that, while a mob was not involved in every lynching, all reflected the social life of the locality in which they took place. Half of these lynchings were carried out by the local elite that had sprung from the Nazi revolution. This holds as much for major lynchings as it does for smaller ones. The general pattern was as follows: airmen came down and were taken to the local "police station," placed under the guard of "rural police" at city hall or held at the village police station to await transfer to military custody. Having also noticed the airmen as they descended, local Gestapo or Nazi Party agents placed a call to the Kreisleiter, the Nazi Party's district chief, so that he might order that the prisoners be handed over to them. Sometimes, the Kreisleiter had already made this call. The airmen awaiting transfer in the premises of city hall had thus often been picked up by rank-and-file Party members or policemen in civilian dress. These prisoners would then be taken by foot or car somewhere a few kilometers distant, where their guards would shoot them dead along the roadside or in the woods. In a few cases, the more scrupulous of these executioners then submitted a report to notify their superiors of an "attempted escape." The population did not fail to notice these comings and goings on foot and in automobile, which often also involved army personnel. Cemeteries and their caretakers were also concerned by these events, as their services were called upon for the burial of bodies. Finally, the local elite – or, as they were known in the language of the Third Reich, the "politische Leitung" – were themselves drawn from the local population. Scattered across the nation's

Table 10.1. *Eleven major lynchings tried by the American Army*

Date	Place	Site	Crowd size	Number of defendants	Mention of bombing	Number of airmen killed
04/08/44	Borkum	Streets, Square	200–300	24	1	7
06/08/44	Lübeck-Siems	Field bordering town	250–300	16	1	1
26/08/44	Rüsselsheim	Streets	100–200	13	1	6
29/08/44	Gross Gerau	Square	300	7	1	2
12/09/44	Bingen	Streets	150–200	6	0	1
21/07/44	Schollach	Woods, Road	Unknown	7	1	5
29/07/44	Ottmannshausen	House, Square	Unknown	3	1	5
31/07/44	Saarbrücken	Woods, Shooting Range	0	8	0	7
01/08/44	Helmstedt	Woods	0	9	0	6
05/08/44	Hohenhausen	Woods	0	4	0	5
21/03/45	Neckarsulm	Square, Street, Woods	Unknown	3	1	6

Sources: Judge Advocate General, Reviews and Recommendations, Flyer Trials, NARA, M-1217. Trial references: 12-1497, 2381, 3245; 12-793, 1, 2; 12-1307; 12-1115; 12-489; 12-1182, (1), (2); 12-779; 12-1395; 12-3205; 12-1247.

Note: This table does not include some murders committed the same day in various places on direct order of the Gauleiter. On 21 June 1944, for example, more than eleven airmen were killed on the direct order of Friedrich Hildebrandt, Gauleiter and Reichsstatthalter of Mecklenburg, in the villages of Veelböken (unknown number of killed), Pingelshagen (two killed) and Klink (nine killed). The Review file does not supply detailed information regarding these actions. NARA, M-1217, trials 12-1368 and 1369.

230 LYNCHING IN GERMANY: DEFENDING THE NAZI STATE

territory, these locally orchestrated murders were thus very much part of the social life of the places where they happened.

The table also demonstrates that the population of those who volunteered to assault downed airmen was numerically significant. These furious mobs were a mix of neighbors, passersby and residents of the street-cum-arena. They formed spontaneously and had neither leader nor hierarchy. These were not processions secretly orchestrated by the authorities but rather mobs that formed in decentralized fashion. The Nazi state did not make the mistake of repeating the technique of Kristallnacht, when orders were given from above to enact destruction across the territory. These crowds entirely retained their freedom of choice and of action and were truly representative of a segment of the German people. Such was their anger that men, women and children made it a point of honor to strike defenseless men. As they were not armed, these crowds produced fewer dead than local elite groups. Crowds like those of Borkum (300 participants, 7 dead) and Rüsselsheim (200 participants, 6 dead) were unusual. In Borkum, it was the result of synergy between the Wehrmacht and the population. In Rüsselsheim, the civilian mob acted alone.

Reprisal Violence and Vendetta Violence

What led these Germans to thus overstep the barriers of everyday civility? Was it a straightforward response to the destruction and mourning caused by bombing? This was the line taken by the Nazi authorities. In the documents of the postwar Allied trials, however, defendants did not always characterize this violence as a response to bombing. Of the eleven major cases of lynching, in which a total of one hundred defendants were tried, the notion that the bombing played a role in motivating violence only explicitly comes up in seven. In these cases, moreover, violence as reprisal (or punishment meted out as a matter of principle) must be distinguished from violence as vendetta (that is, as personal vengeance).

The most obvious example of reprisal violence is that of Rüsselsheim, where the lynching unfolded against the backdrop of several episodes of bombing, the last of which had taken place the night before. Seven of the thirteen defendants lived along the route of the lynching. And the cries that set off the event accused the airmen of having bombed the town. By contrast, none of the defendants had lost a loved one in the bombing nor had any of their homes been destroyed. They seem to have experienced the collective action as an act of justice carried out by proxy on behalf of widows and orphans.

The Borkum lynching, which also took place in August 1944, in some ways resembles that of Rüsselsheim, drawing a large crowd and resulting in the death of a high number of airmen. As in Rüsselsheim, the court proceedings also suggest that none of the defendants had lost loved ones or property as a result of the bombing. The island of Borkum was not a target of bombing nor was it located near any such target. The handful of lone bombs that fell there caused no victims. And yet bombing was indeed mentioned as a motive at the time. The Kriegsmarine captain who laid the groundwork for the lynching was not himself a member of the Party but nevertheless rebuked one of his subordinates for his "rotten German humanitarian ideas at a time when women and children are being killed in Bremen." Located some 300 kilometers away, Bremen was the administrative capital of the Gau. After being thus lectured, the first lieutenant of the Flak helped prepare the lynching and promised a bottle of whiskey to the first guard to fire on an airman.

For the leading protagonists of the Borkum lynching – the Kriegsmarine captain and Borkum's mayor – the "pilots-who-kill-women-and-children" trope seems to have been more of a mobilizing slogan than a reflection of lived experience. On the day in question, Captain Kurt Goebell insisted on the "decree from Reichsminister Dr. Goebbels." This was in fact merely the newspaper article mentioned above, which inspired the leitmotiv of women and children as victims. Informed at the request of the captain, the mayor in his turn mentioned the "decree" when contacting the air raid marshals, asking them to "show what you can do, boys." He personally took up position along the escorted airmen's path to harangue the crowd: "There are the killers! They're the ones who killed your women and children, they're the ones who bombed your homes, beat them, hit them on the neck! There you are, killers! How many women and children have you killed? Beat them to death, civilians, beat them to death!" At the mayor's insistence, a city hall employee who had lost his home and work in the bombing of Hamburg was present in the crowd. His case aside, however, it does not seem that any other member of the lynch mob had been a direct victim of bombing. Rather, they saw themselves as noble defenders of the fatherland. That same day, the town's doctor was rebuked by the mayor, who found it impossible "to understand the doctor's attitude, feeling pity on airmen who kill German women and children and destroy German cities."[27]

If there was vengeance in Rüsselsheim and Borkum, it was not on the part of families who had lost loved ones or been made homeless by the bombing. Rather, the lynching was an act of reprisal. This also seems to have been the case in Schollach and Urach. On 21 July 1944, five airmen were taken prisoner in Schollach and Urach, in the Black Forest. The Kreisleiter gave the task of killing them to his peers, a group of minor civil servants and local officials. They consisted of a tax inspector, a tax secretary, a factory supervisor, a Kreis personnel office manager and a reserve police officer. Before killing one of the prisoners, the policeman asked him: "Were you in Munich?" Munich had just experienced its sixth heavy bombardment in ten days.[28] Among this team of killers, the policeman was the only non-Party member. Perhaps he was seeking to assure himself in his way of the legitimacy of his deed.

232 LYNCHING IN GERMANY: DEFENDING THE NAZI STATE

The case of Ottmannshausen also falls under the technique of reprisal. In this suburb of Weimar, three members of the "politische Leitung" and another member of the Party who worked as a locksmith in the neighboring camp of Buchenwald devised an original lynching in two stages. The five airmen taken prisoner were led to the home of a female inhabitant who had been killed by the air raid. There was no mention of any connection between the perpetrators of the lynching and this bombing victim. Once there, the five prisoners were beaten and tortured by an unknown number of assailants. They were then taken to the town square and publicly shot dead.

Of the eleven major cases of lynching tried by the Americans, only two were instances of eye-for-an-eye justice on the part of direct victims. The deadliest action took place at Neckarsulm, a small industrial town in Baden-Württemberg. Heinz Endress, the district's second-highest-ranking Party official and head of personnel at the local automobile factory, lost his wife in the bombardment of 1 March 1945. His home was destroyed. During his trial, he explained that he wanted to avenge his wife's death. As chance would have it, on 21 March, three weeks after the bombing, a bus transporting six airmen taken prisoner in Italy stopped at Neckarsulm's town square. The airmen were standing, lined up near the bus under the watch of a guard. The Party's second-in-command arrived on the scene with his boss and immediately opened fire on two airmen. He then shot a third man who was attempting to shield himself behind a passerby as well as a fourth as he sought to flee. The two survivors were caught and handed over to the army for the night until their guards could return with them the next morning so that they might take the train to the Luftwaffe Interrogation Center in Frankfurt.

Around 5 a.m. the next morning, the two Party leaders were on the route of the escort and fired at the prisoners. One of them was severely wounded. He was once again handed over to the local military authorities. A doctor recommended that he be operated upon immediately and had an ambulance called to take the wounded man to the hospital. The ambulance left and then returned again after the Wehrmacht lieutenant-colonel responsible for the base, who had been in contact with the Kreisleiter, refused to allow the wounded man to receive medical attention. A meeting was held among the murderers of the previous day, the lieutenant-colonel and other members of the "politische Leitung" in the course of which they discussed the possibility of killing the prisoner with poison or a pistol. Despite the doctor's entreaties, the wounded man received no care throughout the day. Around 7:30 pm, an ambulance picked him up. When the wounded man arrived at the hospital, he was dead, three new bullet holes in his chest. The fate of the sixth airman was more commonplace. He was killed by a pistol shot after having been taken to a neighboring wood, with the same local notables taking part.

The second example of deadly vengeance occurred over a shorter time frame. In Gross Gerau (Hesse), a particularly bloody lynching took place on 29 August 1944. A pair of Luftwaffe first lieutenants brought two arrested airmen to the town's city hall. Three days earlier, Gross Gerau had been struck by bombs intended for the Opel factories at Rüsselsheim. Twenty-nine townspeople lost their lives as a result. The captured airmen arrived there on 29 August, the same day as these victims' funerals. After an exchange between the first lieutenants, the Kreisleiter and the local policeman, it was decided to "give them to the population." A crowd of several hundred people stoned them, slashed them and beat them until the district chief of security police (Sipo) had them taken to the courtyard of city hall to be finished off. Two inhabitants volunteered for this job and got to it with iron bars. One of them, who had insisted he be allowed to take part, was a Luftwaffe sergeant. Before starting, he borrowed a pair of pants from a civilian as he did not believe himself authorized to strike while in uniform. Chatting about it with a companion after he left the scene, the sergeant congratulated himself: "Now, my brother has been avenged."

The lynchings were a form of popular expression and, as such, were neither unpredictable outbursts nor the work of death squads. Rather, they were local collective actions generally approved of by the population. The motive put forward by the national elite – that these were acts of vengeance in keeping with the principle of an eye for an eye – cannot be established in any systematic way and may have only obtained in a minority of cases. To understand the practice, one must attend to other forces as well.

Evidence of Residual Civility

To shed light on some of these forces of death, it is worth pausing to consider three control groups: the general population; the scattered helpers identified by the Allies after the war; and the handful of lynch mob witnesses left untouched by the motives that drove others to take action.

What did those who neither participated in lynching nor helped the Allies think? In the absence of sources, it is for the moment almost impossible to say with any confidence. We can make up for this lacuna by appealing to other indicators, such as acts of violence committed against foreign workers or deportees during death marches. But in what regards the specific issue of lynching airmen, the question remains. This is one reason debate persists over the Nazification of German society.

There were some critical witnesses, to be sure. They lived in the same conditions as the perpetrators of lynching and should therefore have experienced the same accesses of anger and deadly hatred. And yet they behaved with civility, just like their British counterparts, who did not practice lynching. There is a cultural and political factor at work here. Indeed, even Goebbels perceived the cultural dimension of British behavior. In March 1943, in one of

234 LYNCHING IN GERMANY: DEFENDING THE NAZI STATE

his secret daily briefings, he underscored the specificity of propaganda in the
United Kingdom, in particular its reliance on humor:

> One cannot expect the [German] people to burst into cheers after air
> raids. The British propaganda conducted in autumn 1940 to cope with
> their own domestic problems is unsuitable for us. In Germany, any
> propagandist who, like the British in the autumn of 1940, were to ask
> why the next bombs weren't coming yet would simply be given the boot.[29]

Is living through bombardment a preconstructed experience, tinged in
advance by cultural and political variables? Who are these "Englishmen"
among the Germans?

Those who actually helped were very few. Although the Allies did not
systematically tally German helpers after the surrender, they did gather some
data. In June 1945, the US Army extracted a list of thirty-four helpers from a
series of forms filled out by evaders, escapers and liberated prisoners of war.[30]
Most instances of aid dated from the final weeks of the war. The helpers acted
nevertheless at great risk to themselves. The British, for their part, did not
identify helpers but they did occasionally indemnify them. For instance, they
made an "ex-gratia payment" to the group of four exceptional women in
Munich who, for two years, from March 1943 to the city's liberation, sheltered
an escaped prisoner of war.[31]

When reading the debriefings of British or Commonwealth POWs, one
infrequently encounters people willing to lend a helping hand.[32] Over the
course of the war, the roughly 170 soldiers and airmen who escaped Germany
properly so called (1937 borders) and were questioned by the British upon
their arrival in London had escaped, not just from their respective camps, but
also from the German population. Six of them were nevertheless helped by
Germans. The greatest assistance came from women, which is doubtless no
accident. The most astonishing example of this is that of the four Munich
women already mentioned who helped a prisoner escape his camp and then
harbored him for two years between March 1943 and the Allies' arrival, all the
while taking part in small acts of resistance in company of this prisoner.
Another young German woman, this time from Dortmund, took in an escapee
for four days in April 1944. Her address had been given to the escapee while he
was hiding in Poland with the family of a young Polish forced laborer in
Dortmund, who had been arrested for engaging in sexual relations with this
same young woman. She took him in against the will of her parents. Two
German women from Upper Silesia also helped an escapee in August 1944.
There were also men: in November 1944 and again in January 1945, a German
man near Dresden provided assistance. With the Russians just a three-day
march away, in January 1945 a prison camp guard also helped a prisoner
looking to escape. And, on 4 April 1945, a similarly belated gesture – the
British troops were only one day's march away – was made in Messen on

behalf of another downed airman. This handful of rebellious German women and less-than-fanatical German men is evidence that some remnant of another Germany, one distinct from the Third Reich, lived on.

Little is known about the witnesses who attempted to prevent lynching. They were obviously no more English than the perpetrators. How many were there? There were few of them at the scene of lynching.[33] In the midst of crowds or among the lynching groups of the local elite, one occasionally espies a very reserved or even contrasting silhouette. The case of Rüsselsheim offers a nearly complete array of profiles foreign to the lynching dynamic. The best documented is that of the retired school teacher who described himself as an "anti-fascist." He had already been investigated by the police on several occasions in the past, which is why he ultimately left the scene. But he was not alone. At Frankfurterstrasse, a coachbuilder from Flörsheim, on the other side of the Main, also tried to put a stop to the rising violence. Shortly beforehand, a woman tried to convince the two sisters to let up. Another sought to dress the wounds of an airman on Taunusstrasse. Each time, these participants swimming against the current were threatened in their turn. In town for an inspection, the chief of the Mayence fire brigade was more successful in preventing a second lynching thanks to his hierarchical authority over a Luftwaffe first lieutenant and the firetruck driver transporting the airmen.[34]

It is difficult to categorize these grains of sand that never (or rarely) managed to halt the machine. Of these, the most effective were obviously soldiers who had not received – or who ignored? – the orders to let events play out, thus performing their traditional duty. As they were armed, they could threaten the mob or Nazi militants, themselves also armed. In Rüsselsheim, the guards who escorted the lynched airmen let events take their course but the chief of the fire brigade intervened. The proportion of women here is also worth noting, acting as they did in their role as nurses and mothers. In August or September 1944, on the outskirts of Drangstedt, a village not far from Bremerhaven, a matron thus interposed herself when airmen were threatened by a mob in the hospital itself.[35] During the 19 June 1944 air raid over Munich, a mother named Anne Visel revolted against the local NSDAP chief, or Ortsgruppenleiter, who had struck a wounded airman in the cellar of her building as children looked on.[36] With help from the concierge, this woman had herself sought out the airman to bring him into the shelter. When the raid ended, the Ortsgruppenleiter took the airman away in his car, accompanied by the driver and a civilian, and killed him in the forest. These soldiers and women who protected airmen against their German fellow citizens were performing their traditional social roles and relied upon them to act.

Their civility, however, isolated these civilians from their fellows. The mob did not follow their lead and sometimes even threatened them, as a result of which they could find themselves targeted for repression. We possess little

236   LYNCHING IN GERMANY: DEFENDING THE NAZI STATE

information on this point but here are a few examples. Anne Visel, who interposed herself between the Ortsgruppenleiter and the wounded airman in her cellar, subsequently found herself under constant threat. Each time the local leader saw her, he would ask in an ironic and unsettling way whether "she still felt pity for the American airman."[37] More serious was the punishment meted out to Major Kirchner, the Mainz fire brigade chief who prevented a second lynching from following the first in Rüsselsheim. Kirchner found himself under investigation at the request of HSSPF Jürgen Stroop, Gauleiter of Rhine-Westmark (and also, it should be recalled, the man who oversaw the destruction of the Warsaw ghetto). Major Kirchner was so "vigorously reprimanded" by police Major-General and SS-Brigadier Hille that he "suffered a nervous depression" as a result. Our source gives no information as to the exact meaning of this "depression."[38] There was also a certain Josef Lindenbolz. Around 29 July 1944, in Oberweier, a village in the district of Rastatt (Baden-Württemberg), Lindenbolz objected to the killing of a Canadian airman by a Wehrmacht soldier in the presence of the mayor and a small crowd of people.[39] Although he was acquitted by a court in Rastatt, he was nevertheless arrested and interned for two months in a concentration camp. No information is available as to the type of camp to which he was sent nor the identity of the court that tried him. It remains the case, however, that this inhabitant of the town was punished for "misplaced pity."

No collective effort was made to defend airmen. A postwar ruling reports an "indignant crowd" after an airman had been murdered in a field but it largely consisted of Russian and Polish slave laborers.[40] At the very end, with the Allied armies just a few kilometers away, crowds were also sometimes divided between supporters and opponents of lynching. This was the case near Düsseldorf on 16 February 1945, when the Americans were just 30 kilometers away, as well as in Mühldorf (Bavaria) on 15 April, fifteen days before the liberation of Munich.[41] Thanks to the letter of denunciation that followed it, however, we do know of a rare case in which a police unit collectively defended an airman. In February 1945, the head of the Nazi Party for the district of Greater Frankfurt wrote to Jürgen Stroop, Gauleiter for the Rhine-Westmark region, to complain that none of the airmen taken prisoner following the downing of their airplane on 22 February had been abused by the population: "It's almost disgraceful for the community of Mühlheim that none of the six prisoners were harmed."[42] In four separate locations, the policemen of the town had prevented a hate-filled mob from approaching the prisoners. "I know," the party official added, "and there are hundreds of witnesses who can confirm this, that many people brimming with hatred tried to approach the prisoners, that they followed them, armed with stones and buckets of manure to throw at the Americans, and that it was only the police who kept their hatred at bay." The Nazi Party chief expected punishment to be meted out, particularly against the party mainly responsible for this "disgrace," a certain Lieutenant Böhm. It is not known what made the police station of Mühlheim-am-Main an island of impassivity and even resistance to the anger of the population. By contrast, the Nazi vision may be clearly discerned in the words of this informer, whose wife was among the protesters: "her house having been bombed, [she was] consequently brimming with hatred for the enemy." It is this "consequently" that requires our attention. Under a guise of apparent rationality, the word "consequently" is freighted with politics and culture.

The refusal to acknowledge this "consequently" is just as freighted with politics and culture but what is this freight? It does not explicitly appear in the documents. Whatever it is that united the critical witnesses discussed above remains to be determined. Even their partisan commitments lack explanatory power. In Rüsselsheim, Keil was stunned to see a former Social Democratic comrade, a railwayman, take part in the lynching and then threaten him with the same treatment if he did not immediately leave the scene.[43] As we saw earlier, half of all first-rank defendants belonged to the NSDAP, a proportion artificially inflated by the effect of postwar liberal justice, which only charged defendants on the basis of clearly identified individual actions. Easily recognizable by those who participated in or witnessed a lynching, party members were also the focus of the occupying powers' attention. The Allies had declared the NSDAP a criminal organization. If only half of all first-rank defendants were party members, the vast majority of the most active perpetrators of lynching were thus not party members. Lynching was not a matter of political parties but of society.

Mourning and Ruins: A Political and Cultural Experience

Why did the common run of "Volksgenossen" not see justice the same way as this handful of critical witnesses? The reason has to do with the meaning given ruins and mourning. The meaning attributed to the experience of suffering and damage modifies their effect on behavior. In this instance, the precise meaning of bombing depended on who was held to be ultimately responsible for it: the German people and Nazis or the Allies? For our purposes, we shall not consider accounts that postdate the country's capitulation, as they are of very limited value.

As test case, we shall use the contemporaneous account of the Bavarian writer Friedrich Reck-Malleczewen, a monarchist and anti-modernist opponent of the regime.[44] Having died in Dachau in February 1945, Reck-Malleczewen was in no position to modify his judgements or revise his writing after the war. It is not his particular stance that interests us – given his opinions, he was clearly in the minority among critical witnesses. But his journal shines a bright light on the role that conviction played in shaping one's perception of bombing. Reck-Malleczewen saw the air war through a counter-

238 LYNCHING IN GERMANY: DEFENDING THE NAZI STATE

revolutionary, anti-Prussian and ultimately anti-Nazi filter. In his view, Allied responsibility was not an issue. As he noted in his journal in May 1942 following the first heavy bombardments of the ports of Lübeck and Rostock by the RAF:

> Everybody is wailing about the destruction of Lübeck and Rostock and nobody could possibly be more unhappy about the loss of these Gothic masterpieces than I am.
>
> But what happened here? Thirty years ago, Rostock was still the peaceful, self-contained market town of a prosperous farming area. Then, the idea was conceived of filling both Rostock and Lübeck with armament factories. These plants could just as well have been located in some uninteresting and architecturally worthless little towns. But the engineers did not want to be bored in provincial towns and the burgomasters wanted to bring "progress" to their communities. The result was the same as happened in Munich, which can thank Herr Krupp for the fact that it was blessed with its first great industrial complex during World War I and that this was followed by others.
>
> So now people are crying over two cathedrals which we will never have again and which were wrecked by the industrial monomania which is the source of all our unhappiness. They weep but they do not beat their own breasts. Do you keep your domestic tools, your crate openers and your tree saws in costly baroque chests – do you use irreplaceable crystal bowls to stack your hunting cartridges? After the war, will these engineers, these War Production Board generals, these burgomasters and community leaders be called to account for the unspeakable frivolity with which they gambled away the treasures entrusted to them?

As this passage makes clear, the relationship to bombing was not neutral. The perspective of this old Bavarian squire was here tinged by hostility to industrial civilization and Northern Germany. His reaction is worth contrasting with that of the ordinary men of Reserve Police Battalion 101 studied by Christopher Browning.[45] Before they were sent to Poland, these retired policemen were called to Lübeck in the immediate aftermath of the bombing in March 1942. For them, not only was there no doubt as to what the newspapers of the time called the "Judeo-English" nature of the air raid, but this feeling helped justify their active participation in the killing of 1,800 Jewish civilians, four months later in Jósefów, in the first days following their arrival. It was Nazi ideology and not the fact of having witnessed the hardship caused by one or more bombings that created the gulf separating these "ordinary men" from the country squire from Bavaria. The shock caused by a bombing is not commensurate with the civilizational transgression that the activity of genocide represents.

On 20 August 1943, Reck-Malleczeven watched as American airplanes attacked Regensburg. When an airplane came down in flames, he headed to the site. Here, too, his traditionalist culture and belief in the "innate" character of a "good old kernel of civility" made itself known:

> I drove to Seebruck to look at the wreckage. Burning oil bubbled in a crater fourteen feet deep. The engines had bored so deeply into the ground that no attempt was being made to dig them out. Around the crater, pieces of the human body were scattered – a foot, a finger, an arm. The remains were carried off in a small potato sack.
>
> Near W., a couple of Americans were luckier and landed safely. But then, as they were being led off, two refugees tried to spit at them and only the fact that the soldier escorting the Americans declared that he would not allow it and waved his gun saved these defenseless men from this indignity. You really have only to scratch your average non-bourgeois to find underneath that good old substance of human decency and that inborn aversion to the actions of canaille.

In the case of Reck-Malleczewen, the historico-political culture out of which he had developed his perspective did not preclude sensitivity to the fate of the victims of bombing. He continued:

> The news from Hamburg is simply beyond the grasp of the imagination ... And now this is what I saw on a burning-hot day in early August at a little railroad station in Upper Bavaria, where forty or fifty of these miserable people were milling about, scrambling, despite the angry roars of the station-master, into a car through a window they had broken, pushing, kicking, yelling, accustomed by now to fighting for space.
>
> What happened then was inevitable. A suitcase, a miserable lump of cardboard with edges broken off, missed the target, fell back to the platform and broke open, revealing its contents. There was a pile of clothes, a manicure kit, a toy. And there was the baked corpse of a child, shrunk to the proportions of a mummy, which the half-crazed woman had dragged along with her, the macabre remains of what only a few days before had been a family. Horror, screaming, hysterical sobbing, a snorting doggie, finally a compassionate official who takes care of the terrible scene.
>
> Another report I heard was that the firestorm created by the immense conflagration sucked up into it all the oxygen, suffocating people who were far away from the actual flames, and that the rain of phosphorus broiled the corpses of grown men and women into tiny, child-sized mummies, so that countless women are now wandering about the country, their homes in ruins, carrying with them these ghastly relics.

Naturally, this generally accurate information was censored. It was not circulated via the press. Instead, this role was performed by the word-of-mouth characteristic of dictatorships. In the same way, Reck-Malleczewen was very well-informed about the methods of warfare, occupation and genocide that had been elaborated by German forces in Poland and Russia. By contrast, he did not know that extreme heat also caused the bodies of airmen who came down in burning airplanes to mummify and shrink. The British corpse recovery mission found several of these 60cm-long mummies.[46] In the case of this writer, knowledge of the horrors of the air war did not trigger a desire for vengeance against the Allies.

Reck-Malleczewen is an extreme case of cultural resistance to the Nazi world. His was a resistance that grew over time. Drawn from the ranks of the conservative revolution, he initially harbored some sympathy for the regime. Starting in 1936, however, he began to heap scorn on it. His journal is that of a man nearly in despair, one whose only hope is for Allied victory. As he asked in October 1944: "Is it not the absolute height of tragedy, simply inconceivable shame, that just those Germans who are left of the best of them, who have been prisoners of this herd of evil-tempered apes for twelve years, should wish and pray for the defeat of their own country, for the sake of that same country?" Shortly after writing these words, he was arrested for the first time. On 9 January 1945, the Gestapo once again came for him. That February, he died in the Dachau concentration camp.

* * *

This detour by way of a case of cultural and spiritual resistance sheds light on the politico-cultural filter that colored the experience of bombing. This filter (or veil) is essential to understanding events and the interpretation given them at the time. Removing it from the analysis leads one to suppose a uniformity of emotions across political cultures and to draw relations of equivalence between what are very different frameworks of experience. When later testimony is used without care, it is also to forget that emotions have a history of their own and that, whatever might be the unity of the human race, raw, universal and timeless emotion does not exist.

This politico-cultural dimension is lacking in the otherwise thoroughly researched books by Dietmar Süss and Aaron William Moore.[47] As a result, their comparative analyses, whether of life under the bombs in Great Britain and Germany or that of civilian emotion during the air war in Great Britain and Japan, are curiously disembodied. Yet the morale of the population was not politically neutral. The sight of ruins was itself colored by which side one was on. The extensive German literature inspired by war ruins is significant in this respect. Echoing as it were the commentaries that Reck-Malleczewen overheard in Munich and reported with irritation in 1942 ("So now people are crying over two cathedrals ..."), these literary works often evoke the broken silhouette of belltowers and the amputated statues of saints that stood out from the expanses of rubble. The authors do not hide the emotion provoked by these remains, so many witnesses to an earlier life.[48] Yet the ruins of hundreds of Jewish cemeteries and synagogues profaned on Kristallnacht did not leave the same trace in this literature. Nor does the construction of imposing anti-air-raid bunkers on the site of destroyed synagogues seem to have aroused particular emotion.[49] For the post-1945 period, Michael Meng has also shown how sites of Jewish memory were neglected by town councils in the reconstruction years.[50] Until the 1980s and 1990s, bombing commemorations in these towns similarly portrayed the inhabitants as a community of "innocent victims" with no attention given their support for the regime that had started the war, initiated the bombing of the cities of Europe and organized the deportation and genocide of the Jews.[51] Despite the passage of time, emotion remained selective.

Nazi propaganda thus successfully exploited a politico-cultural filter that had become emotional. Lynching represented an expression of support for the National Socialist regime, its interpretation of the war (Germany as victim of an Allied "war of annihilation") and its conception of German citizenship (a *Volksgemeinschaft*, or community fusing race and people in union with the Führer). But the forms that the violence took, the words and actions associated with lynching, also reveal a deeper and deadlier adherence to Nazism via an interiorization of the principle of Race.

11

Race at Heart

Nazism is a form of racism. If one adopts this point of view, which is not always a matter of universal assent, talk of the "living space" to be conquered and the "social harmony" to be achieved by the "community of the *Volk*" are merely its corollaries. These are services due the *Volk*, the people-race of supreme essence. In the 1930s, colonial and social ambitions helped lure imperialist "nationalists" and "socialists" *de ressentiment* into the Nazi camp. But it was Race that supplied the foundation of the regime that came into being in 1933 and Race that offered the "Aryans" a path to such unprecedented promotion in the social and international order alike. This redemption by way of Race goes a long way to explaining the attraction of Nazism. This is not the place to seek out the reasons for the success of Nazi racism in Germany. By comparatively charting the development of eugenics in Europe and the United States in the first half of the twentieth century, Isabel Heinemann has demonstrated the specificity of the German case. Nowhere else was such a diversified, brutal and ultimately murderous array of eugenicist practices so systematically implemented.[1] For Heinemann, this is proof of the "extremely racist" character of German society in this period. To assess and understand the various aspects of this specificity as well as their genesis, proliferation and ultimate disappearance, other comparative-historical studies would be useful. But the fact is that the racism of extermination for Jews and the racism of radical exclusion for blacks were both hugely popular in Nazi Germany. To promote lynching, propaganda deftly played upon these popular undercurrents.

Race, the Hallmark of Lethal Violence

It today seems incredible that representatives of modern civilization could have believed that "the Jews" directed Allied bombing. And yet this fantasy was widespread in Germany. In France, the collaborationist (i.e., French Nazi) short film *Nimbus libéré* (1944) depicted an imaginary Jewish character urging on bombing from behind a London microphone. It exerted no influence on French public opinion. In Germany, by contrast, a poster showing 'the Jew', a

Figure 11.1 "Behind the Enemy Powers: The Jew." Nazi propaganda poster displayed in Germany and in the occupied countries, December 1943. © Gettyimages.

scary figure instigating the war from behind a curtain, was more in sync with the general creed.[2]

Christopher Browning has shown how the genocide of the Jews was closely related to the construction of the *Volksgemeinschaft*, the "community of the people-race."[3] Drawing upon his study of the ordinary men of Reserve Police Battalion 101 sent to the Eastern Front in July 1942, he cites its commander's emotional speech informing his men that they will for the first time have to kill civilians: 1,800 men, women and children. Commander Trapp tried to justify the operation by asking his men to bear in mind three "facts": in Germany, bombs were falling on German women and children; in the United States, the Jews were behind the boycott against Germany; and there, in Poland, the Jews had allied with the partisans. As Christopher Browning underscores, the first argument incriminated the Jews just as much as the next two. The belief that the Jews were behind the Allied bombing campaign had already been

244 LYNCHING IN GERMANY: DEFENDING THE NAZI STATE

established in people's minds in 1942. No reminder was necessary. Nicholas Stargardt and Peter Fritzsche examined the prevalence of this fantasy in the German population. As knowledge of certain forms of genocide became widespread in 1942–43, it became commonplace: bombing represented the Jews' vengeance for "what we've done to them."[4] Writing from Dresden, which was nevertheless spared bombing until February 1945, Victor Klemperer noted rumors of this type. Even some still-living Jews believed them:

> Jacobowicz relates credulously: "In 1938, the Jews of Leipzig were pulled out of their beds at 4:15 A.M. and taken to concentration camps; the English recently attacked the city at 4:15 A.M. and afterward all the electric clocks were stopped at 4:15 A.M."[5]

It is thus not surprising that Reserve Battalion 101 should have seized upon this argument to justify its murder of 83,000 Jewish civilians in seventeen months. The *Volksgemeinschaft* was a *Kampfgemeinschaft*, an anti-Semitic and racist fighting community. Several times a week, vibrating as one behind the *Völkischer Beobachter*, this community was reminded by newspaper headlines that "the Jew" was the enemy. The blame was more often put on "Judeo-Americans" than on the "Judeo-English" but, from July 1943, both were accused of "preparing a Jewish terror and vengeance organization for Europe." "In the event of victory, Jewish emigrants will take control of European 'police'. Judas will vent his hatred." Thus ran a headline in Hesse's regional newspaper.[6] Once again, it was *Der Stürmer* (literally, "the attacker"), a newspaper specializing in anti-Semitism, that was the most explicit. For example, on 25 May 1944:

> Whose fault is it if so many million men are separated from their wives and children? The Jews! Who is responsible for the fact that the people are deprived of comfort and must do the hardest work? The Jews! Whose fault is it if our towns and villages are destroyed by enemy bombing? The Jews! Who is responsible for the heroic death of the best of our people and the murder of countless women and children? The Jew! Yes, the Jew is the germ that has hurled the world into a sickness that inevitably leads to death unless humanity rises up at the last moment, after all ... But if the nations wish to regain their health and stay healthy in the future then the germ of the Jewish world scourge must be destroyed at its root.[7]

Alongside these genocidal war cries, the call for murder issued by Goebbels the following day in the portentous article we saw above may seem almost tactful. Apart from its mention of the Law of Talion, that of eye-for-an-eye, which is clearly there to remind one of the Jews' purported role in bombing, "A Word on the Enemy Air Terror" at first glance appears to be free of anti-Semitic allusion:

> Who is right? The murderers who after their cowardly crimes expect humane treatment from their victims or the victims who wish to defend

RACE AT HEART

245

themselves according to the principle, "an eye for an eye, a tooth for a tooth"? The answer is not difficult.[8]

Victor Klemperer read this article, which had been "circulated everywhere." He immediately understood its meaning, adding this remark: "As far as the 'people's soul drunk with rage' is concerned, we know something about it and we see it before our eyes every day in the Zeughausstrasse: where the Russian [prisoner] barracks are now located is where the synagogue once stood."[9] The latter had been burnt down on Kristallnacht. Its ruins had then been blown up with dynamite and the stones of its façade used to build roads. In drawing a line between anti-Jewish street violence and violence against downed airmen, Victor Klemperer showed no little intuition.

Contrary to what Christopher Browning has claimed, however, the image of "the Jew" was not exactly "militarized." Militarization presupposes a uniform and a rational command structure. In the propaganda, however, the anti-Semitism of extermination remains a matter of fantasy: the Jews are not soldiers but rather the instigators of bombing and manipulators of the Allies. This may be seen in the images mentioned above, where the supreme enemy is depicted standing behind a microphone in London or half-hidden behind a curtain. This depiction is also familiar from the illustrations carried by German newspapers. It is not Jews that one sees flying bombers but rather blacks. Media images recapitulate this phantasmagoric alliance of Jews and blacks in the air war against Germany: the former plan and incite the bombing, the latter carry it out.

To analyze these newspaper illustrations joining murderous anti-Semitism and racism, I have chosen the satirical magazine *Kladderadatsch* ("Crash!," in the dialect of Berlin).[10] The trajectory of this publication is itself an illustration of the German cycle of brutalization from 1860 to 1945. Created in 1848 in the context of the liberal revolution of the "springtime of nations," this weekly took an authoritarian turn under the influence of Bismarck. By the time of the Weimar Republic, it had firmly positioned itself on the far right and rallied to the Nazi cause in 1933.[11] If I have chosen this illustrated weekly, it is also because of the high quality of its illustrations. Its combination of anti-black racism and racial anti-Semitism may also be found in the *Völkischer Beobachter* but the draftsmen there were less talented.

Under the heading "Forward, Christian soldiers!" the cover illustration of *Kladderadatsch* for 18 July 1943 (Figure 11.2) is so charged with meaning that it is worth pausing to consider it. Its creator, Oskar Garvens, was a well-known sculptor, draftsman and caricaturist who first began contributing to *Kladderadatsch* in the 1920s and shared its anti-Semitic and nationalist opinions. Besides the drawing's pared-down aesthetic, which contributes to its powerful impact, its message was calculated to simultaneously target British, Americans, blacks and Jews. On the one hand there is a cleric (glasses, clerical

Figure 11.2 "Forward, Christian Soldiers!" *Kladderadatsch*, 18 July 1943. © Universitätsbibliothek Heidelberg. A Nazi cartoon : A half-Anglican, half-Jewish cleric rejoices behind a black airman who is dropping a bomb on a traditional German town. The silhouette of the church is reminiscent of the cathedral of Cologne.

collar) whom one must suppose English given the origin of the hymn quoted in the illustration's title. In keeping with the Nazi imaginary, he is a figure at once Christian (reference to the Christian hymn) and Jewish (hooked fingers, sardonic smile). On the other hand there is a phantasmagoric black American airman (apelike face). Taken together, this pair represents a condensation of the Reich's Western enemies.[12]

But this political message was overlaid with another: the Christian song that begins "Onward, Christian soldiers" was commonly sung in both English and American churches. In August 1941, Churchill chose it for the religious service that took place on the *Prince of Wales* during the signing ceremony to inaugurate the Atlantic Charter. As the Prime Minister subsequently declared in a radio-broadcast speech: "I felt that it was not a vain presumption but that we had the right to feel that we were serving a cause for which a trumpet sounded on high." It was necessary "to save the world from an immeasurable degradation." When Oskar Garvens drew *Vorwärts, Soldaten Christi!* two years later, he had perhaps some memory of this event in mind. But he had almost certainly seen *Mrs. Miniver*, a great box-office hit on British and American screens in 1942. Goebbels admired it on a technical level as propaganda and discusses it in his Journal at precisely the same moment that the *Kladderadatsch* drawing was going to print.[13] The film ends on a homily celebrating the "People's War" in the bombed-out church of an English village as the congregation strikes up "Onward, Christian Soldiers!" Through the gaping roof of the church, they watch as a V-shaped RAF formation – the V signifying Victory – rises into the sky. As we have seen earlier in this book, British propaganda, unlike its German counterpart, served a pacifying role. Mrs. Miniver did not lynch the German airman who came down in her garden; she took him in, fed him and tended to his wounds.

The "militarization" of the Jews was thus not enshrined in Nazi propaganda. In practice and on the ground, however, the members of the *Volk* drew no distinction between the bombing's instigators and those who carried it out. For them, the Jews were bombing Germany. German civilians thus belonged to the same "fighting community" (*Kampfgemeinschaft*) as soldiers at the front. "The Jew" was the enemy.

Blacks as Auxiliaries to the Jews

The main enemy was not alone; he was served by an inferior race. In anti-bombing propaganda, the combination of Nazi Germany's two racist fears helped trigger violence against downed airmen. A word must be said on anti-black racism in Germany. Nazism did not invent it. In the 1920s, a massive campaign in the press had already capitalized on the abuses committed by French colonial troops participating in the occupation of the Rhineland and Ruhr.[14] With the sole exception of the small Independent Social Democratic

Party of Germany (USPD), all political parties, from the SPD to the conservatives, were united behind this campaign to rouse public opinion against the "Black Horror" ("die schwarze Schande" or "die schwarze Schmach").[15] In 1937, after the Nazis had come to power, nearly 400 mixed-race children born of unions between French colonial troops and German women were forcibly sterilized. "Negrofied" France was a theme common to both Hitler and Goebbels. The report from the Minister of Public Enlightenment and Propaganda's secret conference on 30 May 1940 puts it quite clearly:

> The Minister points out that the most important task for the next few weeks will be to explain to the public in every possible way the need for a radical settling of accounts with France. Articles must keep on explaining in the most popular terms how the French in their relations with Germany have always pursued one aim alone – to divide Germany and then to rule her. By recalling the occupation of the Rhineland and then the Ruhr, the hatred of France is to be fanned afresh; it must be shown how this nation with its declining population is trying to overthrow Germany by using yellow, black and brown people from overseas and what a monstrous crime against culture and race it committed by shamelessly bringing negroes to the Rhine. The French must be pilloried as "niggerized sadists" and, by constantly hammering away at this subject, a state of affairs must be brought about, within a fortnight at the most, in which the entire German nation is consumed with anger and hatred against a France riddled with corruption and freemasonry.[16]

At the time this conference took place (30 May), black prisoners had already been massacred east of Amiens. But it would be another five days before the first great wave of massacres began in earnest. Between 5 and 18 June, some 900 to 3,000 African-origin prisoners of war were murdered.[17] These were massacres, not acts of extermination, for the Wehrmacht had over the same period captured between 16,000 and 20,000 colonial soldiers.

The incrimination of "negro" airmen (Negerpiloten), however, was inspired less by Franco-German relations than by the American model. Two recent books have shown how lynching in the American South played a role in the development of the Nuremberg laws.[18] When jurists first met in Berlin in 1934 to prepare the racial laws under the supervision of the Reichsminister of Justice, they began by reviewing American "Jim Crow" laws. At the time, their goal was to implement anti-Jewish segregation without provoking unrest in the street of the type represented by American lynching. Until 1943, the German press held to an ambiguous line, denouncing the discrimination to which American blacks were subjected while at the same time presenting them as lacking intelligence and waxing indignant over the practice of lynching while showing its victims' bodies in a way that elicited disgust.[19] In August 1943, for example, the Völkischer Beobachter wrote that "negroes" were nothing more than "cannon fodder for the Yankees."[20] The article denounced the

American Army's discrimination against "negroes" and "negresses," who it claimed were confined to the duties of washerwomen. The text ambiguously underscored the "racial tension" that reigned in the United States, depicting it as so intense that the least incident "triggers brutal and lethal instincts in this racial struggle."[21] If it was a "racial struggle," which camp had right on its side?

The American case was not just exploited to legal and cultural ends. It prepared the ground for action. After Kristallnacht, the Ministry of Propaganda began to gather information regarding lynching in the United States.[22] Its aim at the time was to respond to American criticism of the persecution of Jews in Germany by showing that the Americans behaved no better towards blacks. Starting in 1943, by contrast, Nazi propaganda began to use American lynching for purposes of naked incitement. Already fighting with American infantry forces in Italy, in the summer of 1943 African-American airmen (the Tuskegee Airmen) began to take part in bombing raids. For Nazi propaganda, this was an unexpected windfall. It allowed the "Schwarze Schande" – the racist "horror" of an inversion of the racial hierarchy – to be rekindled.

The drawings published in *Kladderadatsch* illustrate this revival of racist propaganda against African Americans. In July 1943, the newspapers wrote ironically of the race riots in Detroit. Entitled "Race Lesson in Detroit (USA)," a full-page depiction of a lynch mob was accompanied by this legend: "Damn niggers! When Roosevelt and his clique prattle on about racial equality, that's meant for Europe, not the USA!"[23] But the tone changed when it seemed the American Air Force was training black pilots. Racism showed itself openly and the irony became grating. The newspaper portrayed Eisenhower "awarding the highest honor for bombing civilians: stars and stripes."[24] This play on words (referencing the American flag) was accompanied by an image depicting two convicts (in striped uniform), one white and one black, as they received a red star (the symbol of Bolshevism) from the general's hands. Eight days later, the newspaper depicted a briefing of black airmen. Under the heading "Scientific Bombing," the instructor addressed the airmen: "Look carefully, boys: all of the churches and national shrines are marked in red on this map."[25] But these American Air Force units did not just destroy sacred historical monuments; they also targeted hospitals, women and children. Eleanor Roosevelt is depicted as a fairground woman operating a *jeu de massacre* stall in which these figures are the targets. The stall is patronized by novice pilots, black and white, who go there to practice their trade. "Three shots for one dollar, my boys, the best practice for terrorist airmen!"[26] The First Lady was known for having encouraged the creation of the Army's first school for black airmen at Alabama's Tuskegee airbase in 1941.

In 1944, the last residues of humor in these caricatures disappeared. The setting was no longer a classroom or fun fair but rather a scene of rape and lynching in the United States or a sacrilegious blessing. Sex, death and the sacred made their entrance almost without mediation. The horror of a mixed couple – forbidden by the Nuremberg laws since 1935 – and the threefold aggression that was represented by a mixed group of black and white airmen as they joyfully engaged in religious-sanctified bombing were depicted for the purpose of inspiring anger and hatred. This time, Eleanor Roosevelt was depicted as a street singer. She recounts the story of a white American woman who saves an African-American man she loves from lynching and encourages him to become a pilot. The next scene portrays him joining "the flying murderers' club."[27] The militant anti-clericalism of the 1930s also resurfaces. In one illustration, a reverend blesses black airmen in these, not especially Christian, terms: "My dear boys! Rise above the terrestrial world and fill the heavens with the weak and the innocent!"[28] Several days after the Normandy landing, the *Völkischer Beobachter* doubled down on the propaganda themes introduced in 1943. Roosevelt was depicted as an enthusiastic supporter of black airmen in the garb of baseball players as they prepared to strafe women and children. The president of the United States exclaims, "Onward, Christian soldiers!"[29] The evolution of these two publications reflected the radicalization of the regime itself. Goebbels' article "Lynch-style" (26 May) and Bormann's circular (30 May) encouraging the lynching of Allied airmen similarly date from spring 1944.

This series of images demonstrates the racialization of Allied airmen by Nazi propaganda. In 1943–44, half of the airmen depicted in the satirical newspaper *Kladderadatsch* were black. In 1943, however, there were only a handful of black airmen and they exclusively flew over Italy. Moreover, for every black airman who saw combat in the American Air Force over the course of the war (355 in total), there were two or three thousand non-black airmen. It is also to be noted that African-American airmen were always represented in a subordinate position. In the Nazi imaginary, they were not as threatening as the Jews.

Airmen Seen as "Jews" and "Negroes"

As Johann Chapoutot has shown, by its violence, this deadly hatred of Jews far exceeded contempt for blacks.[30] In 2020, it is still difficult to believe that the Germans or at least some significant share of them could have believed in the "Jewish desire for annihilation," the "Judeo-Anglo-American" nature of the bombs or the theme of the "Jewish war" being waged via bombing.[31] The point thus bears repeating. The degree to which Jew-hatred – the hyphen is well-deserved, as it constituted a feeling in its own right – had taken root among the people may be illustrated by a passage from a recorded speech that Goebbels delivered to an enthusiastic crowd on 4 June 1944. At the time of this speech, the German people as a whole were aware of the reality of the genocide then unfolding. This cheerful exchange between the speaker and his audience bears witness to that point:

RACE AT HEART

> Before taking power, it would have been ill-advised to fully inform the Jews of what we intended to do to them [young women's laughter]. It was a good thing [applause and cheers continue], it was fine and proper, that at least a portion of the Jews thought: well, it won't be so bad, they talk a lot but we'll see what they actually do. It was a good thing they didn't take the National Socialist movement as seriously as it deserved.[32]

Although this Jew-hatred was unrivaled, the physical violence enacted on the ground against "negro" airmen equaled and even surpassed that inflicted on their supposedly Jewish counterparts. Moreover, this violence did not take exactly the same form in the two cases.

There was nothing new about street violence against Jews in 1943. Michael Wildt has closely studied the public dynamics of violence against Jews in provincial towns in 1933–39.[33] As early as 1933, civilians were active participants in the public shaming parades, public humiliations, assaults, rapes and murders targeting Jews. The quintessential example of Kristallnacht (9–10 November 1938) was anticipated by many precedents. The obvious continuity between the years 1933–39 and 1943–45 is statistical in nature; it does not imply that all of those who engaged in violence in the earlier years were once again perpetrators in 1943–45. Yet if one compares the maps provided in the Appendix to this book, it does indeed appear that the memory of these events increased the likelihood of their recurrence. Of the eleven major cases of lynching studied here, five took place in a town where the synagogue had been totally or partly destroyed on Kristallnacht. This was the case of Lübeck, Rüsselsheim, Gross Gerau, Bingen-am-Rhein and Saarbrücken. The destruction of Jewish places of worship was accompanied by violence against property and persons that sometimes lasted several days. The memory of these actions clearly favored their recurrence. Only by increasing the number and depth of local monographs will we arrive at a more detailed understanding of what transpired in these places. One might start, for example, with the case of the Kreisleiter of Müllheim-im-Breisgau, Hugo Grüner, who successfully evaded prosecution after the war. In 1938, he oversaw Kristallnacht in the neighboring village of Sulzburg and, in October 1944, murdered four British airmen in Rheinweiler, another village in his district.[34] The present study, however, is more interested in civilians in general than in local authorities.

The case described above, that of the August 1944 lynching in Rüsselsheim, seems particularly pertinent. As soon as they came down over the little village of Greven, in Rhineland-Westphalia, the airmen were suspected of being Jews and were humiliated as such. In Rüsselsheim itself, it was two inhabitants residing on the edge of the old Jewish quarter (now *judenrein*, or "free of Jews") who initiated the assault. During the lynching, William Adams was singled out for anti-Semitic insult, as had also happened in Greven. Speaking a little German, he denied being Jewish.[35] In contrast, the Armenian-origin Haigus Tufenkjian was unable to respond. Of all those lynched, his skull was the most shattered.[36] The desire to humiliate was apparent in the gesture of one neighborhood resident, a forty-three-year-old man employed as an instructor of forced laborers at the Opel factory: while they were still on Taunusstrasse, he struck one of the airmen in the area of his rectum with a cudgel.[37] Finally, the fact that the bodies of six victims were thrown onto the bare ground in a grave dug in the former Jewish cemetery, which had been abandoned since its profanation on Kristallnacht, sent the same message of murderous anti-Semitism. Among civilians, word and deed converged.

But to arrive at these conclusions, one must be able to reconstruct the scene on the basis of depositions, the transcripts of court hearings and, if possible, other testimony. It is not enough to merely read court rulings or the Reviews that accompanied them. In the case of three airmen who were murdered in the courtyard of the Hanau Criminal Police station (*Kripo*) in 1945, for example, "several civilians" are mentioned as guarding the airmen alongside soldiers without any information given as to their attitude or the role they played in the course of events.[38] On 17 February 1945, these American airmen parachuted onto the surroundings of Hanau, an industrial and commercial town near Frankfurt. At this time, the town had yet to experience much bombing. Instead of handing the airmen over to the Luftwaffe at the neighboring air base, the policemen held the airmen at the headquarters of the Criminal Police (*Kripo*). The chief of police, Hermann Fehrle, then arrived. Upon discovering that one of the airmen was named Goldstein, he was seized by rage and began to swear and shout. He slapped Goldstein and screamed "murderer!" at him. While interrogating the three men, Fehrle called them "gangsters" and "murderers." When the police doctor suggested that he have Goldstein, whose head was injured, taken to the military hospital, Fehrle replied that "Allied airmen are not to be handed over to the Wehrmacht but are to be held by the police" and that "these Allied airmen must be exterminated." Contemplating the possibility of poisoning them, he asked the doctor if he had any way of preventing them from waking up. The doctor responded that he did not. Fehrle thus ordered his subordinates to shoot the three men, a task that they carried out within the hour (or, more precisely, an hour and a half later) in the building's courtyard with a bullet to the neck from behind.

The manner in which the three men directly responsible for the airmen's death – the three policemen who shot them in the neck in Hanau – defended themselves at their postwar trials suggests that they had a short time before received explicit and insistent orders to kill them. In their defense, they argued that they feared they would be sentenced to death by court-martial (*Standgericht*) or perhaps even be killed by Chief Fehrle had they not obeyed, a fear that does not seem entirely feigned. One of them mentioned a telephone call received shortly before from a superior based in Darmstadt, who explained that the order came from Himmler himself. In his study on "Lynchjustiz" in Austria, the historian Georg Hoffmann advances a similar claim, in particular citing a 25 February 1945, written order from the Gauleiter of South Westphalia, which in a threatening tone reiterated the secret orders given the previous year to the effect that the "people's anger" (*Volksempörung*) was to be given free rein.[39] The more direct order to kill may have orally accompanied the written instruction. Already in June 1944, the Gauleiter of Mecklenburg, Friedrich Hildebrandt, had verbally ordered certain Kreisleiters to kill. More than eleven airmen brought down in western Mecklenburg on 21 June 1944 were thus killed by day's end.[40] Following the bombing of Dresden, the Gauleiter's services may have orally given similar orders to the lower ranks.

It was at this time, as we have seen, that Goebbels and Hitler were considering the possibility of publicly repudiating the Geneva Convention. The Wehrmacht responded that it would be pointless to do so as the population was already taking care of downed pilots on its own. Instead, General Jodl suggested an effort be made to divulge more cases of *Lynchjustiz* "'that could not be avoided'" – the quotation marks are in the original – on the part of the "furious population." As written, this was merely a measure intended to incite the population. The general naturally left the rest to Himmler or Kaltenbrunner, who it was understood would translate these instructions into an order to be delivered orally by telephone via the Gauleiter network.[41]

And yet, when several groups of threatening civilians approached six airmen in the neighboring village of Mühlheim-am-Main on 22 February 1945, five days after the triple murder of Hanau, they were driven off by police Lieutenant Böhm and his men. Policemen were thus not necessarily more inclined to kill than civilians. Under the Nazi terror, there remained a degree of freedom.

Nor did all civilians develop homicidal tendencies towards Allied airmen. In the human sciences, a rate of 100 percent is never scientific. Yet the prevalence of a particular behavior constitutes a fact of society. The calvary of Sergeant Solomon, who was subjected to civilian violence in three separate towns, is another example of this.[42] On 28 July 1944, around thirty American airmen were sent by train from Wilhelmshaven, a naval base on the North Sea, to Frankfurt, the location of the Oberursel interrogation center. At the first stop, the lieutenant in charge of the convoy egged on civilians by telling them that these airmen were murderers. He singled out Sergeant Solomon and presented him as a Jew from Palestine who had emigrated to the United States to become an airman and bomb German women and children. The civilians fell upon the sergeant as the other airmen were forced to stand to attention. At the following stop, the same scenario was repeated. The guard singled out Solomon to a civilian, who began to beat him. At the third stop, in Frankfurt, the sergeant was first pummeled by two young civilians around sixteen years old. A large crowd then set about attacking all of the prisoners after the escorting lieutenant once again incited civilians to action. This time, they were armed with

254   LYNCHING IN GERMANY: DEFENDING THE NAZI STATE

sticks and knives. Sergeant Solomon was once again the main target of their blows. This series of lynchings was not tried for lack of sufficient material evidence and probably also because of the scale of the investigations that it would have required. It is unknown what became of Sergeant Solomon.

The manner in which black airmen or those identified as such were treated on the ground seems to have been stamped with another, bloodier cruelty. In the context of the campaign against the *schwarze Schande* of the 1920s, North Africans counted as "negroes" in the eyes of a segment of German public opinion.[43] In 1944, several airmen of swarthy complexion or merely tanned by the sun were thus perceived as black. This was certainly the misfortune of Haigus Tufenkjian in Rüsselsheim: his swarthy complexion meant that he was taken for Jewish and black at one and the same time. One of the major lynching trials conducted by the Americans offers a similar case. On 6 August 1944, a "dark-skinned" airman lost his life in Lübeck-Siems. As the airman descended in parachute, a crowd of between 250 and 300 people were drawn to the highway. Upon reaching the ground, he was relieved of his flight suit. A worker and member of the NSDAP then struck him on the face and head with a steel helmet. No longer recognizable, the disfigured airman lost consciousness. He was awoken and taken to a neighboring corn field, where he found himself surrounded by civilians as they passed a revolver around. After ten shots or so, the man was dead. His disfiguration and conversion into a target for sport are suggestive of a specific process of dehumanization.

There seem to have been more such cases in Austria, a country over which the Tuskegee Airmen flew from the Italian bases of the USAAF. The historian Georg Hoffmann has compiled a list of eighteen cases in which African-American airmen were abused on the territory of present-day Austria and Hungary.[44] Here is one such example. On 1 April 1945, the newspapers of Oberdonau (region of Linz) published a short article inspired by the frankest racism:

> Not long ago, an enemy terrorist airplane was shot down over Oberdonau. Its keeper, an American pilot, a gift from President Roosevelt, came down in parachute and was taken prisoner. According to the commentaries of the American press, we should expect to see intelligent young men as they are represented in American advertisements for chewing gum or in American films. The American pilot, who, as one can see in this photo, was not lynched by the population, even though he and those like him have brought death and destruction to bear on innocents, resembles this photo! A bastard [*Mischling*] with thick negro lips, a brute's expression, a dull-witted air. Here is the culture they wish to bring us! Here is what the representative of this culture looks like! Europe will remember this.[45]

This article is doubly lethal: it is lethal for what it says but also for what it does not say. The pilot in question may not have been "lynched" in the sense of violently abused but it is likely that he was shot to death the preceding

20 March in Bad Hall, south of Linz.[46] Given the circumstances of the time, moreover, the article constitutes a call for lynching. Three days later, on 4 April, another Tuskegee Airman, Second Lieutenant Manning, was taken from his cell at three a.m. He had come down the day the article appeared and been interned at the Hörsching air base, near Linz. Two Luftwaffe officers ordered the guard to "free" him. Outside, a mob of civilians were waiting for the "negro bastard" (*Negermischling*). Manning was viciously beaten then hanged from a telegraph pole with his hands tied behind his back. At dawn, some civilians later returned to the scene to hang a placard around the pilot's neck: "We look after ourselves" (*Wir helfen uns selbst*). The text was signed "Werwolf," a volunteer militia whose creation was announced in October 1944 and that took the form of several dispersed and ephemeral groups in spring 1945.[47]

A Nazified Society

Given the scale of civilian involvement in the murder of Allied airmen, forced laborers and deportees over the course of the death marches, one may reasonably describe German society as an ever more Nazified one. Allied victory alone was capable of putting an end to this process of ceaseless radicalization. It is no accident that the map of lynching so closely corresponds to that of Kristallnacht, and comparisons with the lynching of blacks in the United States prove well-founded. The transformation of ordinary inhabitants into consenting witnesses or active participants in the policy of exclusion by death was the product of an ever-more interiorized way of thinking, an ever-more deeply rooted vison of the world. Nazi political culture had largely taken hold of people's minds and constantly made new inroads.

This finding regarding the primacy of politics relegates the question of the morale of bombed populations, their willingness to fight and belief in victory, to the background. The primacy of politics also brings a new perspective to bear on the question of the preservation of morale and social conventions under bombing. These debates over morale and morality have given rise to many books, whether on Nazi Germany, the United Kingdom or Japan. Thanks to the work of Andrew Knapp, the literature on France has also recently experienced rapid growth. But as comparisons between wartime societies show, the subject is at its core political in nature. The specificity of the German case resides in ever-rising civilian participation in a lethal dynamic. Until May 1945, the number of civilian attacks on downed airmen, foreign workers and the Jewish and non-Jewish victims of the death marches constantly increased. Taken as a whole, non-Nazified and non-politicized Germany simply did not exist.

After the defeat, civilians forgot the strength of their Nazi engagement. They mainly remembered the good intentions they harbored towards their own kind: the Aryan people-race. But the devotion women felt for Hitler and the camaraderie they enjoyed within National Socialist organizations did not stop them from setting off lynchings with their cries.[48] Weariness with the war and a desire for peace were not indications of disaffection with the regime. Ian Kershaw cites the topical case of a sergeant who, in a December 1944 letter to his family, writes of his hope that someday the fighting will end, something "that all peace-loving people hope and pray for." As the next sentence makes clear, however, this sergeant had a peculiar way of loving peace: "Our enemies do not understand this desire and we, the entire German people, will continue to resist during the holidays in our fierce battle against these degenerates, led by Jewish parasites who know no fatherland and have none."[49] The concerns expressed by educated SS as they drafted their reports on the state of public opinion (*SD-Berichte zu Inlandsfragen*) reveal the fatigue and exhaustion of the population under bombing. But these difficult living conditions in no way blunted the conviction of a large majority that they belonged to an elite race for whom dominating and eliminating others was at once a right and duty. Between 1945 and 1948, more than 50 percent of Germans still believed National Socialism to be a good idea poorly implemented.[50]

Seen from the perspective of the population's behavior towards downed airmen, the following portrait of Nazi Germany in 1943–45 emerges. The fact that the vast majority of airmen were not lynched shows that some respect for the customs of war persisted among German civilians. Yet the number and gravity of the violent acts committed against defenseless men reveals the extent to which civilian anger and the desire for reprisal were constructed. For, as we have seen in our comparisons with periods of heavy bombing in Britain (1940–41, 1942, 1944) and France (1944), popular anger was not a universal given. Almost no lynching took place in these countries. Indeed, quite the contrary obtained in France, where a population that had been subjected to bombing took risks to save airmen from arrest by the forces of occupation. At the same time, the extent of the transgression entailed by deadly lynching and the spread of this practice across the length and breadth of Germany suggests the existence of a National Socialist continuum. Incidents of lynching were at once spontaneous manifestations of popular Nazism and indicative of the degree to which racist obsession had taken root in society. It was only the Allies' victory that put an end to this violence. It would take longer for the ideology upon which it was based to disappear. It did so gradually, just as it had gradually taken hold of the country under the Nazi regime, from 1933 to 1945.

Conclusion

An Archeology of the Moment

The moment is freighted with history and politics: that is the lesson one draws from studying the myriad and most often fleeting microsocial encounters that took place in Europe during the Second World War. In addition to the little facts it reveals that, by virtue of their recurrence, constitute social phenomena, comparative history trains a spotlight on national groupings, redefines the lines dividing friend from enemy and also clarifies certain relations of trans-national friendship. What factors animated the Duponts, Smiths and Schmidts of wartime Europe such that they adopted behaviors that were at once so homogeneous and/or specific at the national level and so contrasting from one country to the next? Ground-level analysis demonstrates that France's "strange defeat" in 1940 may have concealed an insurrection nipped in the bud; that the British "People's War" was more than a myth; that the French Resistance was a nationwide movement, a portion of which – that represented by the helpers – was in direct contact with Allied personnel; and that, in Germany, the "community of the people-race" was indeed a social reality and the driving force of collective violence.

The three pillars of wartime social behavior – the political regime, collective memory and cultural traditions – came together in such a way that civilians confronted with airmen were after their fashion transformed into combatants. In the United Kingdom, the potential for violence against downed German airmen was contained by the maintenance of liberal democratic norms and deliberate recourse to "British humor." In the France of May–June 1940, the Republic's last-minute mobilization of the "Gardes territoriaux" demonstrated the strength of a dynamic predicated on the memory of the invasions of 1870 and 1914 and the culture of mass conscription inherited from the French Revolution. Had the invasion been less rapid and the government chosen to pursue the war, an organized resistance might have been born at this time. Following the armistice, these cultural givens – Germanophobia and the ideal of the people in arms – were enough to immunize a large part of the population against the occupier's presence. The national political culture prevailed over the forces of authority and repression. It structured and supported the evasion of Allied airmen and soldiers. This is the opposite of what took place in Germany, where the National Socialist regime, the traumatic

258   CONCLUSION: AN ARCHEOLOGY OF THE MOMENT

memory of 1918 and hyperbolic ethnocentrism coalesced in response to the bombings. In a spiral of violence that only came to an end with the Allies' arrival, a portion of the population participated in the lynching of British and American airmen.

The present book also stands as a demonstration of civilian involvement in the war. There is nothing anecdotal, as it were, about the tens of thousands of anecdotes inspired by the arrival of downed airmen. History from below here intersects with the history from above of states. Taken by surprise by the newcomer's arrival, the civilian is cut off from his usual arrangements or, indeed, any arrangement. He or she is as it were caught in the act and laid bare. And yet comparative analysis shows that he or she was far from helpless. However much it may have been inspired by the Rousseauian myth of the noble savage, research on civilians in wartime shows them in reality to be highly engaged.

It is thus in the interaction between the microsocial and macrosocial levels that civilian action is defined.[1] Microsocial history portrays individual actors, their subjectivity and their room for maneuver while the overarching macro-social history shows the major, long-term parameters that weigh upon them. Together with a critical reading of sources, my method is thus characterized by a certain to and fro, by an alternation of close-ups and panning shots that, one hopes, ultimately offers a well-tailored appreciation of events. By taking the best of Tocqueville and his well-reasoned analyses with the best of Michelet and his enlightening empathy, I seek to supply an understanding of the period.

British Humor and German Fear of "Francs-Tireurs"

Since the 2000s, comparative history has had a bad press. The comparative approach, it was claimed, in itself reinforced national stereotypes while neg-lecting the reciprocal cultural transfers that also contributed to forming nations. Imitation of, opposition to and transposition of foreign norms all contribute to the development of national identity. Working on Franco-German cultural transfers, Michel Espagne is well-positioned to show the limits of the comparative method insofar as it consists in point-by-point comparison and separates the objects under investigation from their specific histories and environment.[2] A "Jakobiner" in 1790s Germany was not a French Jacobin of the same era. A French resister was not a German resister. The risk of nominalism hangs over comparative history. It is also menaced by nationalism to the degree that it does not always deliver on the decentering it presupposes. But as Hartmut Kaelble underscores, the transnational history that analyzes cultural and social exchanges across national borders can also be tainted with nationalism.[3] The example of the "Westforschung" that rapidly expanded in Germany in the 1920s with the aim of denouncing the Treaty of Versailles is one example of this. The institutes associated with this new

CONCLUSION: AN ARCHEOLOGY OF THE MOMENT   259

discipline flourished under Nazism. Their scholars sought to show how the territories of the "West," from Holland to the Loire, were countries of German origin and language and thus destined for annexation.

Of the various contributions that the comparative method has made to our understanding, two are worth singling out as potentially opening up new avenues of research. The first concerns the use of humor in politics. The example of the United Kingdom shows that a government can play upon humor to discipline its population, give it some breathing space and reduce the violence of its reaction. By calling upon its "sense of humor" – in this case, its practice of understatement and gentle self-mockery – British propaganda helped pacify the behavior of a population faced with imminent invasion and the tragedies caused by bombing. Government policy was facilitated by the fact that "British humor" was among the stereotypes that defined the national character and had been internalized as such.[4] In fall 1945, there was not a single French or German film studio that would have dared produce a fantasy-romance screenplay in which endless lines of fully equipped airmen engage in animated conversation as a giant escalator takes them to Heaven.[5] The memory of those tens of thousands of young men thrown scattershot, as it were, over the seas and continents was nevertheless there.

What was the case on the German side? German humor is not generally acknowledged as among the characteristics of this linguistic space. The question has yet to be studied methodically, however. When Goebbels triggered peels of hysterical laughter among the audience that had gathered to hear him speak at Nuremberg's Adolf Hitler Square in June 1944, he was also using understatement. For what would have happened, he was effectively asking to such great hilarity, had the Jews known "what we were going to do to them" or, in the case of Allied airmen, had one explicitly called for their lynching? Here, "understatement" and irony were a way of using laughter to legitimate genocidal transgression and a violation of the laws of war. In "Race and Humor in Nazi Germany," Martina Kessel offers a convergent analysis.[6] "Contrary," she writes, "to the idea deeply rooted in German cultural memory after 1945 that joking under Nazism was a sign of non-Jewish opposition," the humor of this period was a "communicative contract between non-Jews, who used it to portray inclusion and exclusion" and, from 1941, inclusion and extermination. Self-mockery, by contrast, was entirely absent from the apocalyptic rhetoric of the Third Reich. This was noted by Norbert Elias when he sought to compare British and German humor.[7] For Elias, the German incapacity for self-irony before 1945 stemmed from the relatively recent character of unification, which lent a certain touchiness to the "national consciousness." British humor, by contrast, reflected the greater self-confidence of an old and well-established nation. This is an interesting theory, coming as it does from a sociologist who was forced to flee Nazi Germany in 1933 and took up residence in England, but it does not exhaust the subject.

260   CONCLUSION: AN ARCHEOLOGY OF THE MOMENT

Elias could have looked more closely into the matter in his later work on the German "national habitus" but in the event did not revisit the specific issue of humor.[8] So how is one to interpret these complex and differentiated relations to humor?

Another issue that has already fueled research is the German Army's sustained failure between 1870 and 1945 to respect international law as it relates to the emergency formation of volunteer corps to repel invasion as well as its failure (in the West as elsewhere) to respect laws governing the rights of POWs. A series of conventions – specifically, those of The Hague (1899 and 1907) and Geneva (1929) – had defined these aspects of international humanitarian law and were all signed by Germany. The political scientists Béatrice Heuser and Eitan Shamir have shown how "national styles," "strategic cultures" and even "civilizational differences" can determine policies of insurgency and counter-insurgency.[9] This is a path worth pursuing if one wishes to move beyond the to-and-fro of defenders and detractors of the German Army.

The heated debate that raged in the interwar years between two historiographical currents, one denouncing the "German atrocities" of 1914 and the other denying their existence or justifying them as a legitimate reprisal against the activities of "francs-tireurs," seemed to have subsided over time. The historians John Horne and Alan Kramer have shed light on the summary execution of some 5,000 civilians in Belgium and France during the first month of the war.[10] These civilians, women and children among them, were seen as "francs-tireurs" by the invader. As we saw in Chapter 1, though, the debate resurfaced in 2017. It bounced back also in another direction, this time in the context of efforts to link the wars of 1870, 1914 and 1939. The historian Henning Pieper has drawn a straight line from the fight against francs-tireurs in 1870 and the genocide of 1941–45, passing by way of the genocide of the Hereros and Namas, the "francs-tireurs myth" of 1914 and the collective murder of thousands of civilians during the invasion of Poland in 1939.[11] Drawing exclusively on published sources, the historian Bastian Matteo Scianna has by contrast argued that the counter-insurgency measures taken by the Prussian Army in 1870–71 were in keeping with the norms of the time and in no way set the nation on a special path, or *Sonderweg*, that ultimately led to the genocide of the Jews.[12]

In what concerns their policies towards "francs-tireurs," the controversy remains over the Prussian Army's decision to ignore the uses and customs of war in 1870 or the German Army's decision to ignore international law between 1914 and 1945. For the period 1870–1919, Isabel Hull has shown the peculiarities of the German military culture, which isolated it from its counterparts in Western countries.[13] Drawing upon the remaining local archives, some French specialists of the war of 1870 have underscored the brutality of the Kaiser's army and its fear of "francs-tireurs."[14] The parallel between 1914 and 1939 has been closely studied by Jochen Böhler, who shows that the

CONCLUSION: AN ARCHEOLOGY OF THE MOMENT   261

"francs-tireurs' war" in Poland in 1939 was conducted against an imaginary adversary and that, in waging it, the Wehrmacht had been infected by a "franc-tireur psychosis." In contrast to francs-tireurs past, however, the imaginary franc-tireur of 1940 was now depicted as a Jew.[15] In 1940 France, the Republic's duly established Gardes territoriaux were considered to be "francs-tireurs." Gardes who actually fought downed Luftwaffe airmen found themselves on trial before German military tribunals, which sentenced to death or imprisonment. The military tribunal of the Reich in Paris had even contemplated the possibility of bringing charges against all of the country's mayors and prefects for having ordered the creation of the Gardes territoriales. The imposition of Nazified German criminal law upon the invaded territory before the armistice had even been signed was contrary to international law. Some young men who endeavored to make their way to England in 1940, for example, were condemned to death and executed for "high treason" by German military tribunals. Mention must also be made of the fate of the Spanish republicans who fought in the French Army in 1940. Captured by the German Army, from 1940 they found themselves classified as "Rotspanier" ("Red Spaniards") in the Stalags and were sent to the Mauthausen concentration camp in violation of the Geneva Convention. Thanks to their supposed status as former republican guerilla fighters in the Spanish Civil War – and thus "francs-tireurs" in the Germano-Nazi sense of the term – this would be the fate of more than 7,000 regular combatants of the French Army.[16]

Finally, and though this concerns the East, not the West, one cannot ignore the 3 to 4 million Soviet prisoners of war who died of hunger and abuse in Wehrmacht camps. As with the "francs-tireurs," the German Army did not accord them the status of "belligerent" and thus not that of prisoner of war on the grounds that the USSR had not signed the Geneva Convention. Tsarist Russia had nevertheless signed and ratified the Hague Convention. But the Wehrmacht also did not accord the status of human being to the members of the Red Army who found themselves in its hands and this despite what was known as the "Martens clause," so-named after the Russian diplomat and jurist whose initiative it was at the 1899 Peace Conference.[17] Confirmed in 1907, the "Martens clause" was inserted into the preamble to the Hague Convention, where it remains to this day. It stipulates that:

> populations and belligerents remain under the protection and empire of the principles of international law, as they result from the usages established between civilized nations, from the laws of humanity and the requirements of the public conscience.

The debate may be advanced by appealing to the archives and research into the cultural and even civilizational differences between nations. In the case of France, it is clear that the revolutionary tradition that had been inaugurated by the "volunteers of Year II" was not dead in 1870, 1914 or 1940. In that of the

German Army, it seems that the outrage provoked by the type of guerilla warfare that was waged against its supply lines had deep cultural roots that demand further study. In 1870–71, the official newspaper of the occupying power in Champagne, the *Moniteur officiel du Gouvernement général* [sic] *à Reims*, gave voice to this outrage, insisting that war should be the business of soldiers alone. The *Moniteur* also lashed out at French officers who escaped after being freed on parole as well as at the Parisians who insulted paroled Prussian officers in the cafés of the nation's capital.[18] These themes – that war is strictly a matter for soldiers and that the POW is under an obligation to unconditionally honor his "word" (parole) to the enemy – were still very much alive during the Second World War. They reveal a specific conception of "loyalty" that merits further study. It might exceed the confines of military culture. As if in corroboration of this particularity, the fact that German civilians, militia and soldiers neither put up resistance nor engaged in guerilla warfare following the defeat of 1918 and the arrival of Allied troops in 1945 also raises questions. And though the comparison may be surprising, there is also a link – or at the very least a coincidence – between three fears that may be observed in Germany between 1870 and 1945: that of the franc-tireur; that of the "stab in the back" supposedly dealt to the Kaiser's army by domestic revolutionaries in 1918; and that of the "Jew." A variant of the conspiracy theory, the fear of falling victim to surprise attack by an invisible assailant seems to have been more widespread in this country than elsewhere. An in-depth socio-cultural history would help us understand this phenomenon.

A Franco-Anglo-American Nation

Working on three countries at once while showing the interplay between the micro- and macro-social scales does not necessarily lead to the construction of national stereotypes. To the contrary, the observed differences constitute so many reference points for new avenues of research. Nor does the comparative method prevent one from seeing human and cultural flows between nations. The case of occupied France offers two pertinent examples in this connection.

The systematic reception of Allied airmen by those whom MI9 and MIS-X would later refer to as helpers, the material and moral assistance supplied so that they might return to their units and rejoin the battle, is itself a piece of transnational history. The international solidarity shown by the helpers, often in their very homes and at considerable risk to themselves, was also a pure gesture of national defense on their part. One does not so frequently encounter a civilian population willing to harbor and care for the personnel of a foreign army. In French history, the First World War offers a smaller-scale precedent, with the citizens of occupied Northern France helping evading British soldiers make it to Belgium and, from there, the Netherlands, at that time a neutral

CONCLUSION: AN ARCHEOLOGY OF THE MOMENT 263

power. In general, however, any foreign army that found itself in occupied France was part of an enemy force.

At the same time, the frank internationalism that the helpers' activity entailed had its counterpart in the cooperation of the British and American secret services. The historian Valérie Deacon has noted the discrepancy between the tense dealings of Allied general staffs and the good relations that reigned among the various services involved in exfiltrating soldiers and airmen from the continent.[19] The solidarity between MI9 and MIS-X – and between them and the helpers – did not come to an end with the territorial liberation of France. This is unambiguously demonstrated by the Allies' systematic policy of recognizing the helpers and their families who had suffered repression. Until 1947, the regional press reported on the award ceremonies held by the British and Americans to present helpers with their decorations. Of course, not every ceremony came with the pomp of the "great Franco-American events" of Biarritz, a two-day gathering that brought together the ambassador of the United States, the French Air Force minister, the prefects of the neighboring départements and many figures from the American and British Air Force general staffs. There were nevertheless dozens of such ceremonies. On one Saturday night in February 1947, the town of Biarritz hosted a gala party at the casino as well as a dance party at Bagatelle. The next morning, the population could watch as a procession of soldiers headed to the war memorial. Following a luncheon, a rather grand ceremony was held at the Grande Plage, facing the ocean, where "130 Frenchmen and women" were presented with their decorations in the course of a military review.[20] This concert of nations was not without a sour note, however: in July 1945, the French party to what had up till then been a tripartite body for attributing indemnities to the helpers withdrew from the agreement. The motives for their withdrawal, financial or otherwise, remain unknown as the relevant French archives have yet to be found.

In contrast with this slice of resistant inter- and transnationalism and as it were in opposition to the Franco-Anglo-American triangle, German-origin cultural transfers in the domain of the air war were the object of almost general rejection across the expanse of occupied France. As Robespierre remarked in January 1792 before the course of the Revolution convinced him otherwise, "no one likes armed missionaries." In 1940, the occupying power had to overcome strong public hostility based on the experience of the two preceding wars. Yet this Germanophobia did not prevent the establishment of the Vichy government or the implementation of a policy of Collaboration based on broad acceptance of the principles of National Socialism. The population's behavior vis-à-vis the Allies shows the degree to which an entire swath of society wished to have nothing to do with this dictatorial enterprise.

National Socialist culture similarly had no impact in what concerned assistance to downed Allies. Even French Nazis, who called themselves

264   CONCLUSION: AN ARCHEOLOGY OF THE MOMENT

collaborationists, were only Nazis after their (French) fashion. In 1944, Philippe Henriot's pro-Nazi propaganda against Allied bombing would have lost some of its credibility had he dared present the air raids as the work of "Jews" or depict the airmen as "blacks" after the fashion of German propaganda. In the speeches of the Vichy government's Secretary of State for Information and Propaganda, the Jews governed public life in Britain and the USA, to be sure, and also pulled the strings of that "Judeo-Bolshevik," Joseph Stalin, but they played no particular role in instigating the Allied air strategy nor did they go so far as to wish for the extermination of the French people, their "anti-French hatred" notwithstanding. Blacks, for their part, were absent from these radio-broadcast tirades. Even in the case of this French Goebbels, the German-origin cultural transfer was filtered. Only a portion of the Nazi grotesqueries were deemed suitable for broadcast.

The Making of Civilians

Civilian involvement in the war as it was manifested in their behavior towards downed airmen raises several questions for the historian and suggests that a change of course may be called for.

What is a civilian? The definition depends on the political culture and political regime under consideration. Even in times of peace and freedom, a civilian in France is not the same as a civilian in Britain or in Germany. In each of these countries, one's relationship to civic and political life differs. Rates of political party and associational membership, for example, were traditionally much higher in England and Germany than in France. Nor is the manner in which citizens position themselves in public life identical from one country to the next. For obvious reasons relating to sources, historians struggle to work on civilians. States and organizations leave archives but individuals have only their private correspondence, scattered testimony and literary and artistic works to offer. And when the state takes on a dictatorial or totalitarian form, the possibilities for gaining a purchase on civilian activity are yet further diminished. Were it not for the debriefings of evaded airmen in France and the postwar investigations based upon them, little would be known of the helpers. Were it not for the postwar trials conducted in occupied Germany and later the FRG, we would not be able to assess civilian participation in Kristallnacht, assaults on the deportees and prisoners of the death marches or the lynching of airmen. Since the 2000s, a new historiography has begun to emerge in this connection. Its pioneers are Mary Fulbrook, Sven Keller and Edith Raim (for Germany); Gerwin Strobl, Georg Hoffmann and Eleonore Lappin (for Austria); and Jan Gross and Jan Grabowski (for Poland).[21] Even in the legal sources mentioned above, however, the activities of Mr. and Mrs. John Q. Public do not take center stage and are indeed sometimes relegated to

CONCLUSION: AN ARCHEOLOGY OF THE MOMENT   265

the background behind those of the local leaders of the time. It is thus necessary to decipher them.

The other risk as regards the history of civilians is that they will be reduced to the status of anonymous and transparent individuals with no agenda of their own. Interchangeable and borderless beings, as it were. But universal emotional man has no more claim on reality than the purely rational *Homo oeconomicus* of classical economic theory. In the 1930s and 1940s, the historian Lucien Febvre was already underscoring the relativity of emotions across time and space.[22] A century earlier, the philosopher Alexander Bain also insisted on the socially constructed nature of emotions.[23] If neither of them singled out politics as a factor that imprinted emotions with its stamp, it is doubtless because they saw it as entailed by their use of the term "social."

That civilian emotion was transcended by patriotic-political engagement becomes clear when comparing the on-the-ground reactions elicited by the arrival of airmen. The experience of bombing and that of encountering a downed airman were both colored by specifically civic emotion. During the "People's War," bombing was regarded as a military event and downed Luftwaffe airmen were seen as no more than unlucky aviators. In France during the invasion of 1940, German airmen were looked upon as enemy invaders whom one could legitimately neutralize. During the Occupation, the sight of Allied bombing was often greeted as a happy event to be cheered from one's balcony while to encounter downed airmen was to feel as if freedom were at one's fingertips. In 1944, the intensification of bombing was sharply criticized but did not diminish the population's active support for the Allied cause. In Germany, the perception of bombing began to change in spring 1943. This may be deduced from the civilians' behavior: in the period 1940–42, there was no lynching and thus no racist or apocalyptic interpretation of bombing. The reaction was doubtless one of widespread accommodation. "Das ist Krieg" – "that's war." Against a backdrop of escalating destruction and the Stalingrad effect, however, the civilian perspective on bombing began to change in spring 1943, the will of the people increasingly converging with a policy of incitement to murder. Bombing became an evil enterprise cooked up by the phantasmagoric figure of the "Jew" (the stuff of nightmare for countless German children) with the aim of exterminating the German people. The German civilians of 1943–45 were no longer those of 1940–42. For a part of the population, emotional metamorphosis and behavioral transformation went hand in hand.

There was indeed a civilians' war. In tandem with developments in the broader world and concomitant globalization, the 1990s inaugurated a phase in studies of wartime societies characterized by the denationalization and depoliticization of history's actors. It today seems necessary to repoliticize citizens, restoring both their political assessment of the war and their fighting spirit. The victimological approach, which may be described as empathy for victims wherever they be and whatever their commitments, has allowed us to generally take stock of the suffering and disaster of war. But it must not lead the political filter through which these emotions were experienced to be erased from the portrait. For emotions are not politically neutral, even if they are expressed against the backdrop of a common humanity.

Appendix

Bombardments and On-the-Ground Responses: Maps and Numerical Comparisons

Table App.1. *Bombing victims in the United Kingdom, France and Germany, 1940–45*

Country	Number of civilian victims	Total population in 1940	Victims as share of the total population
Germany (Greater Reich)	353,000	79,000,000	0.4%
United Kingdom	61,000	52,000,000	0.1%
France, May–June 1940	$3500 < N < 16,000$	40,000,000	?
France, July 1940–45	51,000	40,000,000	0.1%

Sources: Germany: Overy, *The Bombing War*, 475–77;

France: Knapp, *Les Français sous les bombes alliées*, 19 (the figure of 3,500 includes 200 people killed by British bombs); the figure of 3,500 only seems to cover urban bombing. Stuka bombing on the roads and the strafing of fleeing civilians do not appear to be included in this total. In the epilogue to *L'exode*, Alary writes that "100,000 people doubtless lost their lives as a result of the exodus." Arzalier, "La campagne de mai–juin 1940," 439, gives the figure of 16,000 French civilians killed in May–June 1940.

United Kingdom: Ministry of Home Security, Statement of civilian casualties in the United Kingdom (Great Britain and Northern Ireland), 31 July 1945. TNA, HO 191/11.

268 APPENDIX

Table App.2. *Tonnage of bombs dropped on the United Kingdom, France and Germany, 1940–45*

Country	Tonnage dropped (all types of bomb included)	Number of tons dropped (all types of bomb) per inhabitant killed
France, May–June 1940	No information	?
United Kingdom	74,000	1
Germany	1,357,000	4
France, July 1940–45	588,000	11

Sources: On the tonnage dropped by the Luftwaffe, Overy, *Air War*, 120, which offers 74,172 tons for the United Kingdom. On the tonnage dropped by the Allies: United States Strategic Bombing Survey, *Over-all Report*, 2.

Table App.3. *Morale on the ground and destruction of cities in Germany*

German towns Percentage of homes destroyed	% of civilians exhibiting low morale	
	Sample A	Sample B
60–80%	55	53
40–59%	58	56
20–39%	59	59
1–19%	43	56
0	–	41

Source: United States Strategic Bombing Survey, *Over-all Report*, 95–96.

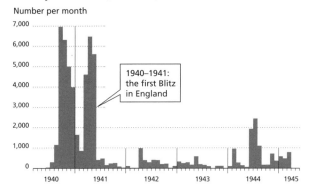

Chart App.1a Victims of German bombing in the United Kingdom: monthly distribution.
Source: Ministry of Home Security, « Statement of civilian casualties in the United Kingdom (Great Britain and Northern Ireland) », 31st July 1945. TNA, HO 191/11. The monthly tonnage dropped over the United Kingdom is not known.

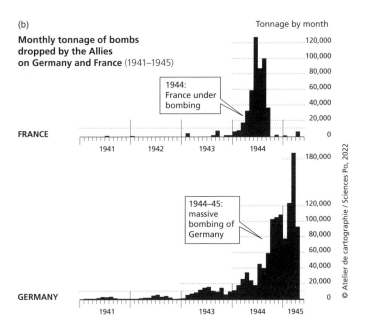

Chart App.1b Monthly tonnage of bombs dropped by the Allies on France and Germany.
Source: US Strategic Bombing Survey, *Over-all report, op.cit.*, p. 7. In this report, tonnage is given as 'short tons' or 'American tons' (2,000 pounds). There are 2,204 pounds in the metric ton.
https://babel.hathitrust.org/cgi/pt?id=mdp.39015049492716&view=1up&seq=23

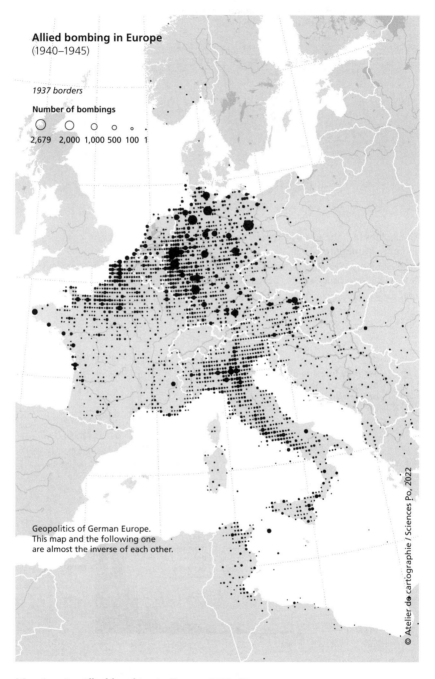

Map App.1 Allied bombing in Europe, 1939–45.
Source: THOR database, Theater History of Operation Reports, US Air Force.

APPENDIX 271

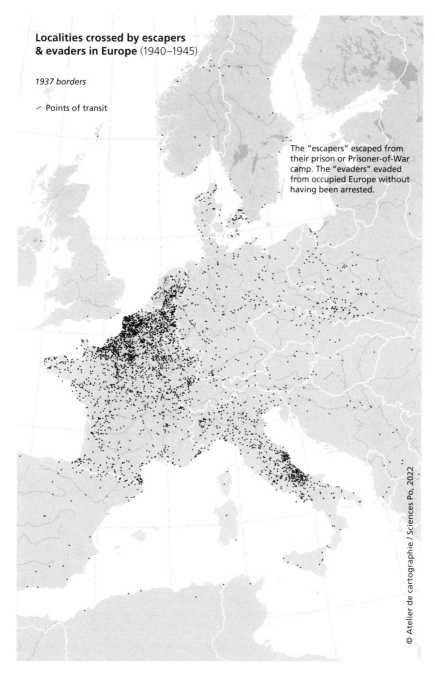

Map App.2 Localities crossed by escapers and evaders in Europe, 1940–45.
Source: TNA, WO208, 3297–3327.

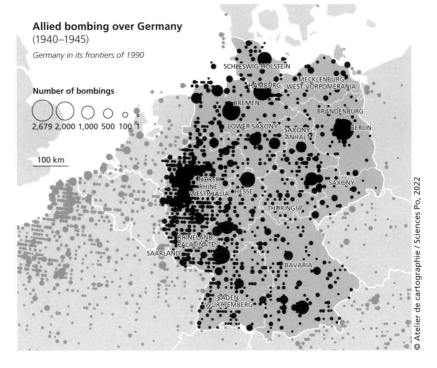

Map App.3 Allied bombing over Germany, 1939–45.
Source: THOR database, Theater History of Operation Reports, US Air Force.

APPENDIX

Map App.4 Lynching of Allied Airmen in Germany, 1943–45.
Source: Deputy Judge Advocate's Office. Reviews and Recommendations, M 1217 Roll 1 à 3, NARA; Index cards of place names for war crimes, WO 353/ 20 and 353/21, The National Archives.

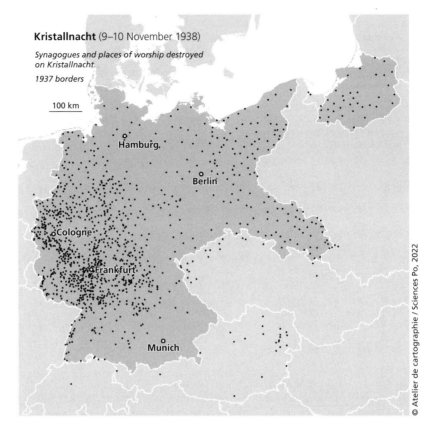

Map App.5 Kristallnacht, 9–10 November 1938.
Source: Stiftung Denkmal für die ermordeten Juden Europas, Berlin.

APPENDIX

Map App.6 Antisemitic violence in Weimar Germany.
Source: Richard Overy, « Racism in the 1920s », The Penguin Historical Atlas of the Third Reich, 1996.

276   APPENDIX

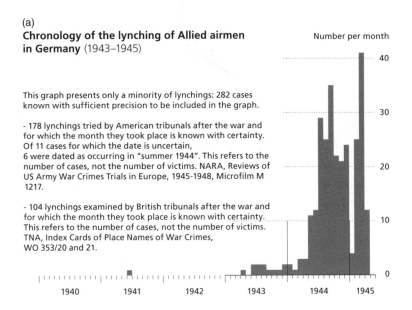

(a)
Chronology of the lynching of Allied airmen in Germany (1943–1945)

Number per month

This graph presents only a minority of lynchings: 282 cases known with sufficient precision to be included in the graph.

- 178 lynchings tried by American tribunals after the war and for which the month they took place is known with certainty. Of 11 cases for which the date is uncertain, 6 were dated as occurring in "summer 1944". This refers to the number of cases, not the number of victims. NARA, Reviews of US Army War Crimes Trials in Europe, 1945-1948, Microfilm M 1217.

- 104 lynchings examined by British tribunals after the war and for which the month they took place is known with certainty. This refers to the number of cases, not the number of victims. TNA, Index Cards of Place Names of War Crimes, WO 353/20 and 21.

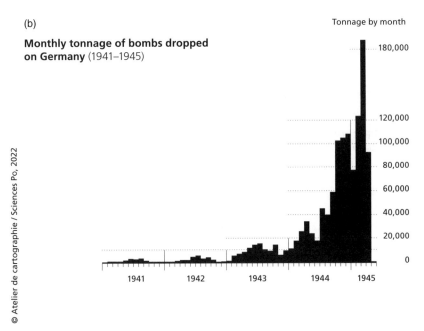

(b)
Monthly tonnage of bombs dropped on Germany (1941–1945)

Tonnage by month

© Atelier de cartographie / Sciences Po, 2022

Chart App.2 (a) Chronology of the lynching of Allied airmen in Germany.
(b) Chronology of the tonnage of bombs dropped on Germany.
Source: NARA, Reviews of US Army War Crimes Trials in Europe, 1945–1948, Microfilm M 1217; TNA, Index Cards of Place Names of War Crimes, WO 353/20 and 21.
Source: US Strategic Bombing Survey, *Over-all report, op.cit.*, p. 7. In this report, tonnage is given in "short", or "American" tons (2,000 pounds) rather than in metric tons (2,204 pounds). https://babel.hathitrust.org/cgi/pt?id=mdp.39015049492716&view=1up&seq=23

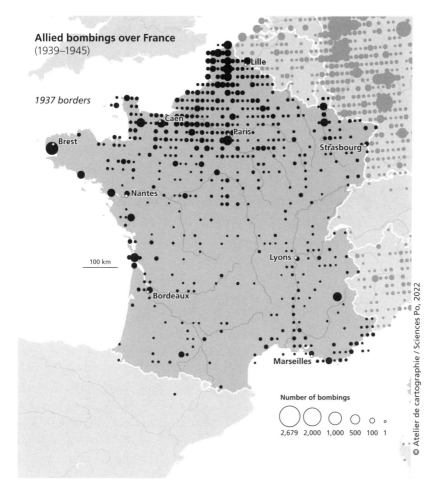

Map App.7 Allied bombing over France.
Source: THOR database, Theater History of Operation Reports, US Air Force.

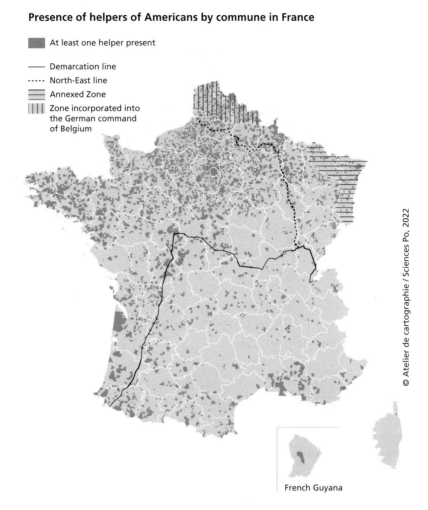

Map App.8 Presence of helpers of Americans by commune in France.
Source: NARA, Master List of MIS-X Awards, France, 1945–1948. Helpers' place of residence in 1945–1946. Recognized helpers.

APPENDIX

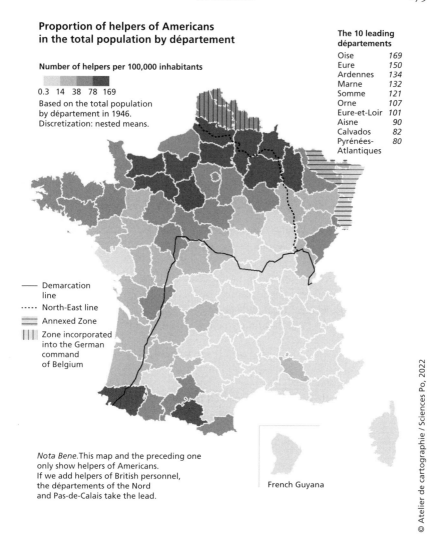

Map App.9 Proportion of helpers of Americans in the total population by département. *NB:* This map and the preceding one only show helpers of Americans. If we add helpers of British personnel, the départements of the Nord and Pas-de-Calais take the lead.
Source: NARA, Master List of MIS-X Awards, France, 1945–1948. Helpers' place of residence in 1945–1946. Only recognized helpers.

ARCHIVAL SOURCES

Archives in France

Paris, Archives nationales

Site Archim	Second World War posters
AJ/40	German delegation to the Armistice Commission
AJ/41	Bodies created by the Armistice of 1940
F/60	French delegation to the occupied territories, DGTO
Z/6	Cour nationale de Justice
Z/5	Chambre civique de la Seine
3W	Haute Cour de Justice, "Berlin" archives

Fort d'Ivry, ECPAD

- AA, German newsreels
- DAA, German air documents. German photographic collection
- Actualités Olympiques (Olympic news items)

Vincennes, Service historique de la Défense

- Files for individual members of the Forces françaises combattantes, GR 28 P4
- Files for individuals having requested recognition as resistants, GR 16 P
- Oberkriegsgerichtsamt bei dem Militärbefehlshaber in Frankreich, case files of trials conducted by German military tribunals, GR 28 P8

Caen, Service historique de la Défense, Division des archives des victimes des conflits contemporains

- Digital database of those deported from France in reprisal, compiled by the Fondation pour la Mémoire de la Déportation, www.bddm.org/liv/index_liv .php
- Files of those deported or interned for acts of resistance

ARCHIVAL SOURCES

Beauvais, Archives départementales de l'Oise
- 33W Archives du cabinet du préfet, 1940–44.

Archives in Great Britain

Colindale, British Newspapers Archive

Peace News, The Daily Worker, The Daily Herald, The Daily Mirror, The Daily Express, The Times, Titbits

Kew, The National Archives

War Office

WO 208	Directorate of Military Intelligence: Escape and Evasion Reports; Register of helpers; Awards Bureau
WO 235	Judge Advocate General's Office: War Crimes Case Files, Second World War
WO 309	Judge Advocate General's Office, British Army of the Rhine War Crimes Group
WO 311	Judge Advocate General's Office, Military Deputy's Department, and War Office

Home Office

HO 191 / 11   Ministry of Home Security

London, Imperial War Museum
- No. 1 Canadian War Crimes Investigation Unit
- Kenneth Hulbert, War Diary

London, Metropolitan Borough of Lambeth Archives
- Civil Defence Emergency Committee, Control Room Diary 1940–45
- South London Press, newspaper.

Maidstone, Kent, Centre for Kentish Studies
- Kent Messenger, newspaper ; brochures

Website: WWII Netherlands Escape Lines

https://wwii-netherlands-escape-lines.com, where the British Register of helpers is available

ARCHIVAL SOURCES

Archives in the United States

Washington, National Archives and Records Administration

European Theater of Operations, Military Intelligence, MIS-X Section, 1944–1948

- Consolidated List of French Helpers, compiled 1945–46, Identifier 5682720
- Case Files Relating to French Citizens Proposed for Awards for Assisting American Airmen, compiled 1945–47, Identifier 5682722
- Captain Tucker's Correspondence Relating to French Aid to American Airmen, compiled 1945–46, Identifier 5682714
- Correspondence Relating to French Aid to American Airmen, compiled 1945–46, Identifier 5682713
- Escape & Evasion Reports (a total of 2,953), Record Group 498, accessible online: https://catalog.archives.gov/id/305270
- Questionnaires relating to Belgian Assistance to British Personnel, compiled 1945–46, Identifier 5701054. Contains correspondence with French people.
- Records Relating to Awards Ceremonies in France, compiled 1946–47, Identifier 5708443
- Escape and Evasion Manual and Service Evasion Forms, compiled 1944–45, Identifier 5701037

German Documents among the War Crimes Records of the Judge Advocate Division,

- Microfilm T 1021

Records of United States Army, Europe, Reviews of US Army War Crimes Trial in Europe, 1945-1948.

- Microfilm Flyer Cases, M 1217. Also online : ICWC, International Research and Documentation Center for War Crime, University of Marburg, Dachau trials, www.uni-marburg.de/icwc/forschung/2weltkrieg/usadachau and Jewish Virtual Library, https://www.jewishvirtuallibrary.org/nazi-war-crimes-trials

World War Two War Crimes Records

- Record Group 153, Record of the Judge Advocate General, War Crimes Branch, Case Files
- Record Group 549, Record of the United States Army, Europe 1942–45. War Crimes Case Files: Cases Tried, Entry A1-2238; and Cases Not Tried, Entry A1-2239

ARCHIVAL SOURCES 283

Archives in Germany

Freiburg-im-Breisgau, Bundesarchiv, Abteilung MilitärArchiv: BA/MA

- Wehrmachtrechtsabteilung, Wehrmacht Legal Service, War Crimes Bureau, RW2
- Generalstab der Luftwaffe, RL-2-II

Berlin, Auswärtiges Amt, Politisches Archiv des Auswärtigen Amtes

- Rechtsabteilung
- Informationsabteilung
- Burö des Staatssekretärs (Ernst Freiherr von Weizsäcker), England
- Botschafter zur besonderen Verwendung (Dr. Karl Ritter), England
- Deutsche Gesandschaft Bern
- Deutsche Botschaft in Paris

Berlin-Lichterfelde, Bundesarchiv

- NS 6 Partei-Kanzlei der NSDAP
- NS 18 Reichspropaganda Leiter der NSDAP
- NS 19 Persönlicher Stab Reichsführer SS
- R 55 Reichsministerium für Volksaufklärung und Propaganda
- R 58 RSHA

Emmendingen, Baden-Württemberg, Deutsches Tagebucharchiv

- Account of Alexandre Meyer, "Mein letzter Feindflug nach England," 1977

Darmstadt, Hessisches Landesarchiv

- *Hessische Landeszeitung*
- *Darmstädter Tagblatt*

Greven, Nordrhein-Westfalen, Stadtarchiv

- NSDAP, Local Police, Air Protection

Münster, Presse und Zeitungen Archiv

- *Münstersche Zeitung*

284   ARCHIVAL SOURCES

Rüsselsheim, Hessen, Stadtarchiv

- *Main-Spitze*
- Many isolated archival items relating to lynching, transcript of the Darmstadt trial, July 1945, and earlier depositions (copy of American archives)
- Archives of the Waldfriedhof cemetery

NOTES

Introduction

1 Kenzaburō Ōe, *The Catch and Other War Stories* (Tokyo, Kondansha International, 1981).

2 Jean-Marie Apostolidès, *Héroïsme et victimisation: une histoire de la sensibilité* (Paris, Cerf, 2011); Michel Messu, *L'ère de la victimisation* (Paris, Payot, 2018); Yana Grinshpun, "Introduction. De la victime à la victimisation: la construction d'un dispositif discursif," *Argumentation et analyse du discours*, 23 (2019), https://journals.openedition.org/aad/3400.

3 Francesca Trivellato, *The Familiarity of Strangers: The Sephardic Diaspora, Livorno and Cross-Cultural Trade in the Early Modern Period* (New Haven, CT: Yale University Press, 2009).

4 Renée Poznanski, "Anti-Semitism and the Rescue of Jews in France: An Odd Couple?" in Jacques Semelin, Claire Andrieu and Sarah Gensburger (eds.), *Resisting Genocide: The Multiple Forms of Rescue* (New York: Columbia University Press, 2011), 83–100.

5 Stanley Milgram, *Obedience to Authority: An Experimental View* (London: Tavistock, 1974), Tables II, III, IV and V, from which experiments 11, 12, 15 and 16 have been removed as not relevant to the present discussion. Out of 476 subjects, 2 refused to participate and 8 limited their participation to light and moderate shocks. See Arthur G. Miller, Barry Collins and Diana Brief (eds.), *Perspectives on Obedience to Authority: The Legacy of the Milgram Experiments*, special issue of *Journal of Social Issues*, 51/3 (Fall 1995); Sophie Richardot, "L'apport de la psychologie sociale à la question de l'obéissance: les travaux de Stanley Milgram sur la soumission à l'autorité," in André Loez and Nicolas Mariot (eds.), *Obéir/Désobéir: les mutineries de 1917 en perspective* (Paris: La Découverte, 2008), 47–59.

6 Gina Perry, *Behind the Shock Machine: The Untold Story of the Notorious Milgram Psychology Experiments* (Brunswick, Victoria: Scribe, 2012).

7 Robert-Vincent Joule and Jean-Léon Beauvois, *Petit traité de manipulation à l'intention des honnêtes gens* (Presses universitaires de Grenoble, 1999); Jean-Léon Beauvois, *Les illusions libérales, individualisme et pouvoir social: petit traité des grandes illusions* (Presses universitaires de Grenoble, 2005).

8 Charles Kiesler, *The Psychology of Commitment: Experiments Linking Behavior to Belief* (New York and London: Academic Press, 1971), 91–99.

9 Michel Espagne, interview with Gérard Noiriel, "Transferts culturels: l'exemple franco-allemand," *Genèses*, 8 (June 1992), 146–54; Michel Espagne, *Les transferts culturels franco-allemands* (Paris: PUF, 1999); Harmut Kaelble, "Les mutations du

286 NOTES TO PAGES 5–10

comparatisme international," in *Histoires croisées: réflexions sur la comparaison internationale en histoire. Les cahiers Irice*, 5 (2010), 9–19; Robert Frank, "Avant-propos: pourquoi une nouvelle revue?," *Monde(s)*, 1 (May 2012), 7–10.

10 Friedrich Nietzsche, *On the Genealogy of Morals* (1887), §11; and on the French: Erwin Scheu, *Frankreich* (Breslau: Ferdinand Hirt, 1923), 120–21, 123, 127. Quoted online at www.deuframat.de.

11 Jean-Noël Jeanneney (ed.), *Une idée fausse est un fait vrai: les stéréotypes nationaux en Europe* (Paris: Odile Jacob, 2000).

12 Marc Bloch, *The Historian's Craft* (Manchester University Press, 1954).

13 Marc Bloch, "Pour une histoire comparée des sociétés européennes," *Revue de synthèse historique*, 46 (1928), 347–80.

14 Michel Boivin, "La Garde territoriale dans la Manche en mai–juin 1940", *Annales de Normandie*, 26 (1995), 571–76.

15 Gaël Eismann, *Hôtel Majestic: ordre et sécurité en France occupée (1940–1944)* (Paris, Tallandier, 2010).

16 Barbara Lambauer, *Otto Abetz et les Français ou l'envers de la Collaboration* (Paris: Fayard, 2001).

17 Simon Paul MacKenzie, *The Home Guard: A Military and Political History* (Oxford University Press, 1995).

18 Richard Overy, *The Battle of Britain* (London, Penguin, 2001), 116. A total of 915 British airplanes were shot down as compared to 1,733 German airplanes.

19 Renate Held, *Kriegsgefangenschaft in Grossbritannien: deutsche Soldaten des Zweiten Weltkriegs in britishem Gewahrsam* (Munich, R. Oldenbourg Verlag, 2008).

20 Jean Quellien, "L'aide aux soldats britanniques," in J.-L. Leleu, F. Passera, J. Quellien and M. Daeffler (eds.), *La France pendant la Seconde Guerre mondiale*, (Paris: Fayard and Ministry of Defense, 2010), 184–85.

21 Laurent Thiéry, *La répression allemande dans le Nord de la France, 1940–1944* (Villeneuve d'Ascq: Presses universitaires du Septentrion, 2013).

22 Jocelyn Leclercq, Antiq'Air Flandre Artois Association, "Les chutes d'avions alliés sur le territoire du Nord-Pas-de-Calais (1940–1944): chronologie, cartographie, bilan humain," in Yves Le Maner (ed.), *Tombés du ciel: les aviateurs abattus au-dessus du Nord-Pas-de-Calais (1940–1944)* (Saint-Omer: Édition La Coupole, 2008), 101–20.

23 Roger Absalom, *A Strange Alliance: Aspects of Escape and Survival in Italy, 1943–1945* (Florence: Leo S. Olschki Editore, 1991).

24 Philippe Burrin, *France under the Germans: Collaboration and Compromise* (New York: New Press, 1996).

25 Robert O. Paxton, *Vichy France: Old Guard and New Order, 1940–1944* (New York: Columbia University Press, 2001; first published 1972), 292.

26 Philippe Burrin, *France under the Germans*.

27 Klaus-Michael Mallmann, "'Volksjustiz gegen anglo-amerikanische Mörder': die Massaker an die westalliierten Fliegern und Fallschirmspringern 1944/45," in Alfred Gottwaldt, Norbert Kampe, and Peter Klein (eds.), *NS-Gewaltherrschaft: Beiträge zur historischen Forschung und juristischen Aufarbeitung* (Berlin, Edition Hentrich, 2005), 202–14; Barbara Grimm, "Lynchmorde an alliierten Fliegern in Zweiten Weltkrieg," in Dietmar Süss (ed.), *Deutschland im Luftkrieg: Geschichte und Erinnerung* (Munich: Oldenburg Wissenschaftsverlag, 2007), 71–84.

NOTES TO PAGES 10–15   287

28 Gerwin Strobl, *Bomben auf Oberdonau: Luftkrieg und Lynchmorde an alliierten Fliegern im 'Heimatgau des Führers'* (Oberösterreichisches Landesarchiv Linz, 2014); Georg Hoffmann, *Fliegerlynchjustiz: Gewalt gegen abgeschossene alliierte Flugzeugbesatzungen 1943–1945* (Paderborn: Ferdinand Schöningh, 2015).

29 Helmut Schnatz, "Lynchmorde an Fliegern," in Franz Seidler und Alfred-Maurice de Zayas (eds.), *Kriegsverbrechen in Europa und im Nahen Osten im 20. Jahrhundert* (Hamburg: Mittler, 2002), 118–21.

30 Kevin T. Hall, "Luftgangster over Germany: The Lynching of American Airmen in the Shadow of the Air War," *Historical Social Research*, 43/2 (2018) 277–312; and Hall, *Terror Flyers: The Lynching of American Airmen in Nazi Germany* (Bloomington: Indiana University Press, 2021). Also of note: Ralph Blank, "Wartime Daily Life and the Air War on the Home Front", in Jörg Echternkamp (ed.), *Germany and the Second World War*, vol. IX-1 (Oxford: Clarendon Press, 2008; first published in German 2004), 464–67.

31 Katrin Hassel, *Kriegsverbrechen vor Gericht: die Kriegsverbrechenprozesse vor Militärgerichten in der britischen Besatzungszone unter dem Royal Warrant vom 18. Juni 1945 (1945–1949)* (Baden-Baden: Nomos, 2009).

32 Bastiaan Robert von Benda-Beckmann, *German Historians and the Bombing of German Cities: The Contested Air War* (Amsterdam University Press, 2015).

33 Presentation of the project on the University of Exeter website, 2006 (URL no longer current).

34 Claudia Baldoli, Andrew Knapp and Richard Overy (eds.), *Bombing, States and Peoples in Western Europe, 1940–1945* (London and New York: Continuum, 2011); Claudia Baldoli and Andrew Knapp, *Forgotten Blitzes: France and Italy under Allied Air Attack, 1940–1945* (London and New York: Continuum, 2012).

35 Martin Francis, *The Flyer: British Culture and the Royal Air Force 1939–1945* (Oxford University Press, 2008).

36 Harald Welzer, Sabine Moller and Karoline Tschuggnall, *Opa war kein Nazi: Nationalsozialismus und Holocaust im Familiengedächtnis* (Frankfurt: Fischer Verlag, 2002).

37 Based on a book by Jan Struther, *Mrs. Miniver* was a Metro-Goldwyn-Mayer Pictures film directed by William Wyler and produced by Sidney Franklin, 1942.

38 Written by Kendal Burt, directed by Roy Ward Baker, *The One that Got Away*, Julian Wintle with the Rank Organisation, 1957.

39 David Croft and Jimmy Perry, *Dad's Army*, BBC Worldwide, 1968–77.

40 *The Enemy within the Gates* (1968), *Man Hunt* (1969), *The Lion has Phones* (1969), *Time on my Hand* (1972), *Come In, Your Time's Up!* (1975).

41 Edgar Reitz, *Heimat: eine deutsche Chronik*, 1984, DVD; and the screenplay published by Greno (Nordlingen, 1985), 266–90; Alan Confino, "Edgar Reitz's *Heimat* and German Nationhood: Film, Memory, and Understandings of the Past," *German History*, 16/2 (1998), 185–208.

42 James Hargest, 1944; Beirne Lay, Jr., 1945; Derrick Nabarro, 1952; Airey Neave, 1953; Jimmy Langley, 1974; Lucien Dumais, 1974; Sir Ronald Ivelaw-Chapman, 1975.

43 Cf. the first-person accounts of Etta Shiber, 1943; Sabine Hoisne, 1945; Drue Tartière, 1946; Rémy Tessonneau, 1946; Louis-Henri Nouveau, 1957; Marie-Thérèse Le Calvez (by Dominique-Martin Le Trividic), 1979; Gabriel Nahas, 1982; André Postel-Vinay, 1997; Georges Broussine, 2000; Odile de Vasselot, 2005.

288   NOTES TO PAGES 15–26

44 Jimmy M. Langley, *Fight Another Day* (London: Collins, 1974), 115–16.
45 *La Grande Vadrouille*, directed by Gérard Oury, produced by Corona/ Lowndes, 1966.
46 One discussion of Mass Observation as a source: Annebella Pollen, "Research Methodology in Mass Observation Past and Present: 'Scientifically, about as valuable as a chimpanzee's tea party at the zoo'?", *History Workshop Journal*, 75/1 (Spring 2013), 213–23. On SD reports, see Christian Ingrao, *Croire et détruire: les intellectuels dans la machine de guerre SS* (Paris: Fayard, 2010), 194–98, 389–93.
47 The British debriefings are numbered from 1 to 3,122 and the American debriefings from 1 to 2,953. But many debriefings from the British series (more than 600) are missing from the boxes in question. TNA, WO 208/3297–327 and NARA, RG 498, UD 133, UD 134, Boxes 516–73.
48 See Chapter 8, Tables 8.1a and 8.1b. TNA, WO 235, WO 309 and WO 353 / 20–21 ; NARA, M-1217 and RG 549, Entry A1-2238, Box 84–255.
49 Archives of the French Zone of Occupation in Germany and Austria, Affaires judiciaires, FRMAE-1AJ.
50 Oberkommando der Wehrmacht (WR), Untersuchungstelle für Verletzungen des Völkerrechts, "Kriegsrechtsverletzungen der britischen Wehrmacht," 1943, 345ff., Bundesarchiv/Militärarchiv (BA/MA), Freiburg, RW2/61.

Part I

1 Cf. Overy, *Battle of Britain*, 116–17.
2 Victor Hugo, *Ô soldats de l'an deux!* (January 1853), published in *Les Châtiments* (1853).

Chapter 1

1 Oberkommando der Wehrmacht (WR), Wehrmacht-Untersuchungsstelle für Verletzungen des Völkerrechts, *Frankreichs völkerrechtswidrige Kriegführung 1939/1940* [*France's Conduct of a War Contrary to International Law, 1939/1940*], vol. 1 (Berlin: Gedrückt in der Reichsdruckerei, November 1940), 223–25.
2 Biger Brewalan and René-Pierre Sudre, "Kérandel, Jean-Marie," in *Le Maitron: dictionnaire des fusillés, 1940–1944*, https://fusilles-40-44.maitron.fr/?article158335.
3 Cf. tables of French aviation victories, in *La Chasse au combat, mai–juin 1940*, *Ciel de guerre* 8 (December 2005 to March–April 2006).
4 Percentage calculated with help from the Office of the Adjutant General, *Army Battle Casualties and Nonbattle Deaths in World War II: Final Report (7 December 1941 – 31 December 1946)* (Washington : Dept. of the Army, 1953), 76–77; Sir Arthur Harris, *Despatch on War Operations, 23rd February 1942 – 8th May 1945*, 18 December 1945 (London: Frank Cass, 1995), 61.
5 Jean-Louis Crémieux-Brilhac, *Les Français de l'an 40*, vol. II: *Ouvriers et soldats* (Paris: Gallimard, 1990), 669. The source is not explicitly mentioned. In his *The Complete War Memoirs of Charles de Gaulle*, vol. I: *The Call to Honor*, trans. Jonathan Griffin and Richard Howard (New York: Carroll & Graf, 2008), De Gaulle mentions 400 German airmen taken prisoner. In *L'armée de l'air dans la tourmente: la bataille de France 1939–1940* (Paris, Economica, 2005), 250, Patrick Facon offers the figure of 1,900 German prisoners of war, 700 of whom were

NOTES TO PAGES 26–28 289

members of the Luftwaffe. His source is the Report drawn up for the Air Force by General Vuillemain in July 1940. The German document, Oberkommando der Wehrmacht (WR), *Frankreichs völkerrechtswidrige Kriegführung*, vol. I, 3, offers the figure of "nearly 10,000 prisoners of war."

6 Karl-Heinz Frieser, *The Blitzkrieg Legend: The 1940 Campaign in the West*, trans. from German (Annapolis, MD: Naval Institute Press, 2013).

7 Karl-Heinz Frieser, "La légende de la 'Blitzkrieg'", in Maurice Vaïsse (ed.), *Mai–Juin 1940: défaite française, victoire allemande, sous l'oeil des historiens étrangers* (Paris: L'Harmattan, 2000), 75–85 (at 84).

8 Christian Malis, "Après le Blitzkrieg: le réveil de la pensée militaire française (juin 1940 – mars 1942). Le rôle de la revue *La France libre*," *Histoire, géopolitique et stratégie*, www.stratisc.org/84-Malis.htm.

9 Dennis Showalter, "Ce que l'armée française avait compris de la guerre moderne," and Martin Alexander, "Gamelin et les leçons de la campagne de Pologne," in Vaïsse (ed.), *Mai–juin 1940*, 29–58 and 59–74.

10 Claire Andrieu, "La nazification de la Wehrmacht durant la campagne de France", in Johann Chapoutot and Jean Vigreux (eds.), *Des soldats noirs face au Reich: les massacres racistes de 1940* (Paris: PUF, 2015), 59–100.

11 Julien Fargettas, *Les tirailleurs sénégalais: les soldats noirs entre légendes et réalités, 1939–1945* (Paris, Tallandier, 2012), 140–68. Cf. also Raffael Scheck, *Hitler's African Victims: The German Army Massacres of Black French Soldiers in 1940* (Cambridge University Press, 2006).

12 The massacres of Paradis, Lestrem, Pas-de-Calais, 27 May 1940, by an SS division: 97 British soldiers. Wormhout massacre in the Nord, 28 May 1940, by a battalion from an SS regiment: 80 British soldiers and a few French ones. Laurent Thiéry, "Les massacres de civils dans le Nord de la France en mai–juin 1940", *La Lettre de la Fondation de la Résistance*, 60 (March 2010), 5–6.

13 The term "normal": Ernst Nolte,*Three Faces of fascism: Action Française, Italian fascism, National Socialism*, trans. Leila Vennewitz (New York: Holt, Rinehart & Winston, 1965; first German edition in 1963); "honorable": Pieter Lagrou, Julie Le Gac, "Guerre honorable sur le front de l'Ouest: crime, punition et reconciliation", in Gaël Eismann and Stefan Martens (ed.), *Occupation et répression militaire allemandes* (Paris: Autrement, 2007), 201–19.

14 Jean Quellien, "Les pertes humaines," in Leleu et al. (eds.), *La France pendant la Seconde Guerre mondiale*, 262–65; Jean-Jacques Arzalier, "La campagne de mai–juin 1940, les pertes?" in Christine Levisse-Touzé (ed.), *La campagne de 1940* (Paris, Tallandier, 2001), 439, cites a total of 21,000 civilians killed, including 16,000 French people, supplied by the Vichy government's Secrétariat general aux anciens combattants, Note of 5 November 1943.

15 Baldoli and Knapp (eds.), *Forgotten Blitzes*, 3 and 261.

16 Marc Bloch, *Strange Defeat*, trans. Gerard Hopkins (Oxford University Press, 1949).

17 Hanna Diamond, *Fleeing Hitler: France 1940* (Oxford University Press, 2007); Eric Alary, *L'exode: un drame oublié* (Paris: Perrin, 2010).

18 Crémieux-Brilhac, *Les Français de l'an 40*.

19 Julian Jackson, *The Fall of France: The Nazi Invasion of 1940* (Oxford University Press, 2003); Julian Jackson and Jérôme Wilson, "Étrange défaite française ou étrange victoire anglaise?" in Vaïsse (ed.), *Mai–juin 1940*, 177–213; Julian Jackson, "Conclusions," in Pierre Allorant, Noëlline Castagnez and Antoine Prost

290   NOTES TO PAGES 28–36

(eds.), *Le moment 1940: Effondrement national et réalités locales* (Paris, L'Harmattan, 2012), 257–64.

20 Philip Nord, *France 1940: Defending the Republic* (New Haven, CT: Yale University Press, 2015.

21 Hanna Diamond, "France in 1940: Images of Refugees", in Stefan Martens and Steffen Prauser (eds.), *La guerre de 40: se battre, subir, se souvenir* (Lille: Presses universitaires du Septentrion, 2014), 195–210.

22 Diamond, *Fleeing Hitler*, 81–85.

23 Figures drawn from ibid., 232 n. 27. Estimates from the Sous-secrétariat d'État aux réfugiés, 2 July 1940, SHAT 1P9; and Note de la Direction des Services de l'Armistice à l'Ambassade de l'Allemagne, 7 March 1941, AN F60 1507. See also Eric Alary, "Evacuations et exode", in Leleu et al. (eds.), *La France pendant la Seconde Guerre mondiale*, 46–47.

24 Jean Vidalenc, *L'exode de mai–juin 1940* (Paris: PUF, 1957), 415–16.

25 Alfred Fabre-Luce, *Journal de la France 1939–1944* (Paris: Fayard, 1969), 235. This journal, first published in 1941, went through several versions. This passage was noted by Alary in *L'exode*, 336.

26 Léon Werth, *33 jours* (Paris: Viviane Hamy, 1992) (first published 1940).

27 Philippe Nivet, "Les populations civiles: le cas de la Somme en 1940," in Allorant, Castagnez and Prost (eds.), *Le moment 1940*, 51–62.

28 These totals are based on comparison of the following sources: the two volumes of the Wehrmacht Rechtsabteilung white book (Wehrmacht Legal Service); archives of the MBF, AN AJ/40/1357 and 1365; archives of the DGTO F60/404 and 1485; DFA volumes with the CAA, 1940–41 (index "gardes territoriales"). Not counted here are the cases of aggression on the part of soldiers (seven cases in the first volume of the white book and nineteen in the second volume) nor the insults and threats voiced by civilians during subsequent transports of airmen taken prisoner (included in the nineteen cases cited in the second volume).

29 Werth, *33 jours*, 41.

30 Cf. website summarizing many texts distributed in the Manche département: www.wikimanche.fr/index.php?title=D%C3%A9fense_passive_%C3%A0_Granville.

31 Captain Moussin, commander of Armes, to the mayor of Landrecies, 4 September 1939, in annexes of Oberkommando der Wehrmacht (WR), *Frankreichs völkerrechtswidrige Kriegführung*, vol. I, 249.

32 Chief warrant officer Huot-Marchand, Gaston, to the mayor of the commune of Auxon, 21 December 1939, in PA-AA, *Deutsche Botschaft Paris*, 2451.

33 Notice in *Le Granvillais*, 25 April 1940, quoted by Michel Boivin, "La garde territoriale dans la Manche en mai–juin 1940," *Cahiers des Annales de Normandie*, 26 (1995), 571–76 (at 571).

34 Préfecture de l'Oise, Cabinet du préfet, Officiel telegram, 19 May 1940, AD Oise, 33 W/8242-1.

35 Décret relatif à la création des formations militaires de gardes territoriaux, 17 May 1940, *Journal officiel de la République française* of 18 May 1940.

36 Instruction pour l'application du décret du 17 mai 1940 portant création des formations militaires des gardes territoriaux, *Journal officiel de la République française*, 21 May 1940.

37 John Horne and Alan Kramer, *German Atrocities 1914: A History of Denial* (New Haven, CT: Yale University Press, 2001), chap. 3: "The German Army and the Myth

NOTES TO PAGES 36–41

of the Francs-tireurs, 1914," and chap. 4: "Memories, Mentalities, and the German Response to the 'Francs-tireurs War'."

38 Ibid., 435–43: "German Atrocities in 1914: Incidents with Ten or More Citizens Killed." Between 5 and 31 August 1914, these massacres have resulted in a total of 4,869 victims.

39 For the specificities of German military culture, see Isabel V. Hull, *Absolute Destruction: Military Culture and the Practices of War in Imperial Germany* (Ithaca, NY: Cornell University Press, 2005), and *A Scrap of Paper: Breaking and Making International Law during the Great War* (Ithaca, NY: Cornell University Press, 2014).

40 Andreas Toppe, *Militär und Kriegsvölkerrecht: Rechtsnorm, Fachdiskurs und Kriegspraxis in Deutschland 1899–1940* (Munich: Oldenburg, 2007).

41 *L'Ouest-Éclair*, 23 May 1940, quoted by Michel Boivin, "La garde territoriale dans la Manche."

42 The prefect of the Oise, telegram to the 702 mayors of the département, 12 May 1940. AD Oise, 33W-8242-1.

43 Peter Jackson, "Returning to the Fall of France: Recent Work on the Causes and Consequences of the 'Strange Defeat' of 1940," *Modern and Contemporary France*, 12/4 (2004), 513–36.

44 Crémieux-Brilhac, *Les Français de l'an 40*, 635–48.

Chapter 2

1 See John Horne and Alan Kramer, "Zur Rezeption des Buches seit 2001," preface to the 2018 German edition of *German Atrocities, Deutsche Kriegsgreuel 1914: die umstrittene Wahrheit* (Hamburg: Hamburger edition, 2018), 3–36; and in contrast: Ulrich Keller, *Schuldfragen: Belgischer Untergrundkrieg und Deutsche Vergeltung im August 1914* (Paderborn : Ferdinand Schöningh, 2017); Gunter Spraul, *Der Franktireurkrieg 1914: Untersuchungen zum Verfall einer Wissenschaft und zum Umgang mit nationalen Mythen* (Berlin : Franck & Timme, 2016).

2 Report of Captain Marchal, Commander of the Compiègne section of gendarmerie, 4 October 1940, drafted on the verbal request of the squadron chief commanding the company and transmitted to the prefect of the Oise in response to his request. AD Oise, 33 W 8242-1.

3 Jacqueline and Paul Martin, "La chute du capitaine Mölders: témoignage des militaires du 195th RALT"(2001), www.aerostories.org.

4 Klaus Schmider, "Werner Mölders und die Bundeswehr: Anmerkungen zum Umgang mit der Geschichte der Wehrmacht" (2016), http://portal-militaergeschichte.de/schmider_moelders.pdf.

5 Eismann, *Hôtel Majestic*; Eismann, "L'escalade d'une répression à visage légal: les pratiques judiciaires des tribunaux du Militärbefehlshaber in Frankreich, 1940–1944", in Eismann and Martens (eds.), *Occupation et répression militaire allemandes*, 127–67.

6 Eismann, "L'escalade d'une répression," 128.

7 Jean Solchany, "Le commandement militaire allemand face aux résistants", in Laurent Douzou et al. (eds.), *La Résistance et les Français: villes, centres et logiques de décision* (Paris : IHTP, 1995), 511–30.

NOTES TO PAGES 41–47

8 Three other Luftwaffe airmen were killed by soldiers at Vimy, in the combat zone, on 18 May 1940.

9 Oberkommando der Wehrmacht (WR), *Frankreichs völkerrechtswidrige Kriegführung*, vol. I (November 1940) and vol. II (April 1941). Cf. Andrieu, "La nazification de la Wehrmacht."

10 Auswärtiges Amt, *Die völkerrechtswidrige Führung des belgischen Volkskriegs* (Berlin: Imprimerie du Reich, 10 May 1915).

11 Cf. Andrieu, "La nazification de la Wehrmacht."

12 "Die französchiche Regierung, die französische Wehrmacht und das französische Volk in weitesten Kreisen haben auch in diesem Kriege das Äusserste getan, den aus Frankreichs eigener Geschichte sich immer wieder ergebenden Gegensatz zwischen humanitärer Dialektik und humanem Handeln von neuem zu beleuchten." Oberkommando der Wehrmacht (WR), *Frankreichs völkerrechtswidrige Kriegführung*, vol. 1, 3.

13 In Wolfgang Geiger, *L'image de la France dans l'Allemagne nazie, 1933–1945* (Presses universitaires de Rennes, 1999), 135: directives from the Armee-OberKommando 2, 12 July 1940, in pursuance of the letter from Goebbels to the OKW, 26 June 1940.

14 Willi A. Boelcke (ed.), *The Secret Conferences of Dr. Goebbels: The Nazi Propaganda War, 1939–1943* (New York: E.P. Dutton, 1970).

15 Ibid., 57, 65, 66, 67: accounts of meetings held on 16 and 18 June and 9 and 15 July 1940.

16 Ibid., 46, 50: 28 May and 9 June 1940; also see Joseph Goebbels, *Journal 1939–1942* (Paris: Tallandier, 2009), 146, 147, 171: 15 and 29 May, 7 July 1940.

17 The majority of deaths were caused by gunfire from the French Army.

18 Nearly 10,000 German prisoners of war: figure given by Oberkommando der Wehrmacht (WR), *Frankreichs völkerrechtswidrige Kriegführung*, vol. I, 3.

19 Fargettas, *Les tirailleurs sénégalais*; Scheck, *Hitler's African Victims*.

20 *Verordnung über das Sonderstrafrecht im Kriege und bei besonderem Einsatz (Kriegssonderstrafrechtsverordnung), vom 17 August 1938* (KSSVO), edict signed by Hitler and published in the *Reichsgesetzblatt* (RGBl), 1 (26 August 1939), 1455–57.

21 Cf. Eismann, *Hôtel Majestic*, 218–22; and "La norme à l'épreuve de l'idéologie: le franc-tireur en droit allemand et la figure du terroriste judéo-bolchévique en France pendant la Seconde Guerre mondiale," in Antoine Mégie and Virginie Sansico (eds.), *Des "terroristes" dans le prétoire: qualifier et punir la violence politique d'hier à aujourd'hui, Histoire@Politique*, 45 (2021), https://journals.openedition.org/his toirepolitique/1874.

22 90,000 French people and residents of France were deported as a measure of repression but only 75,000 from the territory of France (60,400 from the Northern and Southern Zones, and the rest from Nord-Pas-de-Calais and Alsace-Moselle). Around 15,000 were deported while already on German territory. Figures of the Fondation pour la Mémoire de la Déportation, number of deportees sentenced or whose case file was handled by the German military tribunals: see Thomas Fontaine, *Déporter: politiques de déportation et répression en France occupée, 1940–1944* (Paris: Panthéon-Sorbonne, 2013), 1127. Online at HAL.

23 If one adds to this the cases of abuse that took place sometime after arrival on the ground – that is, during interrogation or prisoner convoy transfers – and

NOTES TO PAGES 47–55

committed either by the French Army or by civilians, the total comes to forty cases, fourteen in the first volume of the white book and twenty-four in the second.

24 One trial concerned a French Army captain sentenced to death by the Luftwaffe tribunal in Paris on 25 September 1941, for having killed a German airman. He was executed in January 1943 or shortly beforehand. AN, AJ40/1357.

25 Vidalenc, *L'exode de mai–juin 1940*, 200–04.

26 André Gide, *Ainsi soit-il ou les jeux sont faits*, written in 1950–51 (Paris: Gallimard, 2001), 32 ;Blaise Pascal, *Pensées* (1670), no. 592: "I only believe the stories whose witnesses would have their throats cut."

27 Doubts remain as to the identity of the soldier who killed the airman with a gunshot: he was either a solitary soldier in retreat or a soldier stationed at Rougemaison in the area of Luchy.

28 René Boly, *L'orge et la terre, Mai 1940* (Louvergny: Editions Terres Noires, 2000), 46; André Joncoux, "La Gestapo l'avait condamné, Antenne 2 le retrouve," *Le Courrier picard*, 13 May 1985, 5.

29 Inspector of the security police to the Commissaire Principal in Saint-Quentin, 4 December 1943, AD Oise, 33W 8242-1.

30 Boly, *L'orge et la terre*, 66.

31 Communiqué of the German tribunal of La Rochelle, 13 March 1941, quoted on the website of the community of communes of the canton of Aulnay, Charente-Maritime; see also the weekly summary of the DGTO, AN, AJ41/397, www.ihtp .cnrs.fr/prefets/fr/fzo24034dgto.html.

32 Otto von Stülpnagel, *Die Wahrheit über die deutschen Kriegsverbrechen* (Berlin: Staatspolitischer Verlag, 1920).

33 There is another version of events. It was summarized in late October 1940 by the Direction des Services d'Armistice in a note to the Chief Representative of the French Government for the Occupied Territories (AN, F1a4681) but does not seem to have been verified. According to this version, the airman was killed in his fall and a civilian had shot the corporal in the legs.

34 *Propaganda Kompanien*, documentary film by Véronique Lhorme, ECPAD and La Cuisine aux Images, 2013.

35 Testimony of Mme Mullot, in Joncoux, "La Gestapo."

36 Jean-Paul Pallud, "Show Trial at Luchy," *After the Battle*, 54 (1986), 50–53.

37 ECPAD, DAA-842 and 843.

38 Cf. Joncoux, "La Gestapo."

39 AD Oise, 33W 8242-1, dossier concerning the arrest of gardes territoriaux.

40 "Mullot Alfred" record [October 1940], AD Oise, 33W/8242/1. According to the investigation cited in note 36, the two men who arrived alive on the ground jumped by parachute.

41 Gericht des Kommandanten des rückw, Armeegebiets 580, Doullens, 6 June 1940, PA-AA, R 60636.

42 Feldgericht des Kommandierenden Generals und Befehlshaber im Luftgau Belgien-Nordfrankreich, Feldurteil, 22 April 1941, Brussels. AN, AJ40/1357; "Verordnung gegen Volksschädlinge", 5 September 1939, *Reichsgesetzblatt*, 6 (September 1939).

43 Feldgericht des Kommandierenden Generals und Befehlshaber in Luftgau Belgien-Nordfrankreich, Feldurteil, 23 April 1941, AN, AJ/40/1357; *Nord-Matin*, 9 December 1944.

294 NOTES TO PAGES 55–62

44 A single airman was lynched, not three as Alfred Maurice de Zayas claims in *The Wehrmacht War Crimes Bureau, 1939–1945* (Lincoln: University of Nebraska Press, 1989; first German edn 1979), 197, in a legend accompanying a photograph of the unearthed bodies of three airmen killed on the spot.

45 Cf. AN/AJ/40/1365; and DFA/CAA, Délégation française auprès de la Commission allemande d'armistice, *Recueil de documents*, vol. V, 1959.

46 I.A. gez. Müller, Oberkommando des Heeres, an das Oberkommando der Wehrmacht (WR), 27/11/1940; and Der Chef des Oberkommandos der Wehrmacht, I.A. gez Dr. Lehmann, an den Herrn Reichsminister der Luftfahrt und Oberbefehlshaber der Luftwaffe (ZA R), 24/12/1940. AN AJ/40/1365.

47 Laurent Thiéry, "La répression allemande contre les réseaux d'évasion d'aviateurs alliés," in Le Maner (ed.), *Tombés du ciel*, 139–48; and Thiéry, *La répression allemande*.

48 Eismann, *Hôtel Majestic*, 218.

49 Der Präsident des Reichskriegsgerichts als Gerichtsherr [Admiral Max Bastian], Berlin, to the German Armistice Committee and the military occupation authorities in France (MBF), 9 May 1941. PA-AA, Deutsche Botschaft in Paris, 2451.

50 Cf. Norbert Haase, *Das Reichskriegsgericht und der Widerstand gegen die national-sozialistische Herrschaft*, Katalog zur Sonderausstellung der Gedenkstätte Deutscher Widerstand in Zusammenarbeit mit der Neuen Richtervereinigung (Berlin, 1993).

51 The mayors of 18 communes in the canton of Estrées-Saint-Denis to the prefect, 10 April 1941, AD Oise, 33W 8242-1.

52 Der Militärbefehlshaber in Frankreich an das Oberkommando des Heeres, 21 May 1941, PA-AA, DBP 2451.

53 Artillery General [Oskar] Vogl, an OK W/WR (Oberkommando der Wehrmacht, Wehrmacht Rechtsabteilung), 24 May 1941, PA-AA, Deutsche Botschaft in Paris, 2451.

54 Cf. Délégation française d'armistice auprès de la Commission allemande d'armistice, *Recueil de documents*, vols. IV and V, 1957 and 1959; letter from General Doyen to General Vogl, 3 June 1941,.

55 The sentence of one of them had already been commuted to five years in prison (Cramoisy).

56 Letter from General Doyen to General Vogl, 3 June 1941, PA-AA, DBP, 2451.

57 Marshal Pétain to His Excellency Herr Chancellor, 25 June 1941, ibid.

58 Lambauer, *Otto Abetz*, 462–70.

59 Telegram from Ribbentrop to the German Ambassador in Paris, 5 July 1941, AN, 3W353. Cf. also Vincent Giraudier, *Les Bastilles de Vichy répression politique et internement administratif* (Paris: Tallandier, 2009).

60 Jacques Benoist-Méchin, Secretary of State, letter to Ambassador Otto Abetz, 30 October 1941, PA-AA, DBP, 2451.

61 *Ejusdem*, letter to the ambassador, 17 June 1942, ibid.

62 Rudolf Lehmann (1890–1955) was convicted of war crimes and crimes against humanity, in particular for his participation in drafting the "order regarding commissars" in 1941, and sentenced to seven years' imprisonment by the Nuremberg military tribunal. On his efforts to promote the two volumes of the Investigative Bureau, see Zayas, *Wehrmacht War Crimes Bureau*, 94–99 (first German edition in 1979). The four paragraphs that follow are reprinted from Andrieu, "La nazification de la Wehrmacht."

NOTES TO PAGES 62–74

63 Rudolf Lehmann, memorandum addressed to the Ausland-Abwehr, the Wehrmacht's counter-espionage department, 2 September 1940, quoted by Zayas, *Wehrmacht War Crimes Bureau*, 97.

64 MBF an die deutsche Botschaft, 22 December 1941, ibid.

65 Paul Seabury, *The Wilhelmstrasse: A Study of German Diplomats under the Nazi Regime* (Berkeley: University of California Press, 1954); Christopher R. Browning, *The Final Solution and the German Foreign Office* (London and New York: Holmes & Meier, 1978); Eckart Conze et al., *Das Amt und die Vergangenheit: deutsche Diplomaten im Dritten Reich und in der Bundesrepublik* (Munich: Karl Blessing Verlag), 2010.

66 Conze et al., *Das Amt*, 227–37.

67 Cf. Jean-Nicolas Pasquay, "De Gaulle, les FFL et la Résistance vus par les responsables de la Wehrmacht", *Revue historique des armées*, 256 (2009), 43–65.

68 Décret du 17 mai 1940 relatif à la création de formations militaires de gardes territoriaux, *Journal officiel de la République française*, 18 May 1940, 3692.

69 Lambauer, *Otto Abetz*, 608–12; Jean-Marc Berlière and François Le Goarant de Tromelin, *Liaisons dangereuses: miliciens, truands, résistants, Paris 1944* (Paris: Perrin, 2013).

Chapter 3

1 "We Don't Mind the Jokes," by an LDV, *Daily Herald*, 6 July 1940.

2 Mackenzie, *Home Guard*, 19.

3 Penny Summerfield and Corinna Peniston-Bird, *Contesting Home Defence: Men, Women and the Home Guard in the Second World War* (Manchester University Press, 2007), 37–45.

4 John Langdon-Davies, "Arm the People," *Reynolds News*, 16 June 1940; and Tom Horabin, "Arm the People Now!", *News Chronicle*, 15 June 1940, quoted by Summerfield and Peniston-Bird, *Contesting Home Defence*, 39.

5 Daniel Todman, *Britain's War*, vol. I: *Into Battle, 1937–1941* (Oxford University Press, 2016); Robin Prior, *When Britain Saved the West: The Story of 1940* (New Haven, CT: Yale University Press, 2015).

6 Air Ministry, *The Battle of Britain August–October 1940* (London: Her Majesty's Stationery Office, 1941); and the report drafted in September 1941 by Air Chief Marshal Hugh Dowding, "The Battle of Britain," published in the *Supplement to the London Gazette*, 11 September 1946. On this subject, see Jeremy Crang, "Names of the 'Few'," published at the site of The Battle of Britain London Monument.

7 William L. Shirer, *Berlin Diary: Journal of a Foreign Correspondent 1934–1941* (Mountain View, CA: Ishi Press International, 2010).

8 Klaus A. Maier et al., quoting the journal of General Halder, Army Chief of Staff, 14 September 1940, in *Germany and the Second World War*, vol. II, ed. Militärgeschichtliches Forschungsamt, trans. Dean S. McMurray and Ewald Osers (Oxford: Clarendon Press, 1991), 391. Cf. Karl Klee (ed.), *Dokumente zum Unternehmen 'Seelöwe'* (Göttingen: Muster-Schmidt, 1959), 197–98.

9 Ritchie Calder, *Carry On London* (Bungay: English Universities Press, 1941), 160.

10 Stuart Hylton, *Their Darkest Hour: The Hidden History of the Home Front, 1939–1945* (Stroud: Sutton, 2003); James Heartfield, *Unpatriotic History of the Second World War* (Croydon: Zero Books, 2012).

296   NOTES TO PAGES 75–86

11 Cf. Robert Mackay, *Half the Battle: Civilian Morale in Britain during the Second World War* (Manchester University Press, 2002); Mark Connelly, *We Can Take It: Britain and the Memory of the Second World War* (London: Pearson Education, 2004); John Ramsden, "Myths and Realities of the 'People's War' in Britain," in Jörg Echternkamp and Stefan Martens (eds.), *Experience and Memory: The Second World War in Europe* (New York: Berghahn, 2010), 40–52.

12 Sonya O. Rose, *Which People's War? National Identity and Citizenship in Britain 1939–1945* (Oxford University Press, 2003).

13 Article 2, *Geneva Convention of 27 July 1929 Relative to the Treatment of Prisoners of War*.

14 "Statement of Civilian Casualties in the United Kingdom from 1939 to 1945," TNA, HO 191/11.

15 Ritchie Calder, "London Jokes as It Takes a Knock", *Daily Herald*, 30 August 1940.

16 In order: *Daily Express*, 17 September 1940; *Daily Mirror*, 16 September 1940; *Daily Herald*, 9 September 1940.

17 Winston Churchill, *Into Battle: Speeches* (London: Cassell, 1945).

18 Ibid., 12 June 1941.

19 Winston Churchill, speech delivered separately to the House of Commons and BBC, 18 June 1940. The quoted verses are from Andrew Marvell's "Horatian Ode" to Oliver Cromwell, 1650.

20 Cf. Mackenzie, *Home Guard*, 24–32.

21 Lucy Noakes, "'Serve to Save': Gender, Citizenship and Civil Defence in Britain 1937–1941", *Journal of Contemporary History*, 47/4 (2012), 734–53.

22 Cf. Mackenzie, *Home Guard*, chaps. 2 and 3.

23 Maier et al., *Germany and the Second World War*, 398. 20 September 1940 report.

24 "East-Enders Invade Savoy Hotel," *The Daily Worker*, 16 September 1940.

25 Maier et al., *Germany and the Second World War*, 400.

26 Todman, *Britain's War*, vol. I, 455–56.

Chapter 4

1 All research in the military archives of Freiburg and Wilhelmstrasse (Berlin) proved fruitless in this connection.

2 Amt Ausland/Abwehr in Foreign Armies West, 12 September 1940, BA/MA, RW 2/26.

3 "Francs-Tireurs: German Charges against Britain Repeated," from our special correspondent, German frontier, 31 July, *The Times*, 1 August 1940.

4 Dr. Lehmann, head of the Wehrmacht Legal Department, to L. and Ausl., draft letter in the correct form, 31 March 1941, BA/MA, RW 2/26.

5 Alfred-Maurice de Zayas, "The Wehrmacht Bureau on War Crimes," *Historical Journal*, 35/2 (1992), 383–99.

6 Archives of the German Ministry of Foreign Affairs: "England" files of Secretary of State von Weizsäcker, consulted for 1940; "England" file of Dr. Ritter, ambassador for special interventions, 1942–44; Rechtsabteilung and Informationsabteilung files.

7 Wehrmachtsauskunftstelle für Kriegerverluste und Kriegsgefangene (WASt), Potsdam. Research conducted with the help of Corinna von List.

8 See Sönke Neitzel and Harald Welzer, *Soldaten: On Fighting, Killing and Dying. The Secret World of Transcripts of German POWs* (New York: Alfred A. Knopf, 2012).

NOTES TO PAGES 86–95

9 www.massobs.org.uk.

10 Alfred Guy Kingan L'Estrange, *History of English Humour*, 2 vols. (London: Hurst & Blackett, 1878).

11 "Tractor Drowned Noise of Nazi Plane Crash", *Kent Messenger*, 3 August 1940.

12 Cf. Summerfield and Peniston-Bird, *Contesting Home Defence*, chap. 3.

13 Noakes, "Serve to Save"; and Noakes, *War and the British: Gender and National Identity, 1939–91* (London : I.B. Taurus, 1998).

14 *Kent Messenger*, 21 September 1940.

15 Dr. Alex Wood, president of the Peace Party, "Retrospect and Prospect", *Peace News*, 3 January 1941.

16 "Afterthoughts on Raiding Britain by Five Captured Raiders," *Daily Express*, 13 August 1940; "Six Types of Captured Nazi Airmen", *Daily Express*, 22 August 1940.

17 "Punched Nazi Flyer's Nose", *Newcastle Journal*, 17 August 1940.

18 George L. Mosse, *Fallen Soldiers: Reshaping the Memory of the World Wars* (Oxford University Press, 1990). See the critique of the terms "brutalization" and "war culture" by André Loez, "Petit repertoire critique des concepts de la Grande Guerre," December 2005, www.crid1418.org/doc/textes/repertoire_critique_concepts.pdf.

19 Rose, *Which People's War?*, chap. 5: "Temperate Heroes: Masculinity on the Home Front."

20 Cf. Peter Mandler, *The English National Character: The History of an Idea from Edmund Burke to Tony Blair* (New Haven, CT: Yale University Press, 2006), chap 5: "Little England."

21 "Guns, Pans, Knives Threaten RAF Parachutist", *Daily Express*, 16 August 1940.

22 "Plane Ablaze, Fought On, Baled Out, Shot by Home Guard," *Daily Express*, 15 November 1940; *The London Gazette*, 15 November 1940.

23 "RAF Man Is Mobbed as German," *Daily Mirror*, 2 September 1940.

24 "Our A.A. Guns Stopped as Nazi Baled Out", *Daily Express*, 28 September 1940.

25 "Parachutists Not Always Nazi: Need for Discretion on the Part of the Public," *Kent Messenger*, 14 September 1940.

26 Wehrmachtsauskunftstelle für Kriegerverluste und Kriegsgefangene (WASt), Potsdam.

27 Systematic research in the archives of the BA-MA, Bundesarchiv/Militärarchiv, in Freiburg and Berlin did not turn up anything apart from the few items cited below regarding the publication by F. von Werra of his adventures. Contacts with his widow's daughter yielded no new information.

28 The available documentation is as follows: a study by two British journalists, Kendal Burt and James Leasor, *The One that Got Away: With an Account of Franz von Werra's Experiences as a Prisoner-of-War in England and in Canada* (London: Collins, Michael Joseph, 1956; republished in 2001 by House of Stratus, London) (these journalists met Franz von Werra's widow and saw now missing original documents); the book appeared without further presentation in 1957: anon., *Einer kam durch: Fluchtbericht des Fliegerleutnants Franz von Werra*, Hamburg: Verlag der Sternbücher, 1957). I did not have access to the propaganda brochure written by Joachim Bartsch for the series *Unsere Jagdflieger*, Hefte 12, 1943: *Franz von Werra: sein Leben und seine Leistungen.*

29 Adolf Galland, *The First and the Last: The German Fighter Force in World War II* (London: Methuen, 1955); Hans Ulrich Rudel, *Stuka Pilot*, trans. L. Hudson, New York: Ballantine, 1958).

298   NOTES TO PAGES 95–106

30 Wilfred Meichtry, *Du und ich – ewig eins: die Geschichte der Geschwister von Werra* (Frankfurt: Eichborn, 2001).
31 Ibid., 127–28. And TNA, WO 208/4119. 18 September 1940 listening session.
32 Anon., *Einer kam durch*, 65.
33 Burt and Leasor, *The One that Got Away*, 256–57.
34 Anon., *Einer kam durch*, 171–72.
35 Burt and Leasor, *The One that Got Away*, 253.
36 File of the request to publish addressed to the Reichsschriftumskammer, R 9361/V/ 11845, "Berlin Document Center" collection, Bundesarchiv, Berlin.
37 Burt and Leasor, *The One that Got Away*, 257–58.
38 Kenneth Hulbert, *I Will Lift Up Mine Eyes: The Experience of a Doctor in Peace and War Based on the War Diaries and Early Memoirs of Kenneth Hulbert*, ed. Ann Hulbert (Seal, Kent: Highland Printers, 2003).
39 Jan Harold Brunvand, *The Vanishing Hitchhiker* (New York: W.W. Norton, 1981.
40 Pamela Donovan, *No Way of Knowing: Crime, Urban Legends and the Internet* (New York and London: Routledge, 2004).
41 www.about.com/newsissues
42 Andy Saunders, Luftwaffe and Allied Air Forces Discussion Forum, 2 October 2008.
43 Peter, Axis History Forum, 15 December 2003.
44 Richard T. Eger, 27 December 2000, and "agbrunson," 6 July 2001, LWAG.
45 *Chichester Observer*, 19 February 1971; *Sunday Times*, February 1971. Quoted in anon., "Battle of Britain Investigation," *After the Battle*, 23 (1979), 46–53.
46 Alec Grant, "Was This Our Secret War Crime?" *Tit-Bits*, 30 August to 5 September 1973.
47 Instructions ascribed to Lord Northcliffe, founder of the *Daily Mail*, in 1896.
48 Sergeant Whall, "Combat Report": "This E/A landed on the beach at West Wittering. Circled it and saw Army taking crew prisoners, then climbed to attack single HE 111 flying south below cloud at 1000 ft.", quoted in Matilda Battersby, "Real History: The Battle of Britain – View from a Luftwaffe Air Gunner", *Independent*, 12 August 2010.
49 A.I.1. (k), 27 August 1940, Report no. 310/1940.
50 Quoted in anon., "Battle of Britain Investigation."
51 "The Rudolf Müller Story," *Quinton at War*, www.quintonatwar.org.uk/reminis cences/muller-story/muller-story.html; E.R. Hooton, *Eagle in Flames: The Fall of the Luftwaffe* (Leicester: Brockhampton Press, 1999), 28; Martin W. Bowman, *RAF Escapers and Evaders in World War II* (Barnsley: Pen & Sword, 2014).
52 Alfred Price, *Battle of Britain Day, 15 September 1940* (London: Greenhill Books, 1990), 63. Witness: Walter Chesney, truck driver, Streatham.
53 Martin Smart, 13 December 2000, LWAG.
54 Civil Defence Emergency Committee, Metropolitan Borough of Lambeth, *Control Room Diary*, 15 September 1940, MBL archives, London.
55 A.I.1 (k) Report No. 543/1940, 16 September 1940.
56 Unsigned article, "Troops Save Nazi from Angry Women," *South London Press*, 17 September 1940.
57 Todman, *Britain's War*, vol. I, 522–24.
58 *Daily Express*, 16 November 1940: "It is time for our deepest, most inspired anger. Coventry cries: bomb back and bomb hard!"
59 "Terror Raid," *Daily Mirror*, 12 May 1941.

NOTES TO PAGES 106–13   299

60 Andrew Knapp, "The Allied Bombing Offensive in the British Media, 1942–1945," in Andrew Knapp and Hilary Footitt (eds.), *Liberal Democracies at War* London: Bloomsbury, 2013), 39–66.

61 "Gave Cigarettes For German Ariman. A Son of Kent Charged with Act of Unlawful Benevolence," *Kent Messenger*, 7 April 1944.

62 Hubert Faber, 24 October 2005, account of his arrival on the ground in Bendish, near Hitchin, Hertfordshire, on 8 April 1941. After a few weeks in hospital, he was transferred to the Manchester POW camp with other prisoners. Their escort crossed the town the day following an air raid (date unspecified but sometime between April and 22 December 1941), protecting them from the crowd. Account collected by Hitchin Museum and published on the BBC website, "WW2 People's War," https://www.bbc.co.uk/history/ww2peopleswar/stories/85/a6370085.shtml.

63 Alexander Mayer, "Mein letzte Feindflug nach England," August 1977, account of his arrival on the ground on 3 May 1941 on a mission over Liverpool, Deutsche Tagebucharchiv, Emmendingen; Walter Kempter, account of his arrival on the ground on 14 April 1944, Hill Deverill, Warminster, Wiltshire, *Warminster Journal*, 28 April 1944, Aircrew Remembrance Society, www.aircrewremembrancesociety.co.uk.

64 Joachim Sprenger, testimony on his fall at Harwich, 29 January 1944, with a file constituted by Corinna von List.

65 Richard Overy, *The Bombing War: Europe 1939–1945* (London: Allen Lane, 2013), 169–96.

66 For instance, Todman, *Britain's War*, vol. I, 2016.

Part III

1 Stéphane Longuet and Nathalie Genet-Rouffiac (eds.), *Les réseaux de résistance de la France Combattante* (Paris: Economica; Vincennes: Service historique de la Défense, 2013); and Inventaire des réseaux de la France combattante, SHD, GR28 P 4: Ali-France, Alsace (sub-network of Shelburn), Bénédictine, Bordeaux-Loupiac, Bourgogne, Brandy, Cassagne, CDLL-Évasion, Chartres-Jean-Jacques, Comète, De Larminat, Dutch-Paris, Edouard (Troy), Fan Fan, Félix, Françoise, Kummel, Livry-Gargan, Loyola, Lyon Carter, Marathon, Marie-Claire, Marie-Odile, Maurice, Nevers, Oaktree, Pat O'Leary, Pernod, Porto, Possum, Shelburn, Sibiril, Sylvestre-Farmer, Var, Vic, Wisigoth.

Chapter 5

1 Max Weber, *Economy and Society*, a posthumous work published in 1921, vol. I: *An Outline of Interpretive Sociology* (Berkeley: University of California Press, 1978), 23.

2 Norbert Elias, "Trop tard ou trop tôt: notes sur la classification de la théorie du processus et de la figuration", in *Norbert Elias par lui-même* (Paris: Fayard/Pluriel, 1991), 174.

3 On this subject, see André Ducret, "Le concept de 'configuration' et ses implications empiriques: Elias avec et contre Weber," *SociologieS: La recherche en actes" Régimes d'explication en sociologie*, 11 April 2011, http://journals.openedition.org/sociolo gies/3459.

4 "Escape & Evasion Report" #599. P.F. Allen, brought down over France on 11 September 1941, was taken into the care of helpers and reached England on

300   NOTES TO PAGES 113–20

23 November 1941. *Military Intelligence 9*, 24 November 1941. TNA, WO 208 3307. The remainder of the crew successfully escaped several months later.

5 Historical record of MI9, IS9, RAF Intelligence course B, Awards Bureaus and Screening Commissions, multi-paged file, TNA, WO 208/3242, [1946].

6 "Conduct If Cut Off from Unit or Captured by Enemy," "To All Ranks, All Arms," sd, (source for 90 percent proportion), in Historical record of MI9; and MIS-X, Bulletin #4, 28 May 1943 (source for 99 percent), NARA, RG, 498, 290/55/18/3; and "Evasion in Europe" 11, in "MIS-X Manual on Evasion, Escape and Survival," February 1944, War Department, Washington, multiple pages, which notes "universal solidarity," with the few exceptions to this rule being punished by the inhabitants. NARA, RG 498/ 290/55/21/2.

7 Langley, *Fight Another Day*.

8 Airey Neave, *They Have Their Exits* (London: Hodder & Stoughton, 1953; repr. Barnsley: Leo Cooper, 2002).

9 Langley, *Fight Another Day*; Neave, *They Have Their Exits*; Neave, *Escape Room* (New York: Doubleday, 1970); Donald Darling, *Secret Sunday* (London: William Kimber, 1975).

10 Arthur Harris, *Bomber Offensive* (London: Greenhill, 1998; first edn 1947), 98.

11 "Settlement of claims and bestowal of rewards and awards to French, Belgian and Dutch 'helpers' of Allied escapers or evaders since 1 June 1940", 11 October 1944. TNA, WO 208 3424.

12 Darling, *Secret Sunday*, 152–53.

13 M.R.D. Foot and J.M. Langley, *MI9: Escape and Evasion, 1939–1945* (London: Bodley Head, 1979), Appendix 1, 309–15.

14 MI9, "Attachment A. MI9 Historical Record", 1945, page 14, TNA, WO 208/3242. Quoted by Foot & Langley, *MI9*, 307.

15 Darling, *Secret Sunday*, 164.

16 "Register of Helpers", IS9, Awards Bureau, Paris. TNA, WO208 5465 à 5474.

17 "Master List of MIS-X Awards", 1945–1948, France. NARA, RG 498, ETO, MIS, 290/55/27/1.

18 On 1 June 1946, the number of positively concluded dossiers for all of Europe, Italy included, was 83,262. The same document indicates that the number of helpers recognized for France was still only 12,138, or 36 percent of the final number (33,535). The rule of three thus allows one to estimate at 231,283 the total number of helpers in Europe. By choosing 150,000, I have opted for a known minimum value. "MI9: Amateur Helpers," *Newsletter*, 4 (1 June 1946), TNA AIR20/8912.

19 Paul Lenormand, "Vers l'armée du peuple: autorité, pouvoir et culture militaire en Tchécoslovaquie de Munich à la fin du stalinisme," doctoral thesis, Sciences Po, Paris, 2019.

20 Milgram, *Obedience to Authority*; for a critical analysis, see Perry, *Behind the Shock Machine*.

21 War Department, Military Intelligence Service. Prisoner of War branch, Washington DC. *Bulletin #4*, MIS-X, 28 May 1943: "Ninety-nine out of every 100 Frenchmen will be willing to aid our airmen." RG 498, ETO, MIS-X Section, 290/55/18/3, Box 7.

22 For the first generation of Resistance studies, see the PUF collection, "Esprit de la Résistance"; works on the OCM, Ceux de la Résistance, the Groupes francs of the MUR, Combat, Défense de la France, the Parisian Committee of the Libération, the

CNR, published between 1957 and 1962, and Marie Granet, *Ceux de la Résistance* (Paris: Éditions de Minuit, 1964). For the following generation: Alya Aglan on Libération-nord; Claire Andrieu on the CNR; Laurent Douzou on Libération-sud; Charles Riandey on the Parisian Committee of the Libération; Dominique Veillon on Franc-Tireur; Olivier Wieviorka on Défense de la France and the Resistance as a whole; and Robert Gildea on members of the Resistance as a group.

23 Rémy [Gilbert Renault, dit colonel], *Comment meurt un réseau (novembre 1943 – août 1944)* (Monaco: Éditions Raoul Solar, 1947).

24 Julien Blanc, *Au commencement de la Résistance: du côté du Musée de l'Homme, 1940–1941* (Paris: Seuil, 2010).

25 Claire Andrieu, "Revisiting the Historiography of the Resistance from the Perspective of Its Local Dynamics," in Denis Charbit (ed.), *Revisiting Vichy,* special issue of *Perspectives: revue de l'université hébraïque de Jérusalem,* 26 (2022), 193–208.

26 Georges Broussine, *L'évadé de la France libre: le réseau Bourgogne* (Paris: Tallandier, 2000).

27 Guillaume Pollack, *Les réseaux de la Résistance en France (1940–1945)* (Paris: Tallandier, 2022).

28 Olivier Wieviorka, *The French Resistance* (Cambridge, MA: Harvard University Press, 2016); Robert Gildea, *Fighters in the Shadows: A New History of the French Resistance* (London: Faber & Faber, 2015); Sébastien Albertelli, Julien Blanc and Laurent Douzou, *La lutte clandestine en France: une histoire de la Résistance, 1940–1944* (Paris: Seuil, 2019).

29 Gildea, *Fighters in the Shadows*, 285–90.

30 Around 1,850 escape network agents were interviewed by the DGER in 1945. SHD, inventory of series GR 28 4P. The Allies compiled a list of 34,000 helpers.

31 The "Interrogation Reports" for Germany are to be found in WO 344/1 to 360. There are roughly 16,000 of them. A selection was prepared and placed in WO 208/3336 to 3339. The latter reports, around 1,400 altogether, present at least some of the cases in which the prisoner (POW) had initially avoided capture (and was thus an "evader," particularly in France) before later being made prisoner or had unsuccessfully attempted to escape his prison camp ("attempted escapes"). "Evaded capture in France" represents at least 16 percent of the total. Many reports are missing.

32 There exist many accounts of these three cases. For example, Paul Brickhill, *Reach for the Sky: The Story of Douglas Bader DSO, DFC* (London: Odhams Press, 1954); John Ivelaw-Chapman, *High Endeavour: The Life of Air Chief Marshall Sir Ronald Ivelaw-Chapman, GCB, KBE, DFC, AFC* (London: Leo Cooper, 1993); Arthur G. Kinnis and Stanley Booker, *168 Jump into Hell: A True Story of Betrayed Allied Airmen* (Victoria, Canada: Arthur G. Kinnis, 1999).

33 Debriefings nos. 1878 to 1881 and 1899 to 1900, TNA WO 208/3319; Norman Franks and Simon Muggleton, *Flying among Heroes: The Story of Squadron Leader T.C.S. Cooke DFX AFC DFM AE* (Stroud: Spellmount, 2012).

34 Michèle Agniel (born Moët), in Caroline Langlois and Michel Reynaud, *Elles et eux de la Résistance* (Paris, Tirésias, 2003).

35 CARE International has become a major NGO. www.care-international.org.

36 NARA, RG 498, ETO, MIS, MIS-X Section, Box 1, 290/55/21/4.

302 NOTES TO PAGES 133–44

37 Sgt Jerome J. Bajenski, "Escape and Evasion Report," #715, online at the NARA website; NARA, RG 498, ETO, MIS, MIS-X Section, Box 1, 290/55/21/4; Keith Janes, *They Came from Burgundy: The Story of the Bourgogne Escape Line* (Market Harbourough, Leics: Matador Self-Publishing, 2017).

Chapter 6

1 NARA, European Theater of Operations, Military Intelligence Service, E&E report #260, Evasion in France, Arthur M. Vetter, 14 December 1943.

2 Yves Morat, *A Veules-les-Roses des résistantes de la première heure*, Association pour la sauvegarde du patrimoine veulais, March 2008.

3 German military tribunal ruling, Gericht von Gross-Paris, Abt. B, 31 July 1941. Bundesarchiv Militärchiv Freiburg, RW 35-Gr/365. See also Corinna von List, *Résistantes* (Paris: Alma, 2012).

4 An expression coined by Xavier Vigna and Michelle Zancarini-Fournel. See "Les rencontres improbables dans 'les années 68'," *Vingtième Siècle*, 101/1 (2009), 163–77.

5 The sources vary in what concerns the number and identity of British or Commonwealth soldiers put up by François Le Gac. There were at least three of them (the soldiers Pool and Campbell in 1940 and the pilot Reece) and perhaps as many as six (the soldier Goldney for several months in 1940–41 and the airmen McMillan and Mott, whose airplane came down over Lanvollon on 28 December 1940). Report from the prefect of Côtes du Nord, 22 March 1942; entry for André Marchais, in Jean Maitron and Claude Pennetier, *Dictionnaire biographique du mouvement ouvrier français* (Paris: Éditions Ouvrières, 1988); ruling of the German military tribunal of Greater Paris, 17 July 1942 + Annexes, SHD, GR 28 P 8/44.

6 Documents collected by Maggy de Saint-Laurent, the daughter of a helper from Plestin-les-Grèves, and ruling of the German court of the Greater Paris command, 17 July 1942 + Annexes, SHD, GR 28 P 8/44.

7 RAF Pilot P.F. Allen, "Escape & Evasion report" #599, London, 24 November 1941, TNA, WO 208/3307.

8 Sgt. Worby, Sgt. Campbell, Sg. Christensen, interviewed 6 January1942. TNA, WO 208/3307; and Sgt. Saxton and Sgt. Hickton, interviewed 7 and 8 October 1942, TNA, WO 208/ 3310.

9 Sue Emeny, "Vivid Tale of Capture and Escape," *Manawatu Standard*, 2010; Jimmy Ellingham, "World War II Brushes with Death Preceded Life of Generosity," *Stuff*, 12 July 2017, www.stuff.co.nz/manawatu-standard/news/94534994/world-war-ii-brushes-with-death-preceded-life-of-generosity.

10 Derek Richardson, *Detachment W: Allied Soldiers and Airmen in Vichy France between 1940 and 1942* (s.l.: Paul Mould, 2004), 21–24.

11 Pierre d'Harcourt, *Journal de Buchenwald*, preceded by *Souvenirs de résistance et de prison* (printed without a publisher, 2009; first printing Buzançais, 1988), 2.1, 2009.

12 "The Pat O'Leary (or PAO) Escape Line", *Conscript Heroes* website, www.conscript-heroes.com/Pat-Line.html. There has been no in-depth study of this network. Produced by the son of an evaded soldier, the website *Conscript Heroes* is richly documented. The website was initially based on the book written by father and son. See Peter Scott Janes and Keith Janes, *Conscript Heroes* (Boston: Paul Mould, 2004).

NOTES TO PAGES 144–54

See also Sherri Greene Ottis, *Silent Heroes: Downed Airmen and the French Underground* (University Press of Kentucky, 2001).

13 CNRD brochure. Supplemental online dossier. Fondation de la Résistance.

14 Thiéry, *La répression allemande*, 113–15 and 184–87.

15 William Moore, *The Long Way Round: An Escape through Occupied France* (London: Lee Cooper, 1986).

16 Suzanne Wilborts, *Pour la France: Angers-La Santé-Fresnes-Ravensbrück-Mauthausen*, Preface by General Audibert (Paris, Charles-Lavauzelle, 1946).

17 Catherine Lacour-Astol, *Le genre de la Résistance: la Résistance féminine dans le Nord de la France* (Paris: Presses de Sciences Po, 2015).

18 Nicholas Stargardt, *Witnesses of War: Children's Lives under the Nazis* (Vintage: New York, 2005), and "Jeux de guerre. Les enfants sous le régime nazi," *Vingtième siècle*, 89/1 (2006), 61–76.

19 Quellien, "Les pertes humaines."

20 Eismann, *Hôtel Majestic*; and Gaël Eismann and Corinna von List, "Les fonds des tribunaux allemands (1940–1945) conservés au BAVCC à Caen," *Francia: Forschungen zur Westeuropäischen Geschichte*, 39 (2012), 347–78.

21 Ernst Fraenkel, *The Dual State: A Contribution to the Theory of Dictatorship* (Oxford and New York: Octagon, 1941).

22 Fontaine, *Déporter*.

23 My source for this group of 54 victims of repression is the judgements of the German military tribunal of Greater Paris.

24 Figures established on the basis of the rulings of the German military tribunal of Greater Paris mentioned above; and Fondation pour la mémoire de la Déportation, *Livre-Mémorial des déportés de France*, 4 vols. (Paris: Éditions Tirésias, 2004).

25 Report by Geneviève Fillerin, circa 1945, Service historique de la Défense. Quoted by CNRD brochure. Supplemental online dossier.

26 Renée Guitton, undated intercepted letter in Veules-les-Roses case, Judgement of the German Military Tribunal of Greater Paris, 7 August 1941.

27 Veules-les-Roses case, Judgement of the German Military Tribunal of Greater Paris, 7 August 1941.

28 Brendan Murphy, *Turncoat: The Strange Case of Traitor Sergeant Harold Cole, the Worst Traitor of the War* (London: Macdonald, 1988).

29 The exact figures are unknown. It is known that four people were arrested in Paris but the Note of the German captain responsible for the German section of the prison, dated 18 December 1941, mentions 7 prisoners to be transferred to the Lille GFP. For Lille, it is known that 9 people were arrested and deported but one of the deportees spoke "of 35 from the Cole affair." Archives of the German section of Fresnes prison; ruling of the Berlin Volksgerichtshof, 16 April 1943; testimony of Alfred Lanselle, in Henri Duprez, *1940–45: Même combat de l'ombre et de la lumière – Épisodes de la Résistance dans le nord de la France – Témoignages et souvenirs* (Paris: La pensée universelle, 1979).

30 Cf. Michel Pinault, "Fernand Holweck", in *Le Maitron: Dictionnaire des fusillés, 1940–1944*, https://fusilles-40-44.maitron.fr/spip.php?article149039; and André Postel-Vinay, *Un fou s'évade, 1940–1941* (Paris: Éditions du Félin, 1997).

31 Pinault, "Fernand Holweck."

32 Thiéry, *La répression allemande*, 184–87.

304   NOTES TO PAGES 155–65

33 "Notice" signed by Höhere SS- und Polizeiführer im Bereich des Militärsbefehlshabers in Frankreich, 10 July 1942. Reproduced in Stéphane Marchetti, *Affiches 1939–1945: images d'une certaine France* (Lausanne: Edita, 1982). Published for example in *Le Matin*, 13 July 1942. On its application, see Eismann, *Hôtel Majestic*, 376–82.

34 Jean Guéhenno, *Diary of the Dark Years, 1940–1944*, trans. David Ball (Oxford University Press, 2014), 10 July 1942 (163–64).

35 Leclercq, "Les chutes d'avions alliés," 108 and 115.

36 Sébastien Albertelli, *Histoire du sabotage: de la CGT à la Résistance* (Paris: Perrin, 2016).

37 François Bédarida, "L'histoire de la résistance: lectures d'hier, chantiers de demain, *Vingtième siècle*, 11 (1986), 75–90.

38 Claire Andrieu, "Assistance to Jews and to Allied Soldiers and Airmen in France: a comparative approach," in Semelin, Andrieu and Gensburger (eds.), *Resisting Genocide*, 51–63.

39 Jacques Semelin, *Unarmed against Hitler: Civilian Resistance in Europe, 1939–1943*, trans. Suzan Husserl-Kapit (Westport, CT and London: Praeger, 1993; first published in French 1989), and "Résistance civile" in François Marcot, Christine Levisse-Touzé and Bruno Leroux (eds.), *Dictionnaire historique de la Résistance* (Paris: Robert Laffont, 2006).

40 François Marcot, "Pour une sociologie de la Résistance: intentionnalité et fonctionnalité," in A. Prost (ed.), *La Résistance: une histoire sociale* (Paris: Éditions de l'Atelier, 1997), 21–42.

41 Jacques Semelin, *Face au totalitarisme: la Résistance civile* (Brussels: André Versaille, 2011).

42 The sample is based on a selection of one of every twenty names (scale 1/20) conducted by comparing the list of deportees drawn up by the Fondation pour la mémoire de la Déportation and the list of helpers. Result: 13.4 percent.

43 Survey of a list of 1,071 individuals deported for aiding the enemy. I am grateful to the FMD for sharing this list with me.

44 Bloch, *Strange Defeat*.

Chapter 7

1 Sylvain Auroux (ed.), *Les notions philosophiques: dictionnaire* (Paris: PUF, 1990); Roland Doron and François Parot, *Dictionnaire de psychologie* (Paris: PUF, 2007); Fabien Fenouillet, *Les théories de la motivation* (Paris: Dunod, 2003).

2 Bert Klandermans, "Motivations to action," in Donatella Della Porta and Mario Diani (eds.), *The Oxford Handbook of Social Movements* (Oxford University Press, 2015).

3 François Marcot, "Patriotisme," Serge Wolikow, "Antifascisme," and Denis Peschanski, "Vichysto-résistants," in Marcot, Levisse-Touzé and Leroux (eds.), *Dictionnaire historique de la Résistance,* respectively 649–50, 639–40, 845–47.

4 Alya Aglan, *Le temps de la Résistance* (Aix-en-Provence: Actes Sud, 2008).

5 Dominique Rossignol, *Histoire de la propagande en France de 1940 à 1944: l'utopie Pétain* (Paris: PUF, 1991), 299.

6 Samuel Kitson, "Criminals or Liberators? Public Opinion and the Allied Bombing of France (1940–1945)", in Baldoli, Knapp and Overy (eds.), *Bombing, States and*

NOTES TO PAGES 165–72

Peoples, 279–97; Andrew Knapp, *Les Français sous les bombes alliées, 1940–1945* (Paris: Tallandier, 2014).

7 Jean Quellien, "Les bombardements alliés," in Leleu et al. (eds.), *La France pendant la Seconde Guerre mondiale*, 240–45; and Knapp, *Les Français sous les bombes alliées*.

8 Berthe Auroy, *Jours de guerre: ma vie sous l'Occupation*, presentation and notes by Anne-Marie Pathé and Dominique Veillon (Paris: Bayard, 2008), 209–16; Pauline Corday, *J'ai vécu dans Paris occupé* (Montréal: Éditions de l'Arbre, 1943); G. & W. Fortune, *Hitler Divided France* (London: Macmillan, 1943), 32–36, 95.

9 Fortune, *Hitler Divided France*, 32–33, 102.

10 Etta Shiber, *Paris Underground*, in collaboration with Anne and Paul Dupré, (New York: Charles Scribner's Sons, 1943), 162–63.

11 Auroy, *Jours de guerre*, 209–13, 286–89, 295–300.

12 Knapp, *Les Français sous les bombes alliées*, 438–50.

13 Direction technique des services spéciaux, NM Command Section, "Les bombardements alliés et leur répercussion sur le moral français," 25 April 1944, unpaginated, 24ff.; Presidency of the CFLN, Direction générale des services spéciaux, Documentation Center, signed by the Center's director, Colonel Jousse, "Note sur les répercussions des bombardements anglo-américains sur le moral des populations en France," 26 p. + 5 p. of annexes, 17 May 1944, TNA, FO 371/41384.

14 *La France socialiste*, 22 April 1944, quoted in Direction générale des services spéciaux, "Note sur les répercussions."

15 Philippe Pétain, *Discours aux Français, 1940–1944* [*Speeches to the French, 1940–1944*], presented by J.-C. Barbas (Paris: Albin Michel, 1989), 322.

16 Direction technique des services spéciaux, "Les bombardements alliés," sheet 3.

17 Direction générale des services spéciaux, "Note sur les répercussions," Annex IV.

18 "Ce que doit être l'attitude de la population à l'égard des aviateurs anglo-américains tombés en France" ["What must be the population's attitude towards downed Anglo-American airmen in France"], *Le Matin*, 13 May 1944; *L'Oeuvre, Paris-Soir, L'Action Française, Ouest-Éclair, Le Nouvelliste*, 1 June 1944.

19 Pierre Limagne, *Éphémérides de quatre années tragiques*, vol. III (La Villedieu, Ardèche: Éditions de Candide, 1987), 31 May 1944, 2025–26.

20 "Les raids terroristes anglo-américains ont considérablement modifié l'opinion publique française, déclare-t-on à Berlin," *Paris-Soir*, 1 June 1944; "Le terrorisme aérien ne restera pas impuni," *Le Matin*, 1 June 1944; "L'Allemagne ne laissera pas sans réplique les atrocités des aviateurs anglo-américains, déclare-t-on à Berlin," *Le Petit Parisien*, 1 June 1944.

21 Joseph Goebbels, "Ein Wort zum feindliche Luftterror" [A word regarding the enemy aerial terror],*Völkischer Beobachter*, 26 May 1944 (Berlin edition), 27 May (Vienna edition), 28–29 May (Munich edition); Martin Bormann, Partei-Kanzler, Rundschreiben 125/44 G, "Volksjustiz gegen anglo-amerikanische mörder" ["People's justice against the Anglo-American murderers"], 30 May 1944, in Nuremberg Military Tribunal, *Documents et autre matériel de preuve*, vol. XXV, 1947, PS-057, 112–13.

22 "Pourquoi la chasse allemande n'intervient pas en France," *Paris-Soir*, 1 June 1944.

23 Christian Delporte, "Nimbus contre Mickey: le dessin animé au service de la propagande," in Delporte, *Images et politique en France au XX° siècle* (Paris: Éditions nouveau monde, 2006); Rossignol, *Histoire de la propagande*, 281–90.

306 NOTES TO PAGES 172–78

24 *Die Deutsche Wochenschau*, German news, week of 3 August 1944, ECPAD AA726; this film has also been presented on French screens. The rushes, dated 17 July 1944, are held at INA, Paris.

25 Cf. *La France Socialiste*, 30 June 1944; *Les Actualités olympiques*, [1 May 1945], ECPAD, SA 279; Investigative case file for Jacqueline Lastra, wife of Tessier, Cour de Justice, AN 46/99.

26 Order issued by the chief of the Security Police and SD relating to the treatment of downed aviators, 5 April 1944, *Procès des Grands criminels de guerre devant le Tribunal militaire international de Nuremberg*, vol. XXXIII, Document PS-3855, 243.

27 *Völkischer Beobachter*, 8 July 1944 (Munich edition), and with this title in the Vienna edition: "Pariser Bevölkerung begrüsst ihre Befreier," 6 July 1944.

28 Research conducted on *RétroNews* for "lynching."

29 "Les exploits de la RAF," in *L'Echo annamite: organe des intérêts franco-annamites* (ARIP), 26–27 November 1941.

30 "Les habitants de Laon ont voulu lyncher un aviateur américain," *Le Petit Parisien*, 17 July 1944.

31 Notice from the Oberfeldkommandantur 670 (Lille) singling out the population's "undisciplined" conduct upon the arrest of Allied airmen as well as the expressions of "sympathy" with which the airmen were greeted on these occasions in a "demonstrative form." "Anti-German expression" was grounds for arrest and trial before German military tribunals. Certified copy, 29 March 1943, Auchel, Pas-de-Calais.

32 Air Chief Marshall Commander-in-Chief Arthur Harris, to all units of Bomber Command, 23 September 1944; and to René Massigli, GPRF Ambassador to London, 18 October 1944. TNA, AIR 14/1021. Andrew Knapp has kindly supplied me with copies of these documents. Knapp, *Les Français sous les bombes alliées*, 462–64.

33 Knapp, *Les Français sous les bombes alliées*, 450–60.

34 *Le Havre-Matin*, 13 September 1944.

35 David Colon (ed.), *Histoire Term. L., ES*, Belin, 2011, 83; compared with *Histoire, Term. S*, 2014, 19 and *Histoire Term. L., ES, S*, 2016, 21.

36 Wieviorka, *French Resistance* (2013 for the French edition); Gildea, *Fighters in the Shadows*; Albertelli, Blanc and Douzou, *La lutte clandestine en France*.

37 Gildea, *Fighters in the Shadows*, 285–90.

38 Serge Barcellini and Annette Wieviorka, *Passant, souviens-toi! Les lieux du souvenir de la Seconde Guerre mondiale en France* (Paris: Plon, 1995).

39 These associations include: Antiq'Air Flandre-Artois; Association des Sauveteurs d'Aviateurs Alliés de la Somme, Association des Sauveteurs d'Aviateurs Alliés – Oise, Association normande du Souvenir aérien Orne-Maine, Fédération bretonne du Souvenir aérien. Each has its own website.

40 France-crash-39–45; aide-aviateurs-alliés-ww2.fr; ww2-netherlands-escape-lines. com; conscript-heroes.com (Pat Line); evasioncomete.org (Comète); possumline. net (Possum).

41 Claire Andrieu, "Les résistantes, perspectives de recherche," in Antoine Prost (ed.), *Pour une histoire sociale de la Résistance: le mouvement social*, special issue of *Le mouvement social*, 180/3 (1997), 69–96.

42 Edict no. 45-2717, 2 November 1945, relating to the death certificates of soldiers and civilians who "Died for France." Cf. Serge Barcellini, preface to Mechthild

NOTES TO PAGES 178–86

Gilzmer, *Mémoires de pierre: les monuments commémoratifs en France après 1944* (Paris: Autrement, 2009).

43 Robert Gildea and Ismee Thames (eds.), *Fighters across Frontiers: Transnational Resistance in Europe, 1936–1948* (Manchester University Press, 2020).

44 The history of the Pat O'Leary, Comète and Shelburn networks has been recounted by Ottis, *Silent Heroes*.

45 Herbert Ford, *Flee the Captor: The Story of the Dutch-Paris Underground and Its Compassionate Leader, John Henry Weidner* (Hagerstown, MD: Review and Herald Publishing Association, 1994 (1st edition 1966).

46 On the financing of the Comète network, see Emmanuel Debruyne and Adeline Rémy, "Les réseaux belges et leurs finances, 1940–1944", in Robert Vandenbussche, *La clandestinité en Belgique et en zone interdite (1940–1944)* (Lille: Le Septentrion, 2009), 113–58.

47 Cf. subseries GR 28 P4, Service historique de la Défense.

48 Broussine, *L'évadé de la France libre*, 145.

49 Ibid., 300–05.

Part IV

1 Strobl, *Bomben auf Oberdonau*; Hoffmann, *Fliegerlynchjustiz*.

2 Mallmann, "Volksjustiz gegen anglo-amerikanische Mörder"; Schnatz,"Lynchmorde an Fliegern"; Grimm, "Lynchmorde an alliierten Fliegern."

3 Hall, "Luftgangster over Germany" and *Terror Flyers*. Also of note: Blank, "Wartime Daily Life."

4 Geoff Eley, *Nazism as Fascism: Violence, Ideology and the Ground of Consent in Germany, 1930–1945* (London and New York: Routledge, 2013).

5 Michael Wildt, *Hitler's Volksgemeinschaft and the Dynamics of Racial Exclusion: Violence against Jews in Provincial Germany, 1919–1939* (New York: Berghahn, 2012; first published in German 2007).

6 Michael Burleigh and Wolfgang Wippermann, *The Racial State: Germany, 1933–1945* (Cambridge University Press, 1991).

7 Ralf Dahrendorf, *Gesellschaft und Demokratie in Deutschland* (Munich: Piper, 1965).

8 David Schoenbaum, *Hitler's Social Revolution: Class and Status in Nazi Germany, 1933–1939* (New York: Doubleday, 1966).

9 Devin O. Pendas, Mark Roseman and Richard F. Wetzel (eds.), *Beyond the Racial State: Rethinking Nazi Germany* (Cambridge University Press, 2017).

10 Henry Friedlander, *The Origins of Nazi Genocide: From Euthanasia to the Final Solution* (Chapel Hill: University of North Carolina Press, 1995). The number of those killed by the SA in 1933–34 is unknown.

11 Johann Chapoutot, *La revolution culturelle nazie* (Paris: Gallimard, 2016).

12 Michael Wildt, *Die Ambivalenz des Volkes: die Nationalsozialismus als Sozialgeschichte* (Berlin: Suhrkamp, 2019), "Introduction."

13 *Das Andere Deutschland: für entschiedene republikanische Politik. Keiner Partei dienstbar [The Other Germany: A Resolute Republican Politics. Member of No Party]*, 1925–33.

308   NOTES TO PAGES 188–93

Chapter 8

1 Fliegerhorstkommandantur Ütersen, "Namentliche Verlustmeldung no. 6," 1.12.41
  to 18.4.42, and "Bericht," 11.8.1942. Bundesarchiv/Militärarchiv (BA/MA),
  Freiburg, RL21/119. See also Helmut Schnatz, in "Tiefangriffe, Propagand und
  Lynchjustiz", talk given on 26 October 2001, Air War Studies and Research
  Society, Hetschbach/Odenwald.
2 Letter from Rev. Hauptmann d.SchP, An die Geheime Staatspolizei in Kiel,
  Aussenstelle Itzehoe, 4 July 1944; and on paper bearing the letterhead of the
  Nationalsozialistische Deutsche Arbeiterpartei, Gau Schleswig-Holstein /
  Kreisleitung Pinneberg, letter from the Kreisleiter (represented by the
  Oberabschnittsleiter), An den Herrn Bürgermeister der Stadt Elmshorn, 17 July
  1944. Records of US Army, Operational, Tactical and Support Organizations, micr.
  M-1217, Roll 17.
3 Deputy Judge Advocate's Office, United States v. Wilhelm Langeloh, Case no. 12-
  3121, Review and Recommendations, 5 August 1947, NARA, RG-338, Records of
  US Army Operational, Tactical and Support Organizations, micr. M-1217, Roll-3.
  These "Reviews" have also been placed online by the International War Crimes
  Center, University of Marburg, and the Jewish Virtual Library. Hearing before the
  tribunal, Dachau, 10–11 April 1947, NARA, RG 549, Entry A1–2238, Box 246.
4 Germaine Tillion, "Le procès des assassins de Ravensbrück," Voix et Visages, 7
  (March 1947). Repr. in Marie-Laure Le Foulon, Le procès de Ravensbrück:
  Germaine Tillion: de la vérité à la justice (Paris: Cherche-Midi, 2016), 189–204.
5 Uwe Danker and Astrid Schwabe, Schleswig-Holstein und der Nationalsozialismus
  (Neumünster: Wachholtz, 2005), 151; www.dithmarschen-wiki.de/Jansen_
  Friedrich.
6 Geneva Convention Relative to the Treatment of Prisoners of War, 27 July 1929.
7 WO 309: War Office: Judge Advocate General's Office, British Army of the Rhine
  War Crimes Group (North West Europe) and predecessors; and WO 235: Judge
  Advocate General's Office: War Crimes Case Files, Second World War.
8 Microfilm M-1217: Flyer Cases, Records of the United States Army, Europe,
  Reviews of US Army War Crimes Trials in Europe, 1945–48; RG 549, Record of
  the United States Army, Europe 1942–45. War Crimes Case Files: Cases Tried,
  Entry A1–2238; and Cases Not Tried, Entry A1–2239 ; RG 153, Records of the
  Judge Advocate General, War Crimes Branch, Case Files.
9 Zone Française d'Occupation en Allemagne et en Autriche. Affaires judiciaires.
  Direction générale de la Justice, 1945–55, FRMAE 1 AJ.
10 A portion of the rulings issued after the war by German tribunals were assembled in
   the collection Justiz und NS-Verbrechen: Sammlung deutscher Strafurteile wegen
   nationalsozialistischer Tötungsverbrechen, 1945–2012, ed. Christian F. Rüter and
   Dock W. de Mildt, 21 vols. (Amsterdam University Press, 1968–2012).
11 Paul Brickhill, The Great Escape (New York: W. W. Norton, 1950); Kinnis and
   Booker, 168 Jump into Hell.
12 Deposition of Dr. Karl Helfrich, 15 May 1945, and "List of 47 British, Dutch and
   American airmen who, on the evening of September 5th, 1944, were delivered to the
   camp of Mauthausen (K.L.M.) and who carried heavy rocks, were chased and
   beaten by a chain of guards and were killed by sentries on September 6th and
   7th." NARA, T 1021, Roll 20; and Strobl, Bomben auf Oberdonau, 189–90.

NOTES TO PAGES 194–202

13 An estimate calculated on the basis of the total number (all branches) of those missing in Germany (1,828). Among them, the percentage of downed airmen is estimated at 45 percent (state of New York: 97/205; Illinois: 62/144; Montana: 5/10; Arizona: 5/11. Defense POW/MIA Accounting Agency).

14 Stuart Hadaway, *Missing Believed Killed: The Royal Air Force and the Search for Missing Aircrew, 1939–1952* (Barnsley: Pen & Sword, 2008).

15 Of the 185 defendants about whom I was able to gather information, corresponding to 185 separate trials, only 13 pleaded guilty (7 percent).

16 Flight Lieutenant Colin Mitchell, in Hadaway, *Missing Believed Killed*, 109, Imperial War Museum, 215 (3115).

17 Martha Gellhorn, *The Face of War* (New York: Simon & Schuster, 1959), excerpted in Hans Magnus Enzensberger, *L'Europe en ruines: textes choisis et présentés par l'auteur* (Aix-en-Provence: Solin/Actes Sud, 1995), 110–21.

18 Alexander and Margaret Mitscherlich, *The Inability to Mourn: Principles of Collective Behavior* (New York: Grove Press, 1975; first published in German 1968).

19 Nicholas Stargardt, *The German War: A Nation under Arms, 1939–1945* (London: Bodley Head, 2015).

20 Statistics established on 1 January 1946, by the JAG's Branch (War Crimes Section), HQ British Army of the Rhine, transmitted to the Judge Advocate General of the Forces, London, 7 February 1946, TNA, WO 311/8.

21 Judge Advocate General's Office: Courts Martial Proceedings, two cases of ill-treatment committed by Army officers in Warminster on 17 September 1940 and London on 21 July 1941. TNA, WO 71/1048 and 1061.

22 Dr. Kaltenbrunner, head of the RSHA, Reichssicherheitshauptamt, directive concerning "the treatment of enemy airmen who parachuted," 5 April 1944, Document 3855-PS, Nuremberg trials of major war criminals reprinted in Office of United States Chief of Counsel for Prosecution of Axis Criminality, *Nazi Conspiracy and Aggression*, 3 vols. and Supplement A (Washington, DC: United States Government Printing Office, 1946–47), Supplement A.

23 Office of the Adjutant General, *Army Battle Casualties and Nonbattle Deaths in World War II*, 76–77; Harris, *Despatch on War Operations*, 61. 67 percent of the American airmen who came down in continental Northwestern Europe did so over Germany. German prisoner of war camps contained 35,140 Allied airmen; 67 percent of them, or 23,500, came down over Germany. If one takes into consideration the 1,500 lynched airmen who were subsequently imprisoned and the 1,000 airmen who were killed, the rate of lynching is 10 percent: 2500/ (23,500+1000).

24 National Association for the Advancement of Colored People, *Thirty Years of Lynching in the United States, 1889–1918* (New York: NAACP, 1919), 29.

25 Edith Raim, *Nazi Crimes against Jews and German Post-War Justice: The West German Judicial System during Allied Occupation (1945–1949)* (Berlin: De Gruyter Oldenbourg, 2015), 215–18.

26 Hassel, *Kriegsverbrechen vor Gericht*, 179. This percentage covers all trials, not just the "Flyer trials."

27 JAG, *Reviews and Recommendations*, Flyer Trial no. 12-1542, NARA, M-1217.

28 Calculated on the basis of the age of 163 first-tier defendants.

29 Cf. Raim, *Nazi Crimes against Jews*, 186–265.

30 Goebbels, *The Goebbels Diaries: The Last Days* (London: Secker & Warburg, 1978), 1 April 1945, 292–96.

310 NOTES TO PAGES 202–9

31 Ibid., 28 March 1945, 288; 1 April 1945, 339.
32 Ibid., 4 March 1945, 67; and Joseph Goebbels, *Journal 1942–1945* (Paris: Tallandier, 2005), 6 February 1945, 701.
33 NSDAP, Rundschreiben R 211/45, 15 April 1945, "Circular [from the Party Chancellery] concerning the duty of political leaders." "Die Führernaturen haben alle hemmenden Brücken abgebrochen und sind von äusserster Einsatzbereitschaft." Quoted in Peter Longerich, *Hitler's Vertreter. Führung der Partei und Kontrolle des Staats apparates durch den Stab Hess und die Partei-Kanzlei Bormann* (Munich: Institut für Zeitgeschichte, 1992), 202.
34 Stargardt, *German War*, chap. 11.
35 Dietrich Orlow, *The History of the Nazi Party*, vol. 2: *1933–1945* (University of Pittsburgh Press, 1973).
36 Hans Mommsen, "The Dissolution of the Third Reich: Crisis Management and Collapse, 1943–1945," *Bulletin of the German Historical Institute*, 27 (Fall 2000), 9–24; Doris Bergen, "Death Throes and Killing Frenzies: A Response to Hans Mommsen," *Bulletin of the German Historical Institute*, 27 (Fall 2000), 25–38.

Chapter 9

1 Headquarters Twelfth Air Force, *E&E Bulletin*, 58 (14 March 1945).
2 MIS-X Manual on Evasion, Escape and Survival, February 1944. With Instructions to Briefers. NARA, RG492/290/55/21/2.
3 War Department, Military Intelligence Service, "Captured Personnel and Material Branch," Washington, DC, *Bulletin No. 7*, MIS-X, 15 November 1944. NARA RG 468, ETO, MIS-X Section, General correspondence, 290/55/18/3, Box 8.
4 Headquarters, United States Strategic Air Forces in Europe (REAR). Office of the Director of Intelligence, "Special information on conditions in Germany as they may affect USAAF personnel forced to ground in that country," 26 February 1945.
5 Headquarters European Theater of Operations, US Army, "File of captured air personnel", RG 468, ETO, MIS-X Section, General Correspondence, 290/55/18/3, Box 8.
6 This is the main inspiration of the book edited by Shelley Baranowski, Armin Nolzen and Claus-Christian W. Szejnmann, *A Companion to Nazi Germany* (Oxford: Wiley-Blackwell, 2018).
7 Richard Overy, "The German Home Front Under the Bombs," in Baranowski, Nolzen and Szejnmann (eds.), *Companion to Nazi Germany*, 231–41.
8 Karl Friedrich Stellbrink (1894–1943). www.luebeckermaertyrer.de/en/geschichte/dokumente/vernehmung-stellbrink.html.
9 Benda-Beckmann, *German Historians and the Bombing of German Cities*.
10 Boelcke (ed.), *Secret Conferences of Dr. Goebbels*, 338–39, conference of 10 March 1943.
11 Heinrich Himmler, Reichsführer SS, Persönlicher Stab, Secret, To all SS and Police leaders, 10 August 1943, German text in International Military Tribunal, *Procès des grands criminels*, vol. XXXVIII, 313–14, Document R-110.
12 General Jodl, Wehrmacht General Chief of Staff, "The Continuation of the War against England," 30 June 1940, trans. into English for Office of United States Chief of Counsel for Prosecution of Axis Criminality, *Nazi Conspiracy and Aggression*, Supplement A, Document 1776-PS, 405–06.

NOTES TO PAGES 209–16

13 Victor Klemperer, *The Language of the Third Reich: LTI, Lingua Tertii Imperii. A Philologist's Notebook* (London and New Brunswick, NJ: Athlone Press, 2000; first published in German 1946), 126–28.

14 *Daily Express*, 16 November 1940.

15 *Hessische Landes-Zeitung*, regional newspaper, consulted from 1938 to 1945. Quotations drawn from April 1942 – July 1943. Hessisches Landesarchiv, Darmstadt.

16 Cf. Stargardt, *German War*, 366–81.

17 *Völkischer Beobachter*, 20 December 1943, Berlin edition.

18 Hoffmann, *Fliegerlynchjustiz*, notes the existence of identical articles in *Oberdonau-Zeitung*, Linz, 24 December 1943, *Tages-Post*, Linz, 23 December 1943, and *Marburger-Zeitung*, Maribor, 21 December 1943.

19 Dr. Kaltenbrunner, Chief of Security and SS Police, Berlin, 5 April 1944, "Treatment of Enemy Pilots Who Have Parachuted to the Ground," Document 3855-PS, German text in International Military Tribunal, *Procès des grands criminels*, vol. XXXIII. An English translation is available in Office of United States Chief of Counsel for Prosecution of Axis Criminality, *Nazi Conspiracy and Aggression*, Supplement A, 592–94.

20 Klemperer, *Language of the Third Reich*, chap. 9: "Fanatical."

21 Joseph Goebbels, "A Word on the Enemy Air Terror," *Völkischer Beobachter*, 26 May 1944 (Berlin edition); 27 May (Vienna edition); 28–29 May (Munich edition).

22 Martin Bormann, Partei-Kanzler, Rundschreiben 125/44 G, "Volksjustiz gegen anglo-amerikanische Mörder" ("Popular justice against the Anglo-American murderers"), 30 May 1944, in International Military Tribunal, *Procès des grands criminels*, vol. XXV, PS-057, 112–13.

23 For example, *Hessische Landes-Zeitung*, 27 May 1944, 1: "Behandelt das deutsche Volk wie einem lästigen Eingeborenenstamm!" ("They treat the German people like a tribe of inconvenient natives!").

24 *Die Tagebücher von Joseph Goebbels*, Part II: *Diktate 1941–1945*, ed. Elke Fröhlich et al., 15 vols. (Munich: K.G.Saur, 1993–96), vol. XII, 392, notes dated 3 June 1944.

25 Ibid., 440, 10 June 1944.

26 *Goebbels-Reden*, vol. II: *1939–1945*, ed. Helmut Heiber (Düsseldorf: Droste Verlag, 1972), 336.

27 American military tribunals heard nine cases of lynching committed in May 1944, five of which took place between 28 and 30 May.

28 Martin Bormann, Partei-Kanzler, Rundschreiben 125/44 G, "Volksjustiz gegen anglo-amerikanische Mörder," 30 May 1944, quoted above.

29 Cf. "The Terror Flyer Order," in *Trials of War Criminals before the Nuremberg Military Tribunal under Control Council Law No. 10*, vol. XI (Washington, DC: United States Government Printing Office, 1951), 166–94; and supplementary documents in Office of United States Chief of Counsel for Prosecution of Axis Criminality, *Nazi Conspiracy and Aggression*, vol. III, Documents 728–41, PS, 526–39.

30 News items in the *Deutsche Allgemeine Zeitung*: "With On-board Weapons against Children" (31 May); "The Murderers Are Still Raging" (30 May); "Low-level Attack on Land Dwellers: Shot at with On-board Weapons while Working in the Field" (June 1944).

312   NOTES TO PAGES 217-19

31 The United States Strategic Bombing Survey, *Over-all Report (European War)*, (30 September 1945), 30–33, https://babel.hathitrust.org/cgi/pt?id=mdp .39015049492716;view=1up;seq=7.

32 *Die Tagebücher von Joseph Goebbels*, vol. XIV, 176, notes dated 8 November 1944. On the question of a relationship between low-altitude fire and *Lynchjustiz*, see Helmut Schnatz's paper, "Tiefangriffe, Propaganda, und Lynchjustiz" ("Low-altitude Attacks, Propaganda and Lynchjustiz"), revised version of a conference given on 26 October 2001 in Hetschbacher Kreis, Arbeitskreis für Luftkriegsforschung in Hetschbach/Oldenwald, manuscript.

33 Ronald Schaffer, "American Military Ethics in World War II: The Bombing of German Civilians," *Journal of American History*, 67/2 (September 1980), 318–34.

34 Victor Klemperer, *I Will Bear Witness: A Diary of the Nazi Years, 1942–1945*, trans. Martin Chalmers (New York: Modern Library, 2001), 441, 458, 462 (10, 21 and 22 April 1945).

35 Marlies Adams DiFante with Anne Marie DiFante, *Queen of the Bremen: The True Story of an American Child Trapped in Germany during World War II* (published by the author, 2010), 226–27.

36 *Die Tagebücher von Joseph Goebbels*, vol. XII, 540, notes dated 24 June 1944.

37 Goebbels, *Goebbels Diaries : The Last Days*, 292, 297, 301–10 (1, 2 and 3 April 1945).

38 Ibid., 272, 297, 310 (30 March, 2, 3 and 4 April 1945).

39 Ibid., 28, 36 (3 and 4 March 1945). On 3 March, Goebbels wrote that he was "absolutely furious with the newspaper *Das Reich*"; on 4 March, he criticized an editor-in-chief for "the recent *faux pas* of which the paper has been guilty . . . these will now definitely cease."

40 Ibid., 311–12 (7 April 1945).

41 Ibid., 247–48 (27 March 1945); and also 257–58 (28 March 1945), 289 (31 March 1945).

42 William L. Shirer, *The Rise and Fall of the Third Reich: A History of Nazi Germany* (New York: Simon & Schuster, 1960), 955–56 and 1100; Office of United States Chief of Counsel for Prosecution of Axis Criminality, *Nazi Conspiracy and Aggression*, Supplement A, 894–905; General Jodl, "Geheime Kommandosache," 21 February 1945, in International Military Tribunal, *Procès des grands criminels*, vol. XXXV, D-606, 181–86.

43 Ops. Staff of the Wehrmacht, 20.2.1945. Top secret, "Draft", Ref: "Present value and lack of value of international obligations such as the Geneva Convention, The Hague Land Warfare Regulations, etc.," in Office of United States Chief of Counsel for Prosecution of Axis Criminality, *Nazi Conspiracy and Aggression*, Supplement A, D-606, 900–05.

44 Ibid.

45 General Staff Chief for the Western Front Jodl, Report to Hitler, 21 February 1945. German text: "Auch in diesem Fall escheint es als die beste und schon vielfach bewährte Methode, Terror mit Gegenterror zu bekämpfen und sich nicht auf die für uns meist abschüssige Bahn des Rechts und der Rechtsverletzung zu begeben." International Military Tribunal, *Procès des grands criminels*, vol. XXXV, D-606, 181–86.

46 Norbert Elias, *The Civilizing Process*, trans. Edmund Jephcott, new edn (Oxford: Blackwell, 1994; first published in German 1939).

NOTES TO PAGES 219–22

47 Norbert Elias, *The Germans: Power Struggles and the Development of Habitus in the Nineteenth and Twentieth Centuries* (New York: Columbia University Press, 1996; first published in German 1989).

48 Ibid. See, in particular, "Introduction," 1–20, and "The Breakdown of Civilization," 299–402.

49 Gerald Kirwin, "Allied Bombing and Nazi Domestic Propaganda," *European History Quaterly*, 15 (1985), 341–62.

50 Ian Kershaw, *The End: The Defiance and Destruction of Hitler's Germany, 1944–1945* (London: Penguin, 2012).

51 Dietmar Süss, "The Air War, the Public and Cycles of Memory", in Echternkamp and Martens (eds.), *Experience and Memory*, 180–96.

52 Jörg Friedrich, *The Fire: The Bombing of Germany, 1940–1945* (New York: Columbia University Press, 2008; first published in German 2002).

Chapter 10

1 Quotations from: Correspondence of Rev. Hauptmann d.SchP, An die Geheime Staatspolizei in Kiel, Aussenstelle Itzehoe, 4 July 1944, Records of US Army, micr. M-1217, Roll 17; Martin Bormann, Partei-Kanzler, Rundschreiben 125/44 G, "Volksjustiz gegen anglo-amerikanische Mörder," 30 May 1944: circular relating to the "Justice du peuple contre les assassins anglo-américains," in International Military Tribunal, *Procès des grands criminels*, vol. XXV, Doc. PS-057, 112–13; Joseph Goebbels, "A Word on the Enemy Air Terror," *Völkischer Beobachter*, 28–29 May 1944 (Munich edition), and speech to the inhabitants of Nuremberg, 4 June 1944, in *Goebbels-Reden*, 323–41.

2 Cf. Appendix: Bombardments and On-the-Ground Responses: Comparative Maps and Figures.

3 Ulrich Herbert, *Hitler's Foreign Workers: Enforced Foreign Labor in Germany under the Third Reich* (Cambridge University Press, 1997), 313–76; Nikolaus Wachsmann, *KL: A History of the Nazi Concentration Camps* (New York: Farrar, Strauss and Giroux, 2015).

4 Overy, *Bombing War*, 475–76.

5 Robert Gellately, *Backing Hitler: Consent and Coercion in Nazi Germany* (Oxford University Press, 2001), chap. 7: "Special Justice for Foreign Workers"; Herbert, *Hitler's Foreign Workers*.

6 Daniel Blatman, *The Death Marches: The Final Phase of Nazi Genocide* (Cambridge, MA: Belknap Press of Harvard University Press, 2011).

7 Sven Keller, *Volksgemeinschaft am Ende: Gesellschaft und Gewalt, 1944/1945* (Munich: Oldenbourg Verlag, 2013), 291–305; Keller, "Les marches de la mort: la dimension sociale de la violence dans la phase de la fin de la guerre," *Revue d'histoire de la Shoah*, 209 (October 2010), 545–64; and Keller, "Total Defeat: War, Society and Violence in the Last Year of National Socialism", in Baranowski, Nolzen and Szejnmann (eds.), *Companion to Nazi Germany*, 247–57.

8 Eleonore Lappin, "The Death Marches of Hungarian Jews through Austria in the Spring of 1945," www.yadvashem.org/download/about_holocaust/studies/lappin_full.pdf; first published in German as "Die Todesmärsche ungarisher Jüdinnen und Juden zu Kriegsende," in Thomas Buchner and Heidemarie Uhl (eds.),

314   NOTES TO PAGES 222–31

Amstetten 1945: Kriegsende und Erinnerung (Stadtgemeinde Amstetten, 2015), 91–117.

9 Gerwin Strobl, *Bomben auf Oberdonau*; Hoffmann, *Fliegerlynchjustiz*.

10 Cf. Gregory A. Freeman, *The Last Mission of the Wham Bam Boys: Courage, Tragedy and Justice in World War II* (New York: Palgrave Macmillan, 2011). The author interviewed Forrest W. Brininstool (the wounded airman taken to hospital) and listened to the video testimony of Eugene Brown. Cf. also Winston G. Ramsey, "The Rüsselsheim Death March," *After the Battle*, 57 (1987), 1–21.

11 *Rechenschaftsbericht des Magistrats der Stadt Rüsselsheim a. M.*, Table "Durch Kriegseinwirkung entstandene Schäden," 14 May 1952, Archives of Rüsselsheim.

12 Sidney Eugene Brown, "Perpetuation of Testimony," 4 October 1945, testimony before the Security Intelligence Corps, Eighth Service Command, San Antonio, Texas, October 1945, NARA, RG 153, Entry 143, Box 352.

13 Klaus-Dieter Alicke, *Lexikon der jüdischen Gemeinden im deutschen Sprachraum* (Gütersloher Verlagsaus, 2008), https://jüdische-gemeinden.de.

14 Brown, "Perpetuation of Testimony" (see note 12).

15 William Adams, "Perpetuation of Testimony", 4 October 1945, NARA, RG 153, Entry 143, Box 352; and hearing before the tribunal, testimony of Margrethe Zogner and Hanna Schnur, 13 and 26.

16 Brown, "Perpetuation of Testimony" (see note 12).

17 Christoph Keil, deposition of 22 June 1945, and Tribunal hearing, 25 July 1945, 49–51, and depositions from August Wolf, Karl Fugmann and Johann Opper, 27, 30 and 26 June 1945. NARA, RG-549, Entry A1–2238, Box 167.

18 "Review of the Staff Judge Advocate", Headquarters of the 7th Army, 23 August 1945, NARA, M-1217, ff. 386–93.

19 Adams, "Perpetuation of Testimony" (see note 15).

20 Witness Heinrich Rauch, Court hearing, trial of Otto Stolz, Dachau, 15 May 1947, 45–47.

21 Onsite investigation with help from the town archivist and the deputy director of the cemetery administration; *Sterbebuch* (burial book) and *Totenbuch* (book of the dead) of the Waldfriedhof cemetery for August 1944; and "Exhibit G," map of the cemetery and location of the mass grave by Captain Max Berg, forensic scientist for War Crimes Investigation Team 6830, 28 June 1945, copy in the Stadtarchiv Rüsselsheim.

22 Keil, deposition of 22 June 1945 (see note 17); Albert Noehl, deposition of 2 June 1945, NARA, RG-549, Entry A1–2238, Box 167.

23 Heinrich Himmler, Reichsführer SS, Persönlicher Stab, Secret, To All SS and Police Chiefs, 10 August 1943, repr. in International Military Tribunal, *Procès des grands criminels*, vol. XXXVIII, 313–14.

24 Joseph Goebbels, "A Word on the Enemy Air Terror," *Völkischer Beobachter*, 26 May 1944 (Berlin edition); 27 May (Vienna edition); 28–29 May (Munich edition).

25 Martin Bormann, Partei-Kanzler, Rundschreiben 125/44 G, "Volksjustiz gegen anglo-amerikanische Mörder," 30 May 1944.

26 Exactly 100 trials out of 192 total.

27 The quotations in this paragraph are drawn from Deputy Judge Advocate Office, "Review and Recommendations," Case 12-489, 1 August 1947, NARA, M-1217.

NOTES TO PAGES 231–40

28 Flotillas of several hundred airplanes bombed the Munich area on 11, 12, 13, 16, 19, 21 and 31 July 1944.

29 Boelcke (ed.), *Secret Conferences of Dr. Goebbels*, 339, conference of 10 March 1943.

30 United States Army, Office of the Acting Assistant Chief of Staff, G-2, APO 867, to IS9 WEA, 2 June 1945. TNA, W0 219 /5298.

31 MI9/19, London, to MI9 Officer Commanding, IS9 (Awards Bureaus), Paris, August 1946. NARA, UD163, Box 626, location 290/55/22/2.

32 "Escapers" debriefings, TNA, WO/208/3297–3327.

33 In the trials studied: 27 cases out of 192.

34 RG 549, entry 2238, Box 167: Witness Christopher Keil, Deposition, 22 June 1945; Box 170: Witness Lorenz Wendel, Court hearing, 25 July 1945, 39, Box 169: Witness Hanna Schnur, Deposition, 11 July 1945, Box 170; Witness Anne Willnow, Statement, and Court hearing, July 1945, 74–76.

35 "Mistreatment of an American flyer in a ward in a hospital," RG 549 Entry 2239, Box 227.

36 Anna Visel, deposition regarding the mistreatment of an airman in a cellar located in Tanga Strasse, Munich, 9 June 1944, during an air raid. RG 549 Entry 2239, Box 254.

37 Ibid.

38 Noehl, deposition of 2 June 1945 (see note 22).

39 Archives of the trial relating to the death of a Canadian airman in Oberweier, Case Reference: 67/NEW/92/Oberweier/1. Record of proceedings and evidence for the trial of Wilhelm Jung et al. Donated by Wing Commander O.W. Durdin of the Royal Canadian Air Force, Imperial War Museum, London.

40 Deputy Theater Judge Advocate's Office, "Review and Recommendations," Case 12-1967, 23 December 1946, M-1217. This lynching took place in Elm, Lower Saxony, on 28 May 1944.

41 Deputy Judge Advocate's Office, Case 12-581, Mühldorf; and 12-2067, Düsseldorf, NARA, M-1217.

42 Jordan, NSDAP, district of Greater Frankfurt, letter to the HSSPF, Waffen-SS Major and Gruppenführer Stroop, 23 February 1945, NARA, RG 549. Entry A1 2239. Case not tried, Box 175.

43 Keil, deposition of 22 June 1945 and Tribunal hearing, 150–51 (see note 17); Request for pardon for the defendant Johann Opper, 11 August 1945; "Review of the Staff Judge Advocate," 23 August 1945, Case 12-1497, NARA M-1217.

44 Friedrich Reck-Malleczewen, *Diary of a Man in Despair*, trans. Paul Rubens (New York: Macmillan, 1970; first published in German 1947); and Hélène Camarade, *Écritures de la Résistance: le journal intime sous le Troisième Reich* (Toulouse: Presses universitaires du Mirail, 2007).

45 Christopher R. Browning, "The Holocaust: Basis and Objective of the Volksgemeinschaft?" in Marina Steber and Bernhard Gotto (eds.), *Visions of Community in Nazi Germany: Social Engineering and Private Lives* (Oxford University Press, 2014), 217–25.

46 Hadaway, *Missing Believed Killed*, 105.

47 Dietmar Süss, *Death from the Skies: How the British and the Germans Survived Bombing in World War II* (Oxford University Press, 2014; first published in German 2011); Aaron William Moore, *Bombing the City: Civilian Accounts of the Air War in Britain and Japan, 1939–1945* (Cambridge University Press, 2018).

316   NOTES TO PAGES 240–45

48 For example, Hans Erich Nossack, *The End: Hamburg 1943*, trans. Joel Agee (University of Chicago Press, 2006; written in 1943 and first published in German in 1946), 47–48; Heinrich Böll, *Silent Angel*, trans. Breon Mitchell (New York: St. Martin's Press, 1994; written in 1949 and published in full in German in 1992), chaps. XIII and XIX.

49 Among other places, this was the case in Berlin, Brunswick, Cologne, Emden, Frankfurt, Hamburg, Siegen, Solingen and Wetzlar. Cf. Süss, *Death from the Skies*, 302; and Stargardt, *German War*, 376.

50 Michael Meng, *Shattered Spaces: Encountering Jewish Spaces in Postwar Germany and Poland* (Cambridge, MA: Harvard University Press, 2011).

51 Jörg Arnold, *The Allied War and Urban Memory: The Legacy of Strategic Bombing in Germany* (Cambridge University Press, 2011).

Chapter 11

1 Isabel Heinemann, "Race", in Baranowski, Nolzen and Szejnmann (eds.), *Companion to Nazi Germany*, 499–511.

2 Raymond Jeannin, *Nimbus libéré*, Nova films, March 1944, online; and "Behind the Enemy Powers: The Jew", by Bruno Hanich, December 1943.

3 Browning, "Holocaust."

4 Stargardt, *German War*; Stargardt, "Rumors of Revenge in the Second World War", in B.J. Davis et al. (eds.), *Alltag, Erfahrung, Eigensinn: Historisch-anthropologische Erkundungen* (Frankfurt: Campus Verlag, 2008), 374–89; Peter Fritzsche, "Babi Yar But Not Auschwitz: What Did Germans Know about the Final Solution?" in Susanna Schraftstetter and Alan Steinweis (eds.), *The Germans and the Holocaust: Popular Responses to the Persecution and Murder of the Jews* (New York and Oxford: Berghahn, 2016), 85–104.

5 Klemperer, *I Will Bear Witness*, 281 (27 December 1943). See also 27 January 1944.

6 "USA und England bilden für Europa eine judische Terror- und Rache-Organisation. Im Falle ihres Sieges sollen jüdische Emigranten die europäische 'Polizei' übernehmen – Juda will seinem Hass ausstoben," *Hessische Landes-Zeitung*, 26 July 1943, frontpage headline.

7 *Der Stürmer: German Weekly for the Struggle and the Truth*, 23 (25 May 1944), extracts of an article by Ernst Hiemer. Quoted in Office of United States Chief of Counsel for Prosecution of Axis Criminality, *Nazi Conspiracy and Aggression*, Supplement A, 950.

8 Joseph Goebbels, "A Word on the Enemy Air Terror", *Völkischer Beobachter*, 26 May 1944.

9 Victor Klemperer, *Ich will Zeugnis ablegen bis zum letzten* (Berlin: Aufbau-Verlag, 1996), 523 (notes dated 29 May 1944). This passage is not translated in the English version (*I Will Bear Witness*).

10 *Kladderadatsch*, 1848–1944, online on Universitätsbibliothek Heidelberg: www.ub.uni-heidelberg.de/Englisch/helios/digi/kladderadatsch.html.

11 Jean-Claude Gardes, "Fragilité et force du pouvoir: l'Allemagne, 1933–1939," in *L'image du pouvoir dans le dessin d'actualité. Le temps des monarques. Le temps des chefs. Le temps des leaders*, special issue of *Matériaux pour l'histoire de notre temps*, 28 (1992), 26–30.

NOTES TO PAGES 247–51

12 For press drawings of the same triple inspiration, see "USA-Kulturträger," *Völkischer Beobachter* (Vienna edition), 22 July 1943; and for joint anticlericalism and anti-black racism only, see "Vorwärts, Soldaten Christi!" *Völkischer Beobachter* (Vienna edition), 24 July 1943; and *Völkischer Beobachter* (Berlin edition), 14 June 1944.

13 *Die Tagebücher von Joseph Goebbels*, vol. IX, 64 (8 July 1943) and 104 (15 July 1943).

14 Jean-Yves Le Naour, *La honte noire: l'Allemagne et les troupes coloniales françaises, 1914–1945* (Paris: Hachette, 2003).

15 Julia Roos, "Women's Rights, Nationalist Anxiety, and the 'Moral' Agenda in the Early Weimar Republic: Revisiting the 'Black Horror' Campaign against France's African Occupation Troops", *Central European History*, 42 (September 2009), 473–508 (at 474).

16 Boelcke (ed.), *Secret Conferences of Dr. Goebbels*, 47.

17 Scheck, *Hitler's African Victims*; and Scheck, "Les massacres de prisonniers noirs par l'armée allemande en 1940,", in Chapoutot and Vigreux (eds.), *Des soldats noirs face au Reich*, 59–100.

18 James Q. Whitman, *Hitler's American Model: The United States and the Making of Nazi Race Law* (Princeton University Press, 2017).

19 S. Jonathan Wiesen, "American Lynching in the Nazi Imagination: Race and Extra-Legal Violence in 1930s Germany", *German History*, 36/1 (2018), 38–59.

20 "The Causes of the Racial Combat: Niggers as Yankee Cannon Fodder" ("Ursachen des Rassenkampfes: Neger als Kanonenfutter der Yankees"), *Völkischer Beobachter* (Vienna edition), 15 August 1943, 2.

21 "Um brutale Mordinstinkte in diesem Rassenkampf auszulösen."

22 Reichsministerium für Volksaufklärung. *Gegen Amerika*, no. 1, 9/12/1938 and no. 17, 4/10/1949, Bundesarchiv, Berlin-Lichterfelde, R 55/24843.

23 "Race Lesson in Detroit", *Kladderadatsch*, 28 (11 July 1943).

24 "The Penitentiary Is the Best School for American Soldiers," *Kladderadatsch*, 32 (8 August 1943).

25 "Scientific Bombing," *Kladderadatsch*, 33 (15 August 1943).

26 "Shooting Gallery Granny," *Kladderadatsch*, 48 (28 November 1943).

27 "Lament in Black and White," *Kladderadatsch*, 16 (16 April 1944).

28 "The Satisfied Reverend," *Kladderadatsch*, 20 (14 May 1944).

29 "Roosevelt's Pilots Strafing Women and Children", *Völkischer Beobachter* (Berlin edition), 14 June 1944.

30 Johann Chapoutot, "Le nazisme et les Noirs: histoire d'un racisme spécifique," in Chapoutot and Vigreux (eds.), *Des soldats noirs face au Reich*, 35–58.

31 The idea is omnipresent in speeches and newspaper articles. Explicit citations may be found in: Victor Klemperer, 30 March 1945 radio broadcast, *I Will Bear Witness*; and an SS pamphlet found in Cologne by Jannet Flanner in March 1945, in Enzensberger (ed.), *L'Europe en ruines*, 107; Klemperer, *Language of the Third Reich*, chap. 26: "The Jewish war."

32 Joseph Goebbels, speech to the residents of Nuremberg, 4 June 1944, in *Goebbels-Reden*, 330.

33 Wildt, *Hitler's Volksgemeinschaft*; and Wildt, "La violence contre les Juifs en Allemagne après 1933," *Revue d'histoire de la Shoah*, 209 (October 2010), 97–112.

318   NOTES TO PAGES 251–58

34 Ulrich Baumann, Memorial Foundation for the Jews Killed in Europe, Berlin, kindly brought this case to my attention. Hugo Grüner was sentenced to death by the French military tribunal headquartered in Strasbourg in May 1946 but the Court of Appeal held that he had to be handed over to the British since the event had neither taken place on French territory nor involved French citizens. He then escaped from the Recklinghausen-Hillerheide camp.

35 Recorded interview of Sidney Eugene Brown in the 2000s; RG 549, Entry 2238, Box 170: witnesses Margrethe Zogner and Hanna Schnur, Court hearings, 25 July 1945, pages 13 and 26.

36 Oral testimony of Sidney Eugene Brown, recalled by Madeline Teremy, daughter of the plane's pilot, interviewed 23 September 2017; Gregory Freeman also recounts the incident, albeit in a different version, in *Last Mission*, 62; RG 549, Entry 2238, Box 168. Corroborating analysis provided Gregory Freeman by a forensic scientist.

37 RG 549, Entry 2238, Box 170: witness Gottlieb Wolf, Court hearing, 26 July 1945, 99.

38 NARA, M-1217, Headquarters Third Army, Office of the Staff Judge Advocate, War Crimes Branch, Cases 12-926 and 12-926-1.

39 Georg Hoffmann, *Fliegerjustiz*, 174–75; Blank, "Wartime Daily Life," 466.

40 Deputy Judge Advocate's Office, "Review and Recommendations", Case 12-1368 and 1368. NARA, M-1217.

41 "Nicht zu verhindernden" and "die rasende Bevölkerung," in Jodl, "Beschreibung. Geheime Kommandosache", 21 February 1945, in International Military Tribunal, *Procès des grands criminels*, vol. XXXV, Document D-606, 185.

42 NARA, RG 549, Entry A-2239. Cases Not Tried, Box 85.

43 Le Naour, *La honte noire*, 59.

44 Hoffmann, *Fliegerlynchjustiz*, 292–97.

45 "Thus 'a Representative of Culture'!," *Oberdonau Zeitung*, Austria, 31 March – 1 April 1945, 1, in Hoffmann, *Fliegerlynchjustiz*, interior supplement of photographs.

46 Hoffmann, *Fliegerlynchjustiz*.

47 Ibid., 293–97; and Strobl, *Bomben auf Oberdonau*, 268–72.

48 On the concomitance of feelings of love for some and hatred for others, see Alexandra Przyrembel, "Emotions and National Socialism," in Baranowski, Nolzen and Szejnmann (eds.), *Companion to Nazi Germany*, 399–410.

49 Sergeant Hermann S., letter of 6 December 1944, quoted by Kershaw, *The End*, 206.

50 Result of twenty polls carried out in the American zone over the period November 1945 to January 1948 in response to the question: "Was National Socialism a bad idea or a good idea poorly implemented?" in Anna J. Merritt and Richard L. Merritt, *Public Opinion in Occupied Germany* (Urbana: University of Illinois Press, 1970), 30–39.

Conclusion

1 On the role played by scales of analysis, see Bernhard Struck, Kate Ferris and Jacques Revel, "Introduction: Space and Scale in Transnational History", *Size Matters: Scales and Spaces in Transnational and Comparative History*, special issue of *International History Review*, 33/4 (2011), 573–84; and Sebouh David Aslanian,

NOTES TO PAGES 258–62

"How Size Matters: The Question of Scale in History", AHR Conversation, *American Historical Review*, 118/5 (December 2013), 1443–47, esp. 1445–46.

2 Espagne, *Les transferts culturels*.

3 Hartmut Kaelble, "Comparative and Transnational History," *Ricerche di storia politica*, special issue, 60 (October 2017), 15–24.

4 Mandler, *English National Character*.

5 *A Matter of Life and Death*, by Michael Powell and Emeric Pressburger, Archers Film Production, released in 1946 in the United Kingdom and United States.

6 Martina Kessel, "Race and Humor in Nazi Germany," in Pendas, Roseman and Wetzell (eds.), *Beyond the Racial State*, 381–401.

7 Norbert Elias, "National Peculiarities of British Public Opinion," talk given in October 1960 in Bad Wildungen, Hesse, excerpts in *Essays II: On Civilising Process, State Formation and National Identity* (Dublin: UCD Press, 2008), 230–55; and Wolf Feuerhahn, "Humours nationaux: le regard situé de Norbert Elias" in *Humour "anglais"*, special issue of *Humoresques*, 36 (2012), 67–80.

8 Elias, *The Germans*.

9 Beatrice Heuser and Eitan Shamir (eds.), *Insurgencies and Counter-Insurgencies: National Styles and Strategic Cultures* (Cambridge University Press, 2017).

10 Horne and Kramer, *German Atrocities*.

11 Henning Pieper, "From Fighting 'Francs-Tireurs' to Genocide: German Counterinsurgency in the Second World War," in Heuser and Shamir (eds.), *Insurgencies and Counter-Insurgencies*, 149–67.

12 Bastian Matteo Scianna, "A Predisposition to Brutality? German Practices against Civilians and *Francs-Tireurs* during the Franco-Prussian War 1870–1871 and Their Relevance for the German 'Military *Sonderweg*' Debate,", *Small Wars & Insurgencies*, 30/4–5 (2019), 968–93.

13 Hull, *Absolute Destruction*, and *A Scrap of Paper*.

14 Olivier Berger, "Comment écrire l'histoire de la violence de guerre allemande pendant la guerre de 1870–1871," in Marie-Claude Marandet (ed.), *Violence(s) de la préhistoire à nos jours: les sources et leur interprétation* (Presses universitaires de Perpignan, 2011), 255–72; Armel Dirou, "Les francs-tireurs pendant la guerre de 1870–1871", *Stratégique*, 93–96/1-4 (2009), 279–317; Claude Farenc, "Guerre, information et propagande en 1870–1871: le cas de la Champagne," *Revue d'histoire moderne et contemporaine*, 31/1 (January–March 1984), 27–63.

15 Jochen Böhler, Francine Wernz and Gaël Eismann, "L'adversaire imaginaire: 'guerre des francs-tireurs' de l'armée allemande en Belgique en 1914 et de la Wehrmacht en Pologne en 1939. Considérations comparatives," in Eismann and Martens (eda.), *Occupation et répression militaires allemandes*, 17–40.

16 Michel Fabréguet, "Un groupe de réfugiés politiques: les républicains espagnols des camps d'internement français aux camps de concentration nationaux-socialistes (1939-1941)," *Revue d'histoire de la deuxième guerre mondiale et des conflits contemporains*, 144 (October 1986), 19–38.

17 Rupert Ticehurst, "The Martens Clause and the Laws of Armed Conflict," *International Review of the Red Cross*, 317 (30 April 1997), www.icrc.org/en/doc/resources/documents/article/other/57jnhy.htm.

18 Farenc, "Guerre, information et propagande," 36–37.

320   NOTES TO PAGES 263–65

19 Valérie Deacon, "International Cooperation, Transnational Circulation: Escape, Evasion, and Resistance in France, 1940–1945," *French Politics, Culture & Society,* 37/1 (Spring 2019), 70–89.

20 "Samedi et dimanche, en présence de l'ambassadeur des États-Unis, de grandes manifestations franco-américaines vont se dérouler à Biarritz. 130 Français et Françaises seront décorés au cours d'une prise d'armes," *Sud-Ouest* (Bordeaux), 18 February 1947.

21 Mary Fulbrook, "Social Relations and Bystander Responses to Violence: Kristallnacht, November 1938," in Wolf Grüner and Steven J. Ross, *New Perspectives on Kristallnacht: After 80 Years, the Nazi Pogrom in Global Comparison* (West Lafayette, IN: Purdue University Press, 2019), 69–87; Keller, *Volksgemeinschaft am Ende* (2013); Raim, *Nazi Crimes against Jews* (2015); Strobl, *Bomben auf Oberdonau* (2014); Hoffmann, *Fliegerlynchjustiz* (2015); Lappin, "Death Marches of Hungarian Jews" (2015); Jan T. Gross, *Neighbors: The Destruction of the Jewish Community in Jedwabne, Poland* (Princeton University Press, 2001), and "Opportunistic Killings and Plunder of Jews by Their Neighbors: A Norm or an Exception in German Occupied Europe?", in Christian Wiese and Paul Betts (eds.), *Years of Persecution, Years of Extermination: Saul Friedländer and the Future of Holocaust Studies* (London: Continuum, 2010), 269–86; Jan Grabowski, *Hunt for the Jews: Betrayal and Murder in German-Occupied Poland* (Bloomington: Indiana University Press, 2013).

22 Lucien Febvre, "Une vue d'ensemble: histoire et psychologie," *Encyclopédie française,* vol. VIII (1938), repr. in Febvre, *Combats pour l'histoire* (Paris: Armand Colin, 1953), 207–20; and Febvre, "Comment reconstituer la vie affective d'autrefois? La sensibilité et l'histoire," *Annales d'histoire sociale,* 3/2 (1941), repr. in Febvre, *Combats pour l'histoire,* 221–38.

23 Alexander Bain, *The Emotions and the Will* (London: John Parker, 1859); Rob Boddice, "The History of Emotions," in Sascha Handley, Rohan McWilliam and Lucy Noakes (eds.), *New Directions in Social and Cultural History* (London: Bloomsbury, 2018), 45–62.

BIBLIOGRAPHY

Official Documents and Databases

Air Ministry, *The Battle of Britain August-October 1940*, London, Her Majesty's Stationery Office, 1941.

Auswärtiges Amt, *Die völkerrechtswidrige Führung des belgischen Volkskriegs*, Berlin, 10 May 1915.

Boelcke, Willi A. (ed.), *The Secret Conferences of Dr. Goebbels: The Nazi Propaganda War, 1939– 1943*, New York: E.P.Dutton, 1970.

Fondation pour la mémoire de la Déportation, *Livre-Mémorial des déportés de France*, 4 vols., Paris : Éditions Tirésias, 2004.

Harris, Sir Athur, *Despatch on War Operations, 23rd February 1942 – 8th May 1945*, 18 December 1945 (London: Frank Cass, 1995).

International Military Tribunal, *Procès des grands criminels de guerre devant le Tribunal Militaire International de Nuremberg, 14 novembre 1945 – 1 octobre 1946*, 42 vols. (Nuremberg: Secrétariat du Tribunal, 1947–49). Texts in their original German version.

Klee, Karl (ed.), *Dokumente zum Unternehmen "Seelöwe,"* Göttingen: Muster-Schmidt, 1959).

Oberkommando der Wehrmacht (WR), Wehrmacht-Untersuchungsstelle für Verletzungen des Völkerrechts, *Frankreichs völkerrechtswidrige Kriegführung 1939/1940 [France's Conduct of a War Contrary to International Law, 1939/1940]*, Berlin: Gedrückt in der Reichsdruckerei, vol. I November 1940; vol. II, April 1941.

Office of the Adjutant General, *Army Battle Casualties and Nonbattle Deaths in World War II: Final Report (7 December 1941–31 December 1946)*, (Washington, DC: Dept. of the Army, 1953).

Office of United States Chief of Counsel for Prosecution of Axis Criminality, [International Military Tribunal at Nuremberg], *Nazi Conspiracy and Aggression*, 3 vols. and Supplement A, Washington, DC: United States Government Printing Office, 1946–47.

Pétain, Philippe, *Discours aux Français, 1940–1944*, presented by J.-C. Barbas, Paris: Albin Michel, 1989.

Rüter, Christian F. and de Mildt, Dick W., *Justiz und NS-Verbrechen: Sammlung deutscher Strafurteile wegen nationalsozialistischer Tötungsverbrechen, 1945-2012*, 21 vols., Amsterdam University Press, 1968–2012.

322   BIBLIOGRAPHY

Trials of War Criminals before the Nuremberg Military Tribunal under Control Council Law No. 10, vol. XI, Washington, DC: United States Government Printing Office, 1951.

The United States Strategic Bombing Survey, *Over-all Report (European War)*, 30 September 1945, https://babel.hathitrust.org/cgi/pt?id=mdp.39015049492716;view=1up;seq=7.

Personal Journals, Contemporaneous Writings and Subsequent Testimony

Auroy, Berthe, *Jours de guerre: ma vie sous l'Occupation*, preface and notes by Anne-Marie Pathé and Dominique Veillon, Paris: Bayard, 2008.

Bloch, Marc, *Strange defeat*, trans. Gerard Hopkins, Oxford University Press, 1949.

Brittain, Vera, *Seeds of Chaos: What Mass Bombing Really Means*, London: New Vision, 1944.

Broussine, Georges, *L'évadé de la France libre: le réseau Bourgogne*, Paris: Tallandier, 2000.

Calder, Ritchie , *Carry On London*, Bungay: English Universities Press, 1941.

Churchill, Winston, *Into Battle: Speeches*, London: Cassell, 1945.

Corday, Pauline, *J'ai vécu dans Paris occupé*, Montréal: Éditions de l'Arbre, 1943.

Darling, Donald, *Secret Sunday*, London: William Kimber, 1975.

DiFante, Marlies Adams, with DiFante, Anne Marie, *Queen of the Bremen: The True Story of an American Child Trapped in Germany during World War II*, published by the author, 2010.

Dumais, Lucien, *The Man Who Went Back*, London: Futura, 1975; 1st edn 1974.

Duprez, Henri, *1940–1945: Même combat de l'ombre et de la lumière – Épisodes de la Résistance dans le nord de la France – Témoignages et souvenirs*, Paris: La pensée universelle, 1979.

Enzensberger, Hans Magnus (ed.), *L'Europe en ruines: textes choisis et présentés par l'auteur*, Aix-en-Provence: Solin/Actes Sud, 1995.

Fabre-Luce, Alfred, *Journal de la France 1939–1944*, Paris: Fayard, 1969.

Fortune, G. & W., *Hitler Divided France*, London: Macmillan, 1943.

Galland, Adolf, *The First and the Last: The German Fighter Force in World War II*, London: Methuen, 1955.

Goebbels, Joseph, *The Goebbels Diaries: The Last Days*, London: Secker & Warburg, 1978.

  Goebbels-Reden, vol. II: *1939–1945*, ed. Helmut Heiber, Düsseldorf: Droste Verlag, 1972.

  Journal 1939–1942 (excerpts), Paris: Tallandier, 2009.

  Journal 1942–1945 (excerpts), Paris: Tallandier, 2005.

  Die Tagebücher von Joseph Goebbels, Part II: *Diktate 1941–1945*, ed. Elke Fröhlich et al., 15 vols., Munich: K.G. Saur, 1993–96.

Guéhenno, Jean, *Diary of the Dark Years, 1940–1944*, trans. David Ball, Oxford University Press, 2014.

BIBLIOGRAPHY

Harcourt, Pierre d', *Journal de Buchenwald*, preceded by *Souvenirs de résistance et de prison*, printed without a publisher, 2009. First printing Buzançais, 1988.

Hargest, James, *Farewell Campo 12*, London: Michael Joseph, 1945.

Harris, Arthur, *Bomber Offensive*, London: Greenhill, 1998 (1st edn 1947).

Hoisne, Sabine, *Chambre 535 ou Mes cinq prisons pendant l'occupation: souvenirs des heures tragiques vécues par Sabine Hoisne de l'Union Nationale des Français condamnés par les tribunaux allemands*, Limoges: Société des journaux et publications du Centre, 1945.

Hulbert, Kenneth, *I Will Lift Up Mine Eyes: The Experience of a Doctor in Peace and War. Based on the War Diaries and Early Memoirs of Kenneth Hulbert*, ed. Ann Hulbert, Seal, Kent: Highland Printers, 2003.

Ivelaw-Chapman, John, *High Endeavour: The Life of Air Chief Marshal Sir Ronald Ivelaw-Chapman, GCB, KBE, DFC, AFC*, London: Lee Cooper, 1993.

Klemperer, Victor, *Ich will Zeugnis ablegen bis zum letzten*, Berlin: Aufbau-Verlag, 1996.

I Will Bear Witness: A Diary of the Nazi Years, 1942–1945, trans. Martin Chalmers, New York: Modern Library, 2001.

Langley, Jimmy M., *Fight Another Day*, London: Collins, 1974.

Lay, Beirne, Jr, *Presumed Dead*, New York: Dodd, Mead, 1980; 1st edn 1945 under the title *I've Had It*.

Le Trividic, Dominique-Martin, *Une héroïne de la Résistance, Marie-Thérèse Le Calvez du réseau Shelburn*, Rennes: Ouest-France, 2002; 1st edn 1979.

Limagne, Pierre, *Éphémérides de quatre années tragiques*, vol. III, La Villedieu, Ardèche: Éditions de Candide, 1987.

Moreau, Émilienne, *La guerre buissonnière: une famille française dans la Résistance*, Paris: Solar Éditeur, 1970.

Nabarro, Derrick, *Wait for the Dawn*, London: Cassell, 1952.

Nahas, Gabriel, *La filière du rail*, Paris: Éditions France-Empire, 1982.

Neave, Airey, *Escape Room*, New York: Doubleday, 1970.

They Have Their Exits, London: Hodder & Stoughton, 1953; repr. Barnsley: Leo Cooper, 2002.

Nossack, Hans Erich, *The End: Hamburg 1943*, trans. Joel Agee, University of Chicago Press, 2004; first published in German 1946.

Nouveau, Louis-Henri, dit Saint-Jean, *Des capitaines par milliers: retour à Gibraltar des aviateurs alliés abattus, 1941-42-43*, Paris: Calmann-Lévy, 1957.

Postel-Vinay, André, *Un fou s'évade, 1940–1941*, Paris: Éditions du Félin, 1997.

Reck-Malleczewen, Friedrich, *Diary of a Man in Despair*, trans. Paul Rubens, New York: Macmillan, 1970; first published in German 1947.

Rémy [Gilbert Renault, known as colonel], *Comment meurt un réseau (novembre 1943 – août 1944)*, Monaco: Éditions Raoul Solar, 1947.

Rudel, Hans Ulrich , *Stuka Pilot*, trans. L. Hudson, New York: Ballantine, 1958.

Shiber, Etta, *Paris Underground*, in collaboration with Anne and Paul Dupré, New York: Charles Scribner's Sons, 1943.

324   BIBLIOGRAPHY

Shirer, William L., *Berlin Diary: Journal of a Foreign Correspondent 1934–1941*, Mountain View, CA: Ishi Press International, 2010..

Tartière, Drue, *The House Near Paris: An American Woman's Story of Traffic in Patriots*, written with M.R. Werner, London: Gollancz, 1947.

Tessonneau, Rémy, *Jacques, l'ami d'Achille: un agent français de la Guerre secrète "Réseau Évasions," 1940–1945*, Paris: Chassany Éditeur, 1946. ["Jacques" is the pseudonym of Alexandre Wattebled.]

Vasselot, Odile de, *Tombés du ciel: histoire d'une ligne d'évasion*, Paris: Le Félin, 2005.

Werth, Léon, *33 jours*, Paris: Viviane Hamy, 1992; 1st edn 1940.

Wilborts, Suzanne, *Pour la France: Angers-La Santé-Fresnes-Ravensbrück-Mauthausen*, preface by General Audibert, Paris: Charles-Lavauzelle, 1946.

Films and Television Series

Dad's Army, by David Croft and Jimmy Perry, BBC Worldwide, 1968–77.

Heimat: eine deutsche Chronik, by Edgar Reitz, 1984, DVD. Script published Nordlingen: Greno, 1985.

La Grande Vadrouille, by Gérard Oury, produced by Corona/Lowndes, 1966.

A Matter of Life and Death, by Michael Powell and Emeric Pressburger, Archers Film Production, 1946.

Mrs. Miniver, directed by William Wyler and produced by Sidney Franklin, a Metro-Goldwyn-Mayer Picture, 1942; based on the book by Jan Struther, 1939.

Nimbus libéré, by Raymond Jeannin, Nova films, March 1944.

The One That Got Away, written by Kendal Burt, directed by Roy Ward Baker, Julian Wintler with the Rank Organisation, 1957.

Propaganda Kompanien, documentary film, by Véronique Lhomme, ECPAD and La Cuisine aux Images, 2013.

Books and Articles

Absalom, Roger, *A Strange Alliance: Aspects of Escape and Survival in Italy, 1943–1945*, Florence: Leo S. Olschki Editore, 1991.

Aglan, Alya, *Le temps de la Résistance*, Aix-en-Provence: Actes Sud, 2008.

Alary, Eric, "Evacuations et exode," in Leleu et al. (eds.), *La France pendant la Seconde Guerre mondiale*, 46–47.

    L'exode: un drame oublié, Paris: Perrin, 2010.

Albertelli, Sébastien, *Histoire du sabotage: de la CGT à la Résistance*, Paris: Perrin, 2016.

Albertelli, Sébastien, Blanc, Julien and Douzou, Laurent, *La lutte clandestine en France: une histoire de la Résistance, 1940–1944*, Paris: Seuil, 2019.

Alexander, Martin, "Gamelin et les leçons de la campagne de Pologne," in Vaïsse (ed.), *Mai-juin 1940*, 59–74.

BIBLIOGRAPHY

Alicke, Klaus-Dieter, *Lexikon der jüdischen Gemeinden im deutschen Sprachraum*, Gütersloher Verlaghsaus, 2008, https://jüdische-gemeinden.de.

Allorant, Pierre, Castagnez, Noëlline and Prost, Antoine (eds.), *Le moment 1940: effondrement national et réalités locales*, Paris: L'Harmattan, 2012.

Almond, Gabriel A. and Verba, Sidney, *Civic Culture: Political Attitudes and Democracy in Five Nations*, Princeton University Press, 1963.

Andrieu, Claire, "Assistance to Jews and to Allied Soldiers and Airmen in France: A Comparative Approach," in Semelin, Andrieu, and Gensburger (eds.), *Resisting Genocide*, 52–64.

"La nazification de la Wehrmacht durant la campagne de France," in Chapoutot and Vigreux (eds.), *Des soldats noirs face au Reich*, 59–100.

"La Résistance comme mouvement social," in Michel Pigenet and Danielle Tartakowsky (eds.), *Histoire des mouvements sociaux en France de 1814 à nos jours*, Paris: La Découverte, 2012, 415–26.

"Les résistantes, perspectives de recherche," in Antoine Prost (ed.), *Pour une histoire sociale de la Résistance*, special issue of *Le mouvement social*, 180/3 (1997), 69–96.

"Revisiting the Historiography of the Resistance from the Perspective of Its Local Dynamics," in Denis Charbit (ed.), *Revisiting Vichy*, special issue of *Perspectives: revue de l'université hébraïque de Jérusalem*, 26 (2022), 193–208.

Anon., "Battle of Britain Investigation," *After the Battle*, 23 (1979), 46–53.

Einer kam durch: Fluchtbericht der Fliegerleutnants Franz von Werra, Hamburg, Verlag der Sternbücher, 1957.

Apostolidès, Jean-Marie, *Héroïsme et victimisation: une histoire de la sensibilité*, Paris: Cerf, 2011.

Arzalier, Jean-Jacques, "La campagne de mai–juin 1940: les pertes?" in Christine Levisse-Touzé (ed.), *La campagne de 1940*, 422–47.

Aslanian, Sebouh David, "How Size Matters: The Question of Scale in History," AHR Conversation, *American Historical Review*, 118/5 (December 2013), 1443–47.

Auroux, Sylvain (ed.), *Les notions philosophiques: dictionnaire*, Paris: PUF, 1990.

Bain, Alexander, *The Emotions and the Will*, London: John Parker, 1859.

Baldoli, Claudia and Knapp, Andrew, *Forgotten Blitzes: France and Italy under Allied Air Attack, 1940–1945*, London and New York: Continuum, 2012.

Baldoli, Claudia, Knapp, Andrew and Overy, Richard (eds.), *Bombing, States and Peoples in Western Europe, 1940–1945*, London and New York: Continuum, 2011.

Baranowski, Shelley, Nolzen, Armin and Szejnmann, Claus-Christian W. (eds.), *A Companion to Nazi Germany*, Oxford: Wiley-Blackwell, 2018.

Barcellini, Serge, Preface by Mechthild Gilzmer, *Mémoires de pierre: les monuments commémoratifs en France après 1944*, Paris : Autrement, 2009.

"La Résistance française à travers le prisme de la carte CVR," in Douzou et al. (eds.), *La Résistance et les Français*, 151–81.

BIBLIOGRAPHY

Barcellini, Serge and Wieviorka, Annette, *Passant, souviens-toi! Les lieux du souvenir de la Seconde Guerre mondiale en France*, Paris: Plon, 1995.

Beauvois, Jean-Léon, *Les illusions libérales, individualisme et pouvoir social: petit traité des grandes illusions*, Presses universitaires de Grenoble, 2005.

Bédarida, François, "L'histoire de la résistance: lectures d'hier, chantiers de demain," *Vingtième siècle*, 11 (1986), 75–90.

Benda-Beckmann, Bastiaan Robert von, *German Historians and the Bombing of German Cities: The Contested Air War*, Amsterdam University Press, 2015.

Bergen, Doris, "Death throes and Killing Frenzies: A Response to Hans Mommsen," *Bulletin of the German Historical Institute*, 27 (Fall 2000), 25–38.

Berger, Olivier, "Comment écrire l'histoire de la violence de guerre allemande pendant la guerre de 1870–1871," in Marie-Claude Marandet (ed.), *Violence(s) de la préhistoire à nos jours: les sources et leur interprétation*, Presses universitaires de Perpignan, 2011, 255–72.

Berlière, Jean-Marc, and Le Goarant de Tromelin, François, *Liaisons dangereuses: miliciens, truands, résistants, Paris 1944*, Paris: Perrin, 2013.

Berstein, Serge, "L'historien et la culture politique," *Vingtième Siècle*, 35 (September–December 1992), 67–77.

Blanc, Julien, *Au commencement de la Résistance: du côté du Musée de l'Homme, 1940–1941*, Paris :Seuil, 2010.

Blank, Ralph, "Wartime Daily Life and the Air War on the Home Front," in Jörg Echternkamp (ed.), *Germany and the Second World War*, vol. IX-1, Oxford : Clarendon Press 2008 (first published in German 2004), 464–67.

Blatman, Daniel, *The Death Marches: The Final Phase of Nazi Genocide*, Cambridge, MA: Belknap Press of Harvard University Press, 2011.

Bloch, Marc, *The Historian's Craft*, Manchester University Press, 1954.

  "Pour une histoire comparée des sociétés européennes," *Revue de synthèse historique*, 46 (1928), 347–80.

Boddice, Rob, "The History of Emotions," in Sasha Handley, Rohan McWilliam and Lucy Noakes (eds.), *New Directions in Social and Cultural History*, London: Bloomsbury, 2018, 45–62.

Böhler, Jochen, Wernz, Francine and Eismann, Gaël, "L'adversaire imaginaire: la 'guerre des francs-tireurs' de l'armée allemande en Belgique en 1914 et de la Wehrmacht en Pologne en 1939. Considérations comparatives," in Eismann and Martens (eds.), *Occupation et répression militaire allemandes*, 17–40.

Boivin, Michel, "La Garde territoriale dans la Manche en mai–juin 1940," *Cahiers des Annales de Normandie*, 26 (1995), 571–76.

Böll, Heinrich, *Silent Angel*, trans. Breon Mitchell, New York: St. Martin's Press, 1994; written in 1949 and published in full in German in 1992.

Boly, René, *L'orge et la terre, Mai 1940*, Louvergny: Éditions Terres Noires, 2000.

Bowman, Martin W., *RAF Escapers and Evaders in World War II*, Barnsley: Pen & Sword, 2014.

Brewalan, Biger and Sudre, René-Pierre, "Kérandel, Jean-Marie," in *Le Maitron: dictionnaire des fusillés, 1940–1944*, https://fusilles-40-44.maitron.fr/?article158335.

BIBLIOGRAPHY

Brickhill, Paul, *The Great Escape*, New York: W.W. Norton, 1950.

Reach for the Sky: The Story of Douglas Bader DSO, DFC, London: Odhams Press, 1954.

Broche, François, Caïtucoli, Georges and Muracciole, Jean-François (eds.), *Dictionnaire de la France libre*, Paris: Robert Laffont, 2010.

Browning, Christopher R., *The Final Solution and the German Foreign Office*, London and New York: Holmes & Meier, 1978.

"The Holocaust: Basis and Objective of the Volkgsemeinschaft?" in Steber and Gotto (eds.), *Visions of Community in Nazi Germany*, 217–39.

Ordinary Men: Reserve Police Battalion 101 and the Final Solution in Poland, New York: HarperCollins, 1992.

Brunvand, Jan Harold, *The Vanishing Hitchhiker*, New York: W.W. Norton, 1981.

Burleigh, Michael and Wippermann, Wolfgang, *The Racial State: Germany, 1933–1945*, Cambridge University Press, 1991.

Burrin, Philippe, *France under the Germans: Collaboration and Compromise*, New York: New Press, 1996.

Burt, Kendal and Leasor, James, *The One that Got Away. With an Account of Franz von Werra's Experiences as a Prisoner-of-War in England and in Canada*, London: Collins, 1956. Repr. London: House of Stratus, 2001.

Camarade, Hélène, *Écritures de la Résistance: le journal intime sous le Troisième Reich*, Toulouse: Presses universitaires du Mirail, 2007.

Chapoutot, Johann, "Le nazisme et les Noirs: histoire d'un racisme spécifique," in Chapoutot and Vigreux (eds.), *Des soldats noirs face au Reich*, 35–58.

La révolution culturelle nazie, Paris : Gallimard, 2016.

Chapoutot, Johann and Vigreux, Jean (eds.), *Des soldats noirs face au Reich: les massacres racistes de 1940*, Paris: PUF, 2015.

Confino, Alan, "Edgar Reitz's *Heimat* and German Nationhood: Film, Memory, and Understandings of the Past," *German History*, 16/2 (1998), 185–208.

Connelly, Mark, *We Can Take It: Britain and the Memory of the Second World War*, London: Pearson Education, 2004.

Conze, Eckart, Frei, Norbert, Hayes, Peter and Zimmermann, Moshe, *Das Amt und die Vergangenheit: deutsche Diplomaten im Dritten Reich und in der Bundesrepublik*, Munich: Karl Blessing Verlag, 2010.

Crémieux-Brilhac, Jean-Louis, *Les Français de l'an 40*, vol. II: *Ouvriers et soldats*, Paris: Gallimard, 1990.

Dahrendorf, Ralf, *Gesellschaft und Demokratie in Deutschland*, Munich: Piper, 1965.

Danker, Uwe and Schwabe, Astrid, *Schleswig-Holstein und der Nationalsozialismus*, Neumünster: Wachholtz, 2005.

Deacon, Valérie, "International Cooperation, Transnational Circulation: Escape, Evasion, and Resistance in France, 1940–1945," *French Politics, Culture & Society*, 37/1 (Spring 2019), 70–89.

Debruyne, Emmanuel and Rémy, Adeline, "Les réseaux belges et leurs finances, 1940–1944," in Robert Vandenbussche (ed.), *La clandestinité en Belgique et en zone interdite (1940–1944)*, Lille: Le Septentrion, 2009, 113–58.

328 BIBLIOGRAPHY

Delporte, Christian "Nimbus contre Mickey: le dessin animé au service de la propagande," in Delporte, *Images et politique en France au XX° siècle*, Paris: Éditions nouveau monde, 2006.

Diamond, Hanna, *Fleeing Hitler: France 1940*, Oxford University Press, 2007.

"France in 1940: Images of Refugees," *in* Kesteloot, Martens and Prauser (eds.), *La guerre de 40*, 195–210.

Dirou, Armel, "Les francs-tireurs pendant la guerre de 1870–1871," *Stratégique*, 93–96/1–4 (2009), 279–317.

Dombrowski Risser, Nicole, *France under Fire: German Invasion, Civilian Flight, and Family Survival during World War II*, Cambridge University Press, 2012.

Donovan, Pamela, *No Way of Knowing: Crime, Urban Legends and the Internet*, New York and London: Routledge, 2004.

Doron, Roland and Parot, François, *Dictionnaire de psychologie*, Paris: PUF, 2007.

Douzou, Laurent, Frank, Robert, Peschanski, Denis and Veillon, Dominique (ed.), *La Résistance et les Français: villes, centres et logiques de décision*, Paris: IHTP, 1995.

Ducret, André, "Le concept de 'configuration' et ses implications empiriques: Elias avec et contre Weber," *SociologieS: La recherche en actes: Régimes d'explication en sociologie*, 11 April 2011, http://journals.openedition.org/sociologies/3459.

Echternkamp, Jörg and Martens, Stefan (eds.), *Experience and Memory: The Second World War in Europe*, New York: Berghahn, 2010.

(eds.), *Germany and the Second World War*, vol. IX-1, Oxford: Clarendon Press, 2008; first published in German 2004.

Eismann, Gaël, "L'escalade d'une répression à visage légal: les pratiques judiciaires des tribunaux du Militärbefehlshaber in Frankreich, 1940–1944," in Eismann and Martens (eds.), *Occupation et répression militaire allemandes*, 127–67.

Hôtel Majestic: ordre et sécurité en France occupée (1940–1944), Paris: Tallandier, 2010.

"La norme à l'épreuve de l'idéologie: le franc-tireur en droit allemand et la figure du terroriste judéo-bolchévique en France pendant la Seconde Guerre mondiale," in Antoine Mégie and Virginie Sansico (eds.), *Des "terroristes" dans le prétoire: qualifier et punir la violence politique d'hier à aujourd'hui*, *Histoire@Politique*, 45 (2021), https://journals.openedition.org/histoirepolitique/1874.

Eismann, Gaël and von List, Corinna, "Les fonds des tribunaux allemands (1940–1945) conservés au BAVCC à Caen," *Francia: Forschungen zur Westeuropäischen Geschichte*, 39 (2012), 347–78.

Eismann, Gaël and Martens, Stefan (eds.), *Occupation et répression militaire allemandes*, Paris: Autrement, 2007.

BIBLIOGRAPHY 329

Eley, Geoff, *Nazism as Fascism: Violence, Ideology, and the Ground of Consent in Germany, 1930–1945*, London and New York: Routledge, 2013.

Elias, Norbert, *The Civilizing Process*, trans. Edmund Jephcott, new edn, Oxford: Blackwell, 1994; first published in German 1939.

The Germans: Power Struggles and the Development of Habitus in the Nineteenth and Twentieth Centuries, New York: Columbia University Press, 1996; first published in German 1989.

"National Peculiarities of British Public Opinion," talk given in October 1960 in Bad Wildungen, Hesse, excerpts in *Essays II: On Civilising Process, State Formation and National Identity*, Dublin: UCD Press, 2008, 230–55.

"Trop tard ou trop tôt: notes sur la classification de la théorie du processus et de la figuration," in *Norbert Elias par lui-même*, Paris: Fayard/Pluriel, 1991.

Espagne, Michel, interview with Gérard Noiriel, "Transferts culturels: l'exemple franco- allemand," *Genèses*, 8 (June 1992), 146–54.

Les transferts culturels franco-allemands, Paris: PUF, 1999.

Fabréguet, Michel, "Un groupe de réfugiés politiques: les républicains espagnols des camps d'internement français aux camps de concentration nationaux-socialistes (1939–1941)," *Revue d'histoire de la deuxième guerre mondiale et des conflits contemporains*, 144 (October 1986) 19–38.

Facon, Patrick *L'armée de l'air dans la tourmente: la bataille de France 1939–1940*, Paris: Economica, 2005.

Farenc, Claude, "Guerre, information et propagande en 1870–1871: le cas de la Champagne," *Revue d'histoire moderne et contemporaine*, 31/1 (January–March 1984), 27–63.

Fargettas, Julien, *Les tirailleurs sénégalais: les soldats noirs entre légendes et réalités, 1939–1945*, Paris: Tallandier, 2012.

Febvre, Lucien, "Comment reconstituer la vie affective d'autrefois? La sensibilité et l'histoire," *Annales d'histoire sociale*, 3/2 (1941); repr. in Febvre, *Combats pour l'histoire*, Paris: Armand Colin, 1953, 221–38.

"Une vue d'ensemble: histoire et psychologie," *Encyclopédie française*, vol. VIII (1938); repr. in Febvre, *Combats pour l'histoire*, Paris: Armand Colin, 1953), 207–20.

Fenouillet, Fabien, *Les théories de la motivation*, Paris: Dunod, 2003.

Feuerhahn, Wolf, "Humours nationaux: le regard situé de Norbert Elias," in *Humour "anglais"*, special issue of *Humoresques*, 36 (2012), 67–80.

Flanner, Jannet, *Jannet Flanner's World: Uncollected Writings, 1932–1975*, New York: Harcourt Brace Jovanovich, 1978, article reprinted in Hans Magnus Enzensberger (ed.), *L'Europe en ruines: textes choisis et présentés par l'auteur*, Aix-en-Provence: Solin/Actes Sud, 1995, 101–09.

Florentin, Eddy, *Quand les Alliés bombardaient la France*, Paris: Perrin, 1997.

Fontaine, Thomas, *Déporter: politiques de déportation et répression en France occupée, 1940–1944*, Paris: Panthéon-Sorbonne, 2013, https://tel.archives-ouvertes.fr/tel-01325232/document.

330 BIBLIOGRAPHY

Foot, M.R.D. and Langley, J.M., *MI9: Escape and Evasion, 1939–1945*, London: Bodley Head, 1979.

Ford, Herbert, *Flee the captor: The Story of the Dutch-Paris Underground and Its Compassionnate Leader, John Henry Weidner*, Hagerstown, MD: Review and Herald Publishing Association, 1994; 1st edn 1966.

Fraenkel, Ernst, *The Dual State: A Contribution to the Theory of Dictatorship*, Oxford and New York: Octagon, 1941.

Francis, Martin, *The Flyer: British Culture and the Royal Air Force 1939–1945*, Oxford University Press, 2008.

Frank, Robert, "Avant-propos: pourquoi une nouvelle revue?," *Monde(s)*, 1 (May 2012), 7–10.

Franks, Norman and Muggleton, Simon, *Flying among Heroes: The Story of Squadron Leader T.C.S. Cooke DFX AFC DFM AE*, Stroud: Spellmount, 2012.

Freeman, Gregory A. *The Last Mission of the Wham Bam Boys: Courage, Tragedy, and Justice in World War II*, New York: Palgrave Macmillan, 2011.

Friedlander, Henry, *The Origins of Nazi Genocide. From Euthanasia to the Final Solution*, Chapel Hill: University of North Carolina Press, 1995.

Friedrich, Jörg, *The Fire: The Bombing of Germany, 1940–1945*, New York: Columbia University Press, 2008; first published in German 2002.

Frieser, Karl-Heinz, *The Blitzkrieg legend: The 1940 Campaign in the West*, trans. from German, Annapolis, MD: Naval Institute Press, 2013.

"La légende de la 'Blitzkrieg'," in Vaïsse (ed.), *Mai-juin 1940*, 75–85.

Fritzsche, Peter, "Babi Yar But Not Auschwitz: What Did Germans Know about the Final Solution?" in Susanna Schraftstetter and Alan Steinweis (eds.), *The Germans and the Holocaust: Popular Responses to the Persecution and Murder of the Jews*, New York and Oxford: Berghahn, 2016, 85–104.

Fulbrook, Mary, "Social Relations and Bystander Responses to Violence: Kristallnacht, November 1938," in Grüner and Ross (eds.), *New Perspectives on Kristallnacht*, 69–87.

Gardes, Jean-Claude, "Fragilité et force du pouvoir: l'Allemagne, 1933–1939," in *L'image du pouvoir dans le dessin d'actualité. Le temps des monarques. Le temps des chefs. Le temps des leaders*, special issue of *Matériaux pour l'histoire de notre temps*, 28 (1992), 26–30.

Geiger, Wolfgang, *L'image de la France dans l'Allemagne nazie, 1933–1945*, Presses universitaires de Rennes, 1999.

Gellately, Robert, *Backing Hitler: Consent and Coercion in Nazi Germany*, Oxford University Press, 2001.

Gellhorn, Martha *The Face of War*, New York: Simon & Schuster, 1959, excerpted in Hans Magnus Enzensberger (ed.), *L'Europe en ruines: textes choisis et présentés par l'auteur*, Aix-en-Provence: Solin/Actes Sud, 1995, 110–21.

Gide, André, *Ainsi soit-il ou les jeux sont faits* (written in 1950–51), Paris: Gallimard, 2001.

BIBLIOGRAPHY 331

Gildea, Robert, *Fighters in the shadows: A New History of the French Resistance*, London: Faber & Faber, 2015.

Gildea, Robert and Thames, Ismee (eds.), *Fighters across Frontiers: Transnational Resistance across Europe*, Manchester University Press, 2020.

Giraudier, Vincent, *Les Bastilles de Vichy: répression politique et internement administratif*, Paris: Tallandier, 2009.

Gottwaldt, Alfred, Kampe, Norbert and Klein, Peter (eds.), *NS-Gewaltherrschaft: Beiträge zur historischen Forschung und juristischen Aufarbeitung*, Berlin: Edition Hentrich, 2005.

Grabowski, Jan, *Hunt for the Jews: Betrayal and Murder in German-Occupied Poland*. Bloomington: Indiana University Press, 2013.

Granet, Marie, *Ceux de la Résistance*, Paris: Éditions de Minuit, 1964.

Greene Ottis, Sherri, *Silent heroes: Downed Airmen and the French Underground*, Lexington: University Press of Kentucky, 2001.

Grimm, Barbara, "Lynchmorde an alliierten Fliegern im Zweiten Weltkrieg," in Dietmar Süss (ed.), *Deutschland im Luftkrieg: Geschichte und Erinnerung*, Munich: Oldenburg Wissenschaftsverlag, 2007, 71–84.

Grinshpun, Yana, "Introduction. De la victime à la victimisation: la construction d'un dispositif discursif," *Argumentation et analyse du discours*, 23 (2019), https://journals.openedition.org/aad/3400.

Gross, Jan T., *Neighbors: The Destruction of the Jewish Community in Jedwabne, Poland*, Princeton University Press, 2001.

"Opportunistic Killings and Plunder of Jews by Their Neighbors: A Norm or an Exception in German Occupied Europe?" in Christian Wiese and Paul Betts (eds.), *Years of Persecution, Years of Extermination: Saul Friedländer and the Future of Holocaust Studies*, London: Continuum, 2010, 269–86.

Grüner, Wolf, *The Persecution of the Jews in Berlin 1933–1945: A Chronology of Measures Taken by the Authorities in the German Capital*, Berlin: Stiftung Topographie des Terrors, 2014.

Grüner, Wolf and Ross, Steven J. (eds.), *New Perspectives on Kristallnacht: After 80 years, the Nazi Pogrom in Global Comparison*, West Lafayette, IN: Purdue University Press, 2019.

Guicherd, J. and Matriot, C., "La terre des régions dévastées," *Journal d'agriculture pratique, de jardinage et d'économie domestique*, 34 (February 1921), 154–56.

Haase, Norbert, *Das Reichskriegsgericht und der Widerstand gegen die nationalso-zialistische Herrschaft*, Berlin: Katalog zur Sonderausstellung der Gedenkstätte deutscher Widerstand in Zusammenarbeit mit der Neuen Richtervereinigung, 1993.

Hadaway, Stuart, *Missing Believed Killed: The Royal Air Force and the Search for Missing Aircrew 1939–1952*, Barnsley: Pen & Sword, 2008.

Hall, Kevin T., "Luftgangster over Germany: The Lynching of American Airmen in the Shadow of the Air War," *Historical Social Research*, 43/2 (2018), 277–312.

Terror Flyers: The Lynching of American Airmen in Nazi Germany, Bloomington: Indiana University Press, 2021.

Hassel, Katrin, *Kriegsverbrechen vor Gericht: die Kriegsverbrechenprozesse vor Militärgerichten in der britische Besatzungszone unter dem Royal Warrant vom 18. Juni 1945 (1945-1949)*, Baden-Baden: Nomos, 2009.

Heartfield, James, *Unpatriotic History of the Second World War*, Croydon: Zero Books, 2012.

Heinemann, Isabelle, "Race," in Baranowski, Nolzen and Szejnmann (eds.), *Companion to Nazi Germany*, 499–511.

Held, Renate, *Kriegsgefangenschaft in Grossbritannien: deutsche Soldaten des Zweiten Weltkriegs in britischem Gewahrsam*, Munich: R. Oldenbourg Verlag, 2008.

Herbert, Ulrich, *Hitler's Foreign Workers: Enforced Foreign Labor in Germany under the Third Reich*, Cambridge University Press, 1997.

Heuser, Beatrice and Shamir, Eitan (eds.), *Insurgencies and Counter-Insurgencies: National Styles and Strategic Cultures*, Cambridge University Press, 2017.

Hoffmann, Georg, *Fliegerlynchjustiz: Gewalt gegen abgeschossene alliierte Flugzeugbesatzungen 1943-1945*, Paderborn: Ferdinand Schöningh, 2015.

Hooton, E.R., *Eagle in Flames: The Fall of the Luftwaffe*, Leicester: Brockhampton Press, 1999.

Horne, John and Kramer, Alan, *German Atrocities 1914: A History of Denial*, New Haven, CT: Yale University Press, 2001.

"Zur Rezeption des Buches seit 2001," preface to the 2018 German edition of *German Atrocities, Deutsche Kriegsgreuel 1914: die umstrittene Wahrheit*, Hamburger Edition, 2018, 3–36.

Hull, Isabel V., *Absolute Destruction: Military Culture and the Practices of War in Imperial Germany*, Ithaca, NY: Cornell University Press, 2005.

A Scrap of Paper: Breaking and Making International Law during the Great War, Ithaca, NY: Cornell University Press, 2014.

Hylton, Stuart, *Their Darkest Hour: The Hidden History of the Home Front, 1939-1945*, Stroud: Sutton, 2003.

Ingrao, Christian, *Croire et détruire: les intellectuels dans la machine de guerre SS*, Paris: Fayard, 2010.

Jackson, Julian, "Conclusions," in Allorant, Castagnez and Prost (eds.), *Le Moment 1940*, 257–64.

The Fall of France: The Nazi Invasion of 1940, Oxford University Press, 2003.

Jackson, Julian and Wilson, Jérôme, "Étrange défaite française ou étrange victoire anglaise?" in Vaïsse (ed.), *Mai-juin 1940*, 177–213.

Jackson, Peter, "Returning to the fall of France: Recent Work on the Causes and Consequences of the 'Strange Defeat' of 1940," *Modern and Contemporary France*, 12/4 (2004), 513–36.

Jackson, Robert, *A Taste of Freedom*, London: Arthur Parker, 1964.

Janes, Keith, *They Came from Burgundy: The Story of the Bourgogne Escape Line*, Market Harbourough, Leics: Matador Self-Publishing, 2017.

BIBLIOGRAPHY

Janes, Peter Scott and Janes, Keith, *Conscript Heroes*, Boston: Paul Mould, 2004.

Jeanneney, Jean-Noël (ed.), *Une idée fausse est un fait vrai: les stéréotypes nationaux en Europe*, Paris : Odile Jacob, 2000.

Jordan, Ulrike (ed.), *Conditions of Surrender: Britons and Germans Witness the End of the War*, London and New York: I.B. Tauris, 1997.

Jörg, Arnold, *The Allied War and Urban Memory: The Legacy of Strategic Bombing in Germany*, Cambridge University Press, 2011.

Joule, Robert-Vincent and Beauvois, Jean-Léon, *Petit traité de manipulation à l'intention des honnêtes gens*, Presses universitaires de Grenoble, 1999.

Kaelble, Hartmut, "Comparative and Transnational History," *Ricerche di storia politica*, special issue, 60 (October 2017), 15–24.

"Les mutations du comparatisme international," *Histoires croisées: réflexions sur la comparaison internationale en histoire. Les cahiers Irice*, 5 (2010), 9–19.

Keller, Sven, "Les marches de la mort: la dimension sociale de la violence dans la phase de la fin de la guerre," *Revue d'histoire de la Shoah*, 209 (October 2010), 545–64.

"Total Defeat: War, Society and Violence in the Last Year of National Socialism," in Baranowski, Nolzen and Szejnmann (eds.), *Companion to Nazi Germany*, 247–57.

Volksgemeinschaft am Ende: Gesellschaft und Gewalt, 1944/1945, Munich: Oldenbourg Verlag, 2013.

Keller, Ulrich, *Schuldfragen: Belgischer Untergrundkrieg und deutsche Vergeltung im August 1914*, Paderborn: Ferdinand Schöningh, 2017.

Kershaw, Ian, *The End: The Defiance and Destruction of Hitler's Germany, 1944–1945*, London: Penguin, 2012.

Kessel, Martina, "Race and Humor in Nazi Germany," in Pendas, Roseman and Wetzell (eds.), *Beyond the Racial State*, 381–401.

Kesteloot, C., Martens, S. and Prauser, S. (eds.), *La guerre de 40: se battre, subir, se souvenir*, Lille: Presses universitaires du Septentrion, 2012.

Kiesler, Charles, *The Psychology of Commitment: Experiments Linking Behavior to Belief*, New York and London: Academic Press, 1971.

Kinnis, Arthur G. amd Booker, Stanley, *168 Jump into Hell: A True Story of Betrayed Allied Airmen*, Victoria, Canada: Arthur G. Kinnis, 1999.

Kirwin, Gerald, "Allied Bombing and Nazi Domestic Propaganda," *European History Quaterly*, 15 (1985), 341–62.

Kitson, Samuel, "Criminals or liberators? Public Opinion and the Allied Bombing of France (1940–1945)," in Baldoli, Knapp and Overy (eds.), *Bombing, States and Peoples*, 279–97.

Klandermans, Bert "Motivations to Action," in Donatella Della Porta and Mario Diani (eds.), *The Oxford Handbook of Social Movements*, Oxford University Press, 2015.

Klemperer, Victor, *Language of the Third Reich: LTI, Lingua Tertii Imperii. A Philologist's Notebook*, London and New Brunswick, NJ: Athlone Press, 1999; first published in German 1946.

BIBLIOGRAPHY

Knapp, Andrew, "The Allied Bombing Offensive in the British Media, 1942–1945," in Andrew Knapp and Hilary Footitt (eds.), *Liberal Democracies at War*, London: Bloomsbury, 2013, 39–66.

Les Français sous les bombes alliées, 1940–1945, Paris: Tallandier, 2014.

Lacour-Astol, Catherine, *Le genre de la Résistance: la Résistance féminine dans le Nord de la France*, Paris: Presses de Sciences Po, 2015.

Lagrou, Pieter and Le Gac, Julie, "Guerre honorable sur le front de l'Ouest: crime, punition et réconciliation," in Eismann and Martens (eds.), *Occupation et répression militaires allemandes*, 201–19.

Lambauer, Barbara, *Otto Abetz et les Français ou l'envers de la Collaboration*, Paris: Fayard, 2001.

Langlois, Caroline et Reynaud, Michel, *Elles et eux de la Résistance*, Paris: Tirésias, 2003.

Lappin, Eleonore, "The Death Marches of Hungarian Jews through Austria in the Spring of 1945," www.yadvashem.org/download/about_holocaust/studies/lappin_full.pdf; first published in German in Thomas Buchner and Heidemarie Uhl (eds.), *Amstetten 1945: Kriegsende und Erinnerung*, Stadtgemeinde Amstetten, 2015, 91–117.

Leclercq, Jocelyn, Association Antiq'Air Flandre Artois, "Les chutes d'avions alliés sur le territoire du Nord-Pas-de-Calais (1940–1944): chronologie, cartographie, bilan humain," in Le Maner (ed.), *Tombés du ciel*, 101–20.

Le Foulon, Marie-Laure, *Le procès de Ravensbrück: Germaine Tillion: de la vérité à la justice*. Paris: Cherche-Midi, 2016.

Leleu, J.-L., Passera, F., Quellien, J. and Daeffler, M. (eds.), *La France pendant la Seconde Guerre mondiale*, Paris: Fayard and Ministry of Defense, 2010.

Le Maner, Yves (ed.), *Tombés du ciel: les aviateurs abattus au-dessus du Nord-Pas-de-Calais (1940–1944)*, Saint-Omer: La Coupole, 2008.

Le Naour, Jean-Yves, *La honte noire: l'Allemagne et les troupes coloniales françaises, 1914–1945*, Paris: Hachette, 2003.

Lenormand, Paul, *Vers l'armée du peuple: autorité, pouvoir et culture militaire en Tchécoslovaquie de Munich à la fin du stalinisme*, doctoral thesis, Sciences Po, Paris, 2019.

L'Estrange, Alfred Guy Kingan, *History of English Humour*, 2 vols. London: Hurst & Blackett, 1878.

Levisse-Touzé, Christine (ed.), *La campagne de 1940*, Paris: Tallandier, 2001.

Loez, André, "Petit répertoire critique des concepts de la Grande Guerre," December 2005, http://crid1418.org/espace_scientifique/textes/conceptsgg_01.htm.

Loez, André and Mariot, Nicolas (ed.), *Obéir/Désobéir: les mutineries de 1917 en perspective*, Paris: La Découverte, 2008.

Longerich, Peter, *Hitlers Stellvertreter: Führung der Partei und Kontrolle des Staatsapparates durch den Stab Hess und die Partei-Kanzlei Bormann*, Munich: Institut für Zeitgeschichte, 1992.

BIBLIOGRAPHY

Longuet, Stéphane and Genet-Rouffiac, Nathalie (eds.), *Les réseaux de résistance de la France Combattante*, Paris: Economica; Vincennes: Service historique de la Défense, 2013.

Mackay, Robert, *Half the Battle: Civilian Morale in Britain during the Second World War*, Manchester University Press, 2002.

Mackenzie, Simon Paul, *The Home Guard: A Military and Political History*, Oxford University Press, 1995.

Maier, Klaus A. et al., *Germany and the Second World War*, vol. II, ed. Militärgeschichtliches Forschungsamt, trans. Dean S. McMurray and Ewald Osers, Oxford: Clarendon Press, 1991.

Maitron, Jean and Pennetier, Claude, *Dictionnaire biographique du mouvement ouvrier français*, Paris: Éditions Ouvrières, 1988.

Malis, Christian, "Après le Blitzkrieg: le réveil de la pensée militaire française (juin 1940 – mars 1942). Le rôle de la revue *La France libre*." *Histoire, géopolitique et stratégie*, www.stratisc.org/84-Malis.htm.

Mallmann, Klaus-Michael, "'Volksjustiz gegen anglo-amerikanische Mörder': die Massaker an die westalliierten Fliegern und Fallschirmspringern 1944/45," in Gottwaldt, Kampe and Klein (eds.), *NS-Gewaltherrschaft*, 202–14.

Mandler, Peter, *The English National Character: The History of an Idea, from Edmund Burke to Tony Blair*, New Haven, CT: Yale University Press, 2006.

Marchetti, Stéphane, *Affiches 1939–1945: images d'une certaine France*, Lausanne: Edita, 1982.

Marcot, François, "Comment écrire l'histoire de la Résistance," *Le Débat*, 177/5 (2013), 173–85.

"Patriotisme," in Marcot, Levisse-Touzé and Leroux (eds.), *Dictionnaire historique de la Résistance*, 649–50.

"Pour une sociologie de la Résistance: intentionnalité et fonctionnalité," in Antoine Prost (ed.), *Pour une histoire sociale de la Résistance: le mouvement social*, Paris, Éditions de l'Atelier, 1997, 21–42.

Marcot, François and Levisse-Touzé, Christine, with the collaboration of Bruno Leroux (eds.), *Dictionnaire historique de la Résistance*, Paris: Robert Laffont, 2006.

Martin, Jacqueline and Paul, "La chute du capitaine Mölders: témoignage des militaires du 195th RALT," www.aerostories.org, 2001.

Meichtry, Wilfred, *Du und ich – ewig eins: die Geschichte der Geschwister von Werra*, Frankfurt: Eichborn, 2001.

Meng, Michael, *Shattered Spaces: Encountering Jewish Spaces in Postwar Germany and Poland*, Cambridge, MA: Harvard University Press, 2011.

Merritt, Anna J. and Merritt, Richard L., *Public Opinion in Occupied Germany*, Urbana: University of Illinois Press, 1970.

Messu, Michel, *L'ère de la victimisation*, Paris: Payot, 2018.

Milgram, Stanley, *Obedience to Authority: An Experimental View*, London: Tavistock, 1974.

Miller, Arthur G., Collins, Barry and Brief, Diana (eds.), *Perspectives on Obedience to Authority : The Legacy of the Milgram Experiments*, special issue of *Journal of Social Issues*, 51/3 (Fall 1995).

Mitscherlich, Alexander and Margaret, *The Inability to Mourn: Principles of Collective Behavior*, New York: Grove Press, 1975; first published in German 1968.

Mommsen, Hans, "The Dissolution of the Third Reich: Crisis Management and Collapse, 1943–1945," *Bulletin of the German Historical Institute*, 27 (Fall 2000), 9–24.

Moore, Aaron William, *Bombing the City: Civilian Accounts of the Air War in Britain and Japan, 1939–1945*, Cambridge University Press, 2018.

Moore, William, *The Long Way Round: An Escape through Occupied France*, London: Lee Cooper, 1986.

Mosse, George L., *Fallen Soldiers: Reshaping the Memory of the World Wars*, Oxford University Press, 1990.

Muracciole, Jean-François, "Français libres, définition et décompte," "Français libres, devenir social des," et "Français libres, sociologie des," in François Broche et al. (eds.), *Dictionnaire de la France libre*, 616–22.

Murphy, Brendan, *Turncoat: The Strange Case of Traitor Sergeant Harold Cole: The Worst Traitor of the War*, London: Macdonald, 1988.

National Association for the Advancement of Colored People, *Thirty Years of Lynching in the United States, 1889–1918*, New York: NAACP, 1919.

Neitzel, Sönke and Welzer, Harald, *Soldaten: On Fighting, Killing and Dying. The Secret World of Transcripts of German POWs*, New York: Alfred A. Knopf, 2012.

Nicholls, Anthony J. "The German 'National Character' in British Perspective," in Ulrike Jordan (ed.), *Conditions of Surrender*, 26–39.

Nivet, Philippe, "Les populations civiles: le cas de la Somme en 1940," in Allorant, Castagnez and Prost (eds.), *Le Moment 1940*, 51–62.

Noakes, Lucy, "'Serve to Save': Gender, Citizenship and Civil Defence in Britain 1937–1941," *Journal of Contemporary History*, 47/4 (2012), 734–53.

    War and the British: Gender and National Identity, 1939–91, London: I.B. Taurus, 1998.

Nolte, Ernst, *Three Faces of Fascism: Action Française, Italian Fascism, National Socialism*, trans. Leila Vennewitz, New York: Holt, Rinehart & Winston, 1965.

Nord, Philip, *France 1940: Defending the Republic*, New Haven, CT: Yale University Press, 2015.

Ōe, Kenzaburō, *The Catch and Other War Stories*, Tokyo: Kodansha International, 1981; 1st edn 1957.

Orlow, Dietrich, *The History of the Nazi Party*, vol. II: *1933–1945*, University of Pittsburgh Press, 1973.

Overy, Richard, *The Air War, 1939–1945*, London: Europa, 1980.

    The Battle of Britain, London: Penguin, 2001.

BIBLIOGRAPHY

The Bombing War, Europe 1939–1945, London: Allen Lane, 2013.

"The German Home Front under the Bombs," in Baranowski, Nolzen and Szejnmann (eds.), *Companion to Nazi Germany*, 231–41.

The Penguin Historical Atlas of the Third Reich, London: Penguin, 1996.

Pallud, Jean-Paul, "Show Trial at Luchy," *After the Battle*, 54 (1986), 50–53.

Papp, Julien, *La Résistance dans l'Eure*, Epinal : Éditions du Sapin d'or, 1988.

Pasquay, Jean-Nicolas, "De Gaulle, les FFL et la Résistance vus par les responsables de la Wehrmacht," *Revue historique des armées*, 256 (2009), 43–65.

Patemann, Colin and Clutton-Brock, Oliver, *Unwanted Hero: The Flying Career of Squadron Leader Donald Barnard DFC, 1937–1955*, Stroud: Fonthill, 2012.

Paxton, Robert O., *Vichy France: Old Guard and New Order*, New York: Columbia University Press, 2001; 1st edn 1972.

Pendas, Devin O., Roseman, Mark and Wetzel, Richard F. (eds), *Beyond the Racial State: Rethinking Nazi Germany*, Cambridge University Press, 2017.

Perry, Gina, *Behind the Shock Machine: The Untold Story of the Notorious Milgram Psychology Experiments*, Brunswick, Victoria: Scribe, 2012.

Peschanski, Denis, "Vichysto-résistants," in Marcot, Levisse-Touzé and Leroux (eds.), *Dictionnaire historique de la Résistance*, 845–47.

Pieper, Henning, "From fighting 'Francs-Tireurs' to Genocide: German Counterinsurgency in the Second World War," in Beatrice Heuser and Eitan Shamir (eds.), *Insurgencies and Counter-Insurgencies*, 149–67.

Pinault, Michel, "Fernand Holweck," in *Le Maitron: Dictionnaire des fusillés, 1940–1944*, https://fusilles-40-44.maitron.fr/spip.php?article149039.

Pollack, Guillaume, *Les réseaux de la Résistance en France (1940–1945)*, Paris: Tallandier, 2022.

Pollen, Annebella, "Research Methodology in Mass Observation Past and Present: 'Scientifically, about as valuable as a chimpanzee's tea party at the zoo'?," *History Workshop Journal*, 75/1 (Spring 2013), 213–23.

Poznanski, Renée, "Antisemitism and the Rescue of Jews in France: An Odd Couple?" in Semelin, Andrieu and Gensburger (eds.), *Resisting Genocide*, 83–100.

Price, Alfred, *Battle of Britain Day, 15 September 1940*, London: Greenhill, 1990.

Prior, Robin, *When Britain Saved the West: The Story of 1940*, New Haven, CT: Yale University Press, 2015.

Przyrembel, Alexandra, "Emotions and National Socialism," in Baranowski, Nolzen and Szejnmann (eds.), *Companion to Nazi Germany*, 399–410.

Quellien, Jean, "L'aide aux soldats britanniques" in Leleu et al. (eds.), *La France pendant la Seconde Guerre mondiale*, 184–85.

"Les bombardements alliés," in Leleu et al. (eds.), *La France pendant la Seconde Guerre mondiale*, 240–45.

"Les pertes humaines," in Leleu et al. (eds.), *La France pendant la Seconde Guerre mondiale*, 262–65.

338 BIBLIOGRAPHY

Raim, Edith, *Nazi Crimes against Jews and German Post-War Justice: The West German Judicial System during Allied Occupation (1945-1949)*, Berlin: De Gruyter Oldenbourg, 2015.

Ramsden, John, "Myths and realities of the 'People's War' in Britain," in Echternkamp and Martens (eds.), *Experience and Memory*, 40-52.

Ramsey, Winston G., "The Rüsselsheim Death March," *After the Battle*, 57 (1987), 1-21.

Richardot, Sophie, "L'apport de la psychologie sociale à la question de l'obéissance: les travaux de Stanley Milgram sur la soumission à l'autorité," in Loez and Mariot (eds.), *Obéir/Désobéir*, 47-59.

Richardson, Derek, *Detachment W: Allied Soldiers and Airmen in Vichy France between 1940 and 1942*, s.l.: Paul Mould, 2004.

Roos, Julia, "Women's Rights, Nationalist Anxiety, and the 'Moral' Agenda in the Early Weimar Republic: Revisiting the 'Black Horror' Campaign against France's African Occupation Troops," *Central European History*, 42 (September 2009), 473-508.

Rose, Sonya O., *Which People's War? National Identity and Citizenship in Britain 1939-1945*, Oxford University Press, 2003.

Rossignol, Dominique, *Histoire de la propagande en France de 1940 à 1944: l'utopie Pétain*, Paris: PUF, 1991.

Schaffer, Ronald, "American Military Ethics in World War II: The Bombing of German Civilians," *Journal of American History*, 67/2 (September 1980), 318-34.

Scheck, Raffael, *Hitler's African victims: The German Army Massacres of Black French soldiers in 1940*, Cambridge University Press, 2006.
  "Les massacres de prisonniers noirs par l'armée allemande en 1940," in Chapoutot and Vigreux (eds.), *Des soldats noirs face au Reich*, 59-100.

Scheu, Erwin, *Frankreich*, Breslau: Ferdinand Hirt, 1923.

Schmider, Klaus, "Werner Mölders und die Bundeswehr: Anmerkungen zum Umgang mit der Geschichte der Wehrmacht," 2016, http://portal-militaergeschichte.de/schmider_moelders.pdf.

Schnatz, Helmut, "Lynchmorde an Fliegern," in Franz Seidler and Alfred de Zayas (eds.), *Kriegsverbrechen in Europa und im Nahen Osten im 20. Jahrhundert*, Hamburg: Mittler, 2002, 118-21.

Schoenbaum, David, *Hitler's Social Revolution: Class and Status in Nazi Germany, 1933-1939*, New York: Doubleday, 1966.

Scianna, Bastian Matteo, "A Predisposition to Brutality? German Practices against Civilians and *Francs-Tireurs* during the Franco-Prussian war 1870-1871 and Their Relevance for the German 'Military *Sonderweg*' Debate," *Small Wars & Insurgencies*, 30/4-5 (2019), 968-93.

Seabury, Paul, *The Wilhelmstrasse: A Study of German Diplomats under the Nazi Regime*, Berkeley: University of California Press, 1954.

BIBLIOGRAPHY

Semelin, Jacques, *Face au totalitarisme: la Résistance civile*, Brussels: André Versaille, 2011.

"Résistance civile," in Marcot, Levisse-Touzé and Leroux, *Dictionnaire historique de la Résistance*, 691–93.

Unarmed against Hitler: Civilian Resistance in Europe, 1939–1943, trans. Suzan Husserl-Kapit, Westport, CT and London: Praeger, 1993; first published in French 1989.

Semelin, Jacques, Andrieu, Claire and Gensburger, Sarah (eds.), *Resisting Genocide: The Multiple Forms of Rescue*, New York: Columbia University Press, 2011.

Shirer, William L, *The Rise and Fall of the Third Reich: A History of Nazi Germany*, New York: Simon & Schuster, 1960.

Showalter, Dennis, "Ce que l'armée française avait compris de la guerre moderne," in Vaïsse (ed.), *Mai–juin 1940*, 29–58.

Solchany, Jean, "Le commandement militaire allemand face aux résistants," in Douzou et al. (eds.), *La Résistance et les Français*, 511–30.

"La lente dissipation d'une légende: la Wehrmacht sous le regard de l'histoire," *Revue d'histoire moderne et contemporaine*, 47/2 (2000), 323–53.

Spraul, Gunter, *Der Franktireurkrieg 1914: Untersuchungen zum Verfall einer Wissenschaft und zum Umgang mit nationalen Mythen*, Berlin: Franck & Timme, 2016.

Stargardt, Nicholas, *The German War: A Nation under Arms, 1939–1945*, London: Bodley Head, 2015.

"Jeux de guerre: les enfants sous le régime nazi," *Vingtième siècle*, 89/1 (2006), 61–76.

'Rumors of Revenge in the Second World War', in B.J. Davis, A. Lüdtke, T. Lindenberger and M. Wildt (eds.), *Alltag, Erfahrung, Eigensinn: Historisch-anthropologische Erkundungen*, Frankfurt: Campus Verlag, 2008, 374–89.

Witnesses of war: Children's Lives under the Nazis, New York: Vintage, 2005.

Steber, Martina and Gotto, Bernhard (eds.), *Visions of Community in Nazi Germany: Social Engineering and Private Lives*, Oxford University Press, 2014.

Strobl, Gerwin, *Bomben auf Oberdonau: Luftkrieg und Lynchmorde an alliierten Fliegern im "Heimatgau des Führers"*, Oberösterreichisches Landesarchiv Linz, 2014.

Struck, Bernhard, Ferris, Kate and Revel, Jacques, "Introduction: Space and Scale in Transnational History," *Size Matters: Scales and Spaces in Transnational and Comparative History*, special issue of *International History Review*, 33/4 (2011), 573–84.

Stülpnagel, Otto von, *Die Wahrheit über die deutschen Kriegsverbrechen*, Berlin: Staatspolitischer Verlag, 1920.

Summerfield, Penny and Peniston-Bird, Corinna, *Contesting Home Defense: Men, Women and the Home Guard in the Second World War*, Manchester University Press, 2007.

340 BIBLIOGRAPHY

Süss, Dietmar, "The Air War, the Public and Cycles of Memory," in Echternkamp and Martens (eds), *Experience and Memory*, 180–96.

Death from the Skies: How the British and the Germans Survived Bombing in World War II, Oxford University Press, 2014; first published in German 2011.

Thiéry, Laurent, "Les massacres de civils dans le Nord de la France en mai–juin 1940," *La Lettre de la Fondation de la Résistance*, 60 (March 2010), 5–6.

"La répression allemande contre les réseaux d'évasion d'aviateurs alliés," in Le Maner (ed.), *Tombés du ciel*, 139–48.

La répression allemande dans le Nord de la France, 1940–1944, Villeneuve d'Ascq: Presses universitaires du Septentrion, 2013.

Ticehurst, Rupert, "The Martens clause and the Laws of armed conflict," *International Review of the Red Cross*, 317 (30 April 1997), www.icrc.org/en/doc/resources/documents/article/other/57jnhy.htm.

Tillion, Germaine, "Le procès des assassins de Ravensbrück," *Voix et Visages*, 7 (March 1947). Repr. in Le Foulon, *Le procès de Ravensbrück*, 189–204.

Todman, Daniel, *Britain's War*, vol. I: *Into Battle, 1937–1941*, and vol. II: *A New World, 1942–1947*, Oxford University Press, 2016–20.

Toppe, Andreas, *Militär und Kriegsvölkerrecht: Rechtsnorm, Fachdiskurs und Kriegspraxis in Deutschland 1899–1940*, Munich: Oldenburg, 2007.

Trivellato, Francesca, *The Familiarity of Strangers: The Sephardic Diaspora, Livorno, and Cross-Cultural Trade in the Early Modern Period*, New Haven, CT :Yale University Press, 2009.

Vaïsse, Maurice (ed.), *Mai–juin 1940: défaite française, victoire allemande, sous l'œil des historiens étrangers*, Paris : Autrement, 2012.

Vidalenc, Jean, *L'exode de mai–juin 1940*, Paris : PUF, 1957.

Vigna, Xavier and Zancarini-Fournel, Michelle, "Les rencontres improbables dans 'les années 68'," *Vingtième Siècle*, 101/1 (2009), 163–77.

von List, Corinna, *Résistantes*, Paris: Alma, 2012.

Wachsmann, Nikolaus, *KL: A history of the Nazi Concentration Camps*, New York: Farrar, Straus and Giroux, 2015.

Weber, Max, *Economy and Society*, vol. I: *An Outline of Interpretive Sociology*, Berkeley: University of California Press, 1978; first published in German 1921.

Welzer, Harald, Moller, Sabine and Tschugnall, Karoline, *Opa war kein Nazi: Nationalsozialismus und Holocaust im Familiengedächtnis*, Frankfurt: Fischer Verlag, 2002.

Whitman, James Q., *Hitler's American Model: The United States and the Making of Nazi Race Law*, Princeton University Press, 2017.

Wiesen, S. Jonathan, "American Lynching in the Nazi Imagination: Race and Extra-Legal Violence in 1930s Germany," *German History*, 36/1 (2018), 38–59.

Wieviorka, Olivier, *The French Resistance*, Cambridge, MA: Harvard University Press, 2016.

BIBLIOGRAPHY   341

Wildt, Michael, *Die Ambivalenz des Volkes: die Nationalsozialismus als Sozialgeschichte*, Berlin: Suhrkamp, 2019.

Hitler's Volksgemeinschaft and the Dynamics of Racial Exclusion: Violence against Jews in Provincial Germany, 1919–1939, New York: Berghahn, 2012; first published in German 2007.

"La violence contre les Juifs en Allemagne après 1933," *Revue d'histoire de la Shoah*, 209 (October 2010), 97–112.

Wolikow, Serge, "Antifascisme," in Marcot, Levisse-Touzé and Leroux (eds.), *Dictionnaire historique de la Résistance*, 639–40.

Zayas, Alfred-Maurice de, "The Wehrmacht Bureau on War Crimes," *Historical Journal*, 35/2 (1992), 383–99.

Zayas, Alfred-Maurice de, with the collaboration of Walter Rabus, *The Wehrmacht War Crimes Bureau, 1939–1945*, Lincoln: University of Nebraska Press, 1989; first published in German 1979.

INDEX

Page numbers in **bold** indicate information in tables; those in *italic* refer to figures and maps.

Abetz, Otto
 repression of local administrative
  bodies, 61
 retaliatory repression of French
  civilians, 7
accounts of downed Luftwaffe airmen
 airmen downed in England
  "treatment beyond reproach,"
   96–98
  Wehrmacht Legal Service,
   96–98
 airmen downed in France
  Wehrmacht Legal Service, 23
Air Forces Escape and Evasion Society
 (AFEES), 175
Allied bombing raids in France, *270*
 anger toward Allies, 167
  political risks, 168
 civilian deaths, 168
 incentivizing anti-German feelings,
  164–67, 173
 national historical narrative,
  exclusion from, 173
 tonnage of bombs dropped, **268**, *269*
 victims, **267**
Allied bombing raids in Germany, *272*
 Allied bombing of Dresden, 217–18
 black airmen as executors, 245–47,
  246
 historiography of German bombings,
  11
 intensification, 206, 217, 219–20
 Jews as instigators of, 169–70,
  243–47, *246*

morale-boosting measures by Nazi
 state
 indemnification, 206–7
 propaganda, 207–8, 227–30, 243
 reprisals, 207, 230–33
 state-sanctioned lynching, 208–12
reprisals
 civilian lynching of airmen,
  231–33
 morale-boosting measures by Nazi
  state, 207, 230–33
 retaliation towards Allied airmen,
  187, 192, 202, 217, 230
 strafing, 217
 suffering and damage, impact of
  experience of, 237–40
 tonnage of bombs dropped,
  268, *269*, *276*
 victims, **267**
American Military Intelligence
 Service (MIS-X),
  17, 114, 262
 danger of German civilians to
  airmen, 204–5
 MI9, relationship with, 263
anti-Allied propaganda, 164
 indifference in France, 168–71
 intensification in France,
  169–71
anti-hero narrative of British, 92
appeasement policy, 70, 72, 88, 105
Appen-Etz
 civilian lynching of airmen, 190–91,
  228

INDEX 343

Asia. *See* Pacific War
autonomy of civilians, 1
  civilian lynching of airmen, 212
  downed airmen in France, 1
  downed airmen in Germany, 219
  "helpers," 162, 164
  See also civilian assistance.

Barcelona
  escape networks, 115
Battle of Britain, 21
  Blitzkrieg in France compared,
    70–71
  downed aeroplanes, 8, 81–83, 86, *96*
  intensification of patriotism,
    18, 67
  model for civilian behaviour, 106,
    169
  mythologizing of, 7, 71–73, 75
    contested historiography,
      72–75
Battle of France, 21–22
  Blitzkrieg "strategy" in France,
    26–27, 70
  débâcle, 23
    changing historiography, 26–29,
      63–65
Beauvais
  civilian assistance,
    131, 135–37
  German propaganda, 53
Bégard, Côtes-du-Nord
  civilian assistance, 140–42
Belgium
  escape networks, 144, 180, 262
  exiled government and escape
    networks, 180
  francs-tireurs, history of, 39
  mass exodus of civilians, 29, 52, 64,
    123
  massacres of civilians,
    36, 53, 260
  preparation for war, 38
  recruitment and training of agents by
    MI9, 114
  resistance of civilians, 109, 137, 180
    retaliatory repression, 154
  See also Brussels.
belligerents, 1
  francs-tireurs, 35–36, 45–46, 260

Hague Convention, 35–37, 45, 75,
  261–62
  See also right of the civilian
    population to resist invasion.
Kriegsonderstraftrechtsverordnung,
  46
Biggin Hill airfield, 13
"Blitz spirit," 105
  contested historiography,
    73–75
Blitz policy in England
  bombing civilian populations,
    21, 85
  class divisions, attempted
    incitement of, 72–73, 80
  bombing of Coventry, 106
  tonnage of bombs dropped,
    268
  V1 attacks, 106
  victims, **267**, *269*
  See also Battle of Britain.
Blitzkrieg "strategy" in France, 26–27,
  70
  Battle of Britain compared, 70–71
Bloch, Marc, 6, 30, 161
  social and political weaknesses of
    French society, 28
  strafing by *Luftwaffe*, 27
bombings
  See also Allied bombing raids in
    France; Allied bombing raids in
    Germany; Battle of Britain; Blitz
    policy in England; Blitzkrieg
    "strategy" in France; Caen,
    Calvados; Coventry, bombing
    of; Dresden, bombing of;
    Guernica, bombing of;
    Hamburg, bombing of;
    historiography of Allied
    bombings; historiography of
    German bombings; Lübeck;
    mortality rates; Munich;
    Rostock; Rouen; strafing.
  map of Allied bombing in Europe,
    270
  map of Allied bombing over France,
    277
  map of Allied bombing over
    Germany, *272*
  number of victims, **267**, *272*

344 INDEX

bombings (cont.)
  tonnage of bombs dropped
    Allied bombing raids in France,
      268, *269*
    Allied bombing raids in Germany,
      268, *269*, *276*
    Blitz policy in England, **268**
Bormann, Martin
  Volksjustiz, 214–15, 228, 250
Boulogne-Billancourt, Seine
  civilian casualties of bombing raids,
    165
Bracklesham Bay Beach, West Sussex
  mistreatment of downed Luftwaffe
    airmen, rumors of,
    99–102
Brest, Finistère
  German bombardment of, 24
  German military tribunals, 23, 56
  occupation, 25, 50
Britain
  appeasement policy, 70
  "German" versus "Nazi," 91
  Luftwaffe prisoners, 1, 7–8
  national cohesion, 107
  See also Battle of Britain; Blitz policy
    in England; Churchill, Winston;
    humor as a British
    characteristic.
British Expeditionary Force in France,
    114, 152
British Missing Research and Enquiry
    Service, 194
Browning, Christopher, 243–44
Brussels
  executions of invasion resisters, 55–56
  German military tribunals, 55–56, 123
  internment of invasion resisters, 55
  resistance, 116
  See also Belgium,
Buchenwald concentration camp, 63,
    124, 193
burial of fallen airmen
  Allied airmen in France, 162
  Allied airmen in Germany, 187–90
  Luftwaffe airmen in England, 82

Caen, Calvados
  Allied bombing raids, 173
Calder, Angus, 74

Calder, Ritchie, 74–76
Canet-Plage, Pyrénées-Orientales
  civilian assistance, 142, 153
Chambéry, Savoie
  escape networks, 115
Churchill, Winston, 72
  Home Guard, 70, 79–81
  retaliation for Blitz, 72–73
  rhetoric and British morale
    armed forces, 76–78
    Battle of Britain, 77
    civilians and the People's War,
      78–80
    evacuation of Dunkirk, 77
  Special Operations Executive, 115
cinema
  German control of French cinema,
    171
civilian (national definitions), 264
  "universal emotional man," 265
civilian assistance, 113, 141, 160
  downing of Allied aircraft/escape of
    Allied servicemen (first
    moments), 134–35, 137, *141*,
    145
    Les Riceys/Paris-Vierzon/Ste
      Léocadie/Canet-Plage escapees,
      142–43
    Plestin-les-Grèvres/Bégard
      escapees, 140–41
    Veules-les-Roses/Rouen-St
      Aignan escapees,
      137–38
  establishment of organized networks,
    134–35, 137, 158
    Les Riceys/Paris-Vierzon/Ste
      Léocadie/Canet-Plage escapees,
      143–44
  Germany, 234–35
  locating go-betweens to escort
    fugitives, 134–35, 137
    Les Riceys/Paris-Vierzon/Ste
      Léocadie/Canet-Plage escapees,
      143
    Plestin-les-Grèvres/Bégard
      escapees, 141–42
    Veules-les-Roses/Rouen-St
      Aignan escapees, 138–40
  national historical narrative,
    exclusion from, 173

INDEX

multinational scope, 178
socio-professional composition,
  175–78
transnational nature, 179–81
women, 146–48
civilian behaviour, influences on, 2,
  257–58, 264
  Battle of Britain, 106
  German civilians, 185
  lynchings, 222
  See also propaganda.
civilian emotion, 240, 265
  propaganda, 241
civilian lynching of airmen
  autonomy of civilians, 212
  France, 50–51
    German encouragement of, 171
    pro-lynching propaganda, 172–73
    Vimy (Pas-de-Calais), 55–56
  Germany, 1, 10–11, 19, 183, 188–92,
    197, 200, 230–33, 236, *273*
    anti-black racism, 254–55
    Appen-Etz, 190–91, 228
    black airmen, 251–55
    children, 225–27
    critical witnesses, 233–34
    demographics of perpetrators,
      199–201, **200**
    Elmshorn, 188–90
    extreme danger of, 204–6
    lost information and records, 193
    numbers, 197–98
    post-war trials, **200**, 222, **232**
    racial anti-Semitism, 250–54
    racial dimension, 198
    reference to American South,
      248–50
    Rüsselsheim, 15, 222–27, *226*, 230,
      235, 237
    state sanctioning of, 205–6,
      208–13, 216
    women, 199–201
  laws and customs of war,
    191, 219
  Nazification of German society,
    208–12, 219–20, 256
"clean Wehrmacht" myth, 41
collaboration policy in France, 56, 59,
  63, 154, 263
  national historical narrative, 173

public order and harmonious
  pursuit, 61
comparative approach to history,
  258–59, 262
"conduct of war contrary to
  international law"
  France, 44
  German military tribunal repression,
    56–59
  Wehrmacht repression, 56–57
    calls for moderation, 60
    local administrative bodies,
      repression of, 58–60
    principle of inhabitants' collective
      responsibility, 57–58
contrôle postal, 17
Cooperative for American Remittances
  to Europe (CARE), 131
Coventry, bombing of, 106, 209
Crémieux-Brilhac, Jean-Louis, 28, 38
cultural differences between nations,
  258–62
cultural resistance to the Nazi world,
  237–40
  Allied bombings, experience of,
    240–41
  differences between nations,
    258–62

Darling, Donald, 115
  "helper" investigations, 116–17
de Gaulle, General Charles
  military resistance, 23
  Nazi concerns, 63
  See also Resistance (recognized
    Resistance).
de Saint-Laurent, Marie, 140
death marches
  civilian participation in
    mistreatment, 10, 221–22, 233,
      255, 264
defeat of France. *See* Battle of France
denunciations and treasons, 99, 162, 236
  Déat, Marcel, 166
  Desoubrie, Jacques, 124
deportation of "helpers," 134, 146,
  149–50, 152, 154, 156, 159
Diamond, Hanna, 28, 50
Dijon, Côte d'Or
  escape networks, 113, 142

346 INDEX

direct actors, civilians as, 1
Directorate of Military Intelligence
(DMI) (UK), 114
downed Allied airmen in Germany
examples
Appen-Etz, 190–91
Elmshorn, 188–90
Oberursel, Hesse-Nassau, 187,
223, 253
Ütersen, Schleswig-Holstein,
187–88
German violence towards, 187
Nazi incitement, 187
numbers, 196–97
trials for war crimes, **196, 200**
See also Allied bombing raids in
Germany;civilian lynching of
airmen.
downed Allied airmen in occupied
France, 109
archives, 114
citizen assistance, 122–25
debriefings, 112–13
See also Allied bombing raids in
France.
downed Luftwaffe airmen, 39–41
England
civilian mistreatment of,
92–94
civilian mistreatment of
(balancing risks), 84
civilian mistreatment of (lack of),
106–7
numbers, 81–83, 105
press and media attention (local
press), 87, 106
press and media attention
(national press), 87
rumor and contemporary legend,
98–99
rumor and contemporary legend
(East Wittering, Sussex), 99–102
rumor and contemporary legend
(Kennington Oval, London),
102–4
France
civilian mistreatment of, 31, 47
civilian mistreatment of
(geographical locations), 48–49
conflicting narratives, 39–41

lynching, 50
Plouguerneau (Finistère), 23–26, *25*
Doyen, General Paul-André, 60
Dresden, bombing of, 217–18, 253
Dunkirk, evacuation of, 13, 76, 80, 126
Durkheim, Émile, 6

East Wittering, West Sussex. *See*
Bracklesham Bay Beach, West
Sussex
Eichmann trial, 219
Eisenhower, Dwight D., 249
Eismann, Gaël
German military tribunals, operation
of, 40–41
German repression of French
civilians, 7
judicial violence of German military
tribunals, 41, 58, 149
Elias, Norbert, 111, 219
Escape & Evasion Reports, 114, 123
Escape Lines Memorial Society
(ELMS), 175
escape networks, 109, 111, 114–15,
121–22, 124–25, **136,** *271*
Belgium, 180
Confrérie Notre-Dame (CND),
120
denunciations and treason, 124
emergency service, as a, 122–24
financing of, 180–81
France, 114, 143–44
MI6, 109
MI9, 109, 114–17, 136, 144, 180
Musée de l'Homme network, 121
Netherlands, 180
OCM, 144
"Pat Line," 144–46
popular culture, representation
in, 15
Sidonie/Georges France network, 147
Spain, 115, 123–24, 134, 143–44, 147,
159, 180
Switzerland, 159, 180
See also civilian assistance.
Estrées-Saint-Denis, Oise
downed *Luftwaffe* airmen, 39
incarceration of civilians, 59
"evaders" versus "escapers," 112, 114,
271

INDEX

execution of "helpers," 55–56, *139*, 149–50, 156, 164
experience of invasion
  contact with the evacuees and refugees, 49
  direct contact with German advance, 48–49
  historical impact of WWI, 49

families
  civilian assistance to Allied airmen, 125–29, 148, 159
  economic burden on family life, 130–31
Fifteen Years War. *See* Pacific War
Fillerin, family, 145–46
forced labor
  mortality rates, 222–23
  punishment for assisting British, 146, 155
France
  Allied airmen, 1, 8, 19
    recognition of "helpers," 8–9
  civilian lynching of airmen, 50–51
    German encouragement of, 171
    pro-lynching propaganda, 172–73
    Vimy (Pas-de-Calais), 55–56
  escape networks, 137–40
  Luftwaffe prisoners, 1, 17–18, 39, 47
    Plouguerneau (Finistère), 23–26, *25*
  mass exodus of civilians, 18
  See also Allied bombing raids in France; Battle of France; civilian assistance; downed Allied airmen in occupied France; Paris.
francs-tireurs
  Belgium, 39
  belligerents, as, 35–36, 45–46, 260–61
  criminalization of, 44–47
  German military tribunals, 41
  judicial repression and violence, 41
  Kriegsonderstrafrechtsverordnung, 45–47, 55
  Vichy's defence of, 60–61

Frankfurt am Main
  downed Allied airmen, 187, 223, 232, 253
French Committee of National Liberation (Algiers), 168
  Secret Service Directorate
    divergent reports on impact of Allied bombings on French morale, 168–69
French National Committee (London), 168
Fulbrook, Mary, 264

Gamelin, Maurice Gustave (Chief of Staff), 27
Garde territoriale (Fr), 7, 149
  creation of, 35
  Hague Convention, 36, 149
  local initiatives, 37–38
  reluctance to arm citizens, 35
  repression
    Reynaud and Mandel as bargaining chips, 61–63
Garrow, Ian
  escape networks, 143–44, 152
Geneva Convention on the treatment of prisoners of war (1929), 34–35, 44, 75, 213
  French violations of, 43
  German ratification, 192
  German repudiation, 206, 208, 216, 218–19, 253
  German violations, 39, 149, 170, 206, 208, 213, 216–19, 253, 261
  retaliatory repression of French civilians, 39, 149
  See also laws and customs of war.
genocide of the Jews, 184–85, 239–41
  German population's awareness of, 195, 250
  Lynchjustiz, 234–35
  Sonderweg, 260
  Volksgemeinschaft, as foundation of, 243–44
German military tribunals, 52
  "conduct of war contrary to international law," 56–59
  francs-tireurs, 41

348   INDEX

German military tribunals (cont.)
  judicial repression and violence, 41,
    58, 149
  mistreatment of Luftwaffe airmen,
    32, 40–43
  repression, 18
    civilian resisters in France, 23–26
    civilians killed without trial, 36
  retaliatory repression of French
    civilians, 18, 23–26, 36, 56–59, 149
  trials of French civilians, 17
Germany
  Fliegerlynchjustiz, 10
  German ideology, 183–86
  lost/missing records, 193–96
  Lynchjustiz, 10
  politicians versus military, 215
  Volksjustiz, 10
  See also Allied bombing raids in
    Germany; civilian lynching of
    airmen; German military
    tribunals; Nazification of
    German society.
Gibraltar
  escape networks, 113, 115, 131, 134
  MI9 offices, 115
Gildea, Robert, 122, 174
Goebbels, Joseph, 203, 207–8, 259
  anti-black rhetoric, 248
  "elimination" of France, 43, 202
  lynching of Allied airmen,
    171, 214–15, 217, 221, 227, 250
  radicalization of German society,
    202, 214, 217, 250
  revolutionary fervour,
    217–19, 244
  victim narrative of Wehrmacht, 43
    air war, 212–13
  Werwolf, 217
good manners and civility, 75, 105
  German civilians, 235–36
  See also humor as a British
    characteristic.
Guérisse, Albert (Pat O'Leary), 144, 153
  "Pat Line" (escape network), 144
Guernica, bombing of, 209

Hague, The
  German bombings of, 33

Hague Convention (1907), 26, 65
  humane treatment of prisoners of
    war, 33, 75, 213
  Martens clause, 261
  militias and voluntary corps,
    recognition of, 35, 37, 45, 85,
    149
  prohibition of killing or wounding
    an enemy who has laid down
    his arms, 33, 35, 64, 170
  See also laws and customs of war;
    right of the civilian population
    to resist invasion.
Hall, Kevin T., 10, 183
Hamburg, bombing of, 189, 209, 231
Hanau, Hesse-Nassau
  state-sanctioned lynchings, 252
"helpers"
  certificates of recognition,
    118, 176
  Cooperative for American
    Remittances to Europe, 131
  cost to families, 125–29
    economic burden on family life,
      130–31
  Escape & Evasion Reports, 115, 123
  German helpers, 234–35
  letters of gratitude, 131–33
  numbers, 112, 117, 123–25, 155–59,
    278
    women, 175
  official Allied recognition of, 8–9, 17,
    119, 119–20, 262
    investigations, 115–17
    women, 175
  risks involved, 125–29, 129–30
  transnational networks, 179–81, 263
  See also civilian assistance; resistance
    of civilians; Resistance
    (recognized Resistance).
Himmler, Heinrich, 85, 203
  state-sanctioned lynchings, 208–9,
    211, 227, 252
historiography of Allied bombings, 11
historiography of Battle of Britain,
    72–75
historiography of German bombings, 11
historiography of People's War, 71, 76,
    257

INDEX

historiography of the French
Resistance, 19, 109–10
Battle of France
débâcle, 26–29, 63–65
Hitler, Adolf
anti-black rhetoric, 248
bombing policy, 72–73, 80
Massenpanik, 73
de Gaulle, concerns about, 63
Hitler-Stalin Pact, 81, 163
invasion of USSR, 73
popularity with German civilian
women, 255
"postponement" of invasion of
Britain, 102
repudiation of Geneva Convention, 218
state-sanctioned lynchings, 215–16
Holweck, Fernand
arrest and torture, 153–54
Home Guard (UK), 35, 70, 80, 105
francs-tireurs, as, 85
See also Local Defence Volunteers
(UK).
homogeneous/national behaviours,
1–2, 203, 257
Honfleur, Calvados
escape networks, 144, 147
Horne, John, 36, 39, 260
humor as a British characteristic, 19,
88–89, *90*, *93*, 105, 259–60
categorization of German airmen,
91–92
unifying national identity, 90–91
humor in politics, 259–60

individual and community,
interaction between, 1–3, 111,
219, 258
Intelligence School 9 (IS9) (UK), 114
escapers, 114
evaders, 114
recruitment and training of agents,
114
intelligence-gathering, 143, 147, 158, 164
international law, contraventions of, 19
See also Geneva Convention on the
treatment of prisoners of war
(1929); Hague Convention
(1907); laws and customs of war.

internment policy of Vichy
government, 143
Italy
helpers, 9, 127
resistance of civilians, 109
US air bases, 254

Jackson, Julian, 28, 38, 65
Jews
Allied bombing raids in
Germany, as instigators of.
169–70, 243–47, *246*
See also genocide of the Jews.
judicial repression and violence
francs-tireurs, 41
German military tribunals,
41, 58, 149
Juvisy, Seine-et-Oise
Allied bombing of, 169

Kaltenbrunner, Ernst
state-sanctioned lynching, 172,
211–12, 216
Keller, Sven, 222, 264
Kennington Oval, London
mistreatment of downed Luftwaffe
airmen, rumors of,
102–4
Kershaw, Ian, 220, 256
Kiesler, Charles
commitment theory, 4
Klemperer, Victor, 209, 212, 217, 244–45
Knapp, Andrew, 11, 255
Kramer, Alan, 36, 39, 260
Kriegsonderstrafrechtsverordnung
(KSSVO), 58, 60, 65
belligerents, 46
francs-tireurs, 45–47, 55
German military culture,
36, 45, 149
Kristallnacht, 199, 202, 223, 230, 241, 245,
249, 251–52, 255, 264, *274*

Langley, "Jimmy," 15, 114
laws and customs of war
belligerents, 37, 261
francs-tireurs, 260–61
German civilian lynchings,
191, 219

350 INDEX

laws and customs of war (cont.)
German repudiation of Geneva
Convention, 219
parachutists, 34
violations, 193, 260
See also Geneva Convention on the
treatment of prisoners of war
(1929), Hague Convention
(1907); international law,
contraventions of.
Le Havre, Seine Inférieure
Allied bombing raids, 173
Les Riceys, Aube
civilian assistance, 142–43, 152
women, 146
Local Defence Volunteers (UK), 35, 69,
79–80, 89, 105
See also Home Guard (UK).
Lübeck
Allied bombing of, 207, 209, 238
repression of civilians, 207
Luchy, Oise
mistreatment of Luftwaffe airmen,
51, 53–54
mock trial, 53, 54
Luxembourg
mass exodus of civilians, 29, 123
massacres of civilians, 36
lynch mobs, 201
political ideology, 222–37
women, 199
lynching defined, 192, 196

Madrid
escape networks, 113, 115
Mallmann, Klaus-Michael, 183
Lynchjustiz, 10, 183
Mandel, Georges
incarceration, 7, 60–63
Marden, Kent
Battle of Britain, 13, 96
Marseille, Bouches-du-Rhône
escape networks, 113–14, 140, 143,
147, 152
mass exodus of civilians
Belgium and Luxembourg, 29
France, 13, 18
débâcle historiography, 23, 26,
28–32, 64, 84

moral foundation of the armistice,
as, 29
records of, 27–28
referendum on collaboration, as a,
28–32, 51
"runaways" and "cowards,"
portrayal as, 29
strafing by Luftwaffe, 27, 44, 47
Mass Observation, 17, 86
mass resistance, 109
"résistancialisme" compared,
117–18, 120
massacres and atrocities, 34, 47
Belgian prison inmates by French, 45
black soldiers, 44, 248
civilians, 44
Nazification of the Wehrmacht, 27
prisoners of war, 44, 261
Wehrmacht Legal Department
justification of civilian massacres,
41–43
See also civilian lynching of airmen;
execution of "helpers"
massacres of civilians, 36, 53
Massenpanik policy of Nazis, 73, 88,
105
Mauthausen concentration camp, 27, 261
Militärbefehlshaber in Frankreich
(MBF)
retaliatory repression of French
civilians, 7, 41–42, 56
Military Intelligence 6 (MI6) (UK), 114
escape networks, 109
official recognition of helpers, 115
Military Intelligence 9 (MI9) (UK), 8,
17, 262
escape networks, 109, 114–17, 136
"Pat Line," 144, 180
internal rivalries, 115–16
official recognition of helpers,
114–15, 262–64
militia and volunteer corps
Hague Convention, 36
Wehrmacht's response to, 38
See also Garde territoriale (Fr.);
Home Guard (UK); Local
Defence Volunteers (UK);
retaliatory repression of French
civilians.

INDEX 351

mistreatment of Luftwaffe airmen, 31,
51–54, 57
"absence of superior orders," 52–53
Luchy (Oise), 53–55
Machault (Ardennes), 52
Vimy (Pas-de-Calais), 55–56
German military tribunals, 32, 40–43
See also civilian lynching of airmen.
morale and public opinion
bombings, impact of, 11
Churchill's rhetoric
armed forces, 76–78
Battle of Britain, 77
civilians and the People's War,
78–80
evacuation of Dunkirk, 77
morale-boosting measures by Nazi
state
indemnification, 206–7
propaganda, 207–8, 227–30, 243
reprisals, 207, 230–33
state-sanctioned lynching,
208–12
mortality rates
airmen, 25, **82**, 115
Allied bombing raids in France, 168
Allied bombing raids in Germany,
96–98, 217, 222
deportees on German territory, 222
forced laborers in Germany, 222
foreign workers on German territory,
222
Moulin, Jean
resistance of local administrative
bodies, 23, 30
Mühlheim-am-Main, Hesse-Nassau
defence of Allied airmen, 237
Munich
Allied bombing of, 231, 235
liberation of, 236
Munich Agreement 1938, 163

Nantes, Loire-Inférieure
escape networks, 141, 147
national identity, 5–6
protection of, 90–91
See also good manners and civility;
humor as a British
characteristic.

National Resistance Council, 121
national stereotypes
risks of, 2, 5–6, 257
See also humor as a British
characteristic.
Nazification of German society, 19,
183–86, 190, 202–3, 233
civilian lynching of airmen, 208–12,
219–20, 256
denial post-war, 193–95
massacres and atrocities,
27, 255–56
response to Allied bombings, 206–8
Nazification of the Wehrmacht, 27
Neave, Airey, 15, 115–16
Neckarsulm, Württemberg
Allied bombing of, 232
Netherlands
escape networks, 262
exiled government and escape
networks, 180
mass exodus of civilians, 123
preparation for war, 38
recruitment and training of agents by
MI9114
resistance of civilians, 137
Newcastle-upon-Tyne
downed Luftwaffe airmen, 91
Nord, Philip, 28, 38, 65
Normandy landings, 250
Nuremberg laws, 248, 250

Oberg, Carl, 149, 155
Oberkommando der Wehrmacht
(OKW), 45
altercations between the civilians and
airmen, 216
Gardes territoriaux' repression, 63
Home Guard as francs-tireurs,
85
repression of local administrative
bodies, 58
Oberkommando des Heeres (OKH),
45, 57
Operation Clarion, 217
Operation Sea Lion, 21, 73
opinion and action, 4–5
national identity, 5–6
Overy, Richard, 11, 107, 207

352 INDEX

Pacific War, 2
parachutists
  airmen forced to abandon planes, distinguished, 33–38, 40, 81, 94, 104
  civilian mobilization in France, 32–35, 60
pardoned civilians, 60
Paris
  Allied bombings of, 165–67
  Awards Bureaus for Europe, 116–17
  civilian assistance, 152
  escape networks, 143, 147, 153, 180
  execution of invasion resister, 52
  German military tribunals, 138, 261
  liberation of, 173
  Oberg, 149, 155
  recognizing and compensating helpers
    investigations, 116, 178
  Reichskriegsgericht, 41, 51, 60
  See also Abetz, Otto; France.
passive defence measures, 32
Pat Line (escape network). See Guérisse, Albert (Pat O'Leary)
People's War (UK), 69–81
  anti-hero narrative of British, 92
  contested historiography, 7, 12, 19, 69–71, 74, 76, 247, 257
Perpignan
  escape networks, 113, 115, 142
Pétain, Maréchal Philippe
  Allied bombings of France, 169
  armistice, 37
  defence of francs-tireurs, 61
  incarceration of Mandel and Reynaud, 62
Phony War (Fr), 76
  aerial warfare concerns
    German parachutists, 32–35
Plestin-les-Grèves, Côtes-du-Nord
  civilian assistance, 142, 146, 148
  escape networks, 147
Plouguerneau, Finistère
  downed Luftwaffe airmen, 23–26, 47, 50, 57
politicization of the Wehrmacht, 27, 202

popular cultural history of WWII92
  aviation and airmen, 12–16
Postel-Vinay, André, 15, 143–44, 152
  arrest, 153–54
preparedness for war
  Belgium, 38
  France
    civilian education at the national level, 34
    Garde territoriale, creation of, 35
  Netherlands, 38
press and media
  England
    downed Luftwaffe airmen, 87, 106
    humor, 86–92
  France
    control by German occupiers, 171
  German newspapers
    anti-black lynching, 248
    propaganda, 53, 170, 212, 245–47
prisoners of war, 213, 260–61
  execution, 27, 193, 248
  Geneva Convention, 34–38, 44, 75, 170, 213, 217
  retaliatory repression of French civilians, 39, 149
  Hague Convention, 33–34, 75, 213
propaganda, 158
  anti-Allied hatred, 168–71, *210*, 246
  anti-black racism, 246–50
  German newspapers, 53, 170, 212, 245–47
  German control of French cinema, 171
  German control of French media, 171
  mock trials, *54*
  morale-boosting measures
    by Nazi state, 207–8, 227–30, 243
  portrayal of Jews, 242–43
  pro-lynching propaganda, 172–73, 210, 227–30
  Propaganda Kompanie, 172–73
  racial anti-Semitism, 243–47, 264
  racialization of Allied airmen, 248–50

INDEX

protecting people and property against air attack
French legislation, 32
psychology of resistance, 3–6, 88, 105, 168
  effect of bombings, 83
  motivations, 162–64
  Nazification of German society, 195

racist ideology of Nazis, 242
racist violence
  anti-black racism, 247–50, 254–55
  racial anti-Semitism, 243–47, *275*
  racist lynchings of airmen, 198
    anti-black racism, 254–55
    racial anti-Semitism, 250–54
  Wehrmacht, 27, 184
Raim, Edith, 199, 264
Ravensbrück concentration camp, 15, 148, 191
Reck-Malleczewen, Friedrich, 237, 239
recognizing and compensating helpers, 8–9, 17–18, 115–16, 118, **119**, *176*, 262–63
  investigations, 115–17
  Military Intelligence 6 (MI6) (UK), 115
  Military Intelligence 9 (MI9) (UK), 114–15, 262–64
  women, 147, 175, 234
records of abuse
  Britain, 193
  France, 193
  German tribunals, 193
  Soviet Union/Russia, 193
  USA, 193
Reichskriegsgericht (RKG), 58, 60
Renty, Pas-de-Calais
  escape networks
    women, role of, 144, 146
repression. *See* retaliatory repression of French civilians
reprisals
  Allied bombing raids in Germany
    civilian lynching of airmen, 231–33
    morale-boosting measures by Nazi state, 207, 230–33
  See also retaliatory repression of French civilians.
Resistance (recognized Resistance), 109, **119**, 120–22, 158, 161

national historical narrative, 173–74, 257
National Resistance Council, 121
women
  recognition of participation, 147
  See also escape networks.
resistance of civilians
  France, 7, 109–10, 122
    Allied bombing, impact of, 164–67
    burial of fallen airmen, 162
    evasion assistance, 158–61
    memory, collective, national and local, 173–75
    motivations, 162–64
    political engagement, 120
  Germany
    helpers, 234–35
    lack of collective action, 236–37
    prevention of lynchings, 235–36
    See also civilian assistance.
resistance to invasion, 149
  Britain, 105
  France, 47–51
  "résistancialisme", 19, 110, 181
  mass resistance compared, 117
retaliatory repression of French civilians, 39, 124, 149, *156*
  Abetz, Otto, 7
  Geneva Convention, 39
  German military tribunals, 18, 23–26, 56–59, 149
    civilians killed without trial, 36
  incentivizing effect, 151–54
  intimidatory effect, 150–51, 154
  Militärbefehlshaber in Frankreich (MBF), 7, 155
  Occupied France versus Free France, 154–55
  Wehrmacht repression, 56–57, 149
    aiding Allied airmen, 146
    calls for moderation, 60, 154
    local administrative bodies, repression of, 58–60
    principle of inhabitants' collective responsibility, 57–58
  See also militia and volunteer corps; right of the civilian population to resist invasion.

354 INDEX

Reynaud, Paul
  incarceration, 7, 60–63
Ribbentrop, Joachim von, 61
right of the civilian population to resist
    invasion, 26, 37
  See also militia and volunteer corps;
    retaliatory repression of French
    civilians.
Riom Trial (Feb to Apr 1942), 59,
    61–62
Roosevelt, Eleanor, 249–50
Roosevelt, Franklin D., 73, 249, 254
Rose, Sonya, 75, 92
Rostock
  Allied bombing of, 207, 209, 238
Rouen
  Allied bombing of, 170
Royal Air Forces Escaping Society
    (RAFES), 175
Ruhr
  Allied bombing of, 73
rumor
  contemporary legend
    mistreatment of downed
      Luftwaffe airmen, 98–104, *100,
      103*

sabotage, 155–56, 164, 168
  "elusive sabotage," 158
Saint-Nazaire
  Allied bombing of, 140, 165
Schleswig-Holstein
  downed Allied airmen
    military burials, 187–90
Secret Intelligence Service (SIS) (UK), 114
  See also Military Intelligence 6 (MI6)
    (UK).
Sedan, Ardennes
  downed Luftwaffe airmen, 47
  mass exodus of civilians, 52
Shoah
  national historical narrative,
    centrality of, 174
Sicherheitsdienst (SD), 17
social and political weaknesses of
    French society, 28–29
Spain
  escape networks, 115, 123–24, 134,
    143–44, 147, 159, 180

Special Operations Executive (SOE)
    (UK), 115
  escape networks, 109
specialized escape networks.
  See escape networks
Stalag Luft III (prisoner of war camp),
    124, 193
Stalingrad, defeat of, 202, 209, 265
strafing
  Allied bombing raids in Germany,
    217
  Luftwaffe in France,
    27, 44, 47
submission to authority, 4–5, 71, 79
successful evasions, rates of, 13–15, 124,
    126, 137
Switzerland
  escape networks, 159, 180
  mass exodus of civilians, 123

Toulouse, Haute-Garonne
  escape networks, 115, 144
transnational resistance,
    179–81, 263
Treaty of Versailles, 91, 258

Ütersen, Schleswig-Holstein, 187–88
  lynchings, 191

Veules-les-Roses, Seine-Inférieure
  civilian assistance, 140
  execution of "helpers,"
    150, 154
Vichy government
  collaboration, 9–10
  repression of local administrative
    bodies, awareness of,
    59–60
  See also Pétain, Maréchal Philippe,
victim narrative, 2–3, 241
  Luftwaffe, 26
  Wehrmacht Legal Department
    War Crimes Investigation Office,
    42–43
Vidalenc, Jean, 28–29, 50
  proto-resistance of mass exodus, 30
Vierzon, Cher
  escape networks, 114, 143
Vimy, Pas-de-Calais

INDEX

downed Luftwaffe airmen, 47, 51
lynchings, 55–56, 197
Vogl, General Emil, 60
Volksgemeinschaft, 190, 194–95, 203,
222, 241, 243–47
collective violence, 257
concept, 183
Volksgenossen, 189–90, 208–11, 214, 237
Volksjustiz, 10, 213–14, 228
volunteering tradition in Britain, 70
von Stülpnagel, Otto, 52, 59, 61

Weber, Max, 111
Wehrmacht Legal Department
accounts of downed Luftwaffe
airmen (Eng), 84
accounts of downed Luftwaffe
airmen (Fr), 23
German military tribunals.
See German military tribunals
Home Guard, 85
justification of civilian massacres,
41–43
War Crimes Investigation Office
mistreatment of German airmen
on British soil, 85
testimony of German soldiers, 42,
44–47
Werth, Léon, 30–31
Weygand, General Maxime, 105

Wiesbaden, Hesse-Nassau
German Armistice Commission, 17,
42, 62
Wilhelmshaven, Weser-Ems
downed Allied airmen, 253
Wilhelmstrasse (Ministry of Foreign
Affairs), 42
archives
German airmen in Britain, 86
collaboration policy, 56
conduct of a war contrary to
international law
Belgium (WW1), 42
military trials, 62
Nazi policy in France, 63
Realpolitik policy, 63
women
civilian assistance,
146–48, 175
civilian lynchings of airmen in
Germany, 199–201
contact with airmen post-
war, 133
national defence, 89–90
recognized helpers, 175
Germans, 234
Women's Home Defence Corps
(WHD), 89
Women's Home Defence Corps
(WHD), 89

1